FIDELIS MORGAN has played major roles in plays from Beaumont & Fletcher to Brecht. She was for many years a leading actress with the Glasgow Citizens Company and has since worked at Nottingham and West Yorkshire Playhouses and in the West End production of Noël Coward's *The Vortex*. On TV she played for three years in the children's series *Mr Majeika* as well as roles in *The Bill* and *Jeeves & Wooster*.

Her adaptation (with Giles Havergal) of Samuel Richardson's *Pamela* for Shared Experience won her a nomination as Most Promising Playwright in *Plays and Players*. She has since adapted *Hangover Square* for the Lyric, Hammersmith.

Her other books include *A Woman of No Character: Delarivier Manley* (Faber 1986), *Bluff Your Way in Theatre* (Bluffer's Guides 1986), *The Well-known Troublemaker: Charlotte Charke* (Faber 1988), *A Misogynist's Source Book* (Jonathan Cape 1988), *The Female Tatler* (Dent 1992), and her first novel *My Dark Rosaleen* (Heinemann 1994).

*Fidelis Morgan*

# THE YEARS
# BETWEEN

Plays by Women
on the London Stage
1900–1950

Published by VIRAGO PRESS Limited July 1994
42–43 Gloucester Crescent, London NW1 7PD

*A CIP catalogue record for this book is available from
the British Library*

Typeset by M Rules
Printed in Great Britain by
Cox & Wyman Ltd, Reading, Berkshire

# CONTENTS

# ACKNOWLEDGEMENTS

Permission to reproduce the plays and revue sketches is gratefully acknowledged to the following: to Samuel French Ltd, 52 Fitzroy Street, London W1P 6JR on behalf of the Estate of Cicely Hamilton for *Diana of Dobson's*, and on behalf of the Hermione Gingold Estate and Nina Warner Hooke for the revue sketches by Hermione Gingold and Nina Warner Hooke; to Curtis Brown Group Ltd, 162–168 Regent Street, London W1R 5TB for *The Constant Nymph*, copyright 1926 by Margaret Kennedy and Basil Dean, and behalf of the Estate of Daphne du Maurier for *The Years Between*; to Warner Chappell Plays Ltd, 129 Park Street, London W1Y 3FA for *Black Chiffon*; to MLR, 200 Fulham Road, London SW10 9PN for *Will Shakespeare*, copyright 1924 by Clemence Dane; to Diana Morgan, c/o MLR, 200 Fulham Road, London SW10 9PN for her revue sketches.

Every effort has been made to trace copyright holders in all material in this book. I regret if there has been any oversight and suggest the publisher be contacted in any such event.

All applications for performance for amateur and professional performance rights should be made to the above.

Many thanks to the staff at the British Theatre Museum, Samuel French Ltd., the Mander & Mitchenson Collection and the British Library Manuscript Room. Huge thanks to Diana Morgan and Nora Swinburne for receiving me with so much humour and grace.

# Preface

No common theme strings these plays easily upon a single thread, so disparate are they in character. All of them however, are written by women during the first half of this century and all explore the changing roles of women finding their feet in an emerging suffragette and post-suffragette milieu (in the case of *William Shakespeare* through metaphor). Leading characters are middle-class, and the plays reflect the limitations and tensions beneath the surface of their domestic lives. Theatre-going was then (as it is again now – 60s' radicalism a pale shadow), primarily a bourgeois entertainment and these dramas throw up a circumscribed but illuminating mirror-image of their audiences' world.

The Shavian heroine of *Diana of Dobson's* rebels against the restrictions forced on her by her gender and class. We discover her, fallen on hard times, a victim of petit-bourgeois tyranny; she may not even discuss her wages with co-workers. But she uses a windfall to strike out for freedom ('Money is . . . power! to do what you like, to go where you like, to say what you like!') rather than security, and taken as a heiress, confronts ruthlessness in the shape of the self-made, no-guilt capitalist, Sir Jabez. In Act II Diana discovers that 'the way to make money is to get other people to work for you for as little as they can be got to take, and put the proceeds of their work in your pockets'. 'In every healthy state of society,' replies Jabez, 'the weakest goes to the wall because the wall is his proper place.' 'Back to basics' indeed! and almost a hundred years later women – shelf-shifters, university lecturers, backstreet workers in the rag-trade – are still at the lowest levels of the wage-scale. At the end of the play, windfall spent, wiser in the ways of the world but a pauper again, this thinking young hedonist opts for a marriage of equals.

While Diana of Dobson's consciously grasps her role as activist in this changing world, Diana Wentworth of *The Years Between* has it thrust upon her; but she too advances the female cause when she takes on her husband's role, and hugely succeeds as a parliamentary candidate in wartime England. And although at the end of the play she returns to her marriage, she will continue with her career, her perceptions profoundly changed: neither will things ever be the same for her husband, her lover, her son. Eventually she will have been a small instrument for change, not just for them, but even England.

*Will Shakespeare* is the cuckoo in the nest of these, a play without a drawing room in sight and – a turbulent, picaresque panorama of Elizabethan life – the most ambitious of all in its scope and in the richness of its neo-Shakespearean blank verse. Strongly imagined characters, Mary Fitton, Elizabeth, Kit Marlowe, bound through its pages, and it may not be too fanciful to suppose that Will himself is a self-portrait of its colourful author, Clemence Dane. Our hero(/heroine?) flees the tyranny of domesticity in the provinces, represented by the lovingly abject Anne Hathaway, for urban sophistication and courtly life, learning in his turn to love, and the pain of his love 'dispriz'd'; learning too, like Vanya's Sonya, that his sole solace is to be in work.

Along with *Will Shakespeare*, *The Constant Nymph* enthusiastically pursues the theme of freedom and self-expression. Again a man, a talented composer, is incarcerated by a woman's love, not in a black-beamed sixteenth-century cottage but in the silver style of a 1920's drawing room. When on the eve of his first great success in England, his own Bohemianism finally recognises its twin in the young girl he has known from her childhood, he rejects his wife's ambitions for him within the hidebound mediocrity of the English musical scene ('But we must save ourselves, mustn't we?'), kicking over the traces in a bid to buy back his soul with the generous and free spirited Teresa . . .

*Black Chiffon* is a powerful and tightly written play whose novelty lies in its Freudian undertones. We have an aggressive and jealous father, a rebellious but loving son to the mother Alicia, who – longtime mediator in the family, and apprehended on the eve of the son's wedding in the apparently motiveless theft of a black chiffon nightdress – is desperate to avert a possible imputation of unnatural love. A strong defence is mounted for her on the grounds of emotional disturbance, but rather than the public humiliation a courtcase might bring to her son and her family, she chooses imprisonment.

As part of the historical charting of our theatre this collection makes invaluable reading – but to see the plays would be much finer. I can readily imagine *Black Chiffon* in a commercial revival, but probably only the National or the RSC or Chichester could afford the extravagance of the large casts and/or multiple sets of the others. I'd love to see, though, one of our more enterprising fringe theatres, the King's Head or New End for example take on the colourful tumble of *Will Shakespeare*.

Here are wonderful roles for women: brave characters all, vivid and outgoing (Dobson's Diana, Teresa, Elizabeth, Mary Fitton), repressed women bursting their confines (Diana Wentworth, Alicia), characters that grow, who are bigger than they were when you came in at their beginnings; no shortage of splendid roles for men, too. Here are well-structured, well-written plays with beginnings and middles and ends, full of human interest and possessing every one of them, a narrative drive that gives to the onstage lives a coherence which audiences in these increasingly turbulent times, must long to see reflected in their own. And in the absence of grand ideas or (*Diana of Dobson's* excepted) social comment, here is intimacy, truthfulness, subtlety, with intense, every-day, and sometimes grand, emotions laid bare. Perhaps their time has come again?

*Susannah York, 1994*

# INTRODUCTION

The plays in this book were written in the first half of this century for performance on London's West End stages. They span the years from the death of Queen Victoria to the accession of Queen Elizabeth II; a period between the last plays of Pinero and the coming of Samuel Beckett and the 'Angry Young Men' with their kitchen sinks.

English plays of this time were usually set in airy drawing rooms and for the most part came from the same emotional spring as the film *Brief Encounter*. They are quintessentially English, and their power lies in the reserve of their central characters; the dialogue throbs not because of any surface passion, but through the use of the words not said, the strong undercurrent of the emotional subtext, which is amplified by the typically English reserve of the leading characters.

While continental Europe saw the rise of playwrights on the epic scale (Wedekind, Brecht, Cocteau, Giraudoux, Artaud, Genet, Sartre, Lorca, Pirandello, Gorky, Mayakovsky) and the United States, as well as starting a huge film industry (to which three writers with works in this book contributed) provided the theatrical genius of Eugene O'Neill, Odets, Kaufman and Hart, Thornton Wilder and Lilian Hellman, England boasted Coward, Rattigan, Shaw, Priestley, Agatha Christie and Somerset Maugham.

As the century turned, the leading British playwrights had been Pinero, Wilde and WS Gilbert. Ibsen's works were being translated and performed mainly by a group of actresses and feminist writers like Janet Achurch, Elizabeth Robins, Florence Farr and Eleanor Marx. Robins and Lady Bell collaborated on an Ibsenic type drama, *Alan's Wife* in 1893.

As the twentieth century progressed, in continental Europe onstage walls were tumbling in every corner, and plays were being written with more fragmentary scene structures, allowing a theatrical imagination to take an audience from a ship to a forest in a small scene change (much as Shakespeare had done centuries before). But over here in England, in plays by men and women alike, night after night, the plush curtains rose on yet another room with french windows at the rear and a sofa placed centre stage facing the footlights.

At the same time, apart from some lengthy offerings from George Bernard Shaw, the issues presented within the plays became smaller, more homogenous, and easy to set within the three stage walls of a middle-class drawing room.

Ours was a parochial theatre for and about the middle-classes. Audiences dressed up for the occasion and it would have been unheard of for a member of the public simply to stroll into a theatre in their everyday clothes without feeling very uncomfortable. The theatre was part of a social world rather than a powerhouse of artistic endeavour. This narrowing of theatrical vision was not only due to the stranglehold exerted by the taste of the British middle-class audience, but to the statutory regulation of the Lord Chamberlain's office, which had to grant a license for any performed work, and who stopped many a play which criticised, or even mentioned, living people, politics, the war, the royal family etcetera, as well as cutting to shreds, or simply banning, plays which dealt with unpalatable subjects like homosexuality, adultery and incest.

As far as language control went, 'God!' was rationed (there had to be fewer than six God!s per play), the word 'bloody', described in Lord Chamberlain's notes as 'the sanguinary expression', was occasionally permitted, but 'sod' was unlikely to be allowed (it caused a theatre-goer to write an indignant letter of complaint to the Lord Chamberlain's Office when used in Mary Hayley Bell's play *Men In Shadows* in 1942).

Actors and actresses were expected to be upper-middle-class, if not in reality at least by accent and dress. Actresses were obliged to have thin ankles and flattened vowels, unless they wished to play eccentric support roles and describe themselves as 'character actresses', and even the mildest of bad language was out of the question, either on or offstage. Actors who swore got fined, and a reputation for being weird or difficult. Rehearsals were also a much more formal affair. Directors (sometimes known as producers) were usually addressed as 'Sir', and often actors were addressed as Miss 'X' or Mr 'Y'.

But the British theatre was not unpopular. Most towns, however small, boasted a theatre of some sort, and large cities sported three of four. Demand therefore prompted supply, and thousands of new plays were performed.

Apart from having value as social documents on a section of the public during this time, these plays also exhibit a tightly wrought style which has influenced today's television drama and finds echoes in some of the most popular novelists of the 1990s.

A handful of almost forgotten plays from this period have already enjoyed spirited revivals. These include Terence Rattigan's *The Deep Blue Sea* and *Separate Tables*, J.B. Priestley's *An Inspector Calls*, Rodney Ackland's *Absolute Hell* and *The Dark River*. But there were also successful plays by women which for one reason or another have faded from the repertoire. I have chosen to bring back into print five women's plays and a number of sketches from war-time revues. My only condition in selecting these plays has been each play's potential to stand up to an audience today. The pool from which to choose was vast. But choosing these plays over the others was not difficult. Each in its own way stands head and shoulders above the others.

There were, surprisingly perhaps, scores of women playwrights during this period, I have however ignored most of them as they fall outside the mainstream of the theatrical movement. Women, for instance, wrote hundreds of plays for amateur production, one-act plays and burlesques for insertion within provincial and suburban music hall productions, plays for children, Christmas shows, plays with a message but little dramatic import (e.g. temperance, health information – Dr Marie Stopes wrote plays about contraception), religious dramas (many published by the SPCK and played in church halls), skits for theatrical garden parties and pageants, and tub-thumping propaganda on behalf of the suffrage movement. I started my search for plays by reading everything that had been put on in London, including shows seen only in tiny theatre clubs and arts theatres, hoping that I would stumble across a lost masterpiece. It didn't take long to realise that the likelihood of this was slim, and the task would take a lifetime.

I discounted, at the same time, all translations by women, including accomplished adaptations of Ibsen, Goldoni, Pergolesi, Pirandello, Gogol, Tolstoy and Schnitzler. Nancy Mitford's *The Little Hut*, from the French, played for 1261 performances in 1950 – the longest run of a woman's play in this period; but my quest, I decided, should be for original work only. I further narrowed the field by looking only at plays which had been performed in the West End, and which somehow or other had caused a bit of a stir, either by having a long run or by receiving a controversial batch of criticisms.

To represent the first decade I settled on a play by the suffragette playwright Cicely Hamilton. John Oliver Hobbs (Pearl Mary Craigie), and George Paston (Emily Morse Symons) had hits in 1902 and 1910, and although they have good moments (Paston's *The Naked Truth* has a feeble story, but very good cheeky dialogue is given to the character of a young American girl Sadie Twisden) they do not hold up in comparison with the slight but spirited *Diana of Dobson's*. Gertrude E. Jennings wrote scores of plays in the 20s and 30s, mainly one-acters, with intriguing titles (*Acid Drops*, *Poached Eggs and Pearls*, *Between the Soup and the Savoury*, *The 'Mind-the-Gates' Girl*) but silly plots. She did have two West End successes with *The Young Person in Pink* in 1920 and *Isabel Edward and Ann* in 1923. I chose, over her, the hugely popular Margaret Kennedy adaptation of her own novel, *The Constant Nymph*, which seems to speak colourfully for the flapper generation.

Other novels of the time which made their way to the stage include Mazo de la Roche's adaptation of her own yarn, *Whiteoaks of Jalna*, and thrillers by the detective novelists Dorothy L. Sayers and Agatha Christie. The true-crime writer, F. Tennyson Jesse, co-wrote a number of plays, including an adaptation of her book *A Pin To See The Peepshow* (which was banned by the Lord Chamberlain's office).

The Irish novelist Molly Keane (writing under the pseudonym M.J. Farrell) had an early success with *Spring Meeting* (311 performances in 1938) but the Lord Chamberlain's notes inform us that this was 'a silly Irish comedy appropriately summed up by Major Gwatkin as "tripe",' adding ruefully, 'There is nothing to notice [change or cut] in this balderdash'. There was also the 1931 Daphne du Maurier adaptation of *Rebecca*. Dame Daphne, though, is included as an original playwright with the post-war drama *The Years Between*.

The 1930s I found a particularly dull period. Dodie Smith, now perhaps more famous as the creator of *One Hundred and One Dalmations*, had many successes (under the name C.L. Anthony), *Call It A Day*, *Touch Wood*, *Autumn Crocus* and (as Dodie Smith) *Bonnet Over the Windmill* and *Dear Octopus*. Of her greatest success, *Call It A Day* (which ran for 509 performances in 1935), the censor's notes say 'Like other plays by this author this is competent and natural without being very interesting. It is *terribly* long . . . I confess the "day" . . . seemed like a month to me.' I have to agree with him.

Esther McCracken had huge West End hits with *The Quiet Weekend*, *No Medals* and *A Quiet Wedding*. *The Quiet Weekend*, which ran for over 1000 performances, was the most successful woman's original play of the war (and the entire period). To Londoners going through a blitz it must have been a lovely thing to see a busy and cheerful quiet weekend on stage. I suspect that in peace-time it would not have fared so well. I have chosen instead, to represent both the 30s and the war, with revue sketches from various shows (by Nina Warner Hooke, Diana Morgan and Hermione Gingold) because I think they display the frantic, energetic side of the woman writer in a dense and utterly theatrical form. The writing is necessarily brisk and full of opportunities for the actor.

A genre which essentially speaks for the 20s and 30s, the bio-play, (a play based on a biography of an historical or literary figure) is perhaps best represented in the work of Gordon Daviot (playwriting alias of Elizabeth Mackintosh, the novelist Josephine Tey) who wrote historical dramas about Richard the Second, Mary Queen of Scots and Henri Gaudier-Brzeska. Other writers, both male and female, produced a bundle of unlikely dramas featuring such personages as Clive of India, Queen Anne, Parnell and the Brontë sisters wandering around talking an uncomfortable (and occasionally hilarious) mix of pseudo-historical rant and banal 1930's idiom. The lofty characters and casual naturalism of these plays I found hard to swallow, and have gone instead for Clemence Dane's *Will Shakespeare – an Invention*, which is the only play in the book which neither boasts a glorious stage history nor numerous film adaptations. I chose it over Clemence Dane's other more successful play, *Bill Of Divorcement*, because, though eccentric, it seems more typically Dane, as well as being a daringly theatrical play, with rich language and some electrifying moments. The final play, *Black Chiffon*, I have chosen as a perfect example of a well-wrought domestic drama, with a hint of psycho-jargon (so popular in the post-war years), which proved to be an evergreen not only in the West End but in repertory companies all over the country.

# NOTE ON THE TEXTS
## AND THE
## BIOGRAPHIES

There is a marked difference of attitude to the actor/reader from different playwrights. Clemence Dane and the revue writers (all intimately connected with the theatrical world) have few stage directions, or set descriptions. Others (in particular the novelists Daphne du Maurier and Margaret Kennedy) felt the need to make their roles actor-proof by inserting directions as to how the line must be said: 'dreamily', 'sensitive', 'her voice flat', 'over-strained', 'hurt and bewildered', 'in his polite sleepwalker's tone', 'in a gale of high spirits'. These I have left intact, even although, as an actor, I loathe such limitations being laid onto a playtext.

The plays themselves I reproduce in full, with any lines which were censored by the blue pencil of the Lord Chamberlain's office now restored. The biographical sketches in this book vary greatly in content and length. This is because some of the playwrights had famous literary or theatrical friends who thought highly enough of them to document their failings, foibles and charms in great detail (Clemence Dane is an example of this), while others seemed to have lived completely outside theatrical and literary circles and provided only the skimpiest of information to publications like *Contemporary Authors* or *Who's Who*.

# Cicely Hamilton

## 1872–1952

Daughter of an impoverished Anglo-Scots army officer and an Irish mother, Cicely Mary Hamill was born in London in 1872. She was educated at schools in Malvern and Hoburg, Germany, but as her family fell into poverty she worked from a very early age as a teacher (a job she loathed) in the Midlands. During this time she started writing – novelettes and detective stories at first, and later, while pursuing a busy career as a touring actress, she worked as a journalist.

In 1898 she toured in *The Gamekeeper* as Elfreda Salisbury. She played in Edward Tearle's company, and in 1911 had a success playing Mrs Knox in Bernard Shaw's *Fanny's First Play* at the Little. The same year, at the Kingsway, she played Wilhelmina in *The Workhouse* and Esther in *Esther Waters* at the Apollo. In 1913 she played Lady Sims in *The Twelve Pound Look* by J.M. Barrie at the Duke of York's.

Cicely Hamilton wrote twenty plays. Her first, a one-act play called *The Sixth Commandment*, was produced in 1906. *Diana of Dobson's* was her first full length play. *The Old Adam* (1925), a pessimistic play dealing with the inevitability of war, was very well received (Prime Minister Asquith is reputed to have seen the play three times), and *The Beggar Prince* (1929) was a popular children's Christmas play.

Although a vociferous member of the Suffrage movement before the First World War, Cicely Hamilton was more concerned that women should have equal rights on the job front than in the voting process and, in fact, spoke out against the militant suffragettes. During the First World War she served in a British women's hospital in France, and suddenly became obsessed with the causes of the aggressive instinct. These two subjects – female rights and aggression – dominate her prose work.

Her short novel *William – an Englishman*, a war story written in 1919, won her the *Femina Vie Heureuse* prize; *Theodore Savage*, a futuristic tale of England after a devastating war, was written in 1922. Her other works were mainly travel books written between 1931 and 1951, covering most of the countries in Europe. She wrote an autobiography, *Life Errant*, and also co-wrote, with Lilian Baylis, a history of the Old Vic.

Cicely Hamilton was reputedly a good talker, though not a good listener, and witty, occasionally to the point of acidity. In 1938 she was awarded a Civil List pension for her services to literature. She died on 6 December 1952.

# About *Diana of Dobson's*

*Diana of Dobson's* opened at the Kingsway Theatre on 12 February 1908 and played for over 140 performances. The author was originally billed as C. Hamilton, and only when the reviews were seen to be good was her billing expanded to include her christian name, thus letting the world know she was female.

Lena Ashwell (the actress-manager who both produced the play and played Diana) offered Cicely Hamilton the choice of a percentage of the box office takings or a lump sum. She chose the 'safe option', selling the rights for £100, and therefore did not profit from the play's long and successful run. When Miss Ashwell sold the film rights to the play she did share the profits with Cicely Hamilton, and, although Lena Ashwell's role in the business side of things was much criticised at the time, the two women continued to work together, particularly during the First World War, when they produced plays for the troops in Flanders.

As a full-length play this is perhaps a little thin. There is no complication provided by a sub-plot, and the characters' transformation, leading to the last scene, happens off-stage with little dramatic conflict. But it is fascinating to see the conditions of working girls, people sleeping rough on park benches along the Embankment – the 'cardboard city' of 1908 – on stage at this time in the century. Today it exudes a strange energy, charm and a tender spirit, and one can imagine why Lena Ashwell, a popular and powerful actress, wrote of her long run playing Diana: 'I revelled in every second, enjoyed every line I had to speak!'

# DIANA OF
# DOBSON'S

## Cicely Hamilton

*C.M. Hallard and Lena Ashwell, Act IV*

First acted on 12 February 1908, at the Kingsway Theatre, London, with the following cast:

| | |
|---|---|
| CAPTAIN THE HON. VICTOR BRETHERTON (late of the Welsh Guards) | *C.M. Hallard* |
| SIR JABEZ GRINLEY | *Dennis Eadie* |
| POLICE CONSTABLE FELLOWES | *Norman McKinnel* |
| A WAITER AT THE HOTEL ENGADINE | *W. Lemmon Warde* |
| MRS CANTELUPE (Capt. Bretherton's Aunt) | *Frances Ivor* |
| MRS WHYTE-FRASER | *Gertrude Scott* |
| MISS PRINGLE (Forewoman at Dobson's) | *Ada Palmer* |
| MISS SMITHERS ⎫ | *Nannie Bennet* |
| KITTY BRANT ⎪ Assistants | *Christine Silver* |
| MISS JAY ⎬ at Dobson's | *Muriel Vox* |
| MISS MORTON ⎪ 'Living-in' | *Doris Lytton* |
| DIANA MASSINGBERD ⎭ | *Lena Ashwell* |
| OLD WOMAN | *Beryl Mercer* |

# ACT I

SCENE: *One of the Assistants' Dormitories in the large suburban drapery establishment at Messrs Dobson's Drapery Emporium.*

*As the* CURTAIN *rises the stage is almost in darkness except for the glimmer of a single gas jet turned very low. A door opens – showing light in passage beyond – and* MISS SMITHERS *enters and gropes her way to the gas jet, which she turns full on. The light reveals a bare room of the dormitory type. Very little furniture except five small beds ranged against the walls – everything plain and comfortless to the last degree. On the doors are some pegs.*

*As* MISS SMITHERS *turns away from the gas,* KITTY BRANT *enters, sighs wearily, and flings herself down on her bed.* MISS SMITHERS *is well over thirty, faded and practical-looking.* KITTY BRANT *is about twenty, pretty, but pale and tired.*

SMITHERS. Very tired tonight, Miss Brant? (*Removes ribbon, tie and collar, takes out brush and comb from drawer.*)

KITTY. Oh no, thank you, not more than usual. I'm always glad when bedtime comes round.

SMITHERS (*commencing to undress*). So's most of us. You look white, though – you are not strong enough – (*unhooks dress*) – to stand the long hours, and that's the truth.

KITTY (*smiling shyly*). Well, I shan't have to stand them for so very much longer now, shall I? (*Begins to undo her tie.*)

SMITHERS (*with a half sigh*). That's true. Ah, you're a lucky girl, you are, to be able to look forward to having a little home of your own. (*Looks round the bare walls, then shrugs her shoulders.*) Wish I could. (*Puts waist over foot of bed – returns to bureau and takes out hairpins from puff and switch.*)

KITTY (*unbuttoning dress*). Perhaps you'll be having a home of your own some day, Miss Smithers.

SMITHERS (*back turned to* KITTY *– standing in front of looking-glass*). Me, bless you – no such luck. I'm one of the left ones; I am left high and dry. I made up my mind to that long ago. But what's the use of grumbling? It'll be all the same in a hundred years' time.

KITTY. You don't often grumble.

SMITHERS. No, what's the good? It only makes things more
uncomfortable for yourself and for everybody else. No use
quarrelling with your bread and butter, even if the butter is spread
thin and margarine at that. Not that I wouldn't grumble fast
enough if there was anything to be got by it – except the sack.
When is it coming off – the wedding?

KITTY. He – Fred – wants it to be at the beginning of October.

SMITHERS (*taking off switch, lets down her own hair*). The beginning of
October – that's less than three months! It won't have been a long
engagement.

KITTY. No. You see, Fred has always been very careful and steady,
and he has got a good bit put by.

SMITHERS (*unbraids switch and combs it*). Well – I won't say that I'm
sorry you're leaving Dobson's, because it's about the best thing that
could happen to you. But I do say this, we shall all of us miss you.

KITTY. It's very kind of you to say so, Miss Smithers.

SMITHERS (*combing her switch*). And as for Miss Massingberd, I really
don't know however she'll manage to get on without you – if she
stays on herself, that's to say.

KITTY. Why do you say that? Do you think Mr Dobson is going to
turn her off?

SMITHERS. Oh, I haven't heard anything about it – if that's what you
mean. But it's as plain as the nose on your face that Dobson don't
like her. And she has managed to put up Miss Pringle's back as
well, so she'll have to mind her p's and q's if she wants to stay on.

KITTY. I wish she didn't hate Miss Pringle so.

SMITHERS. Oh, well, of course we all hate Miss Pringle, with her
mean, nagging ways, and her fines and spying, but the rest of us
aren't quite such fools as to let her see it, like Miss Massingberd
does.

KITTY. Poor Di! I really don't think she can help it, Miss Smithers.
She can't keep her feelings in. Even when she doesn't say anything,
you can tell what she's thinking by her face.

SMITHERS. That you can.

KITTY. I wish – now I'm leaving – that you'd try and be a little better
friends with her, Miss Smithers.

SMITHERS. Oh, you mustn't think I dislike her. It's only that she's a
bit – well – queer – what the French call *difficile*.

KITTY. She's had such a hard time. (*Undoing clothes and shaking out
nightdress.*)

SMITHERS (*takes waist and rolls up things*). Well, so have most of us, as far as that goes. And we're having a hard time now, just the same as she is. You get used to anything if you only stick at it long enough. (*Puts roll she has just made on box at foot of bed.*)

KITTY (*puts feet in slippers*). You know Di wasn't brought up to earn her own living.

SMITHERS (*removes shoes and puts on slippers*). Wasn't she? Of course it always falls hardest on that sort.

KITTY (*gets nightgown from under her pillow, stands on bed, and puts on nightgown – speaking quickly*). She told me the other day that her father was a doctor. She kept house for him until he died, six years ago, and never had the least idea, till then, that – (*the nightgown is over her head, and her movements under it show that she is undoing skirts, etc.*) – she would have to turn and work. When he died – quite suddenly – there was nothing for her – nothing at all. She hasn't got a penny in the world except what she earns, or anyone to turn to.

SMITHERS. No relations?

KITTY. None near enough to be of any good to her. She's had an awful struggle these last six years. Oh, I do hope Mr Dobson isn't going to sack her. After she left Grinley's shop at Clapham she was out of work for weeks before she came here, and I don't suppose she has been able to save anything since.

SMITHERS. Not likely. She's always being fined, for one thing – she's careless, and then Miss Pringle's so down on her – hates her like poison. There must have been precious little left out of her screw last week.

KITTY (*takes skirt from under nightgown*). Poor Di – I wish –

(*Enter* MISS JAY.)

MISS JAY. Hallo, girls – aren't you in bed yet? Thought I'd better come up or I shouldn't have taime to put my hair in pins before the gas is turned off. It's just on the quarter to eleven naow. Heard from him today, Miss Brant?

KITTY. No, not today.

MISS JAY. Thought you were looking a bit paile. Cheer up – he's thinking of you so hard he forgot to write. Where's Miss Morton? Oh, I forgot, she's got an evening aeout. (*With skirt loosened about hips looks in mirror, then takes off skirt and tosses it on box.*) My, what a fright I do look tonight – this damp weather takes every bit of curl out of my hair. (*Curls hair vigorously.*) Miss Massingberd not come up yet?

SMITHERS. No.

MISS JAY. I wish she was in somebody else's dormitory and not mine.

KITTY (*hotly*). Why?

MISS JAY (*at glass with back to* KITTY). Oh, she gives me a fair hump, she does – going about with a face as long as a fiddle. I don't laike her.

KITTY. That's only because you don't understand her.

MISS JAY (*turning to* KITTY). Of course it is. I hate things I can't understand – and people I can't understand too.

(*She breaks off as* DIANA MASSINGBERD *walks in.* DIANA *is about twenty-seven or twenty-eight – she is pale with dark lines under her eyes, her movements are nervous and overwrought. She walks to her box at the foot of bed No. 3, sits on it, and begins pulling off her tie and collar with a quick impatient gesture.*)

KITTY (*after* DIANA *is seated*). How are you feeling tonight, Di – any better?

DIANA (*undoing tie with a jerk*). Better – no, I'm feeling murderous.

SMITHERS. Murderous?

DIANA. That's the word.

(KITTY *goes to door and hangs up her skirt and returns to bed.*)

MISS JAY (*putting curlers in her hair*). And who do you want to murder, Miss Massingberd?

DIANA. Anyone – but first and foremost Dobson and the Pringle woman.

KITTY. Has she been fining you again?

DIANA. Fining and nagging.

KITTY (*anxiously*). Oh, Di, you didn't answer her back?

DIANA (*removing shoes – bitterly*). No – I didn't dare.

MISS JAY. What did she fine you for this time?

DIANA. Need you ask? (*Begins to unbutton waist.*) Usual thing – unbusinesslike conduct. According to her, every single thing I do comes under the heading of unbusinesslike conduct. Oh, how I loathe the words – and how I loathe the Pringle. I wish we were living in the Middle Ages. (*Puts belt over foot of bed.*)

SMITHERS. In the Middle Ages – what for?

DIANA. So that I could indulge in my craving for the blood of Miss Emily Pringle.

MISS JAY (*giggling*). You do saiy funny things, Miss Massingberd.

DIANA. They strike you as funny, do they? It must be delightful to

have your keen sense of humour. (*Waist loosened.*) I wish I could
see anything at all humorous about Messrs Dobson's high-class
drapery emporium. Grind and squalor and tyranny and overwork! I
can see plenty of those – but I fail to detect where the humour
comes in. (*Waist off.*) Wonder how long it will be before I get the
sack, Kit?

KITTY. Di, you mustn't –

DIANA. What's the good of saying that to me? You must talk to
Dobson. I can't help getting the sack if he gives it me, can I? And
I'd bet a shilling, if I had a shilling, that I get kicked out within a
fortnight.

KITTY. Oh – Di –

SMITHERS (*has finished mending skirt – rises with work-basket and opens
box*). Well, I don't want to be unkind, Miss Massingberd –

DIANA. That means you are going to say something particularly nasty.
Fire away. (*Begins to undo boots, then puts on pair of slippers.*)

SMITHERS. Well, you've been going on lately as if you rather wanted
to be turned off. Time after time you've given Miss Pringle the
chance to drop on you – and this morning you all but contradicted
Mr Dobson himself about those suede gauntlets.

DIANA. Miss Smithers, I wish I had had the pluck to contradict Mr
Dobson right down – flat – direct – about those suede gauntlets.

SMITHERS. That's where you're a fool, if you'll excuse me saying so.

DIANA. Oh, I'll excuse you – you can call me whatever you like. I
don't mind. I dare say I am a fool – and anyway, I know for
certain that I'm something that's very much worse than a
fool.

MISS JAY. Something that's very much worse than a fool?

DIANA (*takes off skirt*). Yes – a pauper.

(MISS JAY *sniggers.*)

There's another of my funny remarks for you, and it's not only
funny, it happens to be true as well.

SMITHERS. I don't quite understand what you're driving at, Miss
Massingberd, but what I mean to say is that the way you've been
carrying on the last week or two isn't the way to go to work if you
want to stay on with Dobson.

DIANA. The question is – do I want to stay with Dobson?

KITTY. Oh, you do —for the present you do.

DIANA. For the present –

SMITHERS. Of course, you know you own business best.

DIANA. You wouldn't say that if you thought it. (*Puts skirt at foot of bed.*)

SMITHERS. Well, as you said the other day you were all alone in the world with no one to look to, and as I don't imagine you've been able to save very much since you were taken on here –

DIANA. Save – good Lord – me save! On thirteen pounds a year, five bob a week, with all my clothes to find and my fines to pay.

SMITHERS (*stiffly*). I suppose, you know, Miss Massingberd, that the firm prefer that the assistants should not discuss the amount of their salaries.

DIANA. I don't wonder – I'm glad the firm have the grace to be ashamed of themselves sometimes. Well, I'm not bound to consider their feelings, and I shall discuss the amount of my totally inadequate salary as often as I like. I get five bob a week – with deductions – and I don't care who knows it. I only wish I could proclaim the fact from the housetops. Five bob a week for fourteen hours' work a day – five bob a week for the use of my health and strength – five bob a week for my life. And I haven't a doubt that a good many others here are in the same box.

KITTY. Di, what's come over you lately? You usen't to be like this – not so bad. It's only the last fortnight that you've been so dreadfully discontented.

DIANA. Oh, it has been coming on a great deal longer than that – coming on for years.

KITTY. For years?

DIANA. I have fits of this sort of thing, every now and then. I can't help myself. They come and take hold of you – and you realise what your life might be – and what it is – I'm about at the end of my tether, Kit.

KITTY. But why? What is the matter just now, in particular?

DIANA. There isn't anything particular the matter. That's just it.

KITTY. What do you mean, dear?

DIANA. Everything's going on the same as usual – the same old grind. As it was in the beginning, is now, and ever shall be: world without end. Amen.

MISS JAY. Oh, Miss Massingberd – that's in the prayer book.

DIANA. Ow, Miss Jay, you do surprise me – Is it really?

(MISS JAY *turns back to bureau, annoyed.*)

You're going to have done with it, Kitty. In three months' time you'll be married. However your marriage turns out, it will be a change for you – a change from the hosiery department of Dobson's.

KITTY (*hurt*). Di –

DIANA. Oh, I didn't mean to be unkind, Kit. You're a dear, and if I'm nasty to you it's only because I envy you. You're going to get out of all this: in three months' time you'll have turned your back on it for good – you'll have done with the nagging and the standing and this horrible bare room – and the dining-room with the sloppy tea on the table and Pringle's sour face at the end of it. Lucky girl! But I haven't any prospect of turning my back on it, and it doesn't seem to me I ever shall.

SMITHERS. You will, and before very long too, if you don't look out.

DIANA. Oh, I shan't be here much longer – I can quite see that. But when I am fired out I shall only start the same old grind somewhere else – all over again. The delectable atmosphere of Dobson's will follow me about wherever I go. I shall crawl round to similar establishments, cringing to be taken on at the same starvation salary – and then settle down in the same stuffy dormitory, with the same mean little rules to obey – I shall serve the same stream of intelligent customers – and bolt my dinner off the same tough meat in the same gloomy dining-room with the same mustard-coloured paper on the walls. And that's life, Kit! That's what I was born for. Hurrah for life!

MISS JAY. Well, I never, you do –

DIANA. Say funny things – yes, I know.

SMITHERS. Look here, girls, it's only five minutes now till we have to turn the light out. Instead of listening to Miss Massingberd's nonsense, we'd better –

(*Enter* MISS MORTON – *she wears skirt, jacket and hat and white shirt waist. She is unbuttoning jacket as she runs in.*)

MISS MORTON. Hallo, girls! Gas not out yet. (*Closes door, hangs hat on peg.*) That's a blessing.

SMITHERS. Had a nice evening out, Miss Morton?

MISS MORTON. Tip-top, thanks. Been at my cousin's at Balham. I hurried back, though. I was afraid I shouldn't get in till after eleven – and I do so hate having to go to bed in the dark. (*Hangs jacket on a peg.*) Oh, Miss Massingberd, I brought this up for you. (*Gives letter to* DIANA.) It was in the hall. I suppose it came by the last post.

DIANA. A letter for me?

MISS MORTON (*unlacing boots*). My cousin Albert sent his kind regards to you, Miss Jay. Said I was to be sure not to forget 'em.

MISS JAY (*has hung skirt on peg and is now rolling up waist, etc.; giggling*). Ah! Did he?

MISS MORTON. He asked most particular which department you was in.

MISS JAY. Whatever did you say? You never went and told him it was corsets?

MISS MORTON. Didn't I just? (*Getting into slippers.*)

MISS JAY. Well, I never – you are a caution. What did he say when you told him?

MISS MORTON. Said he was downright disappointed, and he wished you'd been in the tie department – then he could have dropped in now and again to buy a new tie and have a chat.

MISS JAY. Oh, go on!

MISS MORTON. He was afraid he'd be too shy to ask to look at a pair of corsets even for the pleasure of seeing you.

MISS JAY (*giggling more than ever*). Well, I must say, he has got a nerve. Did you ever –

DIANA (*who has been standing under the gas reading her letter – then staring at it incredulously*). Girls – girls –

KITTY. Di, what is it?

SMITHERS. What's the matter, Miss Massingberd?

DIANA (*hysterically*). The letter – it says – (*Holding it out.*) Read it – oh no, let me read it again first.

KITTY. It's not bad news, is it?

DIANA. Bad news – bad news. (*She laughs.*)

MISS JAY. She's got hysterics.

MISS MORTON (*moves to and picks up glass of water from washstand*). Have a glass of water, Miss Massingberd, dear.

DIANA. No, no – I'm all right.

(MISS MORTON *returns glass of water to washstand.*)

(DIANA *pulls herself together.*)

KITTY. Tell us what it is?

DIANA. It's this letter – the letter Miss Morton brought up.

MISS MORTON. Yes.

DIANA. It comes from a lawyer – a solicitor in Manchester –

KITTY. Yes?

DIANA. It seems that a cousin of my father's used to live in
Manchester – a distant cousin whom I never knew, and who was in
some sort of business there. He died suddenly a while ago, without
leaving a will. His money is all to be divided up among the next of
kin – and I'm one of them – one of the next of kin – and I get three
hundred pounds!

(*Chorus of* 'Oh! Three hundred pounds! Oh, you lucky girl!')

KITTY. Di, I'm so glad – so glad, dear.

DIANA. I can't believe it yet – I can't get myself to believe it. Read the
letter, someone. (*Gives letter to* SMITHERS.) Read it aloud to me –
and tell me if it is really true.

SMITHERS (*reading*). 'Madam, *re* R.C. Cooper, deceased. I beg to
inform you that, by the recent death of my client, Mr Edward
Chamberlain Cooper, you, as one of his next of kin, are entitled to
a share in his estates –'

DIANA (*snatching letter from her*). It's true then – it is really true.

(*The girls crowd round her.*)

KITTY. Of course it is.

DIANA. Girls, I'm not a pauper any more. I've got three hundred
pounds of my own. Think of it – three hundred golden sovereigns.

MISS JAY. What are you going to do with it?

DIANA. I don't know – I haven't had time to think yet. I'll stand you
all a treat on Sunday, for one thing. (*The girls cheer.*) And Kitty
shall have a wedding present – what shall it be, Kit?

KITTY (*shaking her head*). You mustn't be extravagant and waste your
money. You ought to put it straight in the bank.

DIANA. Put it in the bank – not me. What's the good of that?

SMITHERS. You should invest it in something really safe.

DIANA. And get nine or ten pounds a year for it at the outside. No,
thank you – not good enough. Now I've got three hundred
pounds – three hundred pounds to do as I like with – I intend to
have some fun out of it.

MISS MORTON. You'll chuck Dobson's, I suppose?

DIANA (*scornfully*). What do you think?

MISS MORTON. Tomorrow?

DIANA (*nods*). I can get an advance tomorrow – the solicitor – Mr
Crampton – says so. So this is my last night here, girls. You don't
suppose I'll stay in this beastly den a moment longer than I can
help! Dobson's hosiery department has seen the last of me. I'd

clear out of the place tonight if it wasn't so late. No, I wouldn't, though – if I went tonight I shouldn't be able to have an interview with Mr Septi-mus Dobson – to tell him what I think of him.

(*Chorus of* 'OH!')

MISS JAY. You're not really going to?

DIANA. Not going to – you wait and see. Why, it'll be glorious – glorious. Girls, have you ever grasped what money really is? It's power! Power to do what you like, to go where you like, to say what you like. Because I have three hundred pounds in my pocket, I shall be able tomorrow morning to enjoy the priceless luxury of telling Dobson, to his fat white face, what we all whisper behind his mean old back –

MISS MORTON. Shall you dare?

DIANA. Dare? With three hundred pounds in my pocket I'd dare any mortal thing on earth.

SMITHERS. I think you're forgetting, Miss Massingberd, that three hundred pounds won't last for ever.

DIANA. Oh, no, I'm not. But while it does last, I mean to have everything I want – everything.

KITTY. Oh Di, don't do anything silly –

SMITHERS. It won't last you very long at that rate.

DIANA. I know – but I don't care. Who was it said something about a crowded hour of glorious life? Well, that's just what I'm going to have – a crowded hour, and it *shall* be crowded. For once in my life I'll know what it is to have a royal time – I'll deny myself nothing. I have had six years of scrape and starve – now I'll have a month of everything that money can buy me – and there are very few things that money can't buy me – precious few.

SMITHERS (*sarcastically*). And when it's all spent?

DIANA (*defiantly*). When it is all spent –

SMITHERS. Yes?

DIANA. I shall go back, I suppose – back to the treadmill grind. But I shall have something to remember – I shall be able to look back at my crossing hour – my one little bit of life. For one month I shall have done what I chose – not what I was forced to. For one month I shall have had my freedom – and that will be something to remember. But I'm not going to think of the afterwards yet – I'm going to think of the *now*. What shall I do, Kit? For one thing, I shall travel – I've always longed and craved to see something of the world besides one narrow little piece of it.

MISS MORTON. Where shall you go?

DIANA. Haven't thought yet, but of course I shall begin with Paris.

MISS MORTON. Paris?

DIANA. To buy my clothes. I'll know what it is to wear a decently cut
frock before I die.

MISS JAY. I saiy, you are going it.

DIANA. Also boots that cost more than seven and elevenpence a pair.
I'm going to have the best of everything, I tell you, and I'll start
with Paris for clothes. Then I shall go on – move about –
Switzerland, Italy, where I feel inclined –

KITTY. It will be lovely – but – Diana –

DIANA. No buts – Kitty – for the next month I am not going to have
any buts. For part of the time I think I shall go somewhere in the
mountains – I've always longed to see real mountains – I shall stay
at the best hotels – I shall call myself Mrs Massingberd, I think.
You're ever so much freer when you're married. I shall be a widow.

KITTY. A widow!

(*All laugh.*)

SMITHERS. Mrs Massingberd! Hush, the Pringle!

(*The door is suddenly flung open, and* MISS PRINGLE *enters, middle-
aged, sour-faced, and wearing a palpable transformation. All except*
DIANA *rush to their beds.* DIANA *whistles.*)

MISS PRINGLE. What is all this noise about? It's past eleven, and the
gas ought to have been out long ago. Miss Massingberd – was it
your voice I heard?

DIANA. Miss Pringle, it was.

MISS PRINGLE. Then –

DIANA (*interrupting*). The usual thing, I suppose? We're all of us fined.
Gas burning after eleven o'clock at night – unbusinesslike
conduct – sixpence all round. Never mind, girls, don't you worry.
I'm standing treat for this lot.

MISS PRINGLE. Miss Massingberd!

DIANA. Miss Pringle!

MISS PRINGLE. Do you wish me to report you?

DIANA. For more unbusinesslike conduct? Certainly, if you like.
Please yourself about it – I don't really care a row of brass pins.

MISS PRINGLE. Are you out of your senses?

DIANA. Now you mention it, I do feel rather like it.

MISS PRINGLE. You'll be sorry for your impertinence tomorrow.

DIANA. I assure you, you are entirely mistaken. The combination of fury and astonishment in your face will always remain with me as a pleasing memory – grateful and comforting. I may add that the effect is singularly unbecoming.

(MISS JAY *giggles audibly – then chokes as* MISS PRINGLE *turns round.*)

MISS PRINGLE (*viciously*). Miss Massingberd –

DIANA. Allow me to remind you that you have made that remark before. If you have nothing to add to it, we need not detain you any longer. I'll turn out the gas when I've done with it – which won't be for a few minutes yet.

MISS PRINGLE (*beside herself with fury*). Miss Massingberd – I believe you're drunk.

GIRLS. Oh!

DIANA. You are quite at liberty to believe any mortal thing you like – you are quite at liberty to say any mortal thing you like. What you choose to think and what you choose to say are matters of perfect indifference to me now. It has ceased to matter to me in the very least whether you are satisfied with me or whether you are not – whether you fine me or whether you don't. This morning the stony glare in your eye would have made me shiver – tonight, it merely makes me smile. In short, Miss Pringle, you are no longer in a position to bully me, so take my advice and don't try it on.

MISS PRINGLE. Miss Massingberd, the first thing in the morning – the *very* first thing in the morning – I shall make it my business to inform Mr *Dobson* –

DIANA. *Damn* Mr Dobson.

*Quick Curtain*

# ACT II

*A few bars of waltz music behind scene with rise of* CURTAIN.

*Evening: About 9.30 p.m. A fortnight later.*

SCENE: *Sitting-room Hotel Engadine – three large windows at back looking on to Swiss Mountains.*

MRS CANTELUPE *discovered in window. When Curtain is well up, enter* WAITER.

WAITER. Mrs Whyte-Frazer.

> (*Enter* MRS WHYTE-FRASER.)

(Exit WAITER.)

MRS CANTELUPE. My dear Eleanour – delighted! I was just wondering if you had arrived. And where's the Major? You haven't brought him with you?

MRS WHYTE-FRASER. No. He said he was too dead beat to talk to anyone – even to you. So he sent his love and retired to the smoking-room. And how long have you been here, Mrs Cantelupe?

MRS CANTELUPE. Just over a week.

MRS WHYTE-FRASER. Captain Bretherton is with you, isn't he?

MRS CANTELUPE. Yes, I insisted on his coming to look after me on the journey and keep me company for a little.

MRS WHYTE-FRASER. And like a dutiful nephew, he complied.

MRS CANTELUPE. He couldn't very well refuse, after all I've done for him lately.

MRS WHYTE-FRASER. Indeed!

MRS CANTELUPE. My dear, you know how fond I am of Victor – he has always been my favourite of all the Bretherton boys – but – well – he has cost me a pretty penny lately. His bills, my dear Eleanour, his bills – monstrous. Raynesworth went on strike four years ago – declared he would never pay his brother's debts again. I told him pleasantly that it was impossible for a man with Victor's tastes to keep up the position in the Guards on a miserable six hundred pounds a year.

MRS WHYTE-FRASER. Six hundred pounds a year? Of course he couldn't remain in the Guards on that.

MRS CANTELUPE. He quite saw that, too. And, as I was only willing to pay his debts, he had to send in his papers.

MRS WHYTE-FRASER. I suppose Lord Raynesworth will get him into some sort of government appointment.

MRS CANTELUPE. Oh, of course – it's the only thing he's fit for, poor boy. Meanwhile, I have brought him out here with me – even *he* can't manage to spend anything very outrageous halfway up a Swiss mountain.

MRS WHYTE-FRASER. It's almost a pity you can't establish him halfway up a Swiss mountain for the term of his natural life.

MRS CANTELUPE. I declare, I wish I could – though even then I believe he could get into mischief.

MRS WHYTE-FRASER. Does that mean that he's got into mischief already?

MRS CANTELUPE. Well, to tell you the truth, my dear Eleanour – I am not quite sure.

MRS WHYTE-FRASER. What is the nature of the mischief?

MRS CANTELUPE. Feminine.

MRS WHYTE-FRASER. Oh – who is she?

MRS CANTELUPE. A Mrs Massingberd, who is staying at this hotel.

MRS WHYTE-FRASER. *Mrs* Massingberd?

MRS CANTELUPE. A widow.

MRS WHYTE-FRASER. Genuine or Grass?

MRS CANTELUPE. Oh, genuine – at least I have no reason to suppose otherwise.

MRS WHYTE-FRASER. Young?

MRS CANTELUPE. About eight and twenty, I should say.

MRS WHYTE-FRASER. Any connection of Mrs Jimmy Sinclair's – she was a Massingberd.

MRS CANTELUPE. I don't know. I have never heard her mention any of her people – except her husband.

MRS WHYTE-FRASER. And who was he?

MRS CANTELUPE. That I don't know either; but I understand from Victor that the late Mr Massingberd was considerably older than his wife.

MRS WHYTE-FRASER. What is she like? Pretty – smart?

MRS CANTELUPE. Both.

MRS WHYTE-FRASER. Then what is the objection – no money?

MRS CANTELUPE. That, my dear Eleanour, is exactly what I want to find out before I let things go too far.

MRS WHYTE-FRASER. I see. When did he first meet her?

MRS CANTELUPE. When she arrived here – five days ago.

MRS WHYTE-FRASER. Only five days ago! He isn't usually so susceptible, is he?

MRS CANTELUPE. No – that is what makes me think it is serious. *Apparently* she is very well off.

MRS WHYTE-FRASER. But you are inclined to mistrust appearances?

MRS CANTELUPE. My dear, one has to be so *careful* in these foreign hotels. Of course, an elderly husband *sounds* like money – and if she is as well off as she seems, it would be the best thing that could happen to Victor. A sensible marriage of the kind is what I've always hoped for him. But with only six hundred a year and his extravagant habits, it would be simply madness for him to marry a woman without money.

MRS WHYTE-FRASER. Surely a skilful cross-examination ought to reveal something.

MRS CANTELUPE. I assure you, Eleanour, I have only been waiting for the opportunity, and I am rather relying on your good nature to help me to it.

MRS WHYTE-FRASER. On my good nature?

MRS CANTELUPE. Yes. I have asked Mrs Massingberd to have coffee with us tonight.

MRS WHYTE-FRASER. Here?

MRS CANTELUPE. Yes – I generally sit here after dinner. No one seems to come to this little room. Now – what I want you to do is to carry Victor off with you, as soon as you have swallowed your coffee, and leave me alone for a quite chat with Mrs Massingberd. Will you?

MRS WHYTE-FRASER. I will – even at the risk of earning Captain Bretherton's undying hatred.

(*Enter* SIR JABEZ.)

MRS CANTELUPE. You can set my undying gratitude against it.

SIR JABEZ. Surely that's Mrs Whyte-Fraser?

MRS WHYTE-FRASER. It is. I congratulate you, *Sir Jabez*. My husband and I were delighted to see your name in the Honours list – *really* delighted.

SIR JABEZ. Many thanks – so was I! It is an excellent form of advertisement, and taking all things into consideration, remarkably cheap at the price.

MRS CANTELUPE. An excellent form of advertisement?

SIR JABEZ. That's how I look upon it, Mrs Cantelupe. My new dignity has a direct commercial value.

MRS WHYTE-FRASER. Then will the fact of your having been created a baronet increase the volume of trade at your innumerable shops?

SIR JABEZ. Very considerably, I hope. Whom His Majesty delights to honour, His Majesty's loyal subjects delight to patronize.

(*Pause.*)

MRS CANTELUPE. Do you know if my nephew is still in the garden, Sir Jabez?

SIR JABEZ. He was smoking a cigar there a minute or two ago.

MRS CANTELUPE. We are waiting coffee for him and Mrs Massingberd.

SIR JABEZ. Mrs Massingberd? You're expecting her?

MRS CANTELUPE. I suppose you have never met her before?

SIR JABEZ. No. At first I fancied I had – her face seemed familiar to me somehow – but she assured me she had never seen mine, so I must have been mistaken. I see so many faces. She's quite an acquisition here. Talks well and dresses well and has a style of her own. I like her.

(*Enter* CAPTAIN BRETHERTON.)

MRS CANTELUPE. Oh, here you are, Victor.

BRETHERTON. Ah! how do, Mrs Whyte-Fraser? When did you turn up?

MRS WHYTE-FRASER. Only a couple of hours ago.

BRETHERTON. You don't look any the worse for the journey.

MRS WHYTE-FRASER. That's nice of you.

BRETHERTON. How's the Major?

MRS WHYTE-FRASER. Oh, he says he's worn out, but I believe, if the truth were known, he's only saving himself for his first climb. I forget – are you a climber?

BRETHERTON. No, I'm not keen – I prefer golf. There's some quite decent links at Samaden – eighteen holes – and you can get over there on a bus.

SIR JABEZ. Been golfing this morning?

BRETHERTON. No. Walked to the Morteratsch Glacier with Mrs Massingberd. She's coming in, isn't she?

MRS CANTELUPE. Yes. We're only waiting for coffee till she arrives. Ah! Here she is.

(*Enter* DIANA. *All rise.*)

DIANA. Did I hear you say you were waiting coffee for me, Mrs Cantelupe? I'm afraid that means I've been a hopelessly long time over dinner. But I was so hungry.

MRS CANTELUPE. Not at all. Just ring the bell, will you, Victor? Mrs Whyte-Fraser, Mrs Massingberd. Where will you sit? I am sure you must be tired.

DIANA. Tired? Oh no – why should I be?

MRS CANTELUPE. My nephew was just telling me that you had walked to the Morteratsch Glacier. That's a long way, isn't it?

DIANA. Only six miles there and back. I don't think anything of that.

SIR JABEZ. You're a great walker, I suppose, Mrs Massingberd?

DIANA. I don't know that I should describe myself as a great walker, but I'm used to being on my feet all day.

(*Enter waiter with salver with letters for* MRS CANTELUPE, *and tray with coffee – and exits.*)

MRS WHYTE-FRASER. Really? How delightfully strong you must be.

MRS CANTELUPE. Will you all excuse me if I just glance at my letters – I see they've been sent on from London. You pour out for me, Eleanour. There's one thing about this place, they do give you excellent coffee – otherwise the cooking isn't up to the mark.

BRETHERTON. No, it isn't. The soup tonight was a disgrace – mysterious brown lumps cruising about in a plateful of warm grease. A revoltin' concoction, I call it. Didn't you think so, Mrs Massingberd?

DIANA. The soup? Do you know, I really didn't notice!

BRETHERTON. You don't mean to say you actually swallowed the stuff?

DIANA. I suppose I must have done so. Yes, I remember I did, and that I not only swallowed it, but enjoyed it.

BRETHERTON. Enjoyed it – no!

DIANA. Yes – in the first place, because I was exceedingly hungry, and in the second place, because I came here to enjoy everything – even that revolting soup.

BRETHERTON. What an extraordinary idea!

DIANA. To want to enjoy yourself?

BRETHERTON. No, but the soup –

DIANA. Captain Bretherton, I am not going to allow indifferent soups or anything else to be the fly in my ointment. If the fly gets in without asking my permission, I simply pretend he isn't there.

BRETHERTON. Then I suppose you're a what d'you call it – Christian
Scientist?

DIANA. Oh no, I'm afraid I'm much too material to be a Christian
Scientist. I like the good things of life – when I can get them – and
plenty of them.

SIR JABEZ. While at the same time you don't seem to mind the bad
ones. That's a very comfortable frame of mind.

DIANA. Oh, I assure you, I'm not so philosophical as all that. I hate
the bad things of life when they are really bad. But, just at present,
I'm having a good time, a really good time – and I refuse to allow
any little diagreeables to interfere with it.

BRETHERTON. Bravo! Have some more coffee?

DIANA. Thanks! I will.

SIR JABEZ. You take a holiday in the right spirit, Mrs Massingberd;
you're determined to get your money's worth.

DIANA. That's exactly what I came here for, Sir Jabez – to get my
money's worth, and I'm getting it.

MRS WHYTE-FRASER. What's the matter?

MRS CANTELUPE. My dear Eleanour, what do you think? Milly
Cantelupe, the pretty one, insists on marrying that dreadful Mr
Wilks – you remember him – the man with no eyebrows and
projecting teeth. And Adelaide says he literally hasn't got a penny.

MRS WHYTE-FRASER. Poor Adelaide!

MRS CANTELUPE. She's in despair about it. She's written me pages,
and the letter has been following me about. She'll think it so
unkind of me not to have answered. Will you all forgive me if I
scribble a line, otherwise I shan't catch the early post. You won't
run away till I come back Mrs Massingberd? Poor Adelaide, such a
blow – and Milly is the only good-looking one of all. Those girls!

(*She exits.*)

BRETHERTON. Take 'em all round, Aunt Emma's nephews and nieces
are an awful lot of rotters. You do take sugar?

DIANA. Yes – thanks.

MRS WHYTE-FRASER. So you like Pontresina, Mrs Massingberd?

DIANA. Like it? That's a very mild way of expressing it. I delight in it –
it's a new sensation.

MRS WHYTE-FRASER. A new sensation?

DIANA. Yes – the mountains, the air, everything. You see, I have never
been in Switzerland before.

MRS WHYTE-FRASER. Really?

DIANA. No, and until the other day, except in a picture, I had never
   seen a mountain with snow on it. I haven't got over the thrill
   yet.

BRETHERTON. Ah, now I understand why it is that you're so keen on
   seeing all these glaciers and waterfalls and things round here.

DIANA. Which means, I suppose, that you have reached the blasé stage
   and are no longer keen on seeing them.

BRETHERTON. Well, you know, you find that when once you've got
   used to 'em, one mountain's awfully like another, especially
   when it's got snow on the top. There's a strong family likeness
   about Alps – I can hardly tell which of 'em I'm looking at
   myself.

DIANA. I wish you'd told me that before.

BRETHERTON. Why?

DIANA. Because for the last two or three days, I have been dragging
   you out in different directions to look at what you probably
   imagined was the same monotonous mountain with the same
   identical snow on the top. I really ought to apologise.

BRETHERTON. Oh, come now, Mrs Massingberd, you know I didn't
   mean that. I've enjoyed the walks awfully, even though I'm not so
   great as you are on mountain scenery, and all that sort of thing. It's
   tremendously good of you to let me go with you.

DIANA. Very kind of you to say so, but after the confession you have
   just made, I shan't dare to ask you again.

BRETHERTON. Oh, come now –

DIANA. I shall have to look out for some unsophisticated Cook's
   tourist to keep me company and share my enthusiasms.

BRETHERTON. The sort of cheerful bounder that takes his five guineas'
   worth of lovely Lucerne, eh? Suit you down to the ground.

MRS WHYTE-FRASER. Do you know, I always wonder who those
   extraordinary people can be, and what they do at other times when
   they're not having five guineas' worth of lovely Lucerne? Tom says
   he believes they spend the remaining fifty-one weeks of the year in
   handing stockings or sausages over a counter.

SIR JABEZ. Very likely.

DIANA. Quite likely. You see, that sort of person is usually in the
   unfortunate position of having its living to earn.

MRS WHYTE-FRASER. I have no doubt of it, but need that make the
   poor things so aggressively – unornamental?

DIANA. I am rather inclined to think that there are great difficulties in the way of being useful and ornamental at the same time. Strictly speaking, we of the ornamental class are not useful; and the useful class – the class that earns its own living and other people's dividends – is seldom decorative.

MRS WHYTE-FRASER. Well, it is to be hoped, then, that the five-guinea tourist is only half as useful as he looks. If your theory is correct, his value to the community must be enormous. There were dozens of him – and her – in the train yesterday, and I must say, greatly as I dislike the species, I really pitied them. Nearly all of them staggered ashore, palpably and unbecomingly the worse for the crossing – it was simply atrocious – and were forthwith packed away like sardines into second-class carriages, with the prospect of a night of unmitigated misery before them. I wondered what on earth induced them to spend their money in undergoing all that torture?

SIR JABEZ. Some form of mild insanity, I should say. They'd much better keep their savings in their pockets, and stop at home.

DIANA. I don't agree with you –

SIR JABEZ. Oh!

DIANA. And I know what the inducement was. It was the prospect of a new sensation – of romance –

SIR JABEZ. Romance?

DIANA. Yes, romance. Something that their everyday life fails to give them.

BRETHERTON. And a jolly good thing, too, I should say. You wouldn't like to spend your daily life sitting five a side in a railway carriage, would you?

DIANA. Of course I shouldn't – and no more would they. But I can imagine that there are times when even a night in a stuffy railway carriage would come as a relief to some people – people whose lives have gone on, day after day, in the same dull, mean little round, without any hope of change or betterment or advancement. I'm afraid you don't quite share my sympathy for the globe-trotting counter-jumper and his fellows. You may consider me very extraordinary, but I really like to think that when he gets away from his daily round and common task he really enjoys himself in his own vulgar fashion.

BRETHERTON. Of course – why shouldn't he enjoy himself, poor beggar? As long as he don't spoil the place for other people and get in the way.

DIANA. Of the ornamental classes! I quite agree with you – the two
    don't mix. Their views of life are so hopelessly dissimilar . . .
    Would you mind putting down my cup?

BRETHERTON. I beg your pardon.

MRS WHYTE-FRASER. Is that the right time? I really must be off, or
    Tom will wonder what has become of me. Captain Bretherton,
    whether you like it or not, I am going to drag you to the Victoria
    with me.

BRETHERTON. Me – oh – er – delighted.

MRS WHYTE-FRASER. To see Tom. He told me I was to be sure and
    capture you if I ran across you. So I must absolutely insist on your
    coming in with me . . . I hope *you* will look us up, Mrs
    Massingberd. My husband and I are at the Victoria.

DIANA. Thank you – it is very kind of you.

MRS WHYTE-FRASER. I shall expect you, then . . . any afternoon. Come
    along, Captain Bretherton!

            (*She exits, followed by* CAPTAIN BRETHERTON.)

SIR JABEZ. Would you care to take a turn in the garden, Mrs
    Massingberd? It's a lovely night.

DIANA. No, thank you. I should like it very much, but I think I ought
    to wait till Mrs Cantelupe comes back.

SIR JABEZ. Then perhaps you won't have any objection to my waiting
    and keeping you company?

DIANA. None at all. On the contrary, you interest me very much, Sir
    Jabez.

SIR JABEZ. Delighted to hear it. May I ask why?

DIANA. Oh, certainly. But perhaps you won't be flattered when you
    hear the reason. When I am with you – when I am talking to you –
    I can't help thinking of the hundreds of men and women whose
    lives you control. I mean the people who work for you.

SIR JABEZ. Oh, my employees.

DIANA. Yes . . . that's how you think of them, of course, just as your
    employees. What a different sort of creature you must seem to
    them from what you do to me.

SIR JABEZ. I suppose I do.

DIANA. Of course you do. You strike me as being quite an amiable
    and good-natured person – but I don't imagine that there is a man
    or woman in your employment who has a good word to say for you
    behind your back.

SIR JABEZ. Upon my soul!

DIANA. Well, is there? You are far too clever not to know that you aren't popular with the people who work for you.

SIR JABEZ. Oh yes, *I* know – but I was wondering how *you* did!

DIANA. Feminine intuition, I suppose – I can feel it in my bones. You're quite charming as an equal, but you would be just the reverse as a – tyrant. And you are a tyrant, aren't you? You like to be feared?

SIR JABEZ. By people who have to work for me – yes. It keeps 'em up to the mark. And the business of an employer is to keep his hands up to the mark.

DIANA. Fancy spending one's life in keeping other people's noses to the grindstone! How I should hate it!

SIR JABEZ. Apparently you've got an idea that I'm a regular ogre to my employees. But I assure you I treat 'em just as well as most other firms. They're no worse off than they would be anywhere else. If you're interested in that sort of thing, you must have a look around one of our establishments some day – let me know when you can go and I'll show you over myself – I'm not afraid of inspection, government or otherwise – in the long run it doesn't pay to play tricks with the Factory Acts. And it would be a new experience for you to see one of my shops. Don't suppose you've ever set foot in any of 'em – they're not quite your style.

DIANA. Oh, you're wrong. I used to know one of them very well indeed – the one at Clapham –

SIR JABEZ. Did you?

DIANA. That was in my hard-up days – you may be surprised to hear it, but I was hard up once. At that time I used to – well, I may say I used to frequent your Clapham establishment – especially the mantle department.

SIR JABEZ. You've given up dealing with us now – eh?

DIANA. I must confess I have.

SIR JABEZ. Well, I shan't ask you to continue your esteemed patronage. I frankly admit that Jabez Grinley & Co. couldn't turn you out as you're turned out tonight.

DIANA. No, I don't think you could. You won't mind my saying so, but your latest Paris models at thirty-five shillings and sixpence always struck me as being painfully uncertain with regard to fit.

SIR JABEZ. They are. They are! I've often remarked it myself. But you can't do better at the price. If you're well enough off to avoid our thirty-five-shilling-and-sixpenny reach-me-down made in Shoreditch and labelled Paris – why, avoid 'em! Avoid 'em! But we cater for the woman with the short purse.

DIANA. See advertisement – 'Grinley's is the place where a short purse is as good as a long one anywhere else'.

SIR JABEZ. That's it. The lower-middle-class woman – she's our best customer – and she's quite satisfied with Paris models that don't fit. So she gets 'em. That's business, Mrs Massingberd. Give people what they want – good or bad, silk or shoddy – and give it 'em a halfpenny cheaper than they can get it anywhere else, and you're a made man.

DIANA. The question is – how do you manage to give it them a halfpenny cheaper than anyone else?

SIR JABEZ. That's the secret – organisation – keep down working expenses.

DIANA. Working expenses – that means wages, doesn't it?

SIR JABEZ. Wages is one item.

DIANA. And generally the first to be kept down. Oh, that's the way to make money – to get other people to work for you for as little as they can be got to take, and put the proceeds of their work into your pockets. I sometimes wonder if success is worth buying on those terms.

SIR JABEZ. You're a bit of a sentimentalist, Mrs Massingberd. Not that I object to that – in a woman. On the contrary – But sentiment is one thing and business is another. Business, my dear lady, is war, commercial war, in which brains and purses take the place of machine guns and shells.

DIANA. And in which no quarter is given to the weaker side.

SIR JABEZ. Why should it be? In every healthy state of society the weakest goes to the wall, because the wall is his proper place. If a man isn't fit to be on top, he must go under – if he hasn't the power to rule, he must serve whether he likes it or not. If he hasn't brains enough to lift himself out of the ruck, in the ruck he must stay. That's what makes success all the more worth winning. It's something to have fought your way, under those conditions, step by step, inch by inch, from the foot of the ladder to the top.

DIANA. As you have done.

SIR JABEZ. Yes, as I have done, Mrs Massingberd. I like to remember that I began my career as a brat of a boy running errands.

DIANA. And I like you for remembering it.

SIR JABEZ. I should be a fool to try and forget it; nobody else would. Beside, I'm proud of the fact – proud to think that a little chap who started on two bob a week had grit and push and pluck enough to raise himself out of the ruck and finish at the top. It shows what a man can do when he sets his mind on a thing and sticks to his business.

DIANA. And doesn't indulge in sentiment – or spend his money in cheap trips to the Continent.

SIR JABEZ. Quite so. But I can see that it's the shiftless chap who has your sympathy.

DIANA. Of course he has my sympathy – he wants it.

(*Enter* MRS CANTELUPE.)

MRS CANTELUPE. Oh, they have gone! So sorry to have left you all this time, Mrs Massingberd. I must apologise.

DIANA. Oh, please don't! Sir Jabez has been entertaining me. We've been talking economics.

MRS CANTELUPE. Economics? How very dull!

SIR JABEZ. Then we'd better adjourn the discussion to a more favourable opportunity, Mrs Massingberd. I'll leave you and Mrs Cantelupe to talk chiffons for a change while I have a cigar in the garden. Good night.

DIANA. Good night, Sir Jabez.

(SIR JABEZ 'Good night again' *and exits.*)

MRS CANTELUPE. Dreadful person, isn't he? But one has to know him – everybody does. I'm afraid he must have bored you horribly.

DIANA. Not at all. On the contrary, he rather interests me.

MRS CANTELUPE. You don't mean to say so. Will you have another cup of coffee?

DIANA. No, thank you.

MRS CANTELUPE. Is this your first visit to Pontresina, Mrs Massingberd?

DIANA. My first visit to Switzerland. It is the fulfilment of a dream.

MRS CANTELUPE. You are fond of travelling, I can see.

DIANA. I am – all the more, perhaps, because I have been very little abroad.

MRS CANTELUPE. Circumstances have prevented you, I suppose?

DIANA. Yes, circumstances have always prevented me.

MRS CANTELUPE. I dare say your husband did not share your pronounced taste for globe-trotting?

DIANA. He strongly objected to it.

MRS CANTELUPE. I wonder – Massingberd is not a very common
name –

DIANA. It *is* rather unusual.

MRS CANTELUPE. There was a Mr Massingberd I met seven or eight
years ago at the Wetherbys' place in Lincolnshire – Cyril
Massingberd. Could it have been –?

DIANA. My husband's name was Josiah.

MRS CANTELUPE. Josiah?

DIANA. Josiah Massingberd.

MRS CANTELUPE. Then it could not have been the same.

DIANA. Of course not.

MRS CANTELUPE. Still, they may very possibly have been related.

DIANA. Very possibly.

MRS CANTELUPE. The man I was speaking of – Cyril Massingberd –
was one of the Wiltshire Massingberds, I think.

DIANA. One of the Wiltshire Massingberds? You will probably think
me very extraordinary, Mrs Cantelupe, but I haven't the faintest
idea whether or not my husband was a Wiltshire Massingberd. I
really know hardly anything about his relations.

MRS CANTELUPE. Indeed?

DIANA. You see, our married life was so brief, so very brief.

MRS CANTELUPE. Indeed?

DIANA. So very brief. I sometimes feel as if it had never been – as if
my life with Josiah had been nothing but a dream.

MRS CANTELUPE. May I ask –?

DIANA. Forgive me, but I had rather you didn't – I had so much rather
you didn't . . .

MRS CANTELUPE. I beg your pardon –

DIANA. There are some things which it is painful to recall.

MRS CANTELUPE. My dear Mrs Massingberd, I shall never forgive
myself. I had no idea your bereavement was so recent – I ought not
to have –

DIANA. Oh please, please, Mrs Cantelupe. It is I who ought to
apologise for giving way to my feelings like this. It is very foolish of
me.

MRS CANTELUPE. Foolish of you – no.

DIANA. Oh yes, it is. I ought to have more self-control. But you see,
my attachment to my husband's – to Josiah's memory is –
peculiar.

MRS CANTELUPE. Peculiar?

DIANA. You do not know how much I owe to Josiah, Mrs Cantelupe.
Every day, I realise more and more that everything that makes my
life worth living – comfort, amusements, friends – even, if I may
use the word in connection with myself, social success – that they
are all due solely to my position as Josiah Massingberd's widow. No
wonder that I am grateful to him for all that he has done for me.

MRS CANTELUPE. My dear Mrs Massingberd, surely you are a great
deal too modest. As regards social success, your own very charming
personality – if you will permit an old woman to say so – has had
something to do with that.

DIANA. Personality does not go very far in society as we understand it,
unless it is backed by money.

MRS CANTELUPE. That is true, unfortunately.

DIANA. And I have very good reason to know it. I was not always as
well off as I am now – in fact, I don't mind confessing to you that,
after my father's death and before I – became the wife of Josiah
Massingberd – I was in very straitened circumstances – very
straitened indeed.

MRS CANTELUPE. Dear, dear, how trying.

DIANA. It was – very.

MRS CANTELUPE. But your marriage changed all that, of course?

DIANA. I should not be here otherwise.

MRS CANTELUPE. It must have been a relief to you. Straitened
circumstances are always so very unpleasant.

DIANA. Oh, they are – I assure you they are.

MRS CANTELUPE. You must be thankful to feel you have done with
them. I can quite understand your very right and natural feeling of
gratitude towards a husband who has placed you beyond the need
for petty economies.

DIANA. Yes, petty economies are rather out of my line, just now. Of
course, I don't mean to say that I am a millionaire or anything near
it. On the contrary, I dare say my income would seem
comparatively small to you. But, coming after the period of petty
economies, I find that three hundred pounds a month is quite
adequate for all my little wants.

MRS CANTELUPE. Three hundred pounds a month – that is three
thousand six hundred a year.

DIANA. Yes, I suppose my income is at the rate of three thousand six
hundred pounds a year – for the present.

MRS CANTELUPE. Does that mean –?

DIANA. Yes – you were going to say?

MRS CANTELUPE. I really don't know – perhaps you would consider it an impertinence on my part.

DIANA. Not at all, pray go on.

MRS CANTELUPE. Well – I was going to ask, as you have been so very frank about your affairs and we seem to have become quite old friends during our little chat – but please do not answer the question if you think it impertinent or inquisitive.

DIANA. I am quite sure I shall not.

MRS CANTELUPE. Well, then, by your saying that your income was three thousand six hundred a year for the present, did you mean that your husband imposed any restriction in his will?

DIANA. Restrictions?

MRS CANTELUPE. I mean, with regard to your marrying again?

DIANA. With regard to my marrying again? Oh, dear no – no restrictions whatever. I beg your pardon.

MRS CANTELUPE. It has always seemed to me that such restrictions – and I have known of several cases where they have been imposed by men who left their property to their wives – are so exceedingly unfair. Don't you think so?

DIANA. Oh, certainly. Most unfair.

MRS CANTELUPE. Especially where a young woman is concerned.

DIANA. I quite agree with you. But from what I know of Josiah, I am certain that such an idea would never have entered his head.

MRS CANTELUPE. You forgive my curiosity in asking?

DIANA. I understand that it was entirely prompted by your very kindly interest in myself.

MRS CANTELUPE. Exactly.

DIANA. But at the same time I think it most unlikely that I shall ever marry again.

MRS CANTELUPE. Oh, you will change your mind when the right man comes along.

DIANA. I don't think so.

MRS CANTELUPE. You are not going?

DIANA. Indeed I am. I have two or three letters I must write – and besides, I have stayed an unconscionable time already.

MRS CANTELUPE. On the contrary, it has been very good of you to waste your time chatting with me. You are staying on here for the present, I think you said?

DIANA. Oh yes. These mountains fascinate me; I don't think I can tear myself away from them just yet.

MRS CANTELUPE. Then I hope we shall see more of you – a great deal more of you.

DIANA. It is very sweet of you to say so.

MRS CANTELUPE. By the way, have you made any arrangements for tomorrow?

DIANA. Tomorrow? No.

MRS CANTELUPE. Because I was thinking of asking Eleanour Whyte-Fraser to join me in a little excursion to the Bernina Hospice – carriages to the Hospice and then those who like a scramble can go farther. Victor will come to look after us, and I shall be so pleased if you will make one of the party.

DIANA. It is really very kind of you. I should enjoy it immensely. I haven't been as far as the Bernina Hospice yet.

MRS CANTELUPE. Then that is settled. I shall arrange it with Eleanour and let you know the time we start.

DIANA. Goodbye till then.

MRS CANTELUPE. Au revoir.

(*Exit* DIANA.)

(*Enter* BRETHERTON.)

Ah, Victor.

BRETHERTON. Oh! Mrs Massingberd gone? Can't think what Mrs Whyte-Fraser wanted – dragging me off like that. Said her husband wanted to see me. He didn't at all, though.

MRS CANTELUPE. No?

BRETHERTON. Looked quite surprised when I turned up, and said he hadn't heard I was here.

MRS CANTELUPE. Oh – curious – Eleanour must have made a mistake. I have been chatting with Mrs Massingberd since you went.

BRETHERTON. Have you?

MRS CANTELUPE. She has only just gone. I must say I like her – very charming and very frank about herself. She was telling me that she had quite hard times before her marriage, but it seems that her husband has left her very comfortably off.

BRETHERTON. Oh!

MRS CANTELUPE. She has three thousand six hundred a year, I understand.

BRETHERTON. Lucky woman!

MRS CANTELUPE. I am quite taken with her. I have asked her to drive
  with Eleanour and ourselves to the Bernina Hospice tomorrow.
  You are not doing anything else, I suppose?

BRETHERTON. Oh no – I'll come!

  CURTAIN.


# ACT III

SCENE: *Same as* Act II. *Twelve days later.* DIANA *is discovered seated at table
with a Continental Bradshaw before her, jotting down figures on a piece of
paper. Enter* WAITER.

WAITER. Did you ring, madame?

DIANA. Yes, how long does it take to drive to Samaden Station?

WAITER. A little over half an hour, madame – thirty-five to forty
  minutes.

DIANA. Forty minutes – and the train starts at 2.17. I haven't much
  time, then. Will you order a carriage to take me to the station at
  five and twenty past one.

WAITER. At five and twenty past one – all right, madame.

DIANA. And will you ask Herr Ritter to send me up my bill as soon as
  possible.

WAITER. All right, madame.

DIANA. That's all, thank you.

WAITER. Thank you, madame.

(*He exits.*)

DIANA. Arrive Zurich eight-twenty – leave Zurich nine-twelve – arrive
  Basle eleven-five – leave Basle . . .

(*Enter* MRS CANTELUPE.)

MRS CANTELUPE. My dear Mrs Massingberd, I have been hunting for
  you all over the place.

DIANA. Have you? I'm so sorry.

MRS CANTELUPE. I have just met Eleanour Whyte-Fraser, and she
  horrified me by telling me that you were leaving Pontresina today.
  Surely it isn't true?

DIANA. I'm afraid it is, Mrs Cantelupe.

MRS CANTELUPE. But why?

DIANA. I have stayed a good deal longer than I intended already, and now I find that I must go back to London at once.

MRS CANTELUPE. Dear, dear, that is most unfortunate.

DIANA. I shall never forget the good time I've had at Pontresina – never as long as I live. It will be something to remember, at any rate, even if I never see mountains like that again – and sky and clean air and white snow. Yes, at least it will be something to remember.

MRS CANTELUPE. But there's no reason why you shouldn't see them again, you know. If you like the place so much, why not come back again next year?

DIANA. Why not? Why not indeed?

MRS CANTELUPE. Only if you come back, I should most strongly advise you to try the Hotel Victoria.

DIANA. Thank you. I shall certainly try the Victoria – on my next visit.

MRS CANTELUPE. I can't tell you how distressed I am that you are going. I shall miss you dreadfully.

DIANA. It's very nice of you to say so.

MRS CANTELUPE. And I am sure that Victor will miss you – more than I shall. I know how thoroughly he has enjoyed all your walks and little excursions together.

DIANA. It has been most kind of him to show me my way about.

MRS CANTELUPE. Most kind of him – my dear Mrs Massingberd! Now I hope, I really do hope, that this unexpected departure of yours isn't going to put an end to our very pleasant friendship.

DIANA. Oh – why should it?

MRS CANTELUPE. Exactly – why should it! I shall be at home by the middle of October at latest. But what are your plans?

DIANA. I really hardly know yet. I am very unsettled at present, and I can't tell in the least what I shall do till I get back to England.

MRS CANTELUPE. Well, as soon as you have fixed your plans you must write and let me know. Now will you?

DIANA. Oh, of course I will.

MRS CANTELUPE. That's a promise. Victor will be most anxious to know that you haven't forgotten your Pontresina friends.

(*Clock strikes.*)

DIANA. You can be quite certain I shall not do that. Is that twelve? I must hurry upstairs and see to my packing.

MRS CANTELUPE. So soon?

DIANA. The train starts from Samaden at 2.17, and the carriage is to be round for me at five and twenty past one.

MRS CANTELUPE. And it is twelve o'clock now. Has Victor any idea that you are leaving so soon?

DIANA. I really don't know. It was only this morning that I found it would be necessary for me to start today.

MRS CANTELUPE. And you have not seen him this morning – since you made up your mind?

DIANA. No, I have not seen him.

MRS CANTELUPE. Then of course he doesn't know – I wonder where he is?

DIANA. If he hasn't come back by the time I start you must say goodbye to him for me.

MRS CANTELUPE. But, my dear – I really don't know what he will say – he will never forgive me if I let you go –

DIANA. I'm afraid I can't expect the Zurich train to wait till Captain Bretherton comes back from his walk, can I? If I don't see him, mind you give him a pretty message from me.

(*Enter* SIR JABEZ.)

MRS CANTELUPE. But I – Oh, Sir Jabez, have you seen my nephew anywhere about?

SIR JABEZ. Not a sign of him. Want him particularly?

MRS CANTELUPE. I do. Mrs Massingberd is leaving here suddenly, and I know Victor will be so distressed if – perhaps some of the waiters know where he has gone. (*Rings bell violently.*)

SIR JABEZ. You're leaving today, Mrs Massingberd?

DIANA. Yes, today. Going back to England.

MRS CANTELUPE. Why doesn't the man answer the bell?

(*She exits calling* 'Waiter, waiter!')

SIR JABEZ. You've been called back suddenly?

DIANA. Rather suddenly – but holidays can't last for ever.

SIR JABEZ. No, of course not, of course not – business is business – must be attended to.

DIANA. Goodbye, Sir Jabez – I must run upstairs and pack.

SIR JABEZ. One moment, Mrs Massingberd . . . one moment. I've a question to put to you before you go – a straightforward question –

DIANA. Yes, what is it?

SIR JABEZ. How should you like me for a husband?

DIANA. Sir Jabez!

SIR JABEZ. A plain answer, please – yes or no – I'm a businessman.

DIANA. Then I'm afraid it must be – no! I'm sorry!

SIR JABEZ. Not sorry enough to change your mind?

DIANA. I'm afraid not.

SIR JABEZ. Yet most women would consider it a good offer – an offer worth considering.

DIANA. I have no doubt of that.

SIR JABEZ. Forty thousand a year, to say nothing of the title. It's brand new, of course – but –

DIANA. You wouldn't like me to accept you for what you've got.

SIR JABEZ. I'm not so sure that I shouldn't. If you'd have me now for what I've got I believe I'd chance your caring – later on –

DIANA. Some day you'll be glad that I didn't let you chance it.

SIR JABEZ. It *is* no, then?

DIANA. It *is* no.

SIR JABEZ. That's straightforward, anyhow. Perhaps it's the drapery sticks in your teeth, eh? You look down on it.

DIANA. I – look down on it – oh no. I've no right to look down on the drapery trade.

SIR JABEZ. I believe you're the first woman I ever met who cared nothing for money.

DIANA. That shows how little you understand me. I'm not at all disinterested. I've known the time when I felt as if I could sell my soul for a five-pound note.

SIR JABEZ. Have you? Have you? Then your soul's gone up in price. What's sent the price up so high? Another bidder in the market, eh?

DIANA. Goodbye, Sir Jabez.

SIR JABEZ. There is – you can't deceive me.

DIANA. I haven't the least wish to deceive you, but having refused you as a husband, I am scarcely likely to accept you as a father-confessor.

SIR JABEZ. You're not going to throw yourself away on that fool of a guardsman – a clever woman like you?

DIANA. Sir Jabez!

SIR JABEZ. You are! That brainless puppy who's spent his life playing at soldiers – who hasn't the sense to stick to the little money he's got.

DIANA. Or the heartlessness to grind a fortune out of underpaid work-girls?

SIR JABEZ.  One for me. So you mean to marry him?

DIANA.  That is a grossly impertinent question.

(BRETHERTON *strolls in.*)

BRETHERTON.  Ah, Mrs Massingberd, there you are. I've been looking round for you. Feel inclined for a stroll?

DIANA.  A stroll? No, thank you, Captain Bretherton. I'm afraid I haven't time this morning. I have other things to do.

(*Exit* DIANA.)

BRETHERTON.  Got a match about you?

SIR JABEZ.  Eh?

BRETHERTON.  Match?

SIR JABEZ *feels in pockets, tosses him box silently and takes Bradshaw from table. He looks at* BRETHERTON *for a moment, then snatches box and crosses to take where he sits, consulting Bradshaw. As* SIR JABEZ *snatches box.*

Thanks.

SIR JABEZ.  Ugh!

BRETHERTON.  Thinking of moving on?

SIR JABEZ.  Yes.

BRETHERTON.  Where to?

SIR JABEZ.  London.

BRETHERTON.  What's taking you to London in August?

SIR JABEZ.  Business.

BRETHERTON.  What a beastly nuisance.

SIR JABEZ.  No doubt you'd find it so.

BRETHERTON.  Don't you?

SIR JABEZ.  No.

BRETHERTON.  There's no accounting for tastes.

SIR JABEZ.  There isn't. Your lounging life would knock me out in three months.

BRETHERTON.  Thanks.

SIR JABEZ.  And my sort of life – hard work and stick at it from morning till night – would kill you in three days.

BRETHERTON.  Thanks, awfully.

SIR JABEZ.  Fact! But you needn't mind. It's your sort that gets the best out of life after all – at any rate, as far as the women are concerned.

BRETHERTON.  That's a comfort.

SIR JABEZ.  It's just the shiftlessness and helplessness of you that
appeals to 'em, I suppose – they know you aren't capable of
looking after yourselves, so they take the job on to their own
shoulders. And perhaps they're right. You couldn't get along
without 'em and the rest of us can, if we must. We've always got
our work to turn to, whatever else fails us, and that's something to
be thankful for.

(*Enter* MRS CANTELUPE.)

MRS CANTELUPE.  You haven't found my nephew, Sir Jabez?

SIR JABEZ.  No, madam, I have not, but he's there if you want him.

(*Exit* SIR JABEZ. *Pause.*)

BRETHERTON.  What's the matter with Sir Jabez? – Sun, or liver, or
whisky, or what?

MRS CANTELUPE.  I really don't know. Has he told you?

BRETHERTON.  Told me?

MRS CANTELUPE.  Then he hasn't.

BRETHERTON.  What is it? Anything wrong?

MRS CANTELUPE.  Yes.

BRETHERTON.  What?

MRS CANTELUPE.  Mrs Massingberd is leaving for England by the next
train.

BRETHERTON.  God bless my soul, no!

MRS CANTELUPE.  Yes.

BRETHERTON.  Are you sure?

MRS CANTELUPE.  She is packing her trunks at this moment.

BRETHERTON.  But what – what's taking her away so suddenly?

MRS CANTELUPE.  I can guess easily enough.

BRETHERTON.  What do you mean?

MRS CANTELUPE.  You have said nothing to her?

BRETHERTON.  Said nothing? Oh, you mean . . . why, no – nothing
definite.

MRS CANTELUPE.  Then you ought to have done it; it is disgraceful of
you, Victor – simply disgraceful.

BRETHERTON.  Disgraceful?

MRS CANTELUPE.  To let your opportunities slip in this idiotic manner;
I have no patience with you. And it has been most unfair to her as
well – most unfair.

BRETHERTON.  My dear Aunt Emma, as far as that goes, though I
haven't said anything definite to Dia – to Mrs Massingberd, I'm

sure I have shown her quite plainly what – er – what my feelings
are towards her.

MRS CANTELUPE. My dear Victor, that is not enough. You ought to
have spoken before now.

BRETHERTON. Come now, we haven't known each other so very
long – less than three weeks.

MRS CANTELUPE. That doesn't matter. What does matter is that I am
perfectly certain she is offended by your silence – as she has every
right to be. Her manner was very constrained when I mentioned
you just now – I could see that she did not wish to meet you again
before she went.

BRETHERTON. But why –?

MRS CANTELUPE. You really are hopelessly dense. She feels, of course,
that she has given you plenty of chances, and is naturally piqued
that you have never attempted to take advantage of them.

BRETHERTON. Never attempted – why?

MRS CANTELUPE. Don't argue. Victor . . . listen to me. You have
behaved most foolishly, Victor – most foolishly. You ought to have
realised that a woman in her position, a woman who, to put it
vulgarly, can pick and choose, does not expect to be kept dangling
on in uncertainty while a man is making up his mind whether or
not he means to propose to her.

BRETHERTON. 'Pon my soul. I'm awfully sorry if I've offended her.

MRS CANTELUPE. So you ought to be.

BRETHERTON. I wouldn't have hurt her feelings for the world.

MRS CANTELUPE. You have not only hurt her feelings, my dear boy,
but you have gone within an ace of losing her altogether. I
conclude you do intend to ask her to be your wife?

BRETHERTON. Of course I do. I – well – I don't mind saying it to you,
Aunt Emma – I've got to like her awfully. She's – she's a downright
good sort.

MRS CANTELUPE. Then why on earth haven't you told her so before
now? You've had plenty of opportunity – I've seen to that.

BRETHERTON. It's such a deuced awkward thing to do.

MRS CANTELUPE. Nonsense.

BRETHERTON. I've been just on the point of getting it out half a dozen
times, and then I've either funked it or else something has
happened to put me off my stroke. Once – just when I'd got the
words on the very tip of my tongue – that ass Grinley came
floundering in, and it was all up with me.

MRS CANTELUPE. Really, Victor.

BRETHERTON. Oh, it's all very well for you to be so down on me, but after all, I'm not at all sure in my own mind that she cares a snap of the fingers about me.

MRS CANTELUPE. Of course she does.

BRETHERTON. H'm! I've thought so sometimes, but other times she's different.

MRS CANTELUPE. Different!

BRETHERTON. Yes, seems to shut up and draw into herself – says such queer things –

MRS CANTELUPE. What sort of things?

BRETHERTON. Oh, contemptuous and sarcastic – and I can't exactly explain – but once or twice it has struck me that she was trying to put me off before I had gone too far.

MRS CANTELUPE. Rubbish – all your imagination.

BRETHERTON. Oh, you can call it rubbish if you like, but that doesn't make me any more certain that she'll have me when I do summon up courage to ask her. And, when you come to think of it, why on earth should she? I'm not much of a catch as far as money goes – and even if I were, it strikes me that I'm not half clever enough for her.

MRS CANTELUPE. Nonsense, Victor.

BRETHERTON. And I can tell you that when a man feels that as soon as he opens his mouth he may be told he's not wanted and sent about his business, it – well, it gives him a sinking sensation in the inside.

MRS CANTELUPE. Does it? That must be very uncomfortable, but as far as you are concerned, you will have to get over that sinking sensation in the inside now.

BRETHERTON. What do you mean?

(*Enter* WAITER.)

WAITER. Your ring, madame?

MRS CANTELUPE. Yes. Will you send up to Mrs Massingberd – she is packing in her bedroom – and tell her I shall be exceedingly obliged – Mrs Cantelupe will be exceedingly obliged – if she will spare me a few minutes down here. Say I am sorry to disturb her, as I know she is busy, but it is on a matter of importance.

WAITER. All right, madame.

(*He exits.*)

BRETHERTON. I say, Aunt Emma, you surely don't mean –

MRS CANTELUPE. Now, Victor, no shuffling.

BRETHERTON. Oh, hang it all, you needn't have rushed me into it like this.

MRS CANTELUPE. If I hadn't rushed you into it, my dear boy, it is my firm belief that you would have let her go without a word.

BRETHERTON. But I shouldn't have let her go altogether – I could have written to her.

MRS CANTELUPE. Idiot! My dear Victor, if you are labouring under the delusion that letter-writing is one of your strong points, all I can say is that you are most woefully mistaken; besides, no self-respecting woman likes a man who hasn't the pluck to tell her that he loves her. So take your courage in both hands – you'll find that you'll muddle through somehow.

BRETHERTON. I'm not so sure of that.

MRS CANTELUPE. I shall allow you half an hour. And at the end of that time I shall appear on the scene armed with suitable congratulations.

(*She exits.*)

BRETHERTON. Good Lord!

(DIANA *enters.*)

DIANA. Oh, isn't Mrs Cantelupe here? I heard she wanted to see me.

BRETHERTON. Yes, I know she did – that is to say, she sent a message – I mean, she has just gone out for a stroll –

DIANA. Gone out for a stroll?

BRETHERTON. She'll be back soon – in twenty minutes.

DIANA. In twenty minutes – oh, very well –

BRETHERTON. Don't go for a moment, Mrs Massingberd. I – I want to speak to you.

DIANA. I am rather in a hurry, Captain Bretherton.

BRETHERTON. Yes, I know, but – I – I – I hear you're leaving us.

DIANA. Yes. I find I must get back to London at once.

BRETHERTON. I'm awfully sorry – awfully.

DIANA. It is very nice of you to say so.

BRETHERTON. We – we've had a ripping time together, haven't we?

DIANA. I've enjoyed it immensely.

BRETHERTON. The walks round here are splendid – aren't they?

DIANA. Yes.

(*He attempts to speak and fails.*)

I'm afraid I really must go now, Captain Bretherton. I have to

catch the 2.17 at Samaden, and the carriage will be round for me
directly. Goodbye.

BRETHERTON. Goodbye – I hope you'll have a comfortable journey
and – no, I don't mean that – Mrs Massingberd – Diana – I – oh,
hang it all, what does a fellow say when he wants to ask the nicest
woman in the world to marry him? Diana, do you think you could
possibly manage to put up with me as a husband? I know I'm an
awful fool at putting things into words, but what I mean is that I've
never met a woman like you and – I love you – 'pon my soul, I love
you, Diana.

DIANA. Do you?

BRETHERTON. Diana – does that mean?

DIANA. No, it doesn't – it doesn't – wait.

BRETHERTON. Diana, for heaven's sake, don't keep me in suspense.
Just let me know my fate in one word – tell me one way or the
other.

DIANA. This is just what I can't do.

BRETHERTON. You can't? Why not?

DIANA. Because . . . Captain Bretherton, you have just made me a
proposal of marriage for which I – thank you. But, until you have
heard what I have to say to you, I shall consider that proposal of
marriage unspoken.

BRETHERTON. Unspoken – but it isn't unspoken. What on earth – I
don't understand.

DIANA. Of course you don't understand – yet – but I wish to make the
position clear to you.

BRETHERTON. The position? What position?

DIANA. Will you be good enough to sit down and listen to me
quietly – for a few minutes?

BRETHERTON. Of course – er – certainly – delighted.

DIANA. Do you realise, Captain Bretherton, that we have only been
acquaintances for a little over a fortnight – to be exact, for
seventeen days?

BRETHERTON. Is that all? I feel as if we had been *friends* for seventeen
years.

DIANA. And you know practically nothing about me – nothing, I
mean, of my life and history before I met you here less than three
weeks ago.

BRETHERTON. Er – no – of course not. Except what you have told me
yourself.

DIANA. Let me see – and what have I told you exactly?

BRETHERTON. Well, for one thing, you've told me that you are the widow of Mr Josiah Massingberd.

DIANA. That, of course, was a lie to begin with.

BRETHERTON. Diana, what do you mean?

DIANA. I mean, Captain Bretherton, that the estimable old gentleman, Mr Josiah Massingberd, is in exactly the same position as the celebrated Mrs Harris –

BRETHERTON. Mrs Harris?

DIANA. There never was no such person!

BRETHERTON. What?

DIANA. And that being the case, he couldn't very well have left a widow, could he?

BRETHERTON. What on earth are you saying?

DIANA. Nor, which is more to the point, perhaps, could he have bequeathed the very comfortable income of three thousand six hundred pounds a year to his imaginary relict.

BRETHERTON. His imaginary relict?

DIANA. Those were my words.

BRETHERTON. I say, you're joking!

DIANA. I assure you, I'm not. On the contrary, I'm in black and deadly earnest.

BRETHERTON. Then if you aren't Diana Massingberd, who the deuce are you?

DIANA. Oh, I'm Diana Massingberd right enough. That's my name – my legal and lawful name – and the only thing about me that isn't a snare and delusion.

BRETHERTON. Am I going mad or are you?

DIANA. Neither of us, I hope. I'm perfectly sane. All I'm trying to do is to make you understand that instead of being a rich widow, I'm a poor spinster – a desperately poor spinster.

BRETHERTON. But – then – how?

DIANA. I've been taking you in, of course.

BRETHERTON. Taking me in?

DIANA. You and all your friends – sailing under false colours. No doubt it was a disgraceful thing to do, but before you get angry with me, I have a right to ask you to hear my story. My father was a country doctor – an underpaid country doctor. When he died there was nothing – nothing at all – and I was thrown upon my own resources for a living. I earned it how and where I could –

and a little more than a month ago I was a shop assistant in
London.

BRETHERTON.  A shop assistant – you?

DIANA.  My last situation was at Dobson's – a big draper's. I was in the
hosiery department.

BRETHERTON.  The hosiery department –

DIANA.  Earning five shillings a week and having a hell of a time. I
shan't apologise for the unparliamentary expression – it is justified.
I'd had six years of that sort of slavery – been at it since my father
died. Then one night, I got a solicitor's letter, telling me that a
distant cousin of mine was dead, and that I had come in for three
hundred pounds.

BRETHERTON.  Three hundred pounds?

DIANA.  Of course, if I'd been a sensible woman I should have hoarded
up my windfall - invested it in something safe and got three per cent
for it. But I didn't. I was sick of the starve and the stint and the
grind of it all – sick to death of the whole grey life – and so I settled
to have a royal time while the money lasted. All the things that I'd
wanted – wanted horribly, and couldn't have – just because I was
poor – pretty dresses, travel, amusement, politeness, consideration,
and yes, I don't mind confessing it – admiration – they should be
mine while the cash held out. I knew that I could buy them – every
one – and I wasn't wrong – I have bought them, I've had my royal
time. I've been petted and admired and made much of, and – only
for the sake of my imaginary fortune, I know, but still I have
enjoyed the experience – enjoyed it down to the very ground. . . .
And now, it's over and the money's spent, and . . . I'm going back.

BRETHERTON.  Going back?

DIANA.  Yes. To work – to the old life and the old grind. I've just
enough left out of my three hundred pounds to settle my hotel bill,
tip the servants, and pay for my ticket home. I expect I shall land in
England practically broke to the wide!

BRETHERTON.  Good Lord!

DIANA.  Oh, my dresses will fetch something, of course. In that state of
life to which it will please Providence to call me, I shall have no
further use for smart frocks. They ought to bring me in enough to
live upon until I get work. Well – now you know the whole story –
and having heard it, you are no doubt feeling very much obliged to
me because I refused to allow you to commit yourself a few
minutes ago.

BRETHERTON. You've put me in a deuced awkward position – deuced
    awkward –

DIANA. I assure you, it is just as awkward for me.

BRETHERTON. You had no right to – to –

DIANA. No right to enjoy myself as I pleased for once in my life, and
    to play the fool with my own money? Are you so very scrupulous as
    to the wisdom with which you spend yours?

BRETHERTON. That's not the point. You must see that it was most –
    unfair – to me – to all of us – to deceive us as to your real
    position.

DIANA. In other words, as to the extent of my monetary resources . . .
    Then I am to understand that it was entirely due to my imaginary
    three thousand six hundred a year that I owe all the attention and
    courtesy I have received from you during my stay here. I guessed as
    much from the moment Mrs Cantelupe tried to pump me about
    my income.

BRETHERTON. Oh, it's all very well to talk like that, but surely you
    must realise that you have treated me shamefully.

DIANA. Indeed?

BRETHERTON. Abominably. By deceiving me in this way – by allowing
    me to suppose –

DIANA. That – I was in a position to support a husband?

BRETHERTON. Oh, hang it all, I know I'm no match for you in an
    argument. But however much you may sneer and jeer at me, you
    must know perfectly well that your conduct has been that of an
    adventuress.

DIANA. An adventuress! So I'm an adventuress, am I? Doesn't this
    rather remind you of the celebrated interchange of compliments
    between the pot and kettle? For if I'm an adventuress, Captain
    Bretherton, what are you but an adventurer?

BRETHERTON. I?

DIANA. You were ready and willing and anxious to run after me, so
    long as you believed that I had money and in the hope that I
    should allow you to live upon that money –

BRETHERTON. Diana – Mrs – Miss Massingberd!

DIANA. It's true – and you know it – and what is that, may I ask, but
    the conduct of an adventurer? You are far too extravagant to live
    on your own income – you are far too idle to work to increase it –
    so you look round for a wife who is rich enough to support you in
    idleness and extravagance. You cannot dig, but to sponge on a wife

you would not be ashamed. And what, pray, have you to offer to the fortunate woman in exchange for the use of her superfluous income? Proprietary rights in a poor backboneless creature who never did a useful thing in his life!

BRETHERTON. Miss Massingberd, this is insulting – intolerable.

DIANA. Captain Bretherton, it may be insulting and intolerable, but it is also the truth. Common, vulgar people like me – people who work for their living instead of living on other people's work – have an awkward knack of calling a spade a spade . . . at times. And remember . . . it wasn't I who started calling names . . . Well, goodbye, Captain Bretherton – as I told you just now, my money is spent, and my time here is up. I must hurry off to my room and finish packing all my earthly possessions in a couple of trunks and a handbag. Make my final adieux to Mrs Cantelupe and – tell her – whatever you think fit.

BRETHERTON. Diana – Miss Massingberd . . .

DIANA. Yes?

BRETHERTON. Before you go, I want you to see – I want to tell you that you have been very unjust to me.

DIANA. Unjust . . . how?

BRETHERTON. You can't believe all that you have said about me . . . It is not only money . . . Surely you see that – and surely you must know that I would give a great deal – a very great deal – if circumstances did not keep us apart –

DIANA. Circumstances!

BRETHERTON. If it were not a moral impossibility for a man – a man in my position –

DIANA. If it were not a moral impossibility for a man in your position to marry a shop girl. That's what you mean, isn't it? A shop girl – that is to say, a woman who has so far degraded herself as to work for her own living. Believe me, I quite realise the impossibility of the thing from your point of view – only for the life of me, I cannot understand how you and your like have the impertinence to look down on me and mine? When you thought I had married an old man for his money, you considered that I had acted in a seemly and womanly manner – when you learnt that, instead of selling myself in the marriage market, I have earned my living honestly, you consider me impossible. And yet, I have done for half a dozen years what you couldn't do for half a dozen months.

BRETHERTON. And what's that?

DIANA. Earned my bread, of course – without being beholden to any man and without a penny at my back. I wonder if it has ever entered into your head to ask yourself what use the world would have for you if you hadn't got money enough to pay your own way with?

BRETHERTON. No, it hasn't!

DIANA. Well, it's a question that you might turn over in your mind with considerable advantage to your moral character. Personally I imagine that you would find the answer to be that under those circumstances the world hadn't any use for you at all.

BRETHERTON. Upon my word.

DIANA. If you don't believe me, you have only to try the experiment for yourself. Stand with your back against the wall as I've stood for the last six years, and fight the world for your daily bread on your own hand . . . You simply couldn't do it – you'd throw up the sponge in a week.

BRETHERTON. Do you take me for an absolute fool, then?

DIANA. No. But I take you for a man brought up in sloth and self-indulgence and therefore incapable of seeing life as it really is. Your whole view of life is – must be – false and artificial. What is the meaning to you of the words. 'If a man will not work neither shall he eat?' Just nothing – they have no meaning to you. You don't understand them – and how should you?

BRETHERTON. If I'm the idiot you make out, I wonder you've ever had anything to do with me at all.

DIANA. It would have been very much better for me if I hadn't.

*(She walks rapidly to door and exits.)*

CURTAIN.

# ACT IV

SCENE: *The Thames Embankment in the small hours of a November morning. Fourteen weeks later.*

*As the* CURTAIN *rises, are seen three huddled figures of two sleeping men, and the* OLD WOMAN, *of the hopelessly unemployed class.* POLICE CONSTABLE FELLOWES *enters.*

FELLOWES (*shaking the first loafer by the arm*). Now then – wake up – wake up, d'you hear? This here seat ain't a doss-house – you've got to move on.

(*He repeats the shaking operation. One of them – the extra man – gets up and shuffles away off the Stage; the other,* BRETHERTON, *takes a good deal of rousing.*)

Now then (*shaking him violently*), are you deaf? Move on, when I tell you.

BRETHERTON. Why on earth can't you let me alone? I wasn't doing any harm. This moving on of poor harmless devils is a perfectly inhuman practice.

FELLOWES. Can't help it – it's our orders. Now then, quick march. Why – it's never you, sir – Captain Bretherton. I beg your pardon, sir.

BRETHERTON. Why, who the –

FELLOWES. Don't you remember me, sir? I served in the Welsh Guards afore I got my discharge and joined the force – and in your company, sir – Private Fellowes.

BRETHERTON. Why, of course I remember you, Fellowes. Glad to see you – that's to say, I hope you're doing well.

FELLOWES. Yes, sir, thanks. I – I'm afraid you're not, sir.

BRETHERTON. Well, it doesn't look very much like it, does it?

FELLOWES. I'm sorry to see you come to this, sir – so rejooced in circumstances.

BRETHERTON. Thank you – er – that's very kind of you.

FELLOWES. We all liked you in the regiment, sir. There wasn't an officer that the men thought more of – and if there was anything I could do –

BRETHERTON. Well, if it wouldn't get you into any serious trouble with your superiors, perhaps you'd allow me to resume my seat?

Thank you. And, Fellowes –

FELLOWES. Yes, sir.

BRETHERTON. I suppose you haven't got a morsel – just a morsel of tobacco about you?

FELLOWES. I have, sir. (*Produces tobacco pouch.*)

BRETHERTON. Ah! (*He takes a battered pipe from his pocket, fills and lights it.*) That's good – three days since I had a whiff of the blessed stuff.

FELLOWES. You don't say so, sir.

BRETHERTON. I do. Cash hasn't run to it. Total takings for the last four-and-twenty hours, threepence-halfpenny. And the halfpenny was a French one.

FELLOWES. It's a bad job! 'Eavy financial losses, I suppose, sir?

BRETHERTON. Why, not exactly – light financial gains would be nearer the mark.

FELLOWES. Beg pardon, sir?

BRETHERTON. The truth is, Fellowes, that as regards money I am not quite so badly off as I look.

FELLOWES. I'm very glad to 'ear it, sir – but –

BRETHERTON. But why am I masquerading on this Embankment in these delectable garments, eh? Well, it's on account of what you might call a challenge.

FELLOWES. A challenge, sir?

BRETHERTON. Yes, a – a sort of a bet.

FELLOWES. You're walking about all night with your feet coming through your boots for a bet, sir?

BRETHERTON. For a sort of bet.

FELLOWES. If I was you, sir, I'd stick to the 'orses.

BRETHERTON. I think I will – after next February!

FELLOWES. After next February?

BRETHERTON. Yes. I've got to go on with this sort of thing till then.

FELLOWES. You've got to go on sleeping out till next February, sir. Why, you'll never stand it – it'll be your death.

BRETHERTON. I don't always sleep out, Fellowes. When I possess the necessary twopence, I patronise the doss-house.

FELLOWES. But what's the Hobject of it all, sir? What's the hobject of sleeping in a twopenny doss when you've got a comfortable 'ome of your own?

BRETHERTON. The object, Fellowes, is to discover whether or not I am capable of earning my living by the work of my own unaided hands for the space of six calendar months.

FELLOWES. Well, I'm damn – beg pardon, sir.

BRETHERTON. I suppose, now, you can't give me any tips on how to manage it? How on earth does a man set about earning his livelihood? I don't mean a man who has been through a Board School and has had a trade at his fingers' end, but a man who has muddled through Eton and Oxford and had practically no education at all?

FELLOWES. Why 'is friends usually gets him some sort of berth, don't they, sir?

BRETHERTON. But if he hasn't got any friends – if he has to worry along on his own?

FELLOWES. It's a bit difficult to say. I suppose he looks out for a job.

BRETHERTON. But how the deuce does he get that job? From my experience of the last few weeks, I should say that all trades were closed to the man whose education has cost his father more than five hundred a year. For the last three months I've been trying to earn my living by the sweat of my brow – net result, a few odd jobs at the docks and a shilling for sweeping out an old gentleman's back garden. My present profession is that of a cab chaser.

FELLOWES. That's not much of a trade, sir?

BRETHERTON. I agree with you – it's not. Occasionally, at the end of a two-mile trot, I receive sixpence in return for the privilege of carrying several trunks up four flights of stairs – but more often my services are declined – without thanks.

FELLOWES. I should give it up, sir, if I was you.

BRETHERTON. I'll be hanged if I do, Fellowes.

FELLOWES. Just pride, sir.

BRETHERTON. That's it, I suppose, just pride. Hang it all, it makes a man feel so small when he realises that he hasn't any market value at all.

FELLOWES. I expect it does, sir.

BRETHERTON. I don't mind confessing that if I had known what I was letting myself in for three months ago, I should have thought twice – several times – before I joined the ranks of the unemployed. But now I've started, I've got to see the thing through – somehow. Meanwhile, the devil only knows where my next meal – comes in. I suppose you couldn't suggest any means of acquiring it – honest, if possible?

FELLOWES. I'm afraid I can't at this moment, sir. But I'm sure you won't think it a liberty, sir – if the loan of a shilling – I'd be proud –

BRETHERTON. No – you're a good chap, and thank you – but I won't.

FELLOWES. You'd better, sir – there's a coffee-stall just along there.

BRETHERTON. I know there's a coffee-stall, Fellowes – there's no need to remind me of that fact. For the last half-hour I've been trying not to see it – and smell it. Don't think I'm too proud to accept a loan from you, but I'm playing this game on my own.

FELLOWES. Well, if you won't, sir, I must be moving along my beat. But if you change your mind by the time I'm round this way again –

BRETHERTON. Don't tempt me, Fellowes, don't tempt me.

FELLOWES (*shaking* OLD WOMAN). Come on, Mother. Come on!

BRETHERTON. There's plenty of room for me and that wretched old scarecrow. You'll let her sleep out, eh?

FELLOWES. That's all right, sir.

(*Exit* FELLOWES.)

(OLD WOMAN *starts and wakes.*)

BRETHERTON. Beg pardon.

WOMAN. Is the copper coming back?

BRETHERTON. No, he's gone by.

WOMAN. That's a blessin'. I didn't want to be moved on from this 'ere seat – I chose it pertickler so as to be near the cawfee-stall. I'm 'avin' my brekfus there later on.

BRETHERTON. You're lucky – wish I was.

WOMAN. It's no use 'inting for me to stand yer treat if that's what you're after.

BRETHERTON. Oh, I assure you – I hadn't the least idea.

WOMAN. Not that I wouldn't be willin' if I'd more than enough to pay for myself. What's brought a nice-spoken young man like you down to this?

BRETHERTON. Oh, various things – can't get work.

WOMAN. Take my advice, dearie – an old woman's advice – and leave it alone.

BRETHERTON. What – work?

WOMAN. No, dearie – not the work – the drink.

BRETHERTON. I haven't touched a drop for weeks.

WOMAN. I dessay you haven't – but that's because you haven't had the money. If you'd been flush it 'ud ha' bin another story – I know yer. You take my tip – when the luck turns, leave it alone – leave it alone. And now you an' me 'ull 'ave our forty winks till the copper comes round again. . . . Pleasant dreams, dearie.

BRETHERTON. Oh, Lord!

WOMAN. What's the matter, dearie?

BRETHERTON. I was only thinking what a silly fool I am.

WOMAN. We're all of us that, dearie, or we – we shouldn't be here.

BRETHERTON. Lord, what a fool I am – what a silly fool.

(*Enter* DIANA MASSINGBERD. *She wears a shabby hat and coat, a short skirt, muddy boots and woollen gloves with holes in several of the fingertips. She carries a small brown-paper parcel. Sits on left end of seat.* BRETHERTON's *pipe has gone out – he strikes a match – lights pipe – turns, shades the light from match on to her face with his hand, recognizes her and throws down match.*)

God bless my soul – Miss Massingberd!

DIANA. Who are you?

BRETHERTON. My name's Bretherton.

DIANA. Bretherton – not Vic – Captain Bretherton?

BRETHERTON. The same.

DIANA. What on earth are you doing here?

BRETHERTON. What are you?

DIANA. If you want to know, I'm here because I have no where else to go. I'm resting on this seat until a policeman moves me on.

BRETHERTON. That's exactly my case – only I've got one advantage over you. The policeman on this beat happens to be an old friend of mine and he says I may stay here as long as I like.

DIANA. As you have so much influence with the powers that be, perhaps you'll intercede with them for me.

BRETHERTON. With pleasure.

DIANA. What are you masquerading like this for? Are you trying to eke out your totally inadequate income by sensational journalism?

BRETHERTON. Sensational journalism?

DIANA. I thought perhaps you were writing up the Horrors of Midnight London for the *Daily Mail*. If you are, I dare say I can be of some assistance to you.

BRETHERTON. You know I'm not nearly clever enough for that.

DIANA. Then what are you doing?

BRETHERTON. Looking for work.

DIANA. What? . . . You don't mean to tell me that this is – genuine . . . that you – are penniless – like me?

BRETHERTON. Are you penniless?

DIANA. Quite.

BRETHERTON. My God! . . . Tell me about it.

DIANA. What's the use?

BRETHERTON. Tell me.

DIANA. I've had hard times . . . since I saw you.

BRETHERTON. No work?

DIANA. Very little. I got a job soon after I came back to London, but I only kept it for a fortnight.

BRETHERTON. How was that?

DIANA. Knocked up – got some sort of a chill – and was ill for weeks. That took the rest of my money. Since then – Oh, I've no right to grumble, of course. If I hadn't played the fool with my little fortune – my three hundred pounds – I shouldn't have been turned out of my lodgings . . . But after all; I don't regret it – no, I don't. I had my good time – my one glorious month, when I made fools of you all and – no, I didn't mean that – I oughtn't to have said that to you, now. Forgive me.

BRETHERTON. Of course I forgive you.

DIANA. And now, it's your turn. Tell me, how long is it since you lost your money?

BRETHERTON. I've been at this sort of game for three months now.

DIANA. Three months – why, it's not much more than that since I was at Pontresina.

BRETHERTON. Not much more.

(DIANA *laughs.*)

What's the joke?

DIANA. I can't help it. If anyone who knew us then – at the Engadine – could see us now.

BRETHERTON. They'd notice a difference.

DIANA. We were both rather smart in those days, weren't we?

BRETHERTON. We certainly aren't now.

DIANA. Look at my glove.

BRETHERTON. Not worse than my boots.

DIANA. You poor fellow. You poor fellow. You must find it horribly hard!

BRETHERTON. I do.

DIANA. But won't your people do anything for you? Surely your brother –

BRETHERTON. I haven't asked him.

DIANA. Have you quarrelled with him, then?

BRETHERTON. No. The fact is, he doesn't know. None of them know.

DIANA. They don't know that you have lost your money. But they must know. You must tell them. They'll give you a start –

BRETHERTON. Miss Massingberd, I'm trying to do what you said I couldn't.

DIANA. What's that?

BRETHERTON. Fight the world on my own.

DIANA. You surely don't mean that because of all the ridiculous things I said when I was angry –

BRETHERTON. They were not ridiculous. My own experience has proved that they were perfectly correct – except in one particular. You said that I should throw up the sponge in a week – I haven't done that.

DIANA. Then it is through me – that you have come down to this?

BRETHERTON. Through you.

DIANA. I am – very sorry.

BRETHERTON. Sorry – you ought to be glad.

DIANA. Glad to see you suffer like this – when you might have applied to your friends for help? You must apply to them at once, do you hear?

BRETHERTON. Miss Massingberd, it is only fair to tell you that you have made a mistake.

DIANA. A mistake?

BRETHERTON. A very natural one, of course. Finding me apparently homeless on the Embankment, you have jumped to the conclusion that I am a ruined man. I am not – I have still got six hundred a year when I choose to make use of it.

DIANA. Oh!

BRETHERTON. And six hundred a year seems a great deal more to me now than it did three months ago.

DIANA. But if you have still got all that money, what on earth are you doing on the Embankment at three o'clock in the morning – and in those boots?

BRETHERTON. Don't you remember what you said to me that last day at Pontresina?

DIANA. I remember – some of the things I said.

BRETHERTON. You told me that I wasn't man enough to find myself a place in the world without money to bolster me up – that I was a poor backboneless creature and that I should go to the wall if I were turned out to earn my bread for six months. I didn't believe you then, but I've found out since that you were right, though I set out to prove you wrong.

DIANA. Then do you really mean –

BRETHERTON. I do. Even the ornamental classes have a certain
amount of pride, you know – it isn't only labour that stands on its
dignity. For the last twelve weeks I have been existing on the work
of my two hands and such brains as I possess. I haven't touched a
penny that I haven't earned.

DIANA. You –

BRETHERTON. And you were quite correct – nobody wants my
services. I'm no use to anyone. You were entirely justified in
looking down on me –

DIANA. No, no, I had no right –

BRETHERTON. But you had – All that you said was perfectly true. The
world only tolerated me because I could pay my way – more or
less – with money I never earned. For every useful purpose I'm
a failure. (*Bangs back of seat with his hand, which wakes* OLD
WOMAN.)

WOMAN (*half aroused, drowsily, without opening her eyes*). We're – all of
us – that, dearie – or we shouldn't be here.

DIANA. I've no right to look down on you because you're not
successful. If you're a failure, what else am I? If nobody wants you,
nobody wants me either.

BRETHERTON. I do.

WOMAN (*gives a sort of snort and opens her eyes, looks knowingly from one
to the other, unties a knot in her shawl and takes out a penny*). I think
its abaht time I 'ad my brekfus. The cawfee-stall smells invitin',
don't it, miss? And you two 'ull be able to chat more comfortable
without me sittin' in the middle of yer. Move along, and tike my
plice, dearie.

(*She exits.*)

BRETHERTON. Diana, I remember telling you once that my income
was a miserable pittance, hardly enough for me to live upon. I've
found out my mistake since then. It's not only enough for *one* to
live upon – it's ample for *two*.

DIANA. Do you realise what you're saying?

BRETHERTON. I'm offering you 'proprietary rights in a poor
backboneless creature who never did a useful thing in his life'.

DIANA. Don't.

BRETHERTON. You refuse to – to entertain the idea? I'm sorry.

DIANA. Captain Bretherton – I'm homeless and penniless – I haven't –
tasted food for nearly twelve hours – I've been half starved for days.

And now, if I understand you aright – you offer to make me your wife.

BRETHERTON. You do understand me aright.

DIANA. That is to say, you offer me a home and what is to me a fortune.

BRETHERTON. And myself.

DIANA. And yourself – please don't imagine I forget that important item. But, under the circumstances, don't you think you that you are putting too great a strain upon my disinterestedness.

BRETHERTON. I understand what you mean. Perhaps I ought not to have spoken tonight – perhaps I ought to have waited. It might have been fairer to you – to us both. But –

DIANA. But what?

BRETHERTON. I am going to tell you what is in my mind, even if you are angry with me.

DIANA. Go on.

BRETHERTON. Perhaps, in my blundering conceit, I made a mistake; but it seemed to me that last day at Pontresina, that if I had said to you, 'I care for you, not for your money but for your own sake' – it seemed to me that you would have come to me then . . . Tell me – was I wrong?

DIANA. No – then I would have . . .

BRETHERTON. And now?

DIANA. No.

BRETHERTON. Because you are too proud. Is that it?

DIANA. I suppose so – yes. I *am* too proud.

BRETHERTON. Are you trying to make me still more ashamed of myself?

DIANA. Why?

BRETHERTON. I was willing enough to marry you when you were the plutocrat and I the pauper. Haven't I put my pride in my pocket and for you, Diana? Haven't I trailed about the streets of London for the last three months to justify my existence in your eyes? Diana, a much humiliated failure asks you to lead him in the way he should go.

DIANA. It will be the blind leading the blind, then – and the end of that is the ditch.

BRETHERTON. Never mind. Even the ditch can't be much worse than the Embankment in November.

DIANA. Someone's coming – a policeman.

(*Enter* FELLOWES.)

BRETHERTON. That you, Fellowes?

FELLOWES. Yes, sir.

BRETHERTON. Glad you've come back. Look here, I've changed my mind about that shilling. If you could oblige me with the loan of it for a few hours –

FELLOWES. You're very welcome, sir.

BRETHERTON. Thanks. I've changed my mind on the other point too. I'm going back to civilization in the morning.

FELLOWES. Glad to hear it, sir.

BRETHERTON. And meanwhile this lady and I are going to breakfast off the coffee-stall at your expense.

(*Exits.*)

FELLOWES. Well, I'm blowed!

(*Exit* FELLOWES.)

(*Re-enter* BRETHERTON *carrying two cups of coffee and some thick slices of bread and butter.*)

BRETHERTON. Had rather a difficulty in getting the chap to trust me with the crockery, but I told him we were close by and he could keep an eye on us. Two cups of coffee – and four doorsteps – that's what they call 'em.

DIANA. I know.

BRETHERTON. Do you – poor little woman!

DIANA. Oh! They're not half bad when you're hungry.

BRETHERTON. Not half bad – they're delicious. Good chap, Fellowes, eh? We'll ask him to the wedding.

DIANA. M'm.

(*She nods and smiles over her cup as the* CURTAIN *falls.*)

# C lemence Dane

## 1888–1965

Born Winifred Ashton in 1888 at Blackheath, Clemence Dane took her *nom de plume* from the London church Saint Clements Dane (which was later destroyed by a bomb in the Second World War). Educated at various private schools, at sixteen she taught French in Switzerland, returning to London to study painting under the famous Tonks, at the Slade, and later in Dresden.

From 1907 she taught in Ireland, but left that career in 1913 to become an actress, using the name Diane Cortis. That year she played at the Criterion in *Eliza Comes to Stay*, and at the Queens she played the Baroness des Hebrettes in *This Way, Madam!*. The following year she toured as Sidonie in *Oh, I Say!*

In 1917, at the age of twenty-nine, she started writing. At first she wrote novels – *Regiment of Women*, *First the Blade* and *Legend*, which brought her some success. Her first play, *A Bill of Divorcement*, produced by Basil Dean at the St Martins in March 1921, caused a sensation and ran for over 400 performances. Subsequently she wrote the screenplay for the 1932 George Cukor film of the play, which starred John Barrymore and Billie Burke and introduced Katherine Hepburn. The film was remade in 1940 under the title *Never To Love* starring Maureen O'Hara and Adolphe Menjou.

Throughout the twenties, thirties and forties she wrote plays, novels and screenplays, and won an Oscar in 1945 for her film *Perfect Strangers* (*A Vacation From Marriage*) which was directed by Alexander Korda, and starred Robert Donat and Deborah Kerr.

Her most notable works include the plays *Wild Decembers*

(about the Brontë sisters, which starred Diana Wynward, 1932), *Moonlight is Silver* (starring Gertrude Lawrence and Douglas Fairbanks Jr, 1934), an adaptation of *The Happy Hypocrite* (starring Vivien Leigh and Ivor Novello, 1934), *Cousin Muriel* (starring Edith Evans, 1940), and *Eighty in the Shade* (starring Sybil Thorndike 1958); the books *The Woman's Side* (1926), a plea for equal rights, and *London Has a Garden* (1964), about Covent Garden, where she lived the novels *Broome Stages* (1931), *The Moon is Feminine* (1938) and *He Brings Great News* (1944); and screenplays for *Anna Karenina* (starring Greta Garbo, 1935) *St Martins Lane* (starring Charles Laughton, 1938) and *Fire Over England* (co-written with Sergei Nolbandov, starring Laurence Olivier, Vivien Leigh and Flora Robson, 1937).

She worked frantically hard during the war producing patriotic material for broadcast, film and even a theatrical piece called *Cathedral Steps*, produced by Basil Dean on the steps of St Paul's Cathedral in 1942.

She never again managed to achieve the success of her first play, but towards the end of her career her hopes were set high when the leading West End producer C.B. Cochran chose to produce her new play about Elizabeth and Essex, to star John Mills and Sybil Thorndike. Tragically Cochran's sudden death in January 1951 meant that the show was cancelled. It has never been performed.

Clemence Dane's busts and portraits of her many friends in the arts are still on show at galleries (portrait and bust of Noël Coward at the National Portrait Gallery), and theatres (Ivor Novello at the Theatre Royal, Drury Lane), all over England.

One particular friend, the playwright Noël Coward, regularly visited her at her home in Tavistock Street, Covent Garden. He recalled that her rooms were always crammed with friends – Joyce Grenfell, Richard Adinsell, Katherine Cornell, the Lunts, Douglas Fairbanks Jr, David Niven, Mary Martin – and any Admirals, Generals or firemen who happened to be passing.

At the age of 68 Clemence Dane visited Noël Coward at home in Jamaica, and within days of her arrival he wrote:

She has already painted a large picture of several oranges, very good, told us the plots of several classic novels, recited reams of poetry and dug a fork in her own neck while illustrating the way Shakespeare stabbed Marlowe. Winnie is the supreme dominator. Her vitality is indestructible, her energy fabulous and her untidiness remarkable; she manages to wreak more havoc in a small space of time than an army of delinquent refugees. She talks wisely and informatively up to the point where she gets carried away and begins to show off. Then steps have to be taken. Our evenings are loud with argument. She is a wonderful unique mixture of artist, writer, games mistress, poet and egomaniac. She is infinitely kind, stubborn, and ruthless in her dislikes.

In fact she proved to be the inspiration for Noël Coward's most famous character, Madame Arcati, in *Blithe Spirit*. Miss Dane's frequent use of schoolgirl slang, mixed with unintentional double entendres, kept all of her friends agog: As guests arrived for a dinner party she would cry 'Olwen's got crabs!', or 'We're having roast cock tonight!' When Miss Grenfell asked her how the goldfish (whose pool lay in full sunlight) were doing, received the reply 'They're all right now. They've got a vast erection covered with everlasting pea.' Of the Governor of Jamaica and wife, she inquired 'Do you remember the night we all had Dick on toast?' It was left to Coward to explain to her why she could not include in her latest novel the sentence: 'He stretched out and grasped the other's gnarled, stumpy tool.' As a house-guest she once came down to breakfast and exclaimed 'Oh, the pleasure of waking up to see a row of tits outside your window!' And Coward later admitted that he 'never published a book or produced a play . . . without first indulging myself in the warming radiance of her enthusiasm and the kindly but nonetheless perceptive shrewdness of her criticism. She has enriched my life with her warmth, her vitality, her knowledge and the unfailing generosity of her loving heart.'

She was made President of the Society of Women Journalists

in 1941 and created a CBE in the Coronation Honours of 1953. On 28 March 1965 she died in Chelsea. To everyone's surprise (for she had written a great deal for the lucrative film industry) she only left just over £3000, most of it to her secretary-companion Olwen Bowen-Davies.

# About *Will Shakespeare – An Invention*

Produced by Basil Dean, *Will Shakespeare* opened on 17 November 1921 at the Shaftesbury, a big expensive production in a barn of a theatre (nowadays almost entirely used for musicals).

*The Times* described the play as 'a mighty pretty entertainment', and *Punch* felt that despite an excess of 'wireless voices' the play would be remembered for 'the sustained beauty and nobility of her verse, which shone steadfastly through some rather indifferent delivery.'

Although it was known that the story was fiction, many critics were severe on Miss Dane's cavalier attitude to history, perhaps forgetting that Shakespeare himself was not the most accurate of historians. We know now that as far as historical truth goes Marlowe was highly unlikely to be running off with one of Shakespeare's girlfriends, but we also know that Richard III was probably a good king, as was Macbeth.

The play's opening coincided with the famous epidemic of influenza which killed millions across the world. Not only did this keep the audience away, but it also decimated the cast, and actors often went on in two or more roles to cover for their absent colleagues. One night Flora Robson, instead of playing one of the ghosts, played three, and Philip Merivale, who played Shakespeare, was heard to greet her final appearance with the unscripted line 'Not you again!'

Amazingly, the play's run lasted as long as ten weeks.

By mid-century several of the dramatic critics had revised their original opinions: W. MacQueen-Pope wrote 'It was a play of which any management might have been proud and it shone amongst the welter of mediocrity which surrounded it. Perhaps it was before its time, and the times themselves were out of joint in 1921.' In 1965, in Clemence Dane's obituaries, the critics again re-evaluated the play and thought 'its style, in adorning simple sentiments in colourful language, couples a genuine beauty and bravura with Elizabethan decorousness', and found in it 'an attempt at serious drama at a time when clever triviality was the surest road to popularity.' It was, they trumpeted over her dead body, 'the most distinguished failure of its time.'

For me this is the most exciting play in this book. It ignores the boundaries of the one set fashion and at times flies high. The verse is sinewy and the situations highly charged. The pivotal role of Anne Hathaway echoes nicely throughout the work and Queen Elizabeth's two short scenes are extremely powerful pieces of dramatic writing.

# WILL SHAKESPEARE
## – AN INVENTION

## Clemence Dane

*Mary Clare, Philip Merival and Haidee Wright, Act IV*

First acted at the Shaftesbury Theatre, London, on 17 November 1921, by the Reandean Company, with the following cast:

| | |
|---|---|
| WILL SHAKESPEARE | *Philip Merivale* |
| ANNE | *Moyna Macgill* |
| MRS HATHAWAY | *Mary Rorke* |
| HENSLOWE | *Arthur Whitby* |
| QUEEN ELIZABETH | *Haidee Wright* |
| MARY FITTON | *Mary Clare* |
| KIT MARLOWE | *Claude Rains* |
| A CHILD ACTOR | *Eric Spear* |
| A SECRETARY | *Arthur Bawtree* |
| A STAGE HAND | *Gilbert Ritchie* |
| A BOY | *Eric Spear* |
| A LANDLORD | *Ivor Barnard* |
| A LADY-IN-WAITING | *Joan Maclean* |

*Shadows in Act I*

| | |
|---|---|
| OPHELIA | *Lennie Pride* |
| DESDEMONA | *Gladys Jessel* |
| OTHELLO | *Herbert Young* |
| QUEEN MARGARET | *Flora Robson* |
| PRINCE ARTHUR | *Eric Crosbie* |
| ROSALIND | *Phyllis Fabian* |
| SHYLOCK | *Gilbert Ritchie* |
| CLOWN | *Ivor Barnard* |
| HAMLET | *Neil Curtis* |
| CAESAR | *Arthur Bawtree* |
| CLEOPATRA | *Mai Ashley* |
| KING LEAR | *Fred Morgan* |

The Three Fates
{
*Nora Robinson*
*Gladys Gray*
*Beatrice Smith*
}

*Strolling Players, Beefeaters, Stage Hands, Drinkers,*
*Court Attendants, etc.*

# ACT I

*The* CURTAIN *rises on the living-room of a sixteenth-century cottage. The walls and ceiling are of black beams and whitewashed plaster. On the left is a large oven fireplace with logs burning. Beyond it is a door. At the back is another door and a mullioned window, half open, giving a glimpse of bare garden hedge and winter sky. On the right wall is a staircase running down from the ceiling into the room, a dresser and a light shelf holding a book or two. Under the shelf is a small table piled with papers, inkstand, sandbox, and so on. At it sits* SHAKESPEARE, *his elbows on his papers, his head in his hands, absorbed. He is a boy of twenty, but looks older. He is dark and slight. His voice is low, but he speaks very clearly. Behind him* ANNE HATHAWAY *moves to and fro from dresser to the central table, laying a meal. She is a slender, pale woman with reddish hair. Her movements are quick and furtive, and she has a high sweet voice that shrills too easily.*

ANNE (*hesitating, with little pauses between the sentences*).
        Supper is ready, Will! Will, did you hear?
        A farm-bird – Mother brought it. Won't you come?
        She's crying in for the basket presently.
        First primroses! Here, smell! Sweet, aren't they? Bread?
        Are the snow wreaths gone from the fields? Did you go far?
        Are you wet? Was it cold? There's black frost in the air,
        My mother says, and spring hangs dead on the boughs –
        Oh, you might answer when I speak to you!

  (SHAKESPEARE *gets up quickly.*)

        Where are you going?
SHAKESPEARE.             Out!
ANNE.                 Where?
SHAKESPEARE.                  Anywhere –
ANNE. – away from me! Yes! Say it!
SHAKESPEARE (*under his breath*).    Patience! Patience!
ANNE. Come back! Come back! I'm sorry. Oh, come back!
        I talk too much. I crossed you. You must eat.
        Oh! Oh! I meant no harm – I meant no harm! –
        You know?
SHAKESPEARE.      I know.
ANNE.                 Why then, come back and eat,

And talk to me. Aren't you a boy to lose
All day in the woods?

SHAKESPEARE.                  The town!

ANNE.                            Ah! In the town?

Ah then, you've talked and eaten. Yes, you can talk
In the town!

(*He goes back to his desk.*)

                 More writing? What's the dream today?

(*He winces.*)

       Oh, tell me, tell me!

SHAKESPEARE.             No!

ANNE.                  I want your dreams.

SHAKESPEARE. A dream's a bubble, Anne, and yet a world,
Unsailed, uncharted, mine. But stretch your hand
To touch it – gone! And you have wet your fingers,
Whilst I, like Alexander, want my world –
And so I scold my wife.

ANNE.                   Oh, let me sail
Your world with you.

SHAKESPEARE.         One day, when all is mapped
On paper –

ANNE.         Now!

SHAKESPEARE.       Not yet.

ANNE.            Now, now!

SHAKESPEARE.            I cannot!

ANNE. Because you will not. Ever you shut me out.

SHAKESPEARE. How many are there in the listening room?

ANNE. We two.

SHAKESPEARE. We three.

ANNE.             Will!

SHAKESPEARE.        Are there not three? Yet swift,
Because it is too soon, you shrink from me,
Guarding your mystery still; so must I guard
My dreams from any touch till they are born.

ANNE. What! Do you make our bond our barrier now?

SHAKESPEARE. See, you're a child that clamours – 'Let me taste!'
But laugh and let it sip your wine, it cries –
'I like it not. It is not sweet!' – and blames you.
See! even when I give you cannot take.

ANNE.  Try me!

SHAKESPEARE.  Too late.

ANNE.                    I will not think I know
        What cruelty you mean. What is't you mean?
        What is't?

SHAKESPEARE.        How long since we two married?

ANNE.                                    Why,
        Four months.

SHAKESPEARE.          And are you happy?

ANNE.                                Will, aren't you?

SHAKESPEARE.  I asked my wife.

ANNE.                          I am! I am! I am!
        Oh, how can I be happy when I read
        Your eyes, and read – what is it that I read?

SHAKESPEARE.  God knows!

ANNE.  Yes, God he knows, but He's so far away –
        Tell Anne!

SHAKESPEARE.  Touch not these cellar thoughts, half worm, half weed:
        Give them no light, no air: be warned in time:
        Break not the seal nor roll away the stone,
        Lest the blind evil writhe itself heart-high
        And its breath stale us!

ANNE.                      Oh, what evil?

SHAKESPEARE.                          Know you not?
        Why then I'll say 'Thank God!' and never tell you –
        And yet I think you know?

ANNE.                          Am I your wife,
        Wiser than your own mother in your ways
        (For she was wise for many, I've but you)
        Ways in my heart stored, and with them the unborn
        I feed, that he may grow a second you –
        Am I your wife, so close to you all day,
        So close to you all night, that oft I lie
        Counting your heartbeats – do I watch you stir
        And cry out suddenly and clench your hand
        Till the bone shows white, and then you sigh and turn,
        And sometimes smile, but never ope your eyes,
        Nor know me with a seeking touch of hands
        That bids me share the dream – am I your wife,
        Can I be woman and your very wife

> And know not you are burdened? You lock me out,
> Yet at the door I wait, wringing my hands
> To help you.

SHAKESPEARE.          You could help me; but – I know you!
> You'd help me, in your way, to go – your way!

ANNE. The right way.

SHAKESPEARE.          Said I not, sweetheart – your way?
> So – leave it!

*(He begins to write.* ANNE *goes to the window and leans against it, looking out.)*

ANNE *(softly).*                    Give me words! God, give me words!

SHAKESPEARE. Sweetheart, you stay the light.

ANNE.                                        The pane is cool.

*(She moves to one side.)*

> Can you see now?

SHAKESPEARE.                That's better.

*(The twang of a lute is heard.)*

ANNE.                                        The road dances.

A VOICE *(singing).* Come with me to London,
> Folly, come away!
> I'll make your fortune
> On a fine day –

ANNE. A stranger with my mother at the gate!

*(She opens the door to* MRS HATHAWAY, *who enters.)*

THE VOICE *(nearer).* Daisy leave and buttercup!
> Pick your gold and silver up,
>> In London, in London,
>> Oh, London Town!

ANNE. What have you brought us, Mother, unawares?

MRS HATHAWAY. Why, I met the man in the lane and he asked his way here. He wants Will.

ANNE. Does he, and does he?

SHAKESPEARE *(at the window).* One of the players. In the town I met him
> And had some talk, and told him of my play.

ANNE. You told a stranger and a player? But I –
> I am not told!

THE VOICE *(close at hand).* For sheep can feed

And robins breed
Without you, without you,
And the world get on without you –
Oh, London Town!

(SHAKESPEARE *goes to the door.*)

ANNE (*stopping him*).                    What brings him here?
SHAKESPEARE.                                              I bring him!
To my own house.                                (*He goes out.*)
MRS HATHAWAY.                    Trouble?
ANNE.                                              Why no! No trouble!
I am not beaten, starved, nor put on the street.
MRS HATHAWAY. Be wise, be wise, for the child's sake, be wiser!
ANNE. What shall I do? Out of your fifty years,
What shall I do to hold him?
MRS HATHAWAY.                              A low voice
And a light heart is best – and not to judge.
ANNE. Light, Mother, light? Oh, Mother, Mother, Mother!
I'm battling on the crumble-edge of loss
Against a seaward wind, that drives his ship
To fortunate isles, but carries me cliff over,
Clutching at flint and thistle-hold, to braise me
Upon the barren beaches he has left
For ever.

(SHAKESPEARE *and the player,* HENSLOWE, *come in talking.*)

MRS HATHAWAY (*at the inner door*). Come, find my basket for me. Let
them be!
ANNE. Look at him, how his face lights up!
MRS HATHAWAY.                                        Come now,
And leave them to it!
ANNE.                              I dare not, Mother, I dare not.
MRS HATHAWAY. It's not the way – a little trust –
ANNE.                                              I dare not.

(MRS HATHAWAY *goes out at the door by the fire.*)

HENSLOWE (*in talk. He is a stout, good-humoured, elderly man, with
bright eyes and a dancing step. He wears earrings, is dressed shabby-
handsome, and is splashed with mud. A lute is slung at his shoulder*).
Played? It shall be played. That's why I'm here.
ANNE (*behind them*). Will!

SHAKESPEARE (*turning*). This is my wife.

ANNE (*curtseys. Then, half aside*). Who is the man? Where from? What is his name?

HENSLOWE (*overhearing*). Proteus, Madonna! A poor son of the god.

(SHAKESPEARE *laughs.*)

ANNE. A foreigner?

HENSLOWE. Why, yes and no! I'm from Spain at the moment – I have castles there; but my bed-sitting-room (a green room, Madonna) is in Blackfriars. As to my means, for I see your eye on my travel stains, I have a bank account, also in Spain, a box office, and the best of references. The world and his wife employ me, the Queen comes to see me, and all the men of genius run to be my servants. But as to who I am – O Madonna, who am I not? I've played every card in the pack, beginning as the least in the company, the mere unit, the innocent ace, running up my number with each change of hand to jack, Queen, King, and so to myself again, the same mere One, but grown to my hopes. For Queen may blow kisses, King of Hearts command all hands at court, but Ace in his shirtsleeves is manager and trumps them off the board at will. You may learn from this Ace; for I think, sir, you will end as he does, the master of your suit.

ANNE. A fortune-teller too!

HENSLOWE. Will you cross my palm with a sixpence, Madonna?

ANNE. With nothing.

HENSLOWE. Beware lest I tell you for nothing that you – fear your fortune!

SHAKESPEARE (*spreading his hand*). Is mine worth fearing?

HENSLOWE. Here's an actor's hand, and a bad one. You'll lose your words, King o' Hearts. Your great scenes will break down.

SHAKESPEARE. Then I'll be 'prenticed direct to the Ace.

HENSLOWE. Too fast. You must come to cues like the rest of us, and play out your part, before you can be God Almighty in the wings – as God Himself found out when the world was youngish.

ANNE. We're plain people, sir, and my husband works his farm.

HENSLOWE. And sings songs? I've been trying out a new play in the provinces before we risk London and Gloriana –

ANNE. What! The Queen! The Queen?

HENSLOWE. Oh, she keeps her eye on poor players as well as on Burleigh and the fleet. *There's* God Almighty in the wings if you like! But as I say –

> Whatever barn we storm, here in the west,
> We're marching to the echo of new songs,
> Jigged out in taverns, trolled along the street,
> Loosed under sweetheart windows, whistled and sighed
> Wherever a farmer's boy in Lover's Lane
> Shifts from the right foot to the left and waits –
> 'Where did you hear it?' say I, beating time:
> And always comes the answer – 'Stratford way!'

A green parish, Stratford!

SHAKESPEARE. Too flat, though I love it. Give me hills to climb!

HENSLOWE. Flat? You should see Norfolk, where I was a boy. From sky to sky there's no break in the levels but shockhead willows and reed tussocks where a singing bird may rest. But in which? Oh, for that you must sit unstirring in your boat, between still water and still sky, while the drips run off your blade until, a yard away, uprises the song. Then, flash! part the rushes – the nest is bare and the bird your own! Oh, I know the ways of the water birds! And so, hearing of a cygnet on the banks of Avon –

ANNE. Ah!

HENSLOWE. You're right, Madonna, the poetical vein runs dry. So I'll end with a plain question – 'Is not Thames broader than Avon?'

SHAKESPEARE. Muddier –

HENSLOWE. But a magical water to hasten the moult, to wash white a young swan's feathers.

SHAKESPEARE. Or black, Mephisto!

HENSLOWE. Black swans are rarest. I saw one when I was last in London. London's a great city! Madonna, you should send your husband to market in London, and in a twelvemonth he'll bring you home the world in his pocket as it might be a russet apple.

ANNE. What should we do with the world, sir, here in Stratford?

HENSLOWE. Why, seed it and sow it, and plant it in your garden, and it'll grow into the tree of knowledge.

ANNE (*turning away*). My garden is planted already.

HENSLOWE (*in a low voice*). The black swan seeks a mate, black swan.

SHAKESPEARE.                                                        A woman?

ANNE (*turning sharply*). What did he say to you?

HENSLOWE. Why, that a woman can make her fortune in London as well as man. There's one came lately to court, but sixteen and a mere knight's daughter, without a penny piece, and you should see her now! The men at her feet –

ANNE. And the women –?

HENSLOWE. Under her heel.

ANNE. What does the Queen say?

HENSLOWE.                              Winks and lets her be,
        A fashion out of fashion – gipsy-black
        Among the ladies with their bracken hair,
        (The Queen, you know, is red!)

SHAKESPEARE.                              A vixen, eh?

HENSLOWE. Treason, my son!

ANNE. God made us anyway and coloured us!

SHAKESPEARE. And is he less the artist if at will
        He strings a black pearl, hangs between the camps
        Of day and day the banner of His dark?
        Or that he leaves, when His autumn breath
        He fans the bonfire of the woods, a pine
        Unkindled?

HENSLOWE.           True; and such a black is she
        Among the golden women.

SHAKESPEARE.                              I see your pine,
        Your branching solitude, your evening tree,
        With high, untroubled head, that meets the eye
        As lips meet unseen kisses in the night –
        A perfumed dusk, a canopy of dreams
        And chapel of ease, a harp for summer airs
        To tremble in –

ANNE.                              Barren the ground beneath,
        No flowers, no grass, the needles lying thick,
        Spent arrows –

SHAKESPEARE.            Yes, she knows – we know how women
        Can prick a man to death with needle stabs.

ANNE. O God!

HENSLOWE.      Your wife! She's ill!

SHAKESPEARE.                              Anne?

ANNE.                                   Let me be!

SHAKESPEARE. Come to your mother – take my arm –

ANNE.                                        I'll sit.
        I have no strength.

SHAKESPEARE.                        I'll call her to you. (*He goes out.*)

ANNE.                                   Quick!
        Before he comes, what is her name? Her name?

       Her mood? Her mind? In all the town of Stratford
       As there no door but this to pound at? Quick!
       You know her? Did you see his look? O God!
       The last rope parts. He's like a boat that strains,
       Strains at her moorings. Why did you praise her so?
       And talk of London? What's it all to you?
       Tall, is she? yes, like a tree – a block of wood –
       You said so! (Is he coming?) Tell me quick!
       I've never seen a London lady close.
       She's lovely? So are many! How?

HENSLOWE.                     She's new!
       She's gallant, like a tall ship setting sail,
       And boasts she fears no man. Say 'woman' though –

ANNE. What woman does this woman fear?

HENSLOWE.                  The Queen.
       I've seen it in her eye.

ANNE.             I should not fear.

HENSLOWE. You never saw the Queen of England smile
       And crook her finger, once – and the fate falls.

ANNE. I've seen her picture. She's eaten of a worm
       As I am eaten. I'd not fear the Queen.
       Her snake would know its fellow in my heart
       And pass me. But this woman – what's her name?

HENSLOWE. Mary –

ANNE.            That's 'bitter'. I shall find her so.

   (SHAKESPEARE *comes in with* MRS HATHAWAY.)

       Look at him! Fear the Queen? Did not the Queen,
       My sister, meet a Mary long ago
       That bruised her in the heel?

HENSLOWE.             Man, your wife's mad!
       She says the Queen's her sister.

ANNE.              Mad, noble Festus?
       Not I! But tell him so – he'll kiss you for it.

HENSLOWE. I'll meet you, friend, some other time or place –

SHAKESPEARE. What's this? You're leaving us?

HENSLOWE.              Your wife's too ill –

SHAKESPEARE. Too ill to stand, yet not too ill to – (*Aside*) Anne!
       Why does he stare? What have you told my friend?

ANNE. Your friend!

SHAKESPEARE.    My friend!

ANNE.                                    This once-met Londoner!
　　　What does he want of you, in spite of me?
　　　This bribing tramp, this palpable decoy –
SHAKESPEARE.  Be silent in my house before my friends!
　　　Be silent!
ANNE.              This is your friend!
SHAKESPEARE.                      Silent, I say!
ANNE.  I *will* not! Blows? Would you do that to me, Husband?
SHAKESPEARE.              I never touched you!
ANNE.                                    What! No blow?
　　　Here, where I felt it – here? Is there no wound,
　　　No black mark?
MRS HATHAWAY.          Oh, she's wild! I'll take her. Come!
　　　Come, Anne! It's naught! I know the signs. (*To*
　　　　SHAKESPEARE.)
                                    Stay you!
ANNE.  O Mother, there befell me a strange pang
　　　Here at my heart – (*The two go out together.*)
SHAKESPEARE.                  Oh women! women! women!
　　　They slink about you, noiseless as a cat,
　　　With ready smiles and ready silences.
　　　These women are too humble and too wise
　　　In pricking needle-ways: they drive you mad
　　　With fibs and slips and kisses out of time:
　　　And if you do not trip and feign as they
　　　And cover all with kisses, do but wince
　　　Once in your soul (the soul they shall not touch,
　　　Never, I tell you, never! Sooner the smeared,
　　　The old-time honey death from a thousand stings,
　　　Than let their tongue prick patterns on your soul!)
　　　Then, then all's catlike clamour and annoy!
HENSLOWE.  Cry, 'Shoo!' and clap your hands; for so are all
　　　Familiar women. These are but interludes
　　　In the march of the play, and should be taken so,
　　　Lightly, as food for laughter, not for rage.
SHAKESPEARE.  My mother –
HENSLOWE (*shrugging*).      Ah, your mother!
SHAKESPEARE.                          She's not thus,
　　　But selfless; and I've dreamed of others – tall,
　　　Warm-flushed like pine-woods with their clear red stems,

With massy hair and voices like the wind
Stirring the cool dark silence of the pines.
Know you such women? – beckoning hilltop women,
That sway to you with lovely gifts of shade
And slumber, and deep peace, and when at dawn
You go from them on pilgrimage again,
They follow not nor weep, but rooted stand
In their own pride for ever – demigods.
Are there such women? Did you say you knew
Such women? Such a woman?

HENSLOWE.                              Come to London
And use your eyes!

SHAKESPEARE.                  How can I come to London?
You see me what I am, a man tied down.
My wife – you saw! How can I come to London?
Say to a sick man 'Take your bed and walk!'
Say to a prisoner 'Release your chain!'
Say to a tongue-slit blackbird 'Pipe again
As in the free, the springtime!' You maybe
Have spells to help them, but for me no help.
London!
I think sometimes that I shall never see
This lady in whose lap the weed-hung ships
From ocean-end returning pour their gold,
Myrrh, frankincense. What colour's frankincense?
And how will a man's eye move and how his hand,
Who sailed the flat world round and home again
To London, London of the mazy streets,
Where ever the shifting people flash and fade
Like my own thoughts? You're smiling – why?

HENSLOWE.                                        I live there.

SHAKESPEARE. Oh, to be you!
To read the faces and to write the dreams,
To hear the voices and record the songs,
To grave upon the metal of my mind
All great men, lordlier than they know themselves,
And fowler-like to fling my net o'er London,
And some let fly, and clip the wings of some
Fit for my notes; till one fine day I catch
The Governess of England as she goes

To solemn service with her gentlemen:
(What thoughts behind the mask, beneath the crown?)
Queen! The crowd's eyes are yours, but not my eyes!
Queen! To my piping you shall unawares
Strut on my stage for me! You laugh? I swear
I'll make that thrice-wrapped, politic, vain heart
My hornbook (as you all are) whence I'll learn
How Julius frowned, and Elinor rode her way
Roughshod, and Egypt met ill news. I'll do it,
Though I hold horses in the streets for hire,
Once I am come to London.

HENSLOWE.                                Come with us
And there's no holding horses! Part and pay
Are ready, and we start tonight.

SHAKESPEARE.                            I cannot.
I'm Whittington at crossroads, but the bells
Ring 'Turn again to Stratford!' not to London.

HENSLOWE. Well – as you choose!

SHAKESPEARE.                    As I choose? *I! I* choose?
I'm married to a woman near her time
That needs me! Choose? I am not twenty, sir!
What devil sped you here to bid me choose?
I knew a boy went wandering in a wood,
Drunken with common dew and beauty-mad
And moonstruck. Then there came a nightshade witch,
Locked hands with him, small hands, hot hands, down drew
        him.
Sighing – 'Love me, love me!' as a ringdove sighs,
(How white a woman is, under the moon!)
She was scarce human. Yet he took her home,
And now she's turned in the gross light of day
To a haggard scold, and he handfasted sits
Breaking his heart – and yet the spell constrains him.
This is not I, not I, for I am bound
To a good wife and true, that loves me; but –
I tell you I could write of such a man,
And make you laugh and weep at such a man,
For your own manhood's sake, so bound, so bound.

HENSLOWE. Laugh? Weep? No, I'd be a friend to such a man! Go to

him now and tell him from me – or no! Go rather to this wife of his
   that loves him well, you say –?
SHAKESPEARE.  Too well!
HENSLOWE.  Why, man, it's common! or too light, too low,
         Not once in a golden age love's scale trims level.
SHAKESPEARE.  I read of lovers once in Italy –
HENSLOWE.  You'll write of lovers too, not once nor twice.
SHAKESPEARE.  Their scales were level ere they died of love,
         In Italy –
HENSLOWE.  But if instead they had lived – in Stratford – there'd have
   been such a seesaw in six months as –
SHAKESPEARE.  As what?
HENSLOWE.  As there has been, eh?
         'Seesaw! Margery Daw!
         She sold her bed to lie upon straw.'
   And so – poor Margery! Though she counts me an enemy – poor
   Margery!
SHAKESPEARE.  What help for Margery – and her jack?
HENSLOWE.  None, friend, in Stratford.
SHAKESPEARE.  Do I not know it?
HENSLOWE.  Then – tell Margery!
SHAKESPEARE.  Deaf, deaf!
HENSLOWE.  Not if you tell her how all heels in London
         (And the Queen dances!)
         So trip to the Stratford tune that I hot-haste
         Am sent to fetch the fiddler –
SHAKESPEARE.                              Man, is it true?
         True that the Queen – ?
HENSLOWE.                         I say – tell Margery!
   What! is she a woman, a wife, and will not further her man? I say
   to you – tell Margery, as I tell you –
SHAKESPEARE.  You do?
HENSLOWE.  I do. I do tell you that if you can come away with us now
   with your 'Dream' in your pocket, and teach it to us and learn of
   us while you teach, and strike London in time for the Queen's
   birthday – I tell you and I tell her, Jack's a made man. See what
   Margery says to that, and give me the answer, stay or come, as I
   pass here tonight! And now let me go; for if I do not soon whip my
   company clear of apple-juice and apple-bloom, clear, that is to say,

of Stratford wine and Stratford women, we shall *not* pass here tonight. (*He goes out.*)

SHAKESPEARE. Tonight! (*Calling*) Anne! Anne! (*He walks up and
down.*) Oh, to be one of them tonight on the silver road – to smell
the steaming frost and listen to men's voices and the ring of iron on
the London road! (*Calling*) Anne!

ANNE (*entering*). You called? He's gone? You're angry? Oh, not now,
   No anger now; for, Will, tonight in the sky,
   Our sky, a new star shines.

SHAKESPEARE.       What's that? You know?

ANNE. I know, and oh, my heart sings.

SHAKESPEARE.       Anne, dear Anne,
   You know? No frets? You wish it? Oh, dear Anne,
   How did you guess and know?

ANNE.        My mother told me.

SHAKESPEARE. She heard us? Did she hear – they've read the play,
   And the Queen's asked for me! London, Anne! London!
   I'll send you London home, my lass, by the post –
   Such frocks and fancies! London! London, Anne!
   And you, you know? And speed me hence? By God,
   That's my own wife at last, all gold to me
   And goodness! Anne, be better to me still
   And help me hence tonight!

ANNE.        It dips, it dies,
   A nightlight, Mother, and no star. I grope
   Giddily in the dark.

SHAKESPEARE.     What did she tell you?

ANNE. No matter. Oh, it earns not that black look.
   London? The Queen? I'll help you, oh, be sure!
   Too glad to see you glad.

SHAKESPEARE.     Anne, it's goodbye
   To Stratford till the game's won.

ANNE.       What care I
   So you are satisfied? The farm must go –
   That's little –

SHAKESPEARE.   Must it go?

ANNE.       Dreamer, how else
   Shall we two live in London?

SHAKESPEARE.      *We*, do you say?
   They'd have me travel with them – a rough life –

ANNE.  I care not!

SHAKESPEARE.     – and you're ailing.

ANNE.                                        Better soon.

SHAKESPEARE.  You'll miss your mother.

ANNE.                                        Mothers everywhere
      Will help a girl. I'm strong.

SHAKESPEARE.                    It will not do!
      I have my world to learn, and learn alone.
      I will not dangle at your apron-strings.

ANNE.  I'll be no tie. I'll be your follower
      And scarce your wife; but let me go with you!

SHAKESPEARE.  If you could see but once, once, with my eyes!

ANNE.  Will! Let me go with you!

SHAKESPEARE.                    I tell you – no!
      Leave me to go my way and rule my life
      After my fashion! I'll not lean on you
      Because you're seven years wiser.

ANNE.                                        That too, O God!

SHAKESPEARE.  And if I hurt you – for I know I do,
      I'm not so rapt – think of me, if you can,
      As a man stifled that wildly throws his arms,
      Raking the air for room – for room to breathe,
      And so strikes unaware, unwillingly,
      His lover!

ANNE.                    I could sooner think of you
      Asleep, and I beside you with the child,
      And all this passion ended, as it must
      In quiet graves; for we have been such lovers
      As there's no room for in the human air
      And daylight side of the grass. What shall I do?
      And how live on? Why did you marry me?

SHAKESPEARE.  You know the why of that.

ANNE.                                        Too well we know it,
      I and the child. You have well taught this fool
      That thought a heart of dreams, a loving heart,
      A soul, a self resigned, could better please
      Than the blind flesh of a woman; for God knows
      Your self drew me, the folded man in you,
      Not, not the boy-husk.

SHAKESPEARE.                    Yet the same God knows
          When folly was, you willed it first, not I.
ANNE. Old! Old as Adam! And untrue, untrue!
          Why did you come to me at Shottery,
          Out of your way, so often? Laugh with me
          Apart, and answer for me as of right,
          As if you knew me better (ah, it was sweet!)
          Than my own brothers? And on Sunday eves
          You'd wait and walk with me the long way home
          From church, with me alone, the footpath way,
          Across the fields where wild convolvulus
          Strangles the corn –
SHAKESPEARE.              Strangles the corn indeed!
ANNE. – and still delay me talking at the stile,
          Long after curfew, under the risen moon.
          Why did you come? Why did you stay with me,
          To make me love, to make me think you loved me?
SHAKESPEARE. Oh, you were easy, cheap, you flattered me.
ANNE (*crying out*). I did not.
SHAKESPEARE.              Why, did you not look at me
          As I were God? And for a while I liked it.
          It fed some weed in me that since has withered;
          For now I like it not, nor like you for it!
ANNE. That is your fate, you change, you must ever be changing,
          You climb from a boy to a man, from a man to a god,
          And the god looks back on the man with a smile, and the
                    man on the boy with wonder;
          But I, I am woman for ever: I change not at all.
          You hold out your hands to me – heaven: you turn from
                    me – hell;
          But neither the hell nor the heaven can change me: I love
                    you: I change not at all.
SHAKESPEARE. All this leads not to London, and for London
          I am resolved: if not tonight –
ANNE.                              Tonight?
SHAKESPEARE. As soon as maybe. When the child is born –
          When will the child be born?
ANNE.                        Soon, soon –
SHAKESPEARE.                              How soon?
ANNE. I think – I do not know –

SHAKESPEARE.                    In March?
ANNE.                                    Who knows?
SHAKESPEARE.  Did you not tell me March?
ANNE.                            Easter –
SHAKESPEARE.                            That's May!
          It should be March.
ANNE.                        It – should be – March –
SHAKESPEARE.                                    Why, Anne?
ANNE.  Stay with me longer! Wait till Whitsuntide,
              Till June, till summer comes, and if, when you see
              Your own son, still you'll leave us, why, go then!
              Be sure, you will not go.
SHAKESPEARE.                        Summer? Why summer?
          It should be spring, not summer –
ANNE.                                    I'll not bear
              These questions, like coarse fingers, prying out
              My secrets
SHAKESPEARE.          Secrets?
ANNE.                            Secrets? I've none –
          I never meant – I know not why the word
          Came to me, 'secret'. Yet you're all secret thoughts
          And plans you do not share. Why should not I
          Be secret, if I choose? But see, I'll tell you
          All, all – some other time – were there indeed
          A thing to tell –
SHAKESPEARE.              When will the child be born?
ANNE.  If it were – June? My mother said today
              It might be June – July – This woman's talk
              Is not for you –
SHAKESPEARE.              July?
ANNE.                                Oh, I must laugh
              Because you look and look – don't look at me!
              June! May! I swear it's May! I said the spring,
              And May is still the girlhood of the year.
SHAKESPEARE.  July! A round year since you came to me!
              Then – when you came to me, in haste, afraid,
              All tears, and clung to me, and white-lipped swore
              You had no friend but Avon if I failed you,
              It was a lie?
ANNE.          Don't look at me!

SHAKESPEARE.                              No need?
　　　You forced me with a lie?
ANNE.                              Now there is – now!
SHAKESPEARE.  You locked me in this prison with a lie?
ANNE.  I loved you.
SHAKESPEARE.        And you lied to me –
ANNE.                              To hold you.
　　　I couldn't lose you. I was mad with pain.
SHAKESPEARE.  Are you so weak,
　　　So candle-wavering, that a gust of pain
　　　Could snuff out honour?
ANNE.                              'Ware this hurricane
　　　Of pain! The deserts heed it not, nor rocks,
　　　Nor the perpetual sea; but oh, the fields
　　　Where barley grows and small beasts hide, they fear –
　　　And haggard woods that feel its violent hand
　　　Entangled in their hair and wrestling, shriek
　　　Crashing to ruin. What shall their pensioners
　　　Do now, the rustling mice, the anemones,
　　　The whisking squirrels, ivies, nightingales,
　　　The hermit bee whose summer goods were stored
　　　In a south bank? How shall the small things stand
　　　Against the tempest, against the cruel sun
　　　That stares them, homeless, out of countenance,
　　　Through the day's heats?
SHAKESPEARE.                    Coward! They see the sun
　　　Though they die seeing, and the wider view,
　　　The vast horizons, the amazing skies
　　　Undreamed before.
ANNE.                    I cannot see so far.
　　　I want my little loves, I want my home.
　　　My life is rooted up, my prop is gone,
　　　And like a vine I lie upon the ground,
　　　Muddied and broken.
SHAKESPEARE.                I could be sorry for you
　　　Under the heavy hand of God or man
　　　But your own hand has slain yourself and me.
　　　Woman, the shame of it, to trap me thus,
　　　Knowing I never loved you!

ANNE.                                 Oh, for a month –
        In the spring, in the long grass, under the apple-trees –
SHAKESPEARE. I never loved you.
ANNE.                                 Think, when I hurt my hand
        With the wild rose, it was then you said 'Dear Anne!'
SHAKESPEARE. I have forgotten.
ANNE.                                 On Midsummer Eve –
        There was a dream about a wood you told me,
        Me – not another –
SHAKESPEARE.              *        I was drunk with dreams.
        That night.
ANNE.                       That night, that night you loved me, Will!
        Oh, never look at me and say – that night,
        Under the holy moon, there was no love!
SHAKESPEARE. You knew it was not love.
ANNE.                                 O God, I knew,
        And would not know! You never came again.
        I hoped. I prayed. I hoped. I loved you so.
        You never came.
        And must I go to you? I was ashamed.
        Yet in the wood I waited, waited, Will,
        Night after night I waited, waited, Will,
        Till shame itself was swallowed up in pain,
        In pain of waiting, and – I went to you.
SHAKESPEARE. That lie upon those loving lips?
ANNE.                                 That lie.
SHAKESPEARE. There was no child?
ANNE.                       The hope, the hope of children,
        To bind you to me – a true hope to hold you –
        No lie – a little lie – I loved you so –
        Scarcely a lie – a promise to come true
        Of gifts between us and a love to come.
SHAKESPEARE. You're mad! You're mad!
ANNE.                                 I was mad. I am sane.
        I am blind Samson, shaking down the house
        Of torment on myself as well as you.
SHAKESPEARE. What gain was there? What gain?
ANNE.                                 What gain but you?
        The sight of your face and the sound of your foot on the
                stair,

And your casual word to a stranger – 'This is my wife!'
For the touch of my hand on your arm, as a right, when we
    walked with the neighbours:
For the son, for the son on my heart, with your smile and
    your frown:
For the loss of my name in the name that you gave when you
    said to him – 'Mother! your mother!'
For your glance at me over his head when he brought us his
    toys or his tears:
Have pity! Have pity! Have pity! For these things I did it.

SHAKESPEARE. Words! Words! You lied to me. Go your own road!
I know you not.

ANNE.               But I, but I know you.
Have I not learned my god's face? Have I not seen
The great dreams cloud it, as the ships of the sky
Darken the river? Has not the wind struck home,
The following chill wind that stirs all straws
Of omen? You're to be great, God pity you!
I'm your poor village woman; but I know
What you must learn and learn, and shriek to God
To spare you learning, if you will be great,
Singing to men and women across fields
Of years, and hearing answer as they reap,
Afar, the centuried fields, 'He knew, he knew!'
How will they listen to you – voice that cries
'Right's right! Wrong's wrong! For every sin a stone!'
'Ye shall not plead to any god or man –
'"I flinched because the pain was very great,"
'"I fell because the burden bore me down,"
'"Hungry, I stole."' O boy, ungrown, at judgement,
How will they listen? What? I lied? Oh, blind!
When I, your own, show you my heart of hearts,
A book for you to read all women by,
Blindly you turn my page with – 'Here are lies!'

SHAKESPEARE. Subtle enough – and glitter may be gold
In women's eyes – you say so – though to a man,
Boy rather (boy, you called me) lies are lies,
Base money, though you rub 'em till they shine,
Ill money to buy love with; but – I care not!
So be at ease! My love's not confiscate,

> For none was yours to forfeit. Faith indeed,
> A weakling trust is gone, for though you irked me
> I thought you honest and so bore much from you –
> Your jealous-glancing eye, officious hand
> Meddling my papers, fool's opinion given
> Unasked when strangers spoke with me, and laughter
> Suddenly checked as if you feared a blow
> As a dog does – it made me mad!

ANNE.                                        Go on!

SHAKESPEARE.  For when did I use you ill?

ANNE.                                        Go on!

SHAKESPEARE.                                        What need?
> All's in a word – your ever-presence here
> As if you'd naught in life to do but watch me –

ANNE. Go on!

SHAKESPEARE.  All this, I say, I bore, because at heart
> I did believe you loved me. Well – it's gone!
> And I go with it – free, a free man, free!
> Anne! For that word I could forgive you all
> And go from you in peace.

ANNE (*catching at his arm*).          You shall not go!

SHAKESPEARE. Shall not? This burr – how impudent it clings!

ANNE. You have not heard me –

SHAKESPEARE.                                        Let me go, I say!
> My purse, my papers –

ANNE.                                        Will!

SHAKESPEARE.                                        Talk to the walls,
> For I hear nothing!

ANNE.                                        Why, a murderess
> Has respite in my case – and I – and I –
> What have I done but love you, when all's said?
> You will not leave me now, now when that lie
> Is certain truth at last, and in me sleeps
> Like God's forgiveness? For I felt it stir
> When you were angry – I was angry too,
> My fault, all mine – but I was sick and faint
> And frightened, so I railed, because no word
> Matched with the strong need in me suddenly
> For gentlest looks and your beloved arms
> About this body changed and shaking so;

But why I knew not. But my mother knew
And told me.

SHAKESPEARE.            O wise mother!

ANNE.                                    Will, it's true!

SHAKESPEARE.  Practice makes perfect, as we wrote at school!

ANNE. I swear to you –

SHAKESPEARE.            As then you swore to me.
Not twice, not twice, my girl!

ANNE.                              O God, God Son!
Pitiful God! If there be other lives,
As I have heard him say, as his books say,
In other bodies, for Your Mother's sake
And all she knows (God, ask her what she knows!)
Let me not be a woman! Let me be
Some twisting worm on a hook, or fish they catch
And fling again to catch another year,
Or otter trapped and broiled in the sun three days,
Or lovely bird whose living wing men tear
From its live body, or of Italy
Some peasant's drudge-horse whipped upon its eyes,
Or let me as a heart-burst, screaming hare
Be wrenched in two by slavering deaths for sport;
But let me not again be cursed a woman
Surrendered to the mercy of her man!

(*She sinks down in a crouching heap by the hearth. There has been a
sound of many voices drawing nearer, and as she ceases speaking, the
words of a song become clear.*)

THE PLAYERS (*singing*). Come with us to London,
            Folly, come away!
        We'll make your fortune
            On a summer day.
    Leave your sloes and mulberries!
    There are riper fruits than these,
            In London, in London
            Oh, London Town!
            For winds will blow
            And barley grow
        Without you, without you,
    And the world get on without you –
            Oh, London Town!

(*The voices drop to a low hum.* HENSLOWE *thrusts his head in at the window.*)

HENSLOWE. The sun's down. The sky's as yellow as a London fog. Well, what's it to be?

SHAKESPEARE. London! The future in a golden fog!

HENSLOWE. Come then!

SHAKESPEARE. I'll fetch my bundle. Wait for me! What voices?

HENSLOWE. The rest of us, the people of the plays.

      We're all here waiting for you.

SHAKESPEARE.                   Come in all! all!

HENSLOWE. Does your wife say to us – 'Come in!'?

SHAKESPEARE.                         What wife?

(*He hurries up the stairs and disappears.*)

HENSLOWE (*opening the outer door*). May we come in?

ANNE.                 You heard him.

HENSLOWE.                         We ask you.

ANNE. It's his house.

HENSLOWE (*humming*). While fortune waits.

               Within the gates

                  Of London, of London –

    He must be quick!

ANNE.               Am *I* to tell him so?

HENSLOWE. The new moon's up and reaping in a sky

      Like corn – that's frost! A bitter travelling night

      Before us –

ANNE (*going to the window*). So it is.

HENSLOWE.                 Not through the glass!

      You'll buy ill luck of the moon.

ANNE.                  I bought ill fortune

      Long months ago under the shifty moon,

      I saw her through the midnight glass of the air,

      Milky with light, when trees my casement were,

      And little twigs the leads that held my pane.

      I'm out of luck for ever.

HENSLOWE. Did I not tell you you feared your fortune? But there are some in the company can tell you a better, if you'll let 'em in.

THREE PLAYERS IN MASKS (*tapping at the window*).

      Let us in! Let us in! Let us in!

ANNE. I will not let you in. Wait for your fellow
      On the high road! He'll come to you soon enough.

(*She turns from them and seats herself by the fire.*)

A PLAYER (*dressed as a king, over* HENSLOWE's *shoulder*). Are we never
    to come in? It's as cold as charity since the sun set.
ANNE. It's no warmer here.
A CHILD (poking his head under the PLAYER's arm). I can't feel my
    fingers. (ANNE looks at him. Her face changes.)
ANNE. If the fire warms you, you may warm yourself.

(THE PLAYERS *stream in.*)

It does not warm me. Look! It cannot warm me.

(*She thrusts her hand into the flame.*)

HENSLOWE. God's sake!

(*He pulls her back.* THE PLAYERS *stare and whisper together.*)

ANNE. Eyes! Needle eyes! Why do you stare and point?
      Like you I would have warmed myself. Vain, vain!
      It's a strange hearth. You players are the first
      It ever warmed or welcomed. Charity?
      Who said it – 'Cold as charity'? That's love!
      But there's no love here. Baby, stay away!
      You'll freeze less out in churchyard night than here,
      For here's not even charity.
THE CHILD (*warming his hands*). I'm not a baby. I'm nearly eleven. I've
    played children's parts for years. I'm getting warmer. Are you?
ANNE. No.
CHILD. I like this house. I'd like to stay here. I suppose there are
    things in that cupboard?
THE KING (*overhearing*). Now, now!
CHILD. That's my father. He's a king this week. He's only a duke as a
    rule. Are there apples in that cupboard? Will you give me one?

(ANNE *goes to the cupboard and takes out an apple.*)

ANNE. Will you give me a kiss?
CHILD. For my apple?
ANNE. No, for love.
CHILD. I don't love you.
ANNE. For luck, then.
CHILD. You told him you'd got no luck.

ANNE.  Won't you give me a kiss?

CHILD.  If you like. Don't hold me so tight. Is it true you've no luck?
Shall I tell your fortune?

ANNE.  Can you?

CHILD.  O yes! I've watched the Fates do it in the new play. It's
Orpheus and – it's a long name. But she's his lost wife. Give me a
handkerchief. That's for a grey veil. (*Posing.*) Now say to me –
'Who are you?'

ANNE.  Who are you?

CHILD (*posing*). Fate! Now you must say – 'Whose Fate?'

ANNE.  Whose?

CHILD.  Oh, then I lift the veil and you scream. (*Stamping his feet.*)
Scream!

ANNE.  Why, baby?

CHILD (*frowning*). At my dreadful face. (*But he begins to laugh in spite of
himself.*)

ANNE (*her face hidden*). Oh, child! Oh, child!

CHILD.  That's right! That's the way she cries in the play. You see the
man goes down to hell to find his wife, and the Fates show her
what's going to happen while she's waiting for him. She's in hell
already, waiting and waiting. It takes years to travel through hell.
That's her talking to the old man in rags and a crown.

ANNE.  Who's he?

CHILD.  Oh, he's a poor old king whose daughters beat him. He isn't
in this play. Well, when Orpheus gets to hell – I lead him there,
you know –

ANNE.  A babe in hell – a babe in hell –

CHILD.  I'm the little god of love. I wear a crown of roses and wings.
They do tickle. Soon I'll be too big. So he and I go to the three
Fates to get back his wife. She isn't pretty in that act. She's all
white and dead round her eyes – like you.

ANNE.  Does he find her?

CHILD.  After he sings his beautiful song he does. Everybody has to
listen when he sings. Even the big dog lies down. Your husband
made us a nice catch about it yesterday. I like your husband. I'm
glad he's coming with us. Are you coming with us?

ANNE.  No.

CHILD.  It's a pity. If you were a man you could act in the company.
But women can't act. Even Orpheus's wife is a boy really. So are
the three Fates. They're friends of mine. Would you like to talk to

them, the way we do in the play? Come on! I go first, you see. You
must say just what I tell you.

(*He takes her hands and pulls her to her feet. She stares, bewildered, for
the room has grown dim. The dying fire shines upon the shifting,
shadowy figures of the* PLAYERS. *The crowd grows larger every moment
and is thickest at the foot of the stairs.* SHAKESPEARE *is seen coming
down them.*)

ANNE. The room's so full. I'm frightened. Who are all these people?

CHILD. Hush! We're in hell. These are all the dead people. We bring
'em to life.

ANNE. Who? We?

CHILD. I and the singer. Look, there's your husband coming down the
stairs! That's just the way Orpheus comes down into hell.

ANNE. Will! Will!

CHILD. Hush! You mustn't talk.

ANNE. But it's all dreams – it's all dreams.

CHILD. It's the players.

SHAKESPEARE (*among the shadows*). Let me pass!

THE SHADOWS.                    Pay toll!

SHAKESPEARE.                              How, pay it?

A SHADOW.                                                    Tell my story?

ANOTHER. And mine!

ANOTHER.                    And mine!

ANOTHER.                              And mine!

A ROMAN WOMAN. Pluck back my dagger first and tell my story!

A DROWNED GIRL. Oh, listen, listen, listen, I've forgotten my own
story. It's a very sad one. Remember for me!

SHAKESPEARE. I will remember. Let me pass!

A TROJAN WOMAN (*kissing him*).                    Here's pay!

A VENETIAN. I died of love.

THE TROJAN WOMAN.          Kiss me and tell my story!

A MOOR. Dead lips, dead lips!

A YOUNG MAN.                              This is how Judas kissed.

A QUEEN. My son was taken from me. Tell my story!

ANOTHER. And mine!

ANOTHER.                    And mine!

A YOUNG MAN.                              That son am I!

TWO CHILDREN.                                        I – I –

A SOLDIER. I killed a king.

A CROWNED SHADOW.          He killed me while I slept.

THE SHADOWS. You shall not pass until you tell our story!

A GIRL DRESSED AS A BOY. I lived in a wood and laughed. Sing you my
 laughter
   When the sun shone!

SHAKESPEARE.     I'll sing it. Singing I go,
   What shall I find after the song is over?
   What shall I find after the way is clear?

AN OLD MAN, A JEW. Gold and gold and gold –

A CLOWN.        And a grave untended –

A MAN IN BLACK. Heartbreak –

TWO COUSINS.    A friend or two –

A ROMAN WITH LAURELS.    Oh, sing my story
   Before I had halfway climbed to the nearest star
   My ladder broke.

SHAKESPEARE.   I'll tell all time that story.

THE ROMAN. The stars are dark, seen close.

SHAKESPEARE.     I'll say it.

THE ROMAN.      Pass!

AN EGYPTIAN (*holding a goblet*). He shall not pass. Drink! There are
 pearls in the cup.

A GIRL, A VERONESE (*taking it from her*). No – sleep!

A MAN (*with a wand*).   Dreams!

THE KING IN RAGS.   Frenzy!

A NUN.      Sacrament!

A DRUNKARD.     A jest!

A ROMAN WIFE. Here's coals for bread.

THE EGYPTIAN (*A man in armour has flung his arm about her neck*). Eat,
 drink and pass again
   To the lost sunshine and the passionate nights,
   And tell the world our story!

SHAKESPEARE.    Let me go!

ALL THE SHADOWS. Never, never, never! To the end of time we follow,
   Follow, follow, follow!

SHAKESPEARE.    Threads and floating wisps
   Of being, how they fasten like a cloud
   Of gnats upon me, not to be shaken off
   Unsatisfied –

THE SHADOWS.  Sing! Sing!

 (*There is a strain of music: the crowd hides* SHAKESPEARE: *the three
 masked players have drifted free of the turmoil.*)

CHILD (*delighted*). He does it quite as well as Orpheus.

ANNE. Who are these dreams?

CHILD. The people of the plays. And there are the Fates at last! That's the end of my part. Now you must talk to them till your husband comes. He comes when you scream.

(*He picks up his bow and runs away.*)

ANNE.                                    Come back! Stay by me!

CHILD (*laughing*).                                    Play your part alone.

(*He is lost in the crowd.* THE MASKS *have drawn near. The first is small and closely veiled and carries the distaff. The second is tall: part of her face shows white: her hands are empty. The third is bowed and crowned: she carried the shears.*)

ANNE. These are all dreams or I am mad. Who are you?

FIRST MASK. His fate. I hold the thread.

ANNE.                                    I'll see you!

FIRST MASK.                                    No!

(*As she retreats, the* SECOND MASK *takes the distaff from her.*)

SECOND MASK. I tangle it.

ANNE.                    Who are you?

SECOND MASK.                                    Fate! his fate!

ANNE. Drop the bright mask and let me see!

(*The* SECOND MASK *drops her veil and shows the face of a dark lady.*)

                                                                It needs not!

            I knew, I knew! Barren the ground beneath,
            No flowers, no fruit, spent arrows –

(*The* SECOND MASK *makes way for the* THIRD, *who takes the tangle from her. The* SECOND MASK *glides away.*)

                                                        Not the shears!

THIRD MASK (*winding the thread*)
    Not yet!

ANNE.        Who are you?

THIRD MASK.                    Fate! His fate!

ANNE.                                        A crown!
            My snake should know its fellow – is it so?

(*The mask is lifted and reveals the face of* ELIZABETH.)

            I do not fear the Queen –

THIRD MASK.                    Take back the thread!

(*She gives the distaff to the* FIRST MASK, *who has reappeared beside her and glides away.*)

ANNE.  But you I fear, O shrinking fate! What fate?
          What first and last fate? Show me your face, I say!
(*She tears off the mask. The face revealed is the face of* ANNE. *She screams.*)

          Myself! I saw myself! Will! Will!

(THE CHILD *kneeling at the hearth stirs the fire and a bright flame shoots up that lights the whole room. It is empty save for the few players gathering together their bundles and* SHAKESPEARE, *who has hurried to* ANNE. *His hand, gripping her shoulders, steadies her as she sways.*)

SHAKESPEARE.                                   Still railing?
CHILD (*to his father*). She's a poor frightened lady and she cried. I like her.
ANNE.  Gone! gone! Where are they? Call them back! I saw –
SHAKESPEARE.  What folly! These are players and my friends;
          You could have given them food at least and served them.
ANNE.  I saw – I saw –
HENSLOWE (*coming up to them*). So, are you ready? The moon is high: we must be going.
SHAKESPEARE.  I'll follow instantly.

(THE PLAYERS *trail out by twos and threes. They pass the window and repass it on the further side of the hedge. They are a black, fantastic frieze upon the yellow, winter sky.* HENSLOWE *goes first: the king's crown is crooked, and the child is riding on his back: the masks come last.*)

THE PLAYERS (*singing*). Come away to London,
                    Folly, come away!
               You'll make your fortune
                    Thrice in a day,
          Paddocks leave and winter byres,
          London has a thousand spires,
                    A-chiming, a-rhyming,
                    Oh, London Town!
                    The snow will fall
                    And cover all
               Without you, without you,

And the world get on without you –
　　Oh, London Town!

(SHAKESPEARE *goes hurriedly to the table and picks up his books.*)

ANNE.　　　　　　　　　　　　　Will!
SHAKESPEARE.　　　　　　　　　　　　　For your needs
　　You have the farm. Farewell!
ANNE (*catching at his arm*).　　　　For pity's sake!
　　I'm so beset with terrors not my own –
　　What have you loosed upon me? I'll not be left
　　In this black house, this kennel of chained grief,
　　This ghost-run. Take me with you! No, stay by me!
　　These are but dreams of evil. Shall we not wake
　　Drowsily in a minute? Oh, bless'd waking
　　To peace and sunshine and no evil done!
　　Count out the minute –
SHAKESPEARE.　　　　　　　　If ever I forget
　　The evil done me, I'll forget the spring,
　　And Avon, and the blue ways of the sky,
　　And my own mother's face.
ANNE.　　　　　　　　　　Do I say 'forget'?
　　I say 'remember'! When you've staked all, all,
　　Upon your one throw – when you've lost – remember!
　　And done the evilest thing you would not do,
　　Self-forced to the vile wrong you would not do,
　　Me in that hour remember!
SHAKESPEARE.　　　　　　　Let me go!
ANNE (*she is on the ground, clinging to him*).
　　Remember! See, I do not pray 'forgive'!
　　Forgive? Forgiving is forgetting – no,
　　Remember me! Remember, when your sun
　　Blazes the noon down, that my sun is set,
　　Extinct and cindered in a bitter sea,
　　And warm me with a thought. For we are bound
　　Closer than love or chains or marriage binds:
　　We went by night and each in other's heart
　　Sowed tares, sowed tears. Husband, when harvest comes,
　　Of all your men and women I alone
　　Can give you comfort, for you'll reap my pain
　　As I your loss. What other knows our need?

Dear hands, remember, when you hold her, thus,
Close, close –

SHAKESPEARE.          Let go my hands!

ANNE.                              – and when she turns
To stone, to a stone, to an unvouchsafing stone
Under your clutch –

SHAKESPEARE.                    You rave!

ANNE.                              – loved hands, remember
Me unloved then, and how my hands held you!
And when her face – for I am prophecy –
When her lost face, the woman I am not,
Stares from the page you toil upon thus, thus,
In a glass of tears, remember then that thus,
No other way,
I see your face between my work and me,
Always!

SHAKESPEARE.          Make end and let me go!

ANNE (*she has risen*).                    Why, go!
But mock me not with any 'Let me go'!
I do not hold you. Ah, but when you're old
(You will be old one day, as I am old
Already in my heart), too weary-old
For love, hate, pity, anything but peace,
When the long race, O straining breast! is won,
And the bright victory drops to your outstretched hand,
A windfall apple, not worth eating, then
Come back to me –

SHAKESPEARE (*at the door*).    Farewell!

ANNE.                              – when all your need
Is hands to serve you and a breast to die on,
Come back to me –

SHAKESPEARE.                    Never in any world!

(*He goes out as the last figure passes the window, and disappears.*)

THE PLAYER'S VOICES (*dying away*). For snow will fall
And cover all
Without you, without you –

(*The words are lost.*)

SHAKESPEARE (*joyfully*). Ah! London Town!

(*He is seen an instant, a silhouette with outstretched arms. Then he, too,*

*disappears and there is a long silence. A cold wind blows in through the*
*open door. The room is quite dark and the fire has fallen to ashes.)*

ANNE (*crying out suddenly*).
          The years – the years before me!
MRS HATHAWAY (*calling*).                    Anne! Where's Anne?

(*She comes in at the side door.*)

          Anne! Anne! Where are you? Why, what do you here,
          In the cold, in the dark, and all alone?
ANNE.                                         I wait.


     CURTAIN.


# ACT II

## SCENE 1

*A room at the Palace.* ELIZABETH *sits at a working table. She is upright, vig-*
*orous, with an ivory white skin and piercing eyes. Her hair is dark red and*
*stiffly dressed. She is old, as an oak or a cliff or a cathedral is old – there is no*
*frailty of age in her. Her gestures are measured, she moves very little, and*
*frowns oftener than she smiles, but her smile, when it does come, is kindly. Her*
*voice is strong, rather harsh, but clear. She speaks her words like a scholar, but*
*her manner is that of a woman of the world, shrewd and easy. Her dress is a*
*black-green brocade, stiff with gold and embroidered with coloured stones.*
*Beside her stands* HENSLOWE, *ten years older, stouter and more prosperous. In*
*the background* MARY FITTON, *a woman of twenty-six, sits at the virginals,*
*fingering out a tune very faintly and lightly. She is taller than* ELIZABETH,
*pale, with black hair, a smiling mouth and brilliant eyes. She is quick and*
*graceful as a cat, and her voice is the voice of a singer, low and full. She wears*
*a magnificent black and white dress with many pearls. A red rose is tucked*
*behind her ear.*

ELIZABETH.  Money, money! Always more money! Henslowe, you're a
     leech! And I'm a Gammer Gurton to let myself be bled. Let the
     public pay!
HENSLOWE.  Madam, they'll do that fast enough if we may call
     ourselves Your Majesty's Players.
ELIZABETH.  No, no, you're not yet proven. What do you give me?

Good plays enough, but what great play? What has England, what have *I*, to match against them when they talk to me of their Tasso, their Petrarch, their Rabelais – of Divine Comedies and the plays of Spain? Are we to climb no higher than the Germans with their 'Ship of Fools'?

HENSLOWE. 'The Faerie Queene'?

ELIZABETH. Unfinished.

HENSLOWE. Green – Peele – Kyd – Webster –

ELIZABETH. Stout English names – not names for all the world. I will pay you no more good English pounds a year and fib to my treasurer to account for them. You head a deputation, do you? You would call yourselves the Queen's Players, and mount a crown on your curtains? Give me a great play, then – a royal play – a play to set against France and Italy and Spain, and you can have your patent.

HENSLOWE. There's 'Tamburlaine'!

ELIZABETH. A boy's glory, not a man's.

HENSLOWE. 'Faust' and 'The Jew of Malta'!

ELIZABETH. I know them.

HENSLOWE. He'll do greater things yet.

ELIZABETH. Do you believe that, Henslowe?

HENSLOWE. No, Madam.

ELIZABETH. Then why do you lie to me?

HENSLOWE. Madam, I mark time. I have my man; but he is not yet ripe.

ELIZABETH. How long have you served me, Henslowe?

HENSLOWE. Twelve years.

ELIZABETH. How often have you come to me in those twelve years?

HENSLOWE. Four times, Madam!

ELIZABETH. Have I helped or hindered?

HENSLOWE. I confess it, Madam, I have lived on your wits.

ELIZABETH. Then who's your man?

HENSLOWE. You'll not trust me. He has done little before the world.

ELIZABETH. Shakespeare?

HENSLOWE. Madam, you know everything. Will you see him? He and Marlowe are among our petitioners.

ELIZABETH. H'm! The Stratford boy! I have not forgotten.

HENSLOWE. Who could have promised better? He came to town like a conqueror. He took us all with his laughter. You yourself, Madam –

ELIZABETH. Yes, make us laugh and you may pick all pockets! He helped you to pick mine.

HENSLOWE. So far good. But he aims no higher. Yet what he could do if he would! I have a sort of love of him, Madam. I found him: I taught him: I have daughters enough but no son. I have wrestled with him like Jacob at Peniel, but when I think to conquer he tickles my rib and I laugh. That's his weapon, Madam! With his laughter he locks the door of his heart against every man.

ELIZABETH. And every woman?

HENSLOWE. They say – no, Madam!

ELIZABETH. Then we must find her.

HENSLOWE (*with a glance at* MARY FITTON). They say she is found already. But a court lady – and a player! It's folly, Madam! Now Marlowe would shrug his shoulder and go elsewhere; but Shakespeare – there is about him in little and great a certain dogged and damnable constancy that wrecks all. If he cannot have the moon for his supper, he will starve, Madam, whatever an old fool says to him.

ELIZABETH. Then, Henslowe, we must serve him up the moon. Mary!

MARY (*rising and coming down to them*). Madam?

ELIZABETH. Could you hear us?

MARY. I was playing the new song that the Earl set for you.

ELIZABETH. For me? But you heard?

MARY. Something of the talk, Madam!

ELIZABETH. You go to all the plays, do you not? Which is the coming man, Mary, Shakespeare or Marlowe?

MARY. If you ask me, Madam, I'm all for the cobbler's son.

HENSLOWE. Mistress Fitton should give us a sound reason if she have it, but she has none.

MARY. Only that I don't know Mr Marlowe, and I know my little Shakespeare by heart. I'm an Athenian – I'm always asking for new tunes.

ELIZABETH. Which is Shakespeare? The youngster like a smoking lamp, all aflare?

MARY. No, Madam! That's Marlowe. Shakespeare's a lesser man.

HENSLOWE. A lesser man? Marlowe the lamp, say you?

> He's conflagration, he's 'Armada!' flashed
> From Kent to Cornwall! But this lesser man,
> He's the far world the beacons can outflare
> One little hour, but, when their flame dies down,

> High o'er the embers in the deep of night
> Behold the star!

ELIZABETH. I forget if I ever saw him.

HENSLOWE. Madam, if ever you saw him, you would not forget –
> A small, a proud head, like an Arab Christ,
> And noble, madman's fingers, never still –
> The face still though, mouth hid, the nostril wide,
> And eyes like voices calling, shrill and sad,
> Borne on hot winds from fairyland or hell;
> Yet round the heavy lids a score of lines
> All crisscross crinkle like a score of laughs
> That he has scribbled hastily down himself
> With his quick fingers. No, not tall –

ELIZABETH.                                   But a man!

MARY. Like other men.

ELIZABETH.          Ah?

MARY.                    It was easy.

ELIZABETH.                        Tell!

MARY. He came like a boy to apples. Marlow now –

ELIZABETH. More than a man, less than a man, but not
> As yet a man then? Well, I'll see your Shakespeare:
> Marlowe – some other time.

HENSLOWE.                        I'll fetch him to you.

(HENSLOWE *goes out.*)

ELIZABETH. To you, Mary – to you!

MARY. O Madam, spare me! It's a stiff instrument and once, I think,
has been ill-tuned.

ELIZABETH. Tune it afresh!

MARY. You wish that, Madam?

ELIZABETH. I wish it. Marlowe can wait – and Pembroke.

MARY. Madam?

ELIZABETH. I am blind, deaf, dumb, so long as you practise your new
tune. But the Earl of Pembroke goes to Ireland.

MARY. He's an old glove, Madam.

ELIZABETH. Young or old, not for your wearing. Strip your hand and
finger your new tune!

MARY. Now, Madam?

ELIZABETH. Why not? Why do I dress you and keep you at court?
Here's Spain in the anteroom and France on the stairs – am I to
keep them waiting while I humour a parcel of players?

MARY. Indeed, Madam, I wonder that you have spared half an hour.

ELIZABETH. Wonder, Mary! Wonder! And when you know why I do what I do you shall be Queen instead of me. In the meantime you may learn the trade, if you choose. I give you a kingdom to rule in the likeness of a poor player. Let me see how you do it! Yet mark this – though with fair cheeks and black hair you may come by a coronet (but the Earl goes to Ireland) yet if you rule your kingdom by the glance of your eyes, you will lose it as other Maries have done.

MARY. I must reign in my own way – forgive me, Madam! – not yours.

ELIZABETH. Girl, do you think you could ever rule in mine? Well, try your way! But – between queens, Mary – one kingdom at a time!

(ELIZABETH *goes out.*)

MARY (*she sits on the table edge, swinging her pretty foot*). So Pembroke goes to Ireland! Ay, and comes back, old winter! I can wait. And while I wait – Shakespeare! Will Shakespeare! O charity – I wish it were Marlowe! What did the old woman say? A kingdom in the likeness of a player. I wonder. Well, we'll explore. Yet I wish it were Marlowe. (SHAKESPEARE *enters.*) Ah! here comes poor Mr Shakespeare looking for the Queen and finding –

SHAKESPEARE. The Queen!

MARY. Hush! Palace walls! Well, Mr Shakespeare, what's the news?

SHAKESPEARE. Good, bad and indifferent.

MARY. Take the bad first.

SHAKESPEARE. The bad – that I have not seen you some five weeks! The good – that I have now seen you some five seconds! The indifferent – that you do not care one pin whether I see you or not for the next five years!

MARY. Who told you that, Solomon?

SHAKESPEARE. I have had no answer to –

MARY. Five letters, seven sonnets, two catches and a roundelay!

SHAKESPEARE. Love's Labour Lost!

MARY. Ah, Mr Shakespeare, you were not a Solomon then! There was too much Rosaline and to little Queen in that labour.

SHAKESPEARE. You're right! Solomon would have drawn all Rosaline and no Queen at all. I'll write another play!

MARY. It might pay you better than your sonnets.

SHAKESPEARE. Do you read them – Rosaline?

MARY. Most carefully, Mr Shakespeare – on Saturday nights! Then I make up my accounts and empty my purse, and wonder – must I

pawn my jewels? Then I cry. And then I read your latest sonnet
and laugh again.

SHAKESPEARE.  You should not laugh.

MARY.  Why, is it not meant to move me?

SHAKESPEARE.  You should not laugh. I tell you such a thought,
   Such fiery lava welling from a heart,
   So crystalled in the wonder-working brain,
   Mined by the soul and rough-cut into words
   Fit for a poet's faceting and, last,
   Strung on a string of gold by a golden tongue –
   Why, such a thought is an immortal jewel
   To gild you, living, in men's eyes, and after
   To make you queen of all the unjewelled dead
   Who bear not their least bracelet hence. For I,
   Eternally I'd deck you, were you my own,
   Would you but wear my necklaces divine,
   My rings of sorcery, my crowns of song.
   What chains of emeralds – did you but know!
   My rubies, O my rubies – could you but see!
   And this one gem of wonder, pearl of pearls,
   Hid in my heart for you, could you but take,
   Would you but take –

MARY.        Open your heart!

SHAKESPEARE.          Not so.
   The god who made it hath forgot the key,
   Or lost or lent it.

MARY.      Heartless god! Poor heart!
   Yet if this key – (is there indeed a key?)

SHAKESPEARE.  No lock without a key, nor heart, nor heart.

MARY.  – were found one day and strung with other keys
   Upon my ring?

SHAKESPEARE.   With other – ?

MARY.        Keys of hearts!
   What else?
   Tucked in the casket where my mortals lie –
   Sick pearl, flawed emerald, brooch or coronet –

SHAKESPEARE.  God!

MARY.   Why, Jeweller?

SHAKESPEARE.     Then what they say –

MARY.          They say?

What do they say? And what care I? They say
Pembroke?

SHAKESPEARE.        They lie! You shall not speak. They lie!

MARY. So little doubt – and you a man! It's new.
It's sweet. It will not last. We spoke of keys –
This heart-key, had I found it, would you buy?
Come, tempt me with immortal necklaces!
Come, purchase me with ornaments divine!

SHAKESPEARE. I love you –

MARY.                          Well?

SHAKESPEARE.                        I love you –

MARY.                                      Is that all?

SHAKESPEARE. I love you so.

MARY.                          Why, that's a common cry,
I hear it daily, like the London cries,
'Old chairs to mend!' or 'Sweet, sweet lavender!'
Is this your string of pearls, sixteen a penny?

SHAKESPEARE. D'you laugh at me? I mean it.

MARY.                                      So do they all.
Buy! Buy my lavender! Lady, it's cheap –
It's sweet – new cut – I starve – for Christ's sake, buy!
They mean it, all the hoarse-throat, hungry men
That sell me lavender, that sell me love.

SHAKESPEARE. I put my wares away. I do not sell.

MARY. O pedlar! I had half a mind to buy.

SHAKESPEARE. Too late.

MARY.                    Open your pack again! What haste!
What – not a trinket left me, not a pin
For a poor lady? Does not the offer hold?

SHAKESPEARE. You did not close.

MARY.                            I will.

SHAKESPEARE.                          Withdrawn! Withdrawn!

MARY. Renew!

SHAKESPEARE. Too late.

MARY.              You know your business best;
Yet – what care I?

SHAKESPEARE.          Or I? yet – never again
To buy and sell with you!

MARY.                        Never again.
Heigh-ho! I sighed, sir.

SHAKESPEARE.                                    Yes, I heard you sigh.
MARY. And smiled. At court, sir –
SHAKESPEARE.                          Yes, they buy and sell
  At court. But I know better – give and take!
MARY (*evading him*). What will you give me if I let you take?
SHAKESPEARE. If you will come with me into my mind –
  How shall I say it? Still you'll laugh at me!
MARY. Maybe!
SHAKESPEARE. My mind's not one room stored, but many,
  A house of windows that o'erlook far gardens,
  The hanging gardens of more Babylons
  Than there are bees in a linden tree in June.
  I'm the king-prisoner in his capital,
  Ruling strange peoples of a world unknown,
  Yet there come envoys from the untravelled lands
  That fill my corridors with miracles
  As it were tribute, secretly, by night;
  And I wake in the dawn like Solomon,
  To stare at peacocks, apes and ivory,
  And a closed door.
  And all these stores I give you for your own,
  You shall be mistress of my fairylands,
  I'll ride you round the world on the back of a dream,
  I'll give you all the stars that ever danced
  In the sea o'nights,
  If you will come into my mind with me,
  If you will learn me – know me.
MARY.                                    I do know you.
You are the quizzical Mr Shakespeare of the 'Rose', who never
means a word he says, I've heard of you. All trades hate you
because you are not of their union, and yet know the tricks of each
trade; but your own trade loves you, because you are content with
a crook in the lower branches when you might be top of the tree.
You write comedies, all wit and no wisdom, like a flower-bed raked
but not dug; but the high stuff of the others, their tragedies and
lamentable ends, these you will not essay. Why not, Mr
Shakespeare of the fairylands?
SHAKESPEARE. Queen Wasp, I do not know.
MARY. King Drone, then I will tell you. You are the little boy at
  Christmas who would not play snapdragon till the flames died

down, and so was left at the end with a cold raisin in an empty
dish. That's you, that's you, with the careful fingers and no good
word in your plays for any woman. Run home, run home, there's
no more to you!

SHAKESPEARE. D'you think so?

MARY. I think that I think so.

SHAKESPEARE. I'll show you.

MARY. What will you show me, Will?

SHAKESPEARE. Fairyland, and you and me in it. Will you believe in me
then?

MARY. Not I, not I! I'm a woman of this world. Give me flesh and
blood, not gossamer,
        Honey and heartache, and a lovers' moon

SHAKESPEARE. I read of lovers once in Italy –
        She was like you, such eyes of night, such hair.
        God took a week to make his world, but these
        In four short days made heaven to burn on earth
        Like a great torch; and when they died –

MARY.                                                    They died?

SHAKESPEARE. Like torches quenched in water, suddenly,
        Because they loved too well.

MARY.                              Oh, write it down!
        Ah, could you, Will? I think you could not write it.

SHAKESPEARE. I can write Romeo. Teach me Juliet!

MARY. I could if I would. Was that her name – Juliet?

SHAKESPEARE. Poor Juliet!

MARY. Not so poor if I know her. Oh, make that plain – she was not
poor! And tell them, Will, tell all men and women –

SHAKESPEARE. What, my heart?

MARY. I will whisper it to you one day when I know you better. Oh,
it'll be a play! Will you do it for me, Will? Will you write it for you
and for me? Where do they live?

SHAKESPEARE. Verona. Italy.

MARY. Come to me daily! Read it to me scene by scene, line by line!
How many acts?

SHAKESPEARE. The old five-branched candlestick.

MARY. But a new flame! Will it take long to write?
        It must not.

SHAKESPEARE.           Shall not.

MARY.                              What shall we call it, Will?

The Tragical Discourse? The Famous End?
The Lovers of Verona?

SHAKESPEARE.                    No, no! Plain.
Their two names married – Romeo and Juliet.

(*As they lean towards each other, still talking*)

*the* CURTAIN *falls.*


## SCENE 2

*The first performance of* Romeo and Juliet: *the end of the fourth act. The*
CURTAIN *rises on a small bare dusty office, littered with stage properties and
dresses. When the door at the back of the stage is open there is a glimpse of passage and curtains, and moving figures, with now and then a flare of torchlight.
There is a continuous faraway murmur of voices and, once in a while,
applause. As the* CURTAIN *goes up,* MARY FITTON *is opening the door to go
out.* SHAKESPEARE *holds her back.*

MARY.  Let go! Let me go! I must be in front at the end of that act. I
must hear what the Queen will say to it.

SHAKESPEARE.  But you'll come back?

MARY.  That depends on what the Queen says. I've promised you
nothing if she damns it.

(*The applause breaks out again.*)

SHAKESPEARE.  Listen! Is it damned?

MARY.  Sugar-sweet, isn't it? But that's nothing. That's the mob.
That's your friends. They'll clap *you*. But the Queen, if she claps,
claps your play.

SHAKESPEARE.  Your play!

MARY.  Is it mine? Earnest?

SHAKESPEARE.  My earnest, but your play.

MARY.  Well, good luck to my play!

SHAKESPEARE.  Give me –

MARY.  Oh, so it's not a free gift?

SHAKESPEARE.  Give me a fingertip of thanks!

MARY.  In advance? Not I! But if the Queen likes it – I'm her obedient
servant. If the Queen opens her hand I shan't shut mine. Where
she claps once I'll clap twice. Where she gives you a hand to kiss,
I'll give you – There! Curtain's down! I must go.

SHAKESPEARE.  Mary!

MARY. Listen to it! Listen! Listen! This is better than any poor Mary.

(*She goes out. The door is left open. The applause breaks out again.*)

SHAKESPEARE. Is this the golden apple in my hand
        At last?
        How tastes it, heart, and is it sweet, is it sweet?
        Sweeter than common apples? So many years
        Of days I watched it grow and propped and pruned,
        Besought the sun and watered. O my tree
        When the green broke! That was a morning hour.
        Fool, so to long for fruit! Now the fruit's ripe.
        The tree in spring was fairest, when it flowered,
        And every petal held a drink of dew.
        The bloom went long ago. Well, the fruit's here!
        Hark!

(*The applause breaks out again.*)

        It goes well. Eat up your apple, man!
        This is the hour, the hour! I'm the same man –
        No better for it. When Marlowe praised me so
        He meant it – meant it. I thought he laughed at me
        In his sleeve. Will Shakespeare! Romeo and Juliet!
        I made it – I! Indeed, indeed, at heart –
        (I would not for the world they read my heart:
        I'd scarce tell Mary) but indeed, at heart,
        I know no song was ever sung before
        Like this my lovely song. *I* made it – I!
        It has not changed me. I'm the same small man,
        And yet I made it! Strange!

(*A knock.*)

STAGE HAND (*putting in his head at the door*). You'll not see anyone,
    sir, will you?

SHAKESPEARE. I told you already I'll come to the green-room when
    the show's over. I can see no stranger before.

STAGE HAND. So I've told her, sir, many times. But she says you will
    know her when you see her and she can't wait.

SHAKESPEARE. A lady?

STAGE HAND. No, no, sir, just a woman. I'll tell her to go away again.

SHAKESPEARE. Wait! Did she give no name?

STAGE HAND. Name of Hathaway, sir, from Stratford.

SHAKESPEARE.  Anne! Bring her here! Bring her here quickly, privately!
    You should have told me sooner. Where does she wait? Did any
    see her? Did any speak with her? If anyone asks for me save
    Henslowe or Mr Marlowe, I am gone, I am not in the theatre.
    What are you staring at? What are you waiting for? Bring her here!
STAGE HAND.  Glad to be rid of her, sir! She has sat in the passage this
    hour to be tripped over, and nothing budges her. (*Calling*) Will you
    come this way – this way! (*He disappears.*)
SHAKESPEARE.  Anne? Anne in London? What does Anne in London?
STAGE HAND (*returning*). This way, this way! It's a dark passage. This
    way!

    (MRS HATHAWAY *comes in.*)

SHAKESPEARE.  Not Anne!
MRS HATHAWAY.  Is Mr Shakespeare – ? Will! Is it Will? Oh, how
    you're changed!
SHAKESPEARE.  Ten years change a young man.
MRS HATHAWAY.  But not an old woman. I'm Anne's mother still.
SHAKESPEARE.  I'm not so changed that I forget it. What do you want
    of me, Mrs Hathaway?
MRS HATHAWAY.  I bring you news.
SHAKESPEARE.  Good news?
MRS HATHAWAY.  It's as you take it.
SHAKESPEARE.  Dead?
MRS HATHAWAY.  Is that good news, my half son? She is not so
    blessed.
SHAKESPEARE.  I did not say it so. Is she with you?
MRS HATHAWAY.  No.
SHAKESPEARE.  Did she send you? Oh, so she has heard of this
    business! It's like her to send you now. She is to take her toll of it,
    is she?
MRS HATHAWAY.  You are bitter, you are bitter! You are the east wind
    of your own spring sunshine. She has heard nothing of this
    business or of that – dark lady.
SHAKESPEARE.  Take care!
MRS HATHAWAY.  I saw her come from this room – off her guard. I
    know how a woman looks when a man has pleased her. Oh, please
    her if you must! I am old. I do not judge. And I think you will not
    always. But that's not my news.
SHAKESPEARE.  I can't hear it now. I am pressed. This is not every
    night. I'll see you tomorrow, not now.

MRS HATHAWAY.  My news may be dead tomorrow.

SHAKESPEARE.  So much the better. I needn't hear it.

MRS HATHAWAY.  Son, son, son! You don't know what you say.

SHAKESPEARE.  That is not my name. And I know well what I say. You are my wife's mother and I'll not share anything of hers. But if she needs money I'll send it. Tonight makes me a rich man.

MRS HATHAWAY.  Richer than you think – and tomorrow poorer, if you do not listen to me.

(*There is a roar of applause.*)

SHAKESPEARE.  Listen to you? Why should I listen to you? Can you give me anything to better that?

MRS HATHAWAY.  But if she can? Sixty years I have learned lessons in the world; but I never learned that a city was better than green fields, friends better than a house-mate, or the works of a man's hand more to him than a child of his own flesh.

SHAKESPEARE.  And have I learned it? Do I not know
That when I left her I left all behind
That was my right? See how I live my life –
Married nor single, neither bond nor free,
My future mortgaged for a roofless home!
For though I love I must not say 'I love you,
Come to my hearth!' A child? I have no child:
I hear no voice crying to me o' nights
Out of the frost-bound dark. How can it cry
Or smile at me until I give it lips?
How can it clutch me till I give it hands?
How can it be, until I give it leave?
Small sparrow at the windowpane, a'cold,
Begging your crumb of life from me, indeed
I cannot let you in. Small love, small sweet,
Look not so trustfully! You are not mine,
Not mine, not anyone's. Away, unborn!
Back to the womb of dreams, and never stir,
Never again! How meek the small ghost fades,
Reject and fatherless, that might have been
My son!

MRS HATHAWAY.   Is it possible? Anne knew you best.
She said you did not know. Dear son, too soon
By two last months, yet by these months too late
After you left her, Hamnet, the boy, was born.

SHAKESPEARE. It is not true!

MRS HATHAWAY.                    Ah, ah, she knew you best.
          She said always, weeping she said always
          You would not listen, though she sent you word;
          But when the boy was grown she'd send the boy,
          Then you would listen and come home, come home
          But now that web is tattered in its turn
          By a cold wind, an out-of-season wind,
          Tearing the silver webs, blacking the leaves
          And shaking the first blossoms down too soon,
          Too soon, too soon. He shivered and lay down
          Among pinched violets and the wrack of spring;
          But when the sky drew breath and April came,
          And summer with tanned fingers, beckoning up
          New flowers from the ground, still our flower drooped:
          The sunlight hurt his eyes, his bed's too hot,
          He drinks and will not eat: since Saturday
          There's but one end.

SHAKESPEARE.                    What end?

MRS HATHAWAY.                         You're stubborn as she.
          She will not bow to it. Yet she sent me hither
          To bring you home.

SHAKESPEARE.                    New witch-work!

MRS HATHAWAY.                              Will you not come?

SHAKESPEARE. I will not.

MRS HATHAWAY.              Will you not come? She bade me say
          That the boy cries for you –

SHAKESPEARE.                    A lie! A gross lie!
          He never called me father.

MRS HATHAWAY.                    That he does!
          You are his Merlin and his Arthur too,
          And God-Almighty Sundays. Thus it goes –
          'My Father says –' and 'When my Father comes –'
          'I'll tell my Father!' To his mother's hand
          He clings and whispers in his fever now,
          With bright eyes wide – your eyes, son, your quick eyes –
          That she shall fetch you (she? she cannot speak)
          To bring him wonders home like Whittington,
          (And where's your cat?) and tell the tales you know
          Of Puck and witches, and the English kings,

To whistle down the birds as Orpheus did,
And for a silver penny pick the moon
From the sky's pocket, and buy him gingerbread –
And so he rambles on, breaking her heart
A second time, God help her!

SHAKESPEARE.                              I will come.

A MAN'S VOICE (*off the stage*). Shakespeare! Will Shakespeare! Call Will
    Shakespeare!

SHAKESPEARE (*to* MRS HATHAWAY).                              Here!
    When do we start?

MRS HATHAWAY.              The horses wait at the inn.

VOICE. Will Shakespeare!

SHAKESPEARE.                    Give me an hour. The bridge is nearer.
    On London Bridge at midnight! I'll be there!

MRS HATHAWAY. Not later, I warn you, if you'd see the child alive.

SHAKESPEARE. Fear not, I'll be there. D'you think so ill of me? I could
    have been a good father to my own son – if I had known. If I had
    known! This is a woman's way of enduring a wrong. Oh, dumb
    beast! Could she not send for me – send to me? Am I a monster
    that she could not come to me? 'Buy him gingerbread!' To send
    me no word till he's dying! Would any she-devil in hell do so to a
    man? Dying? I tell you he shall live and not die. There was a man
    once fought death for a friend and held him. Can I not fight death
    for my own son? Can I not beat death off for an hour, for a little
    hour, till I have kissed my only son?

MARLOWE'S VOICE. Shakespeare! The Queen – the Queen has asked
    for you,
            And sent her woman twice. Will Shakespeare! Will!

SHAKESPEARE. At midnight then.

(MRS HATHAWAY *goes out.*)

VOICE.                              Will Shakespeare!

SHAKESPEARE.                              Coming! Coming!

MARY (*in the doorway, followed by* MARLOWE). Is Shakespeare –?

SHAKESPEARE.                              Oh, not now, not now,
    not now!

MARY. Are you mad to keep her waiting? She has favours up her sleeve.
    You are to write her a play for the summer revels. Quick now, ere
    the last act begins! Off you go! (SHAKESPEARE *goes out.*) Look how
    he drags away! What's come to the man to fling aside his luck?

MARLOWE. He has left it behind him.

MARY. Here's a proxy silver-tongue! Are you Mr Marlowe?

MARLOWE. Are you Mistress Fitton?

MARY. So we've heard of each other!

MARLOWE. What have you heard of me?

MARY. That you were somebody's-in-art! What have you heard of me?

MARLOWE. That you were his sister-in-art.

MARY. A man's sister! I'd as soon be a cold pudding! What did he say of his sister, brother?

MARLOWE. That you brought him luck.

MARY. That he leaves behind him!

MARLOWE. Like the blind man's lucky sixpence that the Jew stole when he put a penny in his plate.

MARY. A Jew of Malta?

MARLOWE. What, do *you* read me? You?

A STAGE HAND (*in the passage*). Last act, please! Last act! Last act!

MARY. I must go watch it.

MARLOWE. Don't you know it?

MARY. Oh, by heart! Yet I must sisterly watch it.

MARLOWE. Stay a little.

MARY. Till he comes? Then I shall miss all, for he'll keep me.

MARLOWE. Against your will?

MARY. No, with my Will.

MARLOWE. Is it he or his plays?

MARY.                            Not sure.

MARLOWE.                                          If I were he I'd make you sure.

MARY. I wonder if you could! I wonder – how?

MARLOWE. Too long to tell you here, and – curtain's up!

MARY. Come to my house one lazy day and tell me!

MARLOWE. Hark! That's more noise than curtain!

HENSLOWE'S VOICE. Shakespeare! Shakespeare! (*Entering.*) Here's a calamity! Where's Shakespeare? He should be in the green-room! Why does he tuck away in this rat-hole when he's wanted? And what's to be done? Where in God's name is Shakespeare?

MARY. With the Queen.

MARLOWE. The curtain's up; he'll be here in a minute.

MARY. What's wrong?

HENSLOWE. Everything! Juliet! The clumsy beasts! They let him fall from the bier: they let him fall on his arm! Now he's moaning and wincing and swears he can't go on, though he has but to speak his death scene. I've bid them cut the afterwards.

MARLOWE. Broken?

HENSLOWE. I fear so.

MARY. Let it be broken! Say he must go on!
> What? Spoil the play? These baby-men!

HENSLOWE.                                          He will not.

MARLOWE. The understudy?

HENSLOWE. Playing Paris. Where's Shakespeare? What's to be done?
> The play's spoiled.

MARLOWE. He'll break his heart.

MARY.                          He shall not break his heart!
> This is our play! Back to your Juliet-boy,
> Strip off his wear and never heed his arm!
> Bid them play on and bring me Juliet's robes!
> I'll put them on and put on Juliet too.
> Quick, Henslowe!

HENSLOWE.                    What! a woman play on the stage?

MARY. Ay, when the men fail! Quick! I say I'll do it!

SHAKESPEARE (*entering*). Here still? You've heard?

MARY (*on the threshold*).                    And heeded. Never stop me!
> You shall have Juliet. You shall have your play.

> (*She and* HENSLOWE *hurry out.*)

MARLOWE. There goes a man's master! But does she know the part?

SHAKESPEARE. She knows each line, she knows each word, she
> breathed them
> Into my heart long ere I wrote them down.

MARLOWE. But to act! Can you trust her?

SHAKESPEARE. She? Go and watch! I need not.

MARLOWE. But is it in her? She's Julia, not Juliet, not your young
Juliet, not your June morning – or is she?

SHAKESPEARE. You talk! You talk! You talk! What do you know of
her?

MARLOWE. Or you, old Will?

SHAKESPEARE. I dream her.

MARLOWE. Well, pleasant dreams!

SHAKESPEARE. No more. I'm black awake.

MARLOWE. What's wrong? Ill news?

SHAKESPEARE. From Stratford. Yes, yes, yes, Kit! And it must come
now, just now, after ten dumb years!

MARLOWE. Stratford? Whew! I'd forgotten your nettle-bed. What does
she want of you?

SHAKESPEARE. Hark! Mary's on.

MARLOWE. It's a voice like the drip of a honeycomb.

SHAKESPEARE. Can she play Juliet, man? Can she play Juliet?
    I think she can. Kit?

MARLOWE.             Ay?

SHAKESPEARE.               Oh, is there peace
    Anywhere, Kit, in any, any world?

MARLOWE. What is it, peace?

SHAKESPEARE.               It passeth understanding.
    They round the sermon off on Sunday with it,
    Laugh in their sleeves and send us parching home.
    This is a dew that dries ere Monday comes,
    And oh, the heat of the seven days!

MARLOWE.               I like it!
    The smell of dust, the shouting, and the glare
    Of crowded noon in cities, and such nights
    As this night, crowning labour. What is – peace?

STAGE HAND (*entering*). Sir, sir, sir, will you come down, sir, says Mr
    Henslowe. The end's near and the house half mad. We've not seen
    a night like this since – since *your* night, sir! Your first night, sir,
    your roaring Tamburlaine night! Never anything like it and I've
    seen many. Will you come, sirs?

SHAKESPEARE. You go, Marlowe!

STAGE HAND. There's nothing to fear, sir! It runs like clockwork. The
    lady died well, sir! Lord, who'd think she was a woman! There,
    there, it breaks out. Listen to 'em! Come, sir, come, come!

MARLOWE. We'll come! We'll come!

                            (*The man goes out.*)

SHAKESPEARE. Not I! Oh, if you love me, Marlowe, swear I'm ill, gone
    away, dead, what you please, but keep them away! I can stand no
    more.

MARLOWE. It's as she said – mad – mad – to fling your luck away.

SHAKESPEARE. A frost has touched me, Marlowe, my fruit's black.
    Help me now! Go, go! Say I'm gone, as I shall be when I've seen
    Mary –

MARLOWE. A back stairs? Now I understand.

SHAKESPEARE. Oh, stop your laughter! I'm to leave London in half an
    hour.

MARLOWE. Earnest? For long?

SHAKESPEARE. Little or long, what matter? I've missed the moment.

Who has his moment twice?

MARLOWE. Shall you tell her why you go?

SHAKESPEARE. Mary? God forbid!

VOICES. Shakespeare! Call Shakespeare!

SHAKESPEARE. D'you hear them? Help me! Say I am gone! Oh, go, go!

MARLOWE. Well, if you wish it!

(*He goes out, leaving the door ajar. As* SHAKESPEARE *goes on speaking the murmurs and claps die away and the noises of the stage are heard, the shouts of the scene-shifters, directions being given, and so on. Finally there is silence.*)

SHAKESPEARE. Wish it? I wish it? Have you no more for me
                    Of comfort, Marlowe?
                    Oh, what a dumb and measureless gulf divides
                    Star from twin star, and friend from closest friend!
                    Women, they say, can bridge it when they will:
                    As seamen rope a ship with grappling irons
                    These spinners of strong cords invisible
                    Make fast and draw the drifting glory home
                    In the name of love. I know not. Better go!
                    I am not for this harbour –

(*There is a sound of hasty footsteps and* MARY FITTON *enters in Juliet's robes. She stands in the doorway, panting, exalted, with arms outstretched. The door swings to behind her, shutting out all sound.*)

MARY.                                             Oh, I faced
                    The peacock of the world, the arch of eyes
                    That watched me love a god, the eyes, eyes, eyes,
                    That watched me die of love. Wake me again,
                    O soul that did inhabit me, O husband
                    Whose mind I uttered, to whose will I swayed,
                    Whose self of love I was! Wake me again
                    To die of love in earnest!

SHAKESPEARE.                          Mary! Mary!

MARY. I cannot ride this hurricane. I spin
                    Like a leaf in the air. Die down and let me lie
                    Close to the earth I am! O stir me not
                    With rosy breathings from the south, the south
                    Of sun and wine and peaks that flame to God
                    Suddenly in the dark! O wind, let be
                    And drive me not; for speech lies on my lips

Like a strange finger hushing back my soul
With words not mine, and thoughts not mine arise
Like marsh-flame dancing! As a leaf to a tree
Upblown, O wind that whirls me, I return.
Master and quickener, give me love indeed!

SHAKESPEARE.  These are the hands I never held till now:
These are the lips I never felt on mine:
This is the hour I dreamed of, many an hour:
This is the spirit awake. God in your sky,
Did your heart beat so on the seventh dawn?

MARY.  'Ware thunder!

SHAKESPEARE.          Sweet, he envies and is dumb,
Dumb as His dark. He was our audience.
Now to His blinding centrum home He hies,
Omnipotent drudge, to wind the clocks of Time
And tend His 'plaining universes all –
To us, to us, His empty theatre of night
Abandoning. But we too steal away;
For the play's done,
Lights out – all over – and here we stand alone,
Holding each other in a little room,
Like two souls in one grave. We are such lovers –

ANNE'S VOICE.  As there's no room for in the human air
And green side of the grass –

SHAKESPEARE.                              A voice! A voice!

MARY.  No voice here!

SHAKESPEARE.          In my heart I heard it cry
Like a sick child waked suddenly at night.

(*Crying out.*)

A child – a sick child! Unlink your arms that hold me!

MARY.  Never till I choose.

SHAKESPEARE.                  Put back your hair! I am lost
Unless I lose all gain. O moonless night,
In your hot darkness I have lost my way!
But kiss me, summer, once! On London Bridge
At midnight – I'll be there! Has the clock struck?

MARY.  Midnight long since.

SHAKESPEARE.                  Oh, I am damned and lost
In hell for ever!

MARY.                  Fool, dear fool, what harm?

If this be hell indeed, is not hell kind?
Is not hell lovely, if this love be hell?
Is not damnation sweet?

SHAKESPEARE.                          God does not know
How sweet, how sweet!

MARY.                                  Were they not wise, those two
Whose same blood beats again in you and me,
That chose the desert and the fall and went
Exultant from their garden and their God?
Long shall the sworded angels stand at ease
And idly guard the undesired delight:
Long shall the grasses grow and tall the briars,
And bent the branches of the ancient trees:
And many a year the wilding flowers shall blaze
Under a lonely sun, and fruited sweets
Shall drop and rot, and feed the roots that feed,
And bud again and ripen: long and long
Silent the watchman-lark in heaven shall hang
High over Eden, e'er they come again
Those two, whose blood is our blood, and their love
Our love, our own, that no god gave us, ours,
The venture ours, the glory ours, the shame
A price worth paying, then, now, ever –

SHAKESPEARE.                                        Eve,
Eve, Eve, the snake has been with you! You draw,
You drink my soul as I your body –

MARY.                                  Kiss!

CURTAIN.

# ACT III

## SCENE 1

SHAKESPEARE'S *lodging. It is the plain but well-arranged room of a man of fair means and fine taste. The walls are panelled: on them hang a couple of unframed engravings, a painting, tapestry, and a map of the known world. There is a four-poster bed with a coverlet and hangings of needlework, and on the windowsill a pot of early summer flowers. There is a chair or two of oak and a table littered with papers.* SHAKESPEARE *is sitting at it, a manuscript in his hand. On the arm of the chair lolls* MARLOWE, *one arm flung round* SHAKESPEARE'S *neck, reading over his shoulder.*

SHAKESPEARE. Man, how you've worked! A whole act to my ten lines! You dice all day and dance all night and yet – how do you do it?

MARLOWE. Like it?

SHAKESPEARE. Like it? What a word for a word-master! Consider, Kit! When the sun rises like a battle song over the sea: when the wind's feet visibly race along the treetops of a ten-mile wood: when they shout 'Amen!' in the Abbey, praying for the Queen on Armada Day: when the sky is a brass gong and the rain steel rods, and across all suddenly arch the seven colours of the promise – do I *like* these wonders when I stammer and weep, and know that God lives? Like, Marlowe!

MARLOWE. Yes, yes, old Will! But do you like the new act?

SHAKESPEARE. I like it, Kit! (*They look at each other and laugh.*)

MARLOWE. And now for your scene, ere I go.

SHAKESPEARE. My scene! I give you what I've done. Finish it alone, Kit, and take what it brings! I'm sucked dry.

MARLOWE. I've heard that before.

SHAKESPEARE. I wish I had never come to London.

MARLOWE. Henslowe's back. Seen him?

SHAKESPEARE. I've seen no one. Did the tour go well?

MARLOWE. He says so. He left them at Stratford. Well, I must go.

SHAKESPEARE. Where? To Mary?

MARLOWE. Why should I go to your Mary?

SHAKESPEARE. Because I've asked you to, often enough. Why else? You've grown to be friends. You could help me if you would.

MARLOWE. Never step between a man and a woman!

SHAKESPEARE. But you're our friend! And they say you know women.

MARLOWE. They say many things. They say we're rivals, Will – that I
shall end by having you hissed.

SHAKESPEARE. Let them say! But have you seen Mary? When did you
last see Mary?

MARLOWE. I forget. Saturday.

SHAKESPEARE. Did you speak of me, Kit? Kit, does she speak of me?

MARLOWE. If you must have it – seldom. New songs, new books, new
music – of plays and players and the Queen's tantrums – not of
you.

SHAKESPEARE. I have not seen her three days.

MARLOWE. Why, go then and see her!

SHAKESPEARE. She has company. She is waiting on the Queen. She
gives me a smile and a white cool fingertip, and – 'Farewell, Mr
Shakespeare!' yet a month ago, ay, and less than a month – ! Did
you give her my message? What did she say?

MARLOWE. She laughed and says you dream. She never liked you
better.

SHAKESPEARE. Did she say that?

MARLOWE. She says you cool to her, not she to you.

SHAKESPEARE. Did she say that?

MARLOWE. Swore it, with tears in her eyes.

SHAKESPEARE. Is it so? I wish it were so. Well, you're my good friend,
Marlowe!

MARLOWE. Oh, leave that!

SHAKESPEARE. Kit, do you blame me so much?

MARLOWE. Why should I blame you?

SHAKESPEARE. That I'm here and not in Warwickshire.

MARLOWE. I throw no stones. Why? have you heard aught?

SHAKESPEARE. No, nor dared ask – nor dared ask, Marlowe. The
boy's dead. I know it. But I will not hear it. Marlowe, Marlowe,
Marlowe, do you judge me?

MARLOWE. Ay, that putting your hand to the plough you look back.
Would I comb out my conscience daily as a woman combs out her
hair? I do what I choose, though it damn me! Blame you? The
round world has not such another Mary – or so, had I your eyes, I
should hold. For this prize, if I loved her, I would pay away all I
had.

SHAKESPEARE. Honour, Kit?

MARLOWE. Honour, Will!

SHAKESPEARE.  Faith and conscience and an only son?

MARLOWE.  It's my own life. What are children to me?

SHAKESPEARE.  Well, I have paid.

MARLOWE.  But you grudge – you grudge! Look at you! If you go to her with those eyes it's little wonder that she tires of you.

SHAKESPEARE.  Tires? Who says that she tires? Who says it?

MARLOWE.  Not I, old Will! Not I! Why, Shakespeare?

SHAKESPEARE (*shaken*). I can't sleep, Kit! I can't write. What has come to me? I think I go mad. (*He starts.*) Was that the boy on the stairs? I sent him to her. I wrote. I have waited her will long enough. She shall see me tonight. I'll know what it means. She plays with me, Kit. Are you going?

MARLOWE.  I shall scarce reach Deptford ere dark.

SHAKESPEARE.  How long do you lodge in Deptford?

MARLOWE.  All summer.

HENSLOWE (*pounding at the door*). Who's at home? Who's at home?

MARLOWE.  That's Henslowe.

SHAKESPEARE.  Why does the boy stay so long?

HENSLOWE (*in the doorway*). Gentlemen, the traveller returns! For the last time, I tell you! My bones grow too old for barnstorming. Do you go as I come, Kit? Thank you for nothing!

MARLOWE.  Be civil, Henslowe! 'The Curtain' 's on its knees to me for my next play.

HENSLOWE.  Pooh! This man can serve my turn.

MARLOWE.  You see, they'll make rivals of us, Will, before they've done. I'll see you soon again. (*He goes out.*)

HENSLOWE.  Well, what's the news?

SHAKESPEARE.  I sit at home. You roam England. You can do the talking. How did the tour go?

HENSLOWE.  You're thin, man! What's the matter! Success doesn't suit you?

SHAKESPEARE.  How did the tour go?

HENSLOWE.  By way of Oxford, Warwick, Kenilworth –

SHAKESPEARE.  I said 'how', not 'where'.

HENSLOWE.  – and Leamington and Stratford. We played 'Romeo' every other night – and to full houses, my son! I've a pocketful of money for you. They liked you everywhere. As for your townsfolk, they went mad. You can safely go home, boy! You'll find Sir Thomas in the front row, splitting his gloves. He'll ask you to dinner.

SHAKESPEARE. Were you there long?

HENSLOWE. Two nights.

SHAKESPEARE. Did you see – anyone?

HENSLOWE. Why not say –

SHAKESPEARE. I say, did you pass my house?

HENSLOWE. I had forgot the way.

SHAKESPEARE.                            As I have, Henslowe!

HENSLOWE. Should I have sought her?

SHAKESPEARE.                            No.

HENSLOWE.                                          Yet I did see her.
>           Making for London, not a week ago,
>           Alone on horseback, sudden the long grey road
>           Grew friendly, like a stranger in a dream
>           Nodding 'I know you!' and behold, a love
>           Long dead, that smiles and says, 'I never died!'
>           Then in the turn of the lane I saw your thatch.
>           Summer not winter, else was all unchanged.
>           Still in the dream I left my horse to graze,
>           And let ten years slip from me at your gate.

SHAKESPEARE. Is it ten years?

HENSLOWE.                            The little garden lay
>           Enchanted in the Sunday sloth of noon:
>           In th' aspen tree the wind hung, fast asleep,
>           Yet the air danced a foot above the flowers
>           And gnats danced in it. I saw a poppy-head
>           Spilling great petals, noiseless, one by one:
>           I heard the honeysuckle breathe – sweet, sweet:
>           The briar was sweeter – a long hedge, pink-starred –

SHAKESPEARE. I know.

HENSLOWE.              There was a bush of lavender,
>           And roses, and a bee in every rose,
>           Drowning the lark that fluted, fields away,
>           Up in the marvel blue.

SHAKESPEARE.                            Did you go in?

HENSLOWE. Why, scarce I dared, for as I latched the gate
>           The wind stirred drowsily, and 'Hush!' it said,
>           And slept again; but all the garden waked
>           Upon the sound. I swear, as I play Prologue,
>           It watched me, waiting. Down the path I crept,
>           Tiptoe, and reached the window, and looked in.

SHAKESPEARE.  You saw – ?

HENSLOWE.                        I saw her; though the place was gloom
        After the sunshine; but I saw her –

SHAKESPEARE.                              Changed?

HENSLOWE.  I knew her.

SHAKESPEARE.              Who was with her?

HENSLOWE.                                She was alone,
        Beside the hearth unkindled, sitting alone.
        A child's chair was beside her, but no child.
        Her hands were sleepless, and beneath her breath
        She tuned a thread of song – your song of 'Willow'.
        But when I tapped upon the windowpane,
        Oh, how she turned, and how leaped up! Her face
        Glowed white as iron new lifted from the forge:
        Her hair fled out behind her in one flame
        As to the door she ran, with little cries
        Scarce human, tearing at the bolt, the key,
        And flung it crashing back: ran out, wide-armed,
        Calling your name: then – saw me, and stood still,
        So still you'd think she died there, standing up,
        As a sapling will in frost, so desolate
        She stood, with summer round her, staring –

SHAKESPEARE.                                    Well?

HENSLOWE.  I asked her, did she know me? Yes, she said,
        And would I rest and eat? So much she said
        To the lawn behind me – oh, to the hollyhock
        Stiff at my elbow – to a something – nothing –
        But not to me. I could not eat her food.
        I told her so. She nodded. Oh, she knows
        How thoughts run in a man. No fool, no fool!
        I spoke of you. She listened.

SHAKESPEARE.                        Questioned you?

HENSLOWE.  Never a question.

SHAKESPEARE.                  She said nothing?

HENSLOWE.                                Nothing.

SHAKESPEARE.  Not like her.

HENSLOWE.                  But her eyes spoke, as I came
        By way of London, Juliet, 'The Rose',
        And the Queen's great favour ('And why not?' they said)
        Again to silence; so, as I turned to go

I asked her – 'Any greeting?' Then she said,
Lifting her chin as if she sped her words
Far, far, like pigeons flung upon the air,
And soft her voice as bird-wings – then she said,
'Tell him the woods are green at Shottery,
Fuller of flowers than any wood in the world.'
'What else?' said I. She said – 'The wind still blows
Fresh between park and river. Tell him that!'
Said I – 'No message, letter?' Then she said,
Twisting her hands – 'Tell him the days are long.
Tell him –' and suddenly ceased. Then, with goodbye
Pleasantly spoken, and another look
At some wraith standing by me, not at me,
Went back into the house and shut the door.

SHAKESPEARE. Ay, shut the door, Henslowe; for had she been this she
    Ten years ago and I this other I –
    Well, I have friends to love! Heard Marlowe's news?
    He's three-part through Leander! Oh, this Marlowe!
    I mine for coal but he digs diamonds.

HENSLOWE. Yet fill your scuttle lest the world grow chill! Is the new
  play done?

SHAKESPEARE. No.

HENSLOWE. Much written?

SHAKESPEARE. Not a line.

HENSLOWE. Are you mad? We're contracted. What shall I say to the
  Queen?

SHAKESPEARE. What you please.

HENSLOWE. Are you well?

SHAKESPEARE. Well enough.

HENSLOWE. Ill enough, I think!

SHAKESPEARE. Write your own plays – bid Marlowe, any man
    That writes as nettles grow or rain comes down!
    I am not born to it. I write not so.
    Romeo and Juliet – I am dead of them!
    The pay's too small, good clappers! These ghosts need blood
    To make 'em plump and lively and they know it,
    And seek their altar. Threads and floating wisps
    Of being, how they fasten like a cloud
    Of gnats upon me, not to be shoo'd off
    Unsatisfied – and they drink deep, drink deep;

> For like a pelican these motes I feed,
> And with old griefs' remembrance and old joys'
> Sharper remembrance daily scourge myself,
> And still they crowd to suck my scars and live.

HENSLOWE.  Now, now, now – do I ask another 'Juliet' of you? God
forbid! A fine play, your 'Juliet', but –

SHAKESPEARE.  Now come the 'buts'.

HENSLOWE.  Man, we must live! Can we fill the theatre on love and
longing, and high words? Ay, when Marlowe does it to the sound
of trumpets. But you – you're not Marlowe. You know too much.
Your gods are too much men and women. Who'll pay sixpence for
a heartache? And in advance too! Give us but two more 'Romeo
and Juliet's and you may be a great poet, but we close down.
Another tragedy? No, no, no, we don't ask that of you! We want
light stuff, easy stuff. Oh, who knows as well as you what's wanted?
It's a court play, my man! The French Embassy's to be there and
the two Counts from Italy, and always Essex and his gang, and you
know *their* fancy. Get down to it now, there's a good lad! Oh, you
can do it in your sleep! Lovers and lasses, and quarrels and kisses,
like the two halves of a sandwich! But court lovers, you know, that
talk verse – and between them a green cress of country folk and
country song, daffodils and valentines, and brown bowls of ale –
season all with a pepper of wit – and there's your sandwich, there's
your play, as the Queen likes it, as we all like it!

SHAKESPEARE.  Ay, as you like it! There's your title pat!

> But I'll not serve you. I'm to live, not write.
> Tell that to the Queen!

(*A boy enters whistling and stops as he sees* SHAKESPEARE.)

Well, Hugh, what answer?

BOY.                              None, sir!

SHAKESPEARE.  What? No answer?

HENSLOWE.  See here, Will! If you do not write me this play you have
trice promised, I'll go to the Queen – sick or mad I'll to the Queen
this very day for your physic – and so I warn you.

SHAKESPEARE (*to the boy*). Did you see –?

BOY.  The maid, sir!

HENSLOWE.  I'll not see 'The Rose' in ruins for a mad –

SHAKESPEARE (*to the boy*). But what did I bid you?

BOY.  Wait on the doorstep till Mistress Fitton came out, though I

waited all night. But indeed, sir, she's gone; for I saw her, though
she did not see me.

HENSLOWE. Oh, the Fitton! Now I see light through the wood!

SHAKESPEARE. What's that you say?

HENSLOWE. I say that the Queen shall know where the blame lies.

SHAKESPEARE. You lie. *I* heard you. *I* saw you twist your lips round a
white name.

HENSLOWE. Will! Will! Will!

SHAKESPEARE. Did you not?

HENSLOWE. Why, Will, you have friends, though you fray 'em to the
parting of endurance.

SHAKESPEARE. What's this?

HENSLOWE. I say you have friends that see what they see, and are
sorry.

SHAKESPEARE. Yes, I am blessed in one man and woman who do not
use me as a beast to be milked dry. I have Marlowe and –

HENSLOWE. And I said, God forgive me, that you knew men and
women! Marlowe!

SHAKESPEARE. You speak of my friend.

HENSLOWE. Ay, Jonathan – of David, the singer, of him that took
Bathsheba, all men know how. (SHAKESPEARE *makes a threatening
movement.*) No, no, Will! I am too old a man to give and take with
you – too old a man and too old a friend.

SHAKESPEARE. So you're to lie and I'm to listen because you're an old
man!

HENSLOWE. Lie? Ask any in the town. I'm but a day returned and
already I've heard the talk. Why, man, they make songs of it in the
street!

SHAKESPEARE. It? It? It?

HENSLOWE. Boy?

BOY. Here, sir?

HENSLOWE. What was that song you whistled as you came up the
stairs?

BOY. 'Weathercock', sir?

HENSLOWE. That's it!

BOY. Lord, sir, I know but the one verse I heard a drayman sing.

HENSLOWE. How does it go?

BOY. It goes – (*singing.*)

       Two birds settle on a weathercock –
       How's the wind today – O?

    One shall nest and one shall knock –
     How's the wind today – O?
      Turn about and turn about
      Kit pops in as Will pops out!
    Winds that whistle round the weathercock,
     Who's her love today – O?
It's a good tune, sir!

HENSLOWE. Eh, Will? A good tune! A rousing tune!

SHAKESPEARE (*softly*). 'For this prize, if I loved her, I would pay all I had! I do what I choose though it damn me!'

BOY. May I go, sir?

SHAKESPEARE. Go, go!

BOY. And my pay, sir? Indeed I'd have stopped the lady if I could. But she made as if she were not herself, and rode out of the yard. But I knew her, for all her riding-coat and breeches.

HENSLOWE. What's all this?

SHAKESPEARE ( *to the boy*). You're dreaming –

BOY. No, sir, there was your ring on her finger –

SHAKESPEARE. Be still! Take this and forget your dreams! (*He gives him money.*) Henslowe, farewell! If you've lied to me I'll pay you for it, and if you've spoken truth to me I'll pay you for it no less.

HENSLOWE. Pay? I want no pay. I want the play that the Queen ordered, and will have in the end, mark that! You have not yet served the Queen.

SHAKESPEARE. Boy! Hugh!

BOY. Sir?

SHAKESPEARE. Which way did she ride?

BOY. Am I asleep or awake, sir?

SHAKESPEARE. Which way did she ride?

BOY. Across the bridge, sir, as I dreamt it, along the Deptford road.

SHAKESPEARE. Marlowe! The Deptford road! The Deptford road! (*He rushes out.*)

BOY (*clutching his money*). Dreaming pays, sir! It's gold.

HENSLOWE. Boy, boy. Never trust a man! Never kiss a woman! Work all day and sleep all night! Love yourself and never ask God for the moon! So you may live to be old. This business grows beyond me. I'll to the Queen.

(*He trots out, shaking his head. The boy skips after him, whistling his tune.*)

CURTAIN.

## SCENE 2

*A private room at an inn late at night. Through the door in the right wall is seen
the outer public room, with men sitting drinking. There is a window at the back,
set so low in the wall that, above the windowsill, the heads of summer flowers
glisten in the moonlight. On the left wall is the hearth, and between it and the
window a low bed. In the centre is a table with candle, glasses and mugs, and
two or three men sitting round it drinking.* MARLOWE *stands with his back to
the window, one foot on a chair, shouting out a song as the* CURTAIN *rises.*

MARLOWE (*singing*).
      If Luck and I should meet
        I'll catch her to me crying,
      'To trip with you were sweet,
        Have done with your denying!'
        Hey, lass! Ho, lass!
        Heel and toe, lass!
      Who'll have a dance with me?
ALL TOGETHER. Hey luck! Ho, Luck!
        Ne'er say no, Luck!
      I'll have a dance with thee!
A MAN (*hammering the table*). Again! Again!
LANDLORD (*at the door*). Sir, sir, there's without a young gentleman
    hot with riding –
MARLOWE. Does the hot young gentleman give no name?
LANDLORD. Why yes, sir, Archer, Francis Archer! He said you would
    know him.
MARLOWE. I knew an Archer, but he died in Flanders.
LANDLORD. He may well come from Flanders, sir, for he's muddy.
MARLOWE. Are Flanders' graves so shallow? Tell him if he's alive I
    don't know him, and if he's dead I won't know him, and so either
    way let him go where he belongs.

                          (*The* LANDLORD *goes out.*)

THE MAN. What, Kit! Send him to hell with a dry throat?
MARLOWE. And all imposters with him!
THE MAN. But what if it were a true ghost? Have a heart! You'll be
    one yourself one day, and watch old friends run away from you
    when you come to haunt them in pure good fellowship.
LANDLORD (*at the door*). Sir, he says indeed he knows you. His
    business is private.

MARLOWE. Well, let him come in. No, friends, sit still! If he's the
death he pretends we'll face him together as the song teaches.
(*Singing*.) When Death at last arrives,
   I'll greet him with a chuckle,
  I'll ask him how he thrives
   And press his bony knuckle,
    With – Ho, boy! Hey, boy!
    Come this way, boy!
   Who'll have a drink with me?
MARY'S VOICE (*on the stairs*). Hey, Sir! Ho, Sir!
    No, no, no, Sir!
   Why should he drink with thee?
ALL TOGETHER. Hey, Death! Ho, Death!
    Let me go, Death!
   I'll never drink with thee!
MARLOWE. What voice is that?

(MARY *stands in the doorway. She is dressed as a boy, with cloak, riding
boots, and slouch cap*.)

MARY (*singing*). If Love should pass me by,
   I'll follow till I find him,
  And when I hear him sigh,
   I'll tear the veils that blind him.
    Up, man! Dance, man!
    Take your chance, man!
   Who'll get a kiss from me?
ALL TOGETHER. Hey, Love! Ho, Love!
    None shall know, Love!
   Keep but a kiss for me!

(*They clap*.)

THE MAN (*to* MARLOWE). Ghost of a nightingale! D'you know him?
MARLOWE. I think I do. (*To* MARY *aside*.) What April freak is this?
THE MAN (*with a glass*). Spirits to spirit, young sir! Have a drink!
MARY. I should choke, sir! We drink nectar in my country.
THE MAN. Where's that, ghost?
MARY. Oh, somewhere on the soft side of heaven where the poppies
grow.
THE MAN. He swore you were dead and buried.
MARY. And so I was. But there's a witch in London so sighs for him

and so cries for him, that in the end she whistled me out of my
gravity and sent me here to fetch him home to her.

THE MAN. Her name, transparency, her name?

MARY. Why, sir, I rode in such haste that my memory could not keep
up with me. It'll not be here this half-hour.

MARLOWE. Landlord, pour ale for a dozen, and these friends will
drink to her, name or no name – in the next room.

THE MAN. Kit, you're a man of tact! I'm a man of tact. We're all men
of tact!

>            Ho, boys! Hey, boys!
>            Come this way, boys!
>            Who'll have a drink with me?

(*The door closes on them.*)

MARY. Well, did you ever see a better boy? My hair was the only
trouble.

MARLOWE. Madcap! What does this mean?

MARY. What I said! (*singing*).

>            Moth, where are you flown?
>              To burn in a flame!
>            Moth, I lie alone –

You've not been near me these four days.

MARLOWE. Uneasy days – I could not.

MARY. Are you burned, moth? Are the poor wings a-frizzle?

MARLOWE. Nor mine, dear candle, but a king of moths,

>            But a great hawk-moth, velvet as the night
>            He beats with twilight wings, he, he is singed,
>            Fallen to earth and pitiful.

MARY.                                              Oh, Shakespeare!

>            My dear, I've run away because I hate
>            The smell of burning.

He was to come to me tonight to tell me his tragedies and his
comedies and – oh, I yawn. And I played her so well too at the
first –

MARLOWE. Who?

MARY. The cool nymph under Tiber stairs – what's her name? –
Egeria. Am I your Egeria, Marlowe?

MARLOWE. Something less slippery.

MARY. Oh, she was fun to play – first to please the Queen and then to
please myself. For I was caught, you know. It's something to be
hung among the stars, something to say – 'I was his Juliet!'

MARLOWE.  What, you – you Comedy-Kate?

MARY.  Why, I'm a woman! That is – fifty women!
>     While he played Romeo to my Juliet
>     I could be anything he chose. O Kit!
>     I sucked his great soul out. You never lit the blaze
>     I was for half an hour: then – out I went!

MARLOWE.  He stoops o'er the embers yet.

MARY.                                    But ashes fanned
>     Fly from their centre, lighter than a kiss,
>     And settle – where they please! (*She kisses him.*)
> D'you love me?

MARLOWE.  More than I wish.

MARY.  Would you be cured?

MARLOWE.  Not possible.

MARY (*singing*).  Go to church, sweetheart,
>          A flower in your coat!
>       Your wedding bells shall prove
>     The death of love! The death of love!
>          Ding-dong! Ding-dong!
>           The death of love!
> Or so Will says.

MARLOWE.  He should know.

MARY.  What's that?

MARLOWE.  Nothing.

MARY.  He's married?

MARLOWE.  I do not tell you so.

MARY.  Married! He shall pay me. Married! I guessed it – but he shall
pay me. A country girl?

MARLOWE.  If you must know! He has not seen her these ten years.
She sent for him the night of 'Juliet'.

MARY.  Why now all's plain.
>     So she's the canker that hath drooped our rose!
>     If I had loved him – I do not love him, Marlowe –
>     This would have fanned a flame. Well, we're all cheats!
>     But now I cheat with better conscience. Married!
>     Lord, I could laugh! He must not know I know it.

MARLOWE.  I shan't boast I told you. O Mary, when I first came to
you, it was he sent me. He came like a child and asked me to see
you, to say what good of him I could,

Because I was his friend. And now, see, see,
How I have friended him!

MARY.                                    I love you for it.
He shall not know. Why talk of him? Forget him!

MARLOWE. Can you?

MARY. Why, that I cannot makes me mad –

MARLOWE.                                    Forget him?
As soon forget myself! I am his courage,
His worldly wisdom – Mary, I think I am
The youth he lost in Stratford. Yet we're one age,
And now we write one play. If I died of a sudden,
It seems he'd breathe me as I left my body,
And I should live in him as sunshine lies
Forgotten in a forest, and be found
In slants and pools and patterns, golden still
In all he writes.

MARY. O dull Kit! have I adventured here to hear you talk of dying?

MARLOWE. You borrowed Archer's name.

MARY. I wanted one that would startle you out to me, and you told
me the tale of him once, how young he died.

MARLOWE. And how unwilling! You've set him running in my head
like a spider in a skull,
Spining across the hollows of mine eyes
A web of dusty thought. Sweet, brush him off!
Death's a vile dreg in this intoxicant,
This liquor of the gods, this seven-hued life.
Sometimes I pinch myself, say – 'Can you die?
Is it possible? Will you be winter-nipped
One day like other flies?' I'm glad you came.
Stay with me, stay, till the last minute of life!
Let the court go, the world go, stay with me!

MARY (*her arms round him*). So – quiet till the dawn comes, quiet!
Hark!
Who called? Did you hear it?

MARLOWE.                                    Birds in the ivy.

MARY.                                                            No.
Twice in the road I stopped and turned about
Because I heard my name called. There was nothing;
Yet I had heard it – Mary – Mary – Mary!

MARLOWE. You heard your own heart pound from riding.

MARY.                                                                    Again!
   Open the window! (MARLOWE *rises and goes to the window.*)
                                 Do you see anything?
MARLOWE.  All's sinister. The moon fled out of the sky
   Long since, and the black trees of midnight quake.
MARY.  And the wind! What a wind! It tugs at the window-frame
   Like jealousy, mad to break in and part us.
   Could you be jealous?
MARLOWE.                            If I were a fool
   I'd let you guess it.
MARY.                            Wise, you're wise, but – jealous?
   Too many men in the world! I'd lift no finger
   To beckon back the fool that tired of me,
   Would you? But he, he glooms and says no word,
   But follows with his eyes whene'er I stir.
   I hate those asking eyes. Look thus at me
   But once and – ended, Marlowe! I'll not give
   But when I choose.

   (*He sits beside her.*)

MARLOWE.                            But when *I* choose.

   (*Behind them the blur of the window is darkened.*)

MARY (*in his arms*).                                          Why yes!
   Had he your key-word – ! Sometimes I like him yet,
   When anger comes in a white lightning flash,
   Then he's the man of men still, then with shut eyes
   I think him you and shiver and I like him,
   Held roughly in his arms, thinking of you.
   The Warwick burr is like an afterwards
   Of thunder when he's angry, in his speech.
MARLOWE.  What does he say?
MARY.                            He says he is not jealous!
   He would not wrong me so, nor wrong himself.
   Then the sky lightens and we kiss – or kiss not!
   Who cares?
   Then in come you. It's well he thinks you his
   In friendship –
MARLOWE.                    So I was.

   (SHAKESPEARE *swings himself noiselessly over the sill.*)

MARY.                              And so you are,
And have all things in common as friends should.
Eh, friend?
Oh, stir not! Frowning? If you were a fool –
(How did it run?) you'd let me guess you – jealous!
But you're no fool.

MARLOWE.                    Let's have no more! You know
I loved – I love the man.

MARY.                          Why, so do I.

MARLOWE. You shall not!

MARY.                      Then I will not. Not tonight.

SHAKESPEARE (*standing by the window*).
Why not tonight, my lover and my friend?

(*He comes down into the room as they start up.*)

Will you not give me wine and welcome me?
Sit down, sit down – we three have much to say!
But tell me first, what does that hand of yours
Upon her neck, as there were custom in it?
Part! Part, I say! Part! lest I couple you
Once and for all!

MARY.                    He's armed!

MARLOWE.                          He shall not touch you!

SHAKESPEARE. You, Marlowe! You!

MARLOWE.                    Stand out of her way!

SHAKESPEARE.                          You! You!

MARLOWE. Why then –

(MARLOWE *darts at* SHAKESPEARE *and is thrown off. He staggers against the table, knocking over the candle. As he strikes the second time his arm is knocked up, striking his own forehead. He falls across the bed. There is an instant's pause, then* SHAKESPEARE *rushes to him, slipping an arm under his shoulder.*)

MARY.                    Dead? Is he dead? Oh, what an end!
I never saw a dead man. Will – to me!

SHAKESPEARE. Get help!

MARY.              I dare not.

MARLOWE.                    Oh!

SHAKESPEARE.              What is it?

MARLOWE.                          Oh!
My life, my lovely life, and cast away

           Untasted, wasted –
           Death, let me go!

                                                        (*He dies.*)

MARY.                      What now? Rouse up! Delay
           Is dangerous. Wake! Wake! What shall we do?
SHAKESPEARE. O trumpet of the angels lent to a boy,
           Could I not spare you for the golden blast,
           For the great sound's sake? What have I done?
ANNE'S VOICE.                          Ah! Done
           The thing you would not do –
MARY.                    Rouse! Rouse yourself!
           What now!
ANNE'S VOICE.       Remember –
SHAKESPEARE.               Hark! A sigh!
MARY.                        The wind
           Keening the night –
SHAKESPEARE.            A sound of weeping –
MARY.                       Rain.
           Is this a time for visions? White-cheeked day
           Stares through the pane. Each minute is an eye
           Opening upon us. What shall we do now?
SHAKESPEARE. Weep, clamorous harlot! We have given him death,
           And shall we dock his rights of death, his peace
           Upon his bed, his sun of hair smoothed, hands
           Crossed decently by me, his friend? Close you
           His eyes with kisses, lest I kill you too!
           Give him his due, I say! his woman's tears!
           You were his woman – oh, deny it not!
           You were his woman. Pay him what you owe!
MARY. What? Do you glove my clean hand with your stain,
           Red fingers? Soft! This is your kill, not mine!
           My free soul is not sticky with your sins.
           *You* pinch your lips? *You* singe me with your tongue?
           Your country lilac that you left for me
           Taught you strange names for a woman. Harlot? I?
           Sweep your own stable, trickster, married man!
           Lie, cheat, break faith, until you end a man
           That bettered you as roses better weeds –
SHAKESPEARE. That is well known.
MARY.                      – and now you'll stare and weep

Until the watch comes and the Queen hears all.
Then – ends all!
And I caught with you! She's a devil of ice
Since Leicester died. No man or woman stirs her;
But she must have her toys! London's her doll's house,
Its marts, its theatres. This death was half her pride,
And you the other. Was I not set to mould you?
What will she do to me now her doll's broken,
Broken in my hand? I fear her, oh, I fear her,
The green eyes of her justice and her smile.
Will, if you love me – you who have had my lips,
And more, and more, and shall have all again,
All that you choose, and gladly given – awake!
Fly while there's time to save yourself and me!
Look not on him – he's blind – he cannot speak,
Nor stretch a hand to stay you – he's cold nothing!
But we, we live! Here on my throat, here, here,
(Give me your fingers!) feel the hot pulse live!
Yet I'll die sooner than be pent. You know me!
Must I lie still for ever at his side
Because you will not rouse yourself?

SHAKESPEARE.                                    Who speaks?
O vanished dew, O summer sweetness gone,
O perfume staled in a night, that yesterday
Was fresh as morning roses – do you live?
Are you still Mary? O my shining lamp
Of love put out, how dark the world has grown!
Did you want him so? Did it come on you suddenly,
And shake you from your north –

MARY.                                    The dawn! the dawn!
SHAKESPEARE. Or did you never love me – where do you point?
MARY. To save ourselves comes first!
SHAKESPEARE.                        To answer me!
MARY. Fool! Fool! Will you hang? Let go, fool!
SHAKESPEARE.                                    Answer me!
MARY. Will, for the love of living –
SHAKESPEARE.                        Answer me!
MARY. I never loved you. Are you answered?
ANNE'S VOICE.                                    Oh –
For a month – in the spring –

SHAKESPEARE.                               Is it a month ago?
     The trees are not yet metalled with the dust
     Of summer, that were greening when we two –
MARY.  Oh, peace!
SHAKESPEARE.     – in a night of spring –
MARY.                               Ah, was it love?
SHAKESPEARE.  Remember, beauty, when you came to me,
     As came the beggar to Cophetua,
     As queens came conquered to the Macedon,
     As Cressid came by night to Diomed,
     As night comes queenly to the bed of day
     Enmantled in her hair, so you to me,
     Juliet, and all your night of hair was mine
     To curtain me and you –
MARY.                               Forgotten, forgotten –
SHAKESPEARE.  That night you loved me –
ANNE'S VOICE.                               I was drunk with dreams
     That night.
SHAKESPEARE.        That night of victory you loved me!
     I have my witnesses. O watching stars –
MARY.  The eyes, the eyes, the arch of eyes!
SHAKESPEARE.                               – speak for me!
     Once was a taper that outshone you all,
     It burned so bright. Oh, how you winked and pried!
     I saw you through the tatters of the dark
     And mocked you in my hour. Yet speak for me,
     Eternal lights, for now my candle's blown
     Past envy! But she loved me then!
MARY.                               I know not.
SHAKESPEARE.  Though god and devil deny – you loved me then!
MARY.  But was it love?
     I could have loved if you had taught me loving.
     Something I sought and found not; so I turned
     From searching. I have clean forgotten now
     That ever I sought – and so live merrily –
     And so will live! Why wreck myself for you?
SHAKESPEARE.  O heart's desire, and eyes', desire of hands,
     Self of myself, have pity!
MARY.                               What had you?
     If I had borne you children (but I was wise,

Knowing my man, as men have taught me men)
What name had you to give them, to give me?
No, no, I wrong you, for you christened me
But now, first having slain him who had struck
The rankness from your mouth.

SHAKESPEARE.                                        What I have done –

MARY.  Lied, lied to me!
                          – and if I did –

ANNE'S VOICE.                                      To hold you!
I couldn't lose you. I was mad with pain.

MARY.  Tricked me –

SHAKESPEARE.            To hold – listen to me – to hold you!
Lest I should lose you. I was mad with pain.

MARY.  Are you so womanish that a breath of pain –

SHAKESPEARE.  A breath! God, listen! A breath, a summer breath!

MARY.  – could blow away your honour?

SHAKESPEARE.                                        Once it was mine.
I laid it up with you. Where is it now?
I'm stripped of honour like an oak in June
Whose leaves a curse of caterpillars eat,
That stands a mockery to flowers and men,
With naked arms praying the lightning down.

ANNE'S VOICE.  At Shottery the woods are green –

SHAKESPEARE.                                        My God!

ANNE'S VOICE.  And full of flowers –

SHAKESPEARE.                            Let be, let be! My honour?
I bought it with a woman – not like you,
A faithless-faithful woman – not like you;
But weak as I'm weak, loving as I love,
God help her! not like you – no black-eyed Spain
Whose cheeks hang out their red to match the red
When bull meets man – no luxury that wears
A lover like new clothes, and all the while
Eyes other women's fashions; but a woman
That should have loved me less, poor fool, and less –

MARY.  You should have loved me less, my fool, and less!

SHAKESPEARE.  Yet from this folly all the music springs
That is in the world, and all my hopes that ranged
Lark-high in heaven! Yet murder comes of it.
Look where he lies! he was true friend to me,

And I to him, until you came, you came.
MARY. I came and I can go.
SHAKESPEARE.                    Mary! (*There is a clatter of hoofs.*)
MARY.                              D'you hear?
Horses! What do they seek? You, Marlowe, me?
SHAKESPEARE. This they call conscience.
MARY.                         Take your hand away!
I'll slip through yet; nor shall you follow me;
You had your chance. Listen! A boy was here;
One Francis Archer. Say it after me –
No woman, but a boy, a stranger to you!
SHAKESPEARE. Strange to me, Mary.

(*There is a sound of voices in the yard.*)

MARY.                          If you hold me now
I'll scream and swear you stabbed him as he slept,
They're drinking still. (*She opens the door.*)
VOICES (*in the outer room*).
           Hey, boy! Ho, boy!
           Heel and toe, boy!
           Who'll have a drink with me?
MARY.                         If you should get away.
Send me no message, come not near me! Now!

(*She slips into the room.* SHAKESPEARE *stands at the half-open door, watching.*)

A MAN. Sing another verse!
ANOTHER. There's the boy back. Make him sing it!
MARY. I'm to fetch more wine first.
THE MAN. Sing another verse!
ANOTHER. If Love and I should meet,
           I'll catch her to me –
ANOTHER. Luck, you fool, not love!
ANOTHER. Where's the difference? If you're in love you're in luck.
ANOTHER. Here, stop the boy!
MARY. Let me pass, gentlemen!
THE MAN. Sing another verse!
ANOTHER.                 If Love and I –
ANOTHER. Shut up now and let the kid sing it!
MARY. Why yes, if you'll let me pass afterwards, sir, like love in the
       song.

THE MAN. Sing another verse! Sing twenty other verses!
MARY (*singing*). If Love should pass me by,
    I'll follow till I find him,
   And when I hear him cry,
    I'll tear the veils that blind him!
THE MAN. Now then, chorus!
ALL TOGETHER. Hey, Love! Ho, Love!
    None shall know, Love!
   Keep but a kiss for me!

(MARY *disappears in the crowd. The door swings to as* SHAKESPEARE
*turns back into the room.*)

SHAKESPEARE. Marlowe! Marlowe!
   She is gone, Marlowe, that was a fume of wine
   Between us. Marlowe, Marlowe, speak to me!
   Never a sound. We have seen many a dawn
   Creep like a housewife on the drunken night,
   And tumble him from heaven with work-day hand
   And bird-shrill railing; but such a waking up
   As this we never knew. Sorry and cold
   I look on you. Kit, Kit, this mark of the knife
   Is the first blot I ever saw in you,
   The first ill-writing. Kit, for your own sake,
   You should have wronged a stranger, not your friend;
   For like a looking-glass my heart still served you
   To see yourself, and when you struck at me,
   You struck yourself, and broke this mirror too.

(*A knock.*)

   Mary? Is it Mary? Lie you quiet, Marlowe!
   We will not let her in.
HENSLOWE. Within, who's within there?
SHAKESPEARE.         Two dead men.
HENSLOWE.            Is it Marlowe?
   Is Shakespeare there?
SHAKESPEARE.     Come in, come in, come in!

(HENSLOWE *comes in hurriedly. He leaves the door half open behind
him.*)

VOICES (*singing*). Ho, boy! Hey, boy!
>           Come this way, boy!
>           Who'll have a drink with me?

HENSLOWE. Why, here's a bird of wisdom sitting in the dark! Shut
your eyes, man, and use candles or you'll scorch out your own
sockets! What's wrong now? But tell me that as we ride; for the
Queen wants you in a hurry, and what's more an angry Queen. I'd
not be you! Here I've hunted London for you from tavern to lady's
lodging till I ferreted out that Marlowe was here, and so I followed
him for news.

SHAKESPEARE. Here's news enough. Henslowe, look here!

HENSLOWE.                                                    Who did it?

SHAKESPEARE. We – he and I. There was another in it.

HENSLOWE. Was it the youngster passed me in the yard,
>           Caught at his horse and rose like fear away?

SHAKESPEARE. Was't a pale horse?

HENSLOWE.                                    I saw not. In the dark
>           A voice cried 'Hurry!'

SHAKESPEARE.                        That was she.

HENSLOWE.                                                    Who? Who?

SHAKESPEARE. Death. She has fled and left her catch behind.
>           Can you do anything?

HENSLOWE.                                For the living scarce –
>           You must be got away. Are you known here?

SHAKESPEARE. As men know Cain. All, all is finished, Henslowe!

LANDLORD (*putting his head in at the door*). Is anything wrong, sir?

HENSLOWE. Wrong? What should be wrong? But we're in haste. Call
the ostler! We want a second horse.

(*He slips his arm through* SHAKESPEARE'*s and tried to lead him to the
door.*)

LANDLORD. Is the gentleman ill, sir. He sways.

HENSLOWE. Your good wine, host.

A MAN (*over the* LANDLORD'*s shoulder*). The best on the Surrey side!

HENSLOWE. He'll tell the Queen so in an hour if you'll make way.

MEN (*crowding into the doorway*). The Queen
>           Did you hear?
>           He's been sent by the Queen!

HENSLOWE. Keep your people back, landlord!

THE MAN (*staggering into the room*). I say, three cheers for the Queen!

ANOTHER. The Queen! The Queen! Three cheers for Bess!

(*Singing*).    Hey, Bess! Ho, Bess!
                        Heel and toe, Bess!
Ladies and gentlemen, here's a man on the bed.

HENSLOWE. Ay! My friend! Let him be!

THE MAN. Is he drunk too?

THE OTHER. If I were a judge I'd say 'Very drunk'! He's spilled his
wine on his clothes. What I say is 'Waste not, want not!'

LANDLORD. Come now, come away! You hear what the gentleman
says.

THE MAN (*throwing him off*).
                        Hey, Death! Ho, Death!
                        Let me go, Death!
Shall I wake him?

SHAKESPEARE (*turning in the doorway*). Ay, wake him, wake him, old
trump of judgement! Wake him if you can,
                        And if you cannot let him sleep his sleep
                        And envy him that he can sleep so sound!

THE MAN. Ay sir, he shall sleep till he wakes. But we, sir, we'll sing
you off the premises, for the love of Bess.
                        Hey, Bess? Ho, Bess!

ANOTHER (*hammering the table*). Death, not Bess! Death! Death!
Death! Come along, chorus!

TWO OR THREE (*as they lurch out of the room*).
                        Ho, boy! Hey, boy!
                        Come this way, boy!
                        Who'll have a drink with me?

ALL (*following*). Hey, Death! Ho, Death!
                        Out you go, Death!
                        We'll never drink with thee!

(*The door swings to and quiet settles on the lightening room. The first ray
of sunlight touches the bed. Outside the birds are beginning to sing.*)

CURTAIN.

# ACT IV

*A room in the palace, hung with tapestries. On the right wall is a heavy, stud-
ded door, on the left, a great raised seat on a low platform. On the back wall
is a small curtained door and a large window. A girl in a primrose-coloured
gown stands at it, holding back its curtain. Set slantwise in front of it, nearer
the centre of the stage, is a writing-table with scattered papers. At it sits* ELIZ-
ABETH, *a secretary beside her. The Queen's dress is of dull grey brocade with
transparent lawn and jewels of aquamarine; but as the evening deepens its
colour becomes one with the dusk, and only her white face and hands are
clearly seen.*

A HAWKER (*chanting in the street far away*).
> Cress! Buy cress!
> Who'll buy my cress-es?

(ELIZABETH *lays down her pen.*)

ELIZABETH. These three are signed. Take them to Burleigh. This I'll
> not grant. Tell him so! (*The man bows and goes out.*)

HAWKER (*nearer*). Cress! Buy cress!

ELIZABETH. There! Put the papers by!

(*The girl at the window comes down to the table and begins to sort
them.*)

ANOTHER HAWKER. Strawberries! Ripe strawberries!

THE GIRL. I wonder, Madam, that you choose this room
> Here on the noisy street.

ELIZABETH.                              Child, when you marry
> Who'll rule your nursery, you or your maids?

GIRL. Why, that I will!

ELIZABETH. Then you must sit in it daily. Where's Mary Fitton?

GIRL. In waiting, Madam, and half asleep. She was up early today. I
> saw her from my window by the little garden door and called to
> her. She had been out to pick roses, as you bade her, ere the dew
> dried on them.

ELIZABETH. As I bade her?

GIRL. Yes, Madam, she said so.

HAWKER (*close at hand*). Cress! Buy cress!
> Fit for Queen Bess!

ELIZABETH. Open the window! (*The girl opens it.*)

HAWKER. Cress! Buy cress!
    Who'll buy my cress-es?
ELIZABETH. Fetch me my purse!

(*The girl goes out by the little door. As she does so,* ELIZABETH *takes her purse from a drawer and, going to the window, throws out a coin.*)

HAWKER.                              Cress! Buy cress!
    Are you there, lady? (ELIZABETH *throws out another coin.*)
        I plucked my riches
        From Deptford ditches,
    I came by a Deptford Inn;
        Where a young man lies,
        With pennies on his eyes –
    Murdered, lady, and none saw who did it!
        Cress! Buy cress!

(ELIZABETH *flings out another coin.*)

There was a boy that ran away, and Henslowe the Queen's man, and a third –
        Cress! Buy cress!
        A supper for Queen Bess!

(ELIZABETH *lays down the purse on the table as the girl comes back.*)

GIRL (*distressed*). Madam –
ELIZABETH. It was here. That cress-seller has a sweet voice. Fling her a coin and ask her where she lives!
GIRL (*going to the window*). Hey, beggar!
HAWKER. Bless you, lady!
GIRL. Where do you come from with your green stuff?
HAWKER. Marlow, lady, Marlow!
        Down by the river where the cresses grow,
        And buttercups like guineas.
            Cress! Buy cress!
            Who'll buy my cress-es?

(*Her voice dies away in the distance.*)

GIRL. She has come a long way.
        Marlow's across the river, far from us.
ELIZABETH. Marlowe's across the river, far from us. If any ask to speak with me, let me know it!
GIRL. Why, Madam, Henslowe, the old player, has been waiting since noon, and Mr Shakespeare with him.

ELIZABETH. The name's not written here. Whose duty?

GIRL. Mary Fitton's.

ELIZABETH. Send Henslowe! And when I ring, let Mary Fitton
answer!

GIRL. I'll tell her, Madam.

(*She goes out.* ELIZABETH *rises and goes slowly across the room to the
dais, and seats herself. There is a pause. Then a page throws open the
big door facing the dais and* HENSLOWE *enters.*)

ELIZABETH.                              Henslowe, you're not welcome
    For the news you bring.

HENSLOWE.                              Madam, that Marlowe's dead
    I know because I found him – I am new come from
        Deptford –
    But how you know I know not.

ELIZABETH.                              Why, not a keel
    Grounds on the Cornish pebbles, but the jar
    Thrills through all English earth home to my feet.
    No riderless horse snuffs blood and gallops home
    To a girl widowed, but I the sparking hoofs
    Hear pound as her heart pounds, waiting; for my spies
    Are everywhere. Do not my English swifts
    Report to me at dusk, eavesdropping low,
    The number of my English primroses
    In English woods all spring? The gulls on Thames
    Scream past the Tower 'Storm in Channel! Storm!'
    And if I hear not, sudden my drinking glass
    Rings out 'Send help, lest English sailors drown!'
    The lantern moon swings o'er unvisited towns
    Signalling 'Peace!' or a star shoots out of the west
    Across my window, flashing 'Danger here!'
    And is it Ireland rising, or a child
    On chalk-pit roof after the blackberries,
    I'm warned, and bid my human servants haste.
    The flat-worn stones, the echoes of the streets
    At night when drunkards tumble, citizens
    In the half-silence and half-light trot home,
    Reveal the well, the ill in my own land.
    I am its eyes, its pulse, its fingertips,
    The wakeful partner of its married soul.

> I know what darkness does, what dawn discovers
> In all the English country. I am the Queen.
> You have done my errand? Shakespeare the player is with you?

HENSLOWE. He waits without.

ELIZABETH. Then he too was at Deptford last night.

HENSLOWE. None knows it.

ELIZABETH. That's well! But was it he, Henslowe – he?

HENSLOWE. No, no, no! I'll swear it.

ELIZABETH. But will he swear it?

HENSLOWE. He's dazed, he will say anything – yes – no –
> Just as you prompt him, as if one blow had struck
> His soul and Marlowe's body. Madam, he's not his witness!
> Yet if t'were true, if he has lost us Marlowe,
> Must we lose him? Then has the English stage
> Lost both her hands and cannot feed herself,
> Starves, Madam!

ELIZABETH. You're honest, Henslowe! Your son's son one day
> May help a king to thread a needle's eye.
> But do you think he did it?

HENSLOWE.                              No, though he says it,
> For he loved him.

ELIZABETH.                    Loved him, but a woman better.

HENSLOWE. There was no woman with them.

ELIZABETH. So I hear; but a boy!

HENSLOWE. Unknown.

ELIZABETH. Did you see him?

HENSLOWE. Not his face. He was past me in a flash, crying 'Hurry!'

ELIZABETH. Well, I'll see Shakespeare.

HENSLOWE. Madam –

ELIZABETH. I thread my own needles, Henslowe, being a woman.
(MARY FITTON *enters.*) Send Mr Shakespeare to me! (*Then, as*
MARY *turns to go* –) Mary!

MARY. Madam?

ELIZABETH. Bid him hurry! (MARY *turns to the door.*) Mary!

MARY. Madam?

ELIZABETH. What did I tell you but now?

MARY. Madam, to bid him hurry.

HENSLOWE (*recognising the voice*). 'Hurry!'

ELIZABETH. Wait. Daylight, Henslowe? Girl, you're slow. You go
heavily. Have you not slept? Let Henslowe do your errand! (*To*

HENSLOWE.) Let him wait at hand!

MARY.  Madam, I can well go.

ELIZABETH.  No hurry now. (HENSLOWE *goes out*.) D'you guess why I
send for your teller of tales?

MARY.  No, Madam.

ELIZABETH.  He has told a tale, it seems, that I'd hear told again.

MARY.  Told?

ELIZABETH.  Why are you not in black, Mary?

MARY.  I, Madam?

ELIZABETH.  Marlowe is dead.

MARY.  I grieve to hear it.

ELIZABETH.  When did you hear?

MARY.  Why, Madam, now – you tell me!

ELIZABETH.  Then I tell you wrong. He is alive and has told all.

MARY.  Alive? They lie to you, Madam! What has he told? Who says it?

ELIZABETH.  You, Mary Fitton! For by your dark-ringed eyes
  Your dreaming service and those blind hands of yours
  Seeking a hold, I think you saw him die,
  Ere you passed Henslowe in the dark, crying 'Hurry!'

MARY.  Madam, it was your errand. For this Shakespeare,
  This quill you thrust on me to sharpen up,
  Jealous of Marlowe, though he had no cause
  (What! must I live his nun, his stay-at-home?
  Your servant and a lady of the court!),
  Sent me a letter –

ELIZABETH.     Let me read!

MARY.         I tore it!

– so inked in threat that I post-haste for Deptford –

ELIZABETH.  Ill judged!

MARY.    I know! I followed my first fear.
  – rode to warn Marlowe. Shakespeare following,
  Spying upon us, spying upon us, Madam!
  Found us in counsel. Then, with a hail of words
  That Marlowe would not bear, with 'stale' and 'harlot',
  He beat me down, till Marlowe flung 'em back;
  Then like two dogs they struggled. Marlowe fell.

ELIZABETH.  Struck down?

MARY.    Struck down, but blindly, not to kill –
  I will not think to kill – as he fell
  His own knife caught him, here.

ELIZABETH.                                    What did you then?

MARY. I, Madam?

ELIZABETH.             You, Madam? Did you fold your hands
                And watch this business as you'd watch a play,
                And clap them on? Or, as a short month since
                You played a part I think, did you strike in
                And play a part? Why did you call for help?

MARY. I did not, Madam!

ELIZABETH.                  Why did not Mary Fitton
                Cry help against – which lover?

MARY.                                     Lover, madam?

ELIZABETH. There's tinker, tailor, soldier – the old rhyme –
                There's Pembroke, Marlowe, Shakespeare –

MARY.                                         Madam! Madam!
                I'll not bear this!

ELIZABETH.                  Ay, you have fierce black eyes –
                What will you do then if you will not bear it?
                You have leave to show.

MARY.                          I say I did cry out
                To both that they should cease.

ELIZABETH.                            So you cried out!
                Bring up your witnesses that heard you cry!

MARY. I did not stand and watch. I ran upon them.
                I was flung off and bruised.

ELIZABETH.                        Show me the bruise!

MARY. High on my arm –

ELIZABETH.              Rip up your sleeve and show me!
                You stand, you stare, you're white. I think you shake.

MARY. Anger not fear, though you were ten times Queen
                Of twenty Englands!

ELIZABETH.                    Quiet, and quiet, my girl!
                This ill-spent night has left you feverish.
                You are too free for court,
                Too bruised and tousled for my gentlemen.
                You shall go home, I think, to heal this bruise,
                To cleanse your body and soul in country air
                And banished quiet till I send for you.

MARY. Upon what count?

ELIZABETH.              On none. But I've no time,
                No room for butterfingers. Here's a man slain

Upon your lap that England needed. Go!
Go, blunted tool! (*She touches a bell.*)

MARY.                    Madam! Madam! You wrong me!

ELIZABETH.  I've wronged your betters, Mary, Mary Fitton,
As tide wrongs pebble, or as wind wrongs chaff
At threshing time.

(*A page enters at the great door on the right.*)

                              Send Mr Shakespeare to me!

MARY.  This is the justice of the Queen of England!

ELIZABETH.  My justice.

MARY.                Have I not served you?

ELIZABETH.                              All things serve me.
They choose their path. I use them in their path.

MARY.  As once you used, they say –

ELIZABETH.                      Do not dare! Do not dare!

MARY.  Dare, Madam? May I not wonder, like another.
Why you have used me thus?

ELIZABETH.                        I used you, dirt,
To show a man how foul the dirt can be;
But now I brush you from him.

(*The main door opens and* HENSLOWE *enters, followed by*
SHAKESPEARE. *She beckons to* HENSLOWE.)

                        Henslowe!

HENSLOWE.                          Madam?

(*The speak privately for a moment, then* HENSLOWE *goes out by the
small door.*)

MARY (*to* SHAKESPEARE). You come to cue!

SHAKESPEARE.                    What has fallen?

MARY.                                Sent away
Because of you, because my name is Mary!

SHAKESPEARE.  Go to my lodging! Wait for me! I'll follow,
For where you go I go.

MARY.                    Ay, bring your wife!
This act is over! There are other men!

                              (*She goes out.*)

SHAKESPEARE.  Mary! Love, life, the breath I breathe, come back!
Mary, you have not heard me! Mary! Mary!
Come back! (*The door shuts with a clang.*)

ANNE'S VOICE.     Come back!

ELIZABETH.             Never in any world!
      Fasten the door there!

SHAKESPEARE (*struggling to open it*). Open! Open, I say!

ELIZABETH. Beat, beat your heart out! Let me watch you beat
      Those servants of your soul until they bleed,
      Mash, agonise, against a senseless door!
      Beat, beat your weaker hands than that dead tree,
      Tear, tear your nails upon its nails in vain.
      Beat, beat your heart out – you'll not pass the door!
      Can you not come at her? She goes – beat, beat!
      The distance widens, like a ship she goes
      Utterly from you. Follow! Beat your hands!
      What? Are you held, you who bow men with words
      Windily down like cornfields? Is she gone?
      Call up the clouds to carry you who walk
      Sky-high, star-level, eyeing the naked sun.
      Where are your wings? Beat, beat your heart out! Beat!
      Where is your strength? Will not the wood be moved?
      Cannot your love-call reach her, you who know
      The heart of the lark and how the warm throat thrills
      At mating-time? Is there a living thing
      You do not dwell in, cannot stir, and yet
      You cannot move this door?

SHAKESPEARE.             I am not so bound –

ELIZABETH. Why, yes, there's the window! You may cast down and be
   done with it all – done with it all! I'll not stop you. Who am I to
   keep a man from his sweet rest? And yet – what of me, my son,
   before you do it? What of me and this England that I am?

SHAKESPEARE. Madam, I have not slept these five nights. I do not
   know what you say.

ELIZABETH. Or care?

SHAKESPEARE. Or care, Madam, forgive me! God's pity, Madam,
   open the door!

ELIZABETH. It shall not serve you.

SHAKESPEARE. I know it.

ELIZABETH. She has sold you, man.

SHAKESPEARE. I know it. Open the door!

ELIZABETH. Come here, my son! Why do I hold you here, think you?

SHAKESPEARE. Marlowe –

ELIZABETH.  Tell me nothing! I'll know nothing! Mr Shakespeare,
    where is the work I should have from you? Where is the new play?
    You sold and I bought. Give me my goods! Then go!

SHAKESPEARE.  A play? You are Queen, Madam, you do not live our
    lives; so I call you not pure devilish to keep me here for so little a
    thing.

ELIZABETH.  Yet I will have it from you! There's paper, pen –
        I'll have your roughed-out scene ere Henslowe leaves
        Tonight. And ere the ended month this play,
        This English laughter, ringing all her bells,
        Before the pick of Europe at my court
        Performed, shall link our hands with Italy,
        With old immortal Athens. This you'll do,
        For this you can.

SHAKESPEARE (*crying out*).   I am to live, not write,
        To love, not write of love, to live my life
        As others do, to live a summer life
        As all the others do!

ELIZABETH.                I thought so too
        When I was young. Then, 'mid my state affairs
        And droning voices of my ministers,
        The people's acclamation and the hiss
        Of treacheries to England and to me,
        Ever I heard the momentary clock
        Ticking away my girlhood as I reigned;
        While she – while she –
        Mary of Scotland, Mary of delight,
        (I know her sweetheart names) Maybird, May flower.
        The three-times-married honeysuckle queen,
        She had her youth. Think you I'd not have changed,
        Sat out her twenty years a prisoner,
        Ridden her road from France to Fotheringay,
        To have her story? Am I less woman, I,
        That I'd not change with her? For the high way
        Is flowerless, and thin the mountain air
        And rends the lungs that breathe it; and the light
        Spreading from hill to everlasting hill,
        Welling across the sky as from a wound,
        A heart of blood between the breasts of the world,
        Is not much nearer, no, nor half as warm

As the kissing sun of the valleys: and we climb
(You'll climb as I do) not because we will,
Because we must. There is no virtue in it;
But some pride. Fate can force but not befool me!
I am not drunken with religious dream
Like the poor blissful fools of kingdom come:
I know the flesh is sweetest, when all's said,
And summer's heyday and the love of men:
I know well what I lose. I'm head of the Church
And stoop my neck on Sunday – to what Christ?
The God of little children? I have none.
The God of love? What love has come to me?
The God upon His ass? I am not meek,
Nor is he meek, the stallion that I ride,
The great white horse of England. I'll not bow
To the gentle Jesus of the women, I –
But to the man who hung 'twixt earth and heaven
Six mortal hours, and knew the end (as strength
And custom was) three days away, yet ruled
His soul and body so, that when the sponge
Blessed his cracked lips with promise of relief
And quick oblivion, he would not drink:
He turned his head away and would not drink:
Spat out the anodyne and would not drink.
This was a god for kings and queens of pride,
And him I follow.

SHAKESPEARE.            Whither?

ELIZABETH.                              The alley's blind.
For the cross rules us or we rule the cross,
Yet the cross wins in the end.
For night is older than the daylight is:
The slack string will not quiver for the hand
Of cunningest musician.
Does the cross care, a chafer or a pin,
Whether Barabbas writhe, or very God?
All's one to the dead wood! Dead wood, dead wood,
It coffins us in the end. God, you and me
And everyone – the dead wood baffles all.
And why I care I know not, but I know
That I'll die fighting – and the fight goes on.

Yet not uncaptained shall the assault go on
Against dead wood fencing the hearts of men.
For this I chose you.
I am a barren woman. Mary's child
Reigns after me in England. Yet, tonight,
I crown my heir. I, England, crown my son.

SHAKESPEARE. There was a better man but yesterday –
To him the crown! King was he of all song.

ELIZABETH. He's king now of the silence after song,
When the last bell-note hovers, like a high
And starry rocket that dissolves in stars,
Lost ere they reach us. He is lord of that
For ever.

SHAKESPEARE.      He – he had the luck; but I,
But England was not lucky.

ELIZABETH.                          Be assured
Had England chosen Marlowe, here tonight
England had crowned him, and you in Surrey ditch
Had lain where he lies, dead, my dead son, dead.
Take you the kingship on you!

SHAKESPEARE.                          A player-king –

ELIZABETH. As I player-queen! I play my part
Not ill, not ill. Judge me, my English peer,
And witness for me, that I play not ill
My part! And if by night, unseen, I weep,
Scourging my spirit down the track of the years,
Hating the name of Mary, as she said;
Yet comes and goes my hour, and comes again,
My hour, when I bear England in my breast
As God Almighty bears His universe,
England moves in me, I for England speak,
As I speak now. It is not the shut door,
But I, but England, holds you prisoner.

SHAKESPEARE. But to what service, England, and what end?

ELIZABETH. I send my ships where never ships have sailed,
To break the barriers and make wide the ways
For the afterworld.
Send you your ships to the hidden lands of the soul,
To break the barriers and make plain the ways
Between man and man. Why else were we two born?

SHAKESPEARE. What's the worth of a play?

ELIZABETH.                                     My ships are not so great
          And ride not like firm islands of dry land
          As Philip's do; yet these my cockle-boats
          Have used the vast world as a village pond,
          And fished for treasure above the planets' bed
          In the drowned palaces where, water-bleached,
          Atlantis gleams as gleams the skull-white moon,
          Rolled in the overwhelming tides of time
          Hither and down the beaches of the sky.
          Send out your thoughts as I send out my men,
          To earn a world for England! – paying first
          The toll of the pioneer. I do not cheat.
          Here is the bill – reckon it ere you pay!

SHAKESPEARE. Have I not paid?

ELIZABETH.                          Nay, hourly, till you die.
          I tell you, you shall toss upon your bed
          Crying 'Let me sleep!' as men cry 'Let me live!'
          And sleeping you shall still cry 'Mary! Mary!'
          This will not pass. Think not the sun that wakes
          The birds in England and the daisy-lawns,
          Draws up the meadow fog like prayer to heaven,
          And curls the smoke in cottage chimneystacks,
          Shall once forget to wake you with a warm
          And kissing breath! The four walls shall repeat
          The name upon your lips, and in your heart
          The name, the one name, like a knife shall turn.
          These are your dawns. *I* tell you, I who know.
          Nor shall day spare you. All your prospering years,
          The tasteless honours for yourself – not her –
          The envy in men's voices, (if they knew
          The beggar that they envied!) all this shall stab,
          Stab, stab, and stab again. And little things
          Shall hurt you so: stray words in books you read,
          And jests of strangers never meant to hurt you:
          The lovers in the shadow of your fence,
          Their faces hid, shall thrust a spare hand out,
          The other held, to stab you as you pass:
          And oh, the cry of children when they play!
          You shall put grief in irons and lock it up,

And at the door set laughter for a guard,
Yet dance through life on knives and never rest,
While England knows you for a lucky man.
These are your days. I tell you, I, a queen,
Ruling myself and half a world. I know
What fate is laid upon you. Carry it!
Or, if you choose, flinch, weaken, and fall down,
Lie flat and howl, and let the ones that love you
(Not burdened less) half carry it and you!
Will you do that? Proud man, will you do that?

SHAKESPEARE.  Because you are all woman –

ELIZABETH.                                    Have you seen it?
None other sees.

SHAKESPEARE.                              – and not as you're the
Queen,
I'll let you be the tongue to my own soul,
Yet not for long I'll bear it.

ELIZABETH.                          To each his angel
For good or ill.
Women to a man, the man to a woman ever
Mated or fated. I am this fate to you,
As to me once a fallen star you knew not.
It's long ago. You should have known the man.
He was the glory of the English night,
Its red star in decline. For see what came –
His fires were earthy and he choked himself
In his own ash. Not good but goodly was he,
A natural prince of the world: and he had been one
Had he been other, or I blind, or – Mary.
Lucifer! Lucifer! He loved me not,
But would have used me. Well – he used me not.
He died. I loved him. This between us two.
Bury it deep!

SHAKESPEARE.          Deep as my sorrow lies.
But Queen, what cometh after?

ELIZABETH.                              Work.

SHAKESPEARE.                                    And after?

ELIZABETH. Sleep comes for me.

SHAKESPEARE.                  And after?

ELIZABETH.                                    Sleep for you.

SHAKESPEARE. And after?

ELIZABETH.                          Nothing. Only the blessed sleep.

SHAKESPEARE. And so ends all?

ELIZABETH.                     And so all ends.

SHAKESPEARE.                                    Love ends?

ELIZABETH. And so love ends.

SHAKESPEARE.                     I have a word to say.
    Give me this crown and reach the sceptre here!
    The end's not yet, but yet the end is mine;
    For I know what I am and what I do
    At last! Give me my pen, ere the spark dies
    That lights me! And now leave me!

(*He turns to the table and his work.*)

ELIZABETH (*loudly*).                          Open the door!

SHAKESPEARE. Sesame, sesame! A word to say –

(*The door is flung open and the long passage is seen.*)

    O darkness, did she pass between your walls,
    And left no picture on the empty air,
    No echo of her step that waits for mine
    To wake it in a message? What do I here?
    'A word to say!' There's nothing left but words.

(ELIZABETH *has descended from her throne and, crossing the room,
pauses a moment beside him.*)

ELIZABETH. Is the harness heavy – heavy?

SHAKESPEARE.                          Heavy as lead.
    Heavy as a heart.

ELIZABETH.                     It will not lighten.

SHAKESPEARE.                          Go! (*She goes out.*)
    I had a word to say.
    Oh, spark that burned but now –!

ANNE'S VOICE.                          It dips, it dies –

SHAKESPEARE. A nightlight, fool, and not a star. I grope
    Giddily in the dark. I shall grow old.
    What is my sum? I have made seven plays,
    Two poems and some sonnets. I have friends
    So long as I write poems, sonnets, plays.
    Earn then your loves, and as you like it – write!
    Come, what's your will?

Three sets of lovers and a duke or two,
Courtiers and fool – We'll set it in a wood,
Half park, half orchard, like the woods at home.
See the house rustle, pit gape, boxes thrill,
As though the trees, boyishly, hand on hip,
Knee-deep in grass, zone-deep in margarets,
Comes to us – Mary!

ANNE'S VOICE.                    Under the apple-trees,
In the spring, in the long grass – Will!

SHAKESPEARE.                         Still the old shame
Hangs round my neck with withered arms and chokes
Endeavour.

ANNE'S VOICE.          Will!

SHAKESPEARE.                    At right wing enter ghost!
It should be Marlowe with his parted mouth
And sweep of arm. Why should he wake for me?
That would be friendship, and what a friend was I!
Well – to the work!

ANNE'S VOICE.                    Will! Will!

SHAKESPEARE.                              What, ghost? Still there?
Must I speak first? That's manners with the dead;
But this haunt lives – at Stratford, by the river.
Maggot, come out of my brain! Girl! Echo! Wraith!
You've had free lodging, like a rat, too long.
I need my room. Come, show yourself and go!
'Changed?' 'But I knew her!' – Say your say and go!
You'd a tongue once.

ANNE'S VOICE.                    You're to be great –

SHAKESPEARE.                              Stale! Stale!
That's the Queen's catchword.

ANNE'S VOICE.                         But I know, I know,
I'm your poor village woman, but I know
What you must learn and learn, and shriek to God
To spare you learning –

SHAKESPEARE.                    Ay, like wheels that shriek,
Carting the grain, their dragged unwilling way
Over the stones, uphill, at even, thus,
Shrieking, I learn –

ANNE'S VOICE.                    When harvest comes –

SHAKESPEARE.                                                    Is come!
         Sown, sprouted, scythed and garnered –
ANNE'S VOICE.                                                  I alone
         Can give you comfort, for you reap my pain,
         As I your loss – loss – loss –
SHAKESPEARE.                        Anne, was it thus?
ANNE'S VOICE.  No other way –
SHAKESPEARE.                   Such pain?
ANNE'S VOICE.                                    Such pain, such pain!
SHAKESPEARE.  I did not know. O tortured thing, remember,
         I did not know – I did not know! Forgive –
ANNE'S VOICE.  Forgiving is forgetting – no, come back!
         I love you. Oh, come back to me, come back!
SHAKESPEARE.  I cannot.
ANNE'S VOICE.                 Oh, come back! I love you so.
SHAKESPEARE.  Be still, poor voice, be still!
ANNE'S VOICE.                                  I love you so.
SHAKESPEARE.  What is this love?
         What is this awful spirit and unknown,
         That mates the suns and gives a bird his tune?
         What is this stirring at the roots of the world?
         What is this secret child that leaps in the womb
         Of life? What is this wind, whence does it blow,
         And why? And falls upon us like the flame
         Of Pentecost, haphazard. What is this dire
         And holy ghost that will not let us two
         For no prayers' sake nor good deeds' sake nor pain
         Nor pity, have peace, and live at ease, and die
         As the leaves die?
ANNE'S VOICE.                 I know not. All I know.
         Is that I believe because I know, I know,
         Being in hell, paying the price, alone,
         Licked in the flame unspeakable and torn
         By devils, as in the old tales that are true –
         All true, the fires, the red-hot branding irons,
         The thirst, the laughter, and the filth of shame,
         All true, O fellow men! All true, all true –
         Down through the circles, like a mangled rat
         A hawk lets fall from the far towers of the sky,
         Down through the wakeful æons of the night,

Into the Pit of misery they call
Bottomless, falling – I believe and know
That the Pit's bottom is the lap of God,
And God is love.

ANNE'S VOICE.                 Is love, is love –

SHAKESPEARE.                                        I know.
And knowing I will live my dark days out
And wait for His own evening to give light.
And though I may not fill the mouth I love,
Yet will I sow and reap and bind my sheaves,
Glean, garner, mill my corn, and bake and cast
My bread upon the waters of the age.
This will I do for love's sake, lest God's eyes,
That are the Judgement, ask her man of her
One day, and she be shamed – as I am shamed
Ever, in my heart, by a voice witnessing
Against me that I knew not love.

PAGE (*entering with lights*).                 The Queen, sir,
Has sent you candles, now the sun is down,
That you may see to work.

SHAKESPEARE.                          I thank the Queen.
Tell her the work goes well!

(*He sits down at the table.*)

                                        Act one, scene one,
Oliver's house. It *shall* go well. I have
A strength that comes I know not whence. It *shall*
Go well. And then I'll give the Roman tale
I heard at school – a tale of men, not women:
That easies all. But Antony goes on
To Egypt and a gipsy: leaves his pale wife
At home to scald her eyes out. Mary – Mary –
Will you not let me be? It *shall* go well.
And after Antony some Twelfth Night trick
To please our gods and give my pregnancy
Its needed peace. How many months for Denmark?
And then? A whole man laughs, and so will I.
Oh, Smile behind the thunder, teach me laughter,
And save my soul! –
The knockabout fat man, try him again!
He'll take a month or less – candles are cheap,

Cheaper than sleep these dreaming nights. That done,
I'll sink another shaft in Holinshed –
Marlowe, your diamonds! Your diamonds!
The king and his three daughters – he's been shaped
Already. True! But rough-cut only. Wait!
Give me that giant cluster in my hand
To cut anew, in its own midnight set,
It shall outshine Orion! Afterwards,
A fairytale maybe, and after that –
And after that – and after – after? God!
The years before me! And no Mary! Mary –

ANNE'S VOICE. When her lost face –

SHAKESPEARE.                         It shall, it shall go well.

ANNE'S VOICE. – stares from the page you toil upon, thus, thus,
      In a glass of tears –

SHAKESPEARE.                  They scald, they blind my view,
      No comfort anywhere.

ANNE'S VOICE.                  I love you so.

SHAKESPEARE. The work, the work remains.

ANNE'S VOICE.                              But when you're old,
      For work too old, or pity, love or hate,
      For anything but peace, and in your hand
      Lies the crowned life victorious at last –

SHAKESPEARE. Like the crowned Indian fruit, the voyage home
      Rots while it gilds, not worth the tasting –

ANNE'S VOICE.                              Then,
      Remember me! Then, then, when all your need
      Is hands to serve you and a breast to die on,
      Come back to me!

SHAKESPEARE.            God knows – some day?

ANNE'S VOICE.                              I wait.

(*As he stoops over his work again*)

the CURTAIN *falls*.

# Margaret Kennedy

## *1896–1967*

The daughter of Charles Moore Kennedy and his wife Elinor, Margaret Kennedy was born on 23 April (Shakespeare's supposed birthday) 1896 in London. In 1922, after an education at Cheltenham Ladies' College and Somerville College, Oxford (where she read history), she published a history textbook *A Century of Revolution: A History of Europe between 1789-1922*, and the following year produced a novel, *The Ladies of Lyndon*.

In 1924 her novel *The Constant Nymph* became not only an intellectual, but also an internationally popular, success. Basil Dean (who had produced Clemence Dane's *Bill of Divorcement*, *Will Shakespeare* and other projects) persuaded her to adapt the novel for the stage, with his help. In 1925 she married David Davies, a barrister (like her father) who became a KC (later QC) and County Court Judge.

For twenty years she continued writing plays: *Come With Me*; *Escape Me Never* (which starred Elisabeth Bergner and ran for 230 performances in 1933); *Autumn* and *Happy with Either*; as well as novels: *Red Sky at Morning*; *The Fool of the Family* (a sequel to *The Constant Nymph*); *Return I Dare Not*; *A Long Time Ago*; *The Oracles* and *The Heroes of Clone*.

Between 1938 and 1950 she wrote no fiction because, she said, 'I was not obliged to do so . . . I had twelve years in which to stroll about and look at things, without being obliged to rush off and turn the *chose vue* into the *chose imaginée* in a sort of pressure cooker.'

Later, during the war, she lived in the country with her three children, but travelled back and forth to London to see her husband. Their home was destroyed in the blitz.

Her return to the literary world began with *The Feast* and a biography of Jane Austen (1950), followed in 1951 by *Lucy Carmichael*. Two years later she published *Troy Chimneys* (which won the James Tait Black award) and in 1955, *Act of God*. In 1958 she wrote *The Outlaw on Parnassus*, a study of twentieth-century fiction and its degeneration in public esteem – a book noted for its intellectual austerity. She also wrote an autobiography called *Where Stands a Winged Sentry*.

Margaret Kennedy was described as 'rather tall, neither fat nor thin . . . nervous and talkative', and as one of the 'brilliant women novelists of the twentieth century . . . distinguished by this hardness, gaiety and firm moral stamina.' And the *Observer* review in 1926 of *The Constant Nymph* points out the 'curious fact that nearly all the books and plays about free and unfettered people, blithely acting on impulse and always indulging their desires in disregard of other persons, are written by authors who are themselves almost over-disciplined.'

Margaret Kennedy died on 31 July 1967.

# Basil Dean

## *1888–1978*

Co-adapter of *The Constant Nymph* for the stage, Basil Dean CBE was one of the most important figures of the time in English theatre. Born in Croydon in September 1888, he became an actor with Miss Horniman's Repertory Company. He went on to help found the Reps at Liverpool and Birmingham. He worked as assistant to Sir Herbert Tree before the First World War, in which he served as a gazetted Captain in the Cheshire Regiment. He was soon appointed head of the entertainment branch of the Navy and Army Canteen Board, running ten companies.

In 1919, with Alec L. Rea, he founded Reandean, which produced many West End shows including *A Bill of Divorcement* and *Will Shakespeare*. In 1926 he set up Basil Dean Productions which produced many plays by women including *The Constant Nymph* and *Autumn* (Margaret Kennedy), *Autumn Crocus*, *Touch Wood* and *Call It A Day* (C.L.Anthony/Dodie Smith).

During the Second World War Basil Dean helped found ENSA and produced many patriotic anthologies, including Clemence Dane's *Cathedral Steps*. He directed films of *Lorna Doone* and *The Constant Nymph*, as well as many of Gracie Fields's comedies.

This is how Noël Coward described Basil Dean: 'As a man he was pleasant, occasionally gay with an almost childish abandon, and in his more relaxed moments exceedingly good company. As a producer he could be and frequently was a fiend . . . Basil's only real failing in the theatre was lack of psychological perceptiveness. His actors on the whole were terrified of him; frequently even stars of big reputation quailed before him.'

He married and divorced three times.

# About *The Constant Nymph*

*The Constant Nymph* first opened on 14 September 1926 at the New Theatre, transferred to the Garrick in 1928 and achieved a run of 587 performances, despite mixed reviews. The bad reviews mainly concentrated on the everlasting gripe that novels cannot successfully be translated for the stage.

The *Observer* disagreed, and thought it 'a job well done. The play is good, the acting is good, the production is good.' Other papers, despite commenting that the play was too long (it ran over three and a half hours), hailed it as 'a play you must see', in which 'remarkable things were happening . . . with a Tchekovian grace'. '*The Constant Nymph*', they cried, 'is the play in London to go to, and the enthusiasm at the end was immense.' It became the theatre's greatest success of 1926, as well as the most discussed play of the year.

Noël Coward, who took the role of Lewis Dodd, was not happy in the part, and described moving through the opening night 'in a dull coma of depression'. He later explained that his unhappiness had a lot to do with Basil Dean trying to rob him 'quite rightly' of his 'Noël Coward mannerisms', together with 'a series of ghastly thirty-second changes . . . so that when [he] wasn't actually on the stage, which was for most of the play, [he] was gasping away at the side, putting on [his] shoes or something.'

The ascerbic, ageing actress Mrs Patrick Campbell did not help his confidence by phoning him after the dress rehearsal and asking him why he had accepted the part: 'You're the wrong type! You have no glamour and you should wear a beard.' After a month, John Gielgud took over from Coward.

Coward thought Edna Best, in the role of Tessa, 'was so gallant and moving in the death scene at the end that she almost made me forget my own dreariness.' It was filmed by Basil Dean at Ealing Studios in 1934, and also in 1943 in Hollywood directed by Edmund Goulding with Charles Boyer, Joan Fontaine, Alexis Smith and Peter Lorre.

The *Constant Nymph* has a mad energy and gushing sentimentality which, in the right hands, could be irresistible. The bustling scenes from bohemian life provide a vivid backdrop to the more tender love story of Tessa, the constant nymph herself, and Lewis Dodd the concert pianist.

# THE CONSTANT NYMPH

## Margaret Kennedy
## and
## Basil Dean

*The Supper Scene, Act I. Noël Coward is second from the right.*

First acted at the New Theatre, London, on 14 September 1926, with the following cast:

| | |
|---|---|
| LEWIS DODD | *Noël Coward* |
| LINDA COWLAND | *Mary Clare* |
| KATE SANGER | *Marie Ney* |
| KIRIL TRIGORIN | *Aubrey Mather* |
| PAULINA SANGER | *Helen Spencer* |
| TERESA SANGER | *Edna Best* |
| JACOB BIRNBAUM | *Keneth Kent* |
| ANTONIA SANGER | *Elissa Landi* |
| ROBERTO | *Tony de Lungo* |
| SUSAN | *Elsie Clarke* |
| FLORENCE CHURCHILL | |
| (afterwards wife of Lewis Dodd) | *Cathleen Nesbitt* |
| CHARLES CHURCHILL | *Cecil Parker* |
| MILLICENT GREGORY | *Marie Ney* |
| SIR BARTLEMY PUGH | *Aubrey Mather* |
| PEVERIL LEYBURN | *Harold Scott* |
| ERDA LEYBURN | *Margot Sieveking* |
| DR DAWSON | *Craighall Sherry* |
| LYDIA MAINWARING | *Marjorie Gabain* |
| ROBERT MAINWARING | *David Hawthorne* |
| AN USHER | *Guy Pelham Boulton* |
| A FIREMAN | *Charles Garry* |
| A CITY CLERK | *Philip Wade* |
| MADAME MARXSE | *Margaret Yarde* |

*Subsequently taken by John Gielgud.

# ACT I

SCENE 1

SCENE: *The Karindehütte on a spring afternoon. At the back a large door Centre, with windows on either side giving a lovely view of the Austrian Tyrol in spring. It is apparent that the house is at a considerable elevation: there are views of the upper parts of hillsides. The rear portion of the room is raised about a foot, forming a sort of dais. Above this raised portion is a wooden gallery with doors to the bedrooms, two of which face the audience. The remaining rooms are beyond an archway at the head of the staircase Right. A large doorway down Right, leading to music-room. On the opposite side is a large fireplace Left. Door to the kitchen is under the staircase up Right. On the dais at back Left a grand piano, keyboard at right angles to audience. On Right side of dais a shabby leather screen, in one fold a round hole in which to insert one's head. Right down the centre of the lower portion of the room is a large oblong table, with* SANGER's *chair at head, facing the audience. The whole place is shockingly untidy, books, music, manuscript, articles of clothing, flowers, satchels, shoes, etc., strewn everywhere. And yet the whole place has a distinct atmosphere of its own, artistic feeling fighting the squalor.*

LINDA *is half asleep in a hammock chair on the verandah formed by the projecting portion of the bedrooms on the first floor. These are supported by wooden pillars seen through the windows.* LEWIS *is trying over his Opera at the piano, humming and strumming and writing corrections into his manuscript.* KATE's *voice is heard off, practising agility exercises. In the rare silences, the faint, intermittent tinkle of cow bells is heard, as though the animals were all round the house, straying and browsing on the steep Alpine meadow.*

LEWIS (*humming*). Gentle earth, more lightly lie, on a maid untimely
  slain – unti-imely slain –
LINDA (*bawling*). Kate!
LEWIS. Damn! Damn! (*Bangs again.*) Three damns!
LINDA. Ka-ate!
LEWIS (*to himself*). Oh, shut up!
LINDA. Kate!
LEWIS. Not here! (*Hums.*) Gentle earth – (*Writes in MS.*)
KATE (*singing off*). La, la, la, la-a-a! La, la, la, la, la, la, la!
LEWIS. Ten million devils! Kate!

# About *The Constant Nymph*

*The Constant Nymph* first opened on 14 September 1926 at The New Theatre, transferred to the Garrick in 1928 and achieved a run of 587 performances, despite mixed reviews. The bad reviews mainly concentrated on the everlasting gripe that novels cannot successfully be translated for the stage.

The *Observer* disagreed, and thought it 'a job well done. The play is good, the acting is good, the production is good.' Other papers, despite commenting that the play was too long (it ran over three and a half hours), hailed it as 'a play you must see', in which 'remarkable things were happening . . . with a Tchekovian grace'. '*The Constant Nymph*', they cried, 'is the play in London to go to, and the enthusiasm at the end was immense.' It became the theatre's greatest success of 1926, as well as the most discussed play of the year.

Noël Coward, who took the role of Lewis Dodd, was not happy in the part, and described moving through the opening night 'in a dull coma of depression'. He later explained that his unhappiness had a lot to do with Basil Dean trying to rob him 'quite rightly' of his 'Noël Coward mannerisms', together with 'a series of ghastly thirty-second changes . . . so that when [he] wasn't actually on the stage, which was for most of the play, [he] was gasping away at the side, putting on [his] shoes or something.'

The acerbic, ageing actress Mrs Patrick Campbell did not help his confidence by phoning him after the dress rehearsal and asking him why he had accepted the part: 'You're the wrong type! You have no glamour and you should wear a beard.' After a month, John Gielgud took over from Coward.

LEWIS. Then I should certainly sit down.

TRIGORIN. This moment, you can imagine, my dear sir, is for me a very great one. I go to visit Mr Sanger, I meet Mr Dodd. I find myself in the company of two most distinguished composers all in the one time. I am astonished.

LEWIS. H'm! Nothing to what you will be.

TRIGORIN. I must make my salutes to the family. It is a large family? Yes?

LEWIS. Well, yes. (*Smiling.*) Pretty big.

TRIGORIN. How many are now here?

LEWIS. Well, there's Madame. (*Indicating with his thumb over his shoulder the slumbering* LINDA.)

TRIGORIN (*cautiously peeping at her*). Madame! You would say – Mrs Sanger?

LEWIS. Yes, if you like. Then there's the children.

TRIGORIN. Many children?

LEWIS. Dozens!

TRIGORIN. *Tiens!* And all the children of Madame?

LEWIS. No! Not all. Only one.

TRIGORIN. Then the rest – they have had another mother?

LEWIS. Several!

TRIGORIN. *Par exemple?*

LEWIS. He collects children without meaning to. They're not all here. There isn't room.

TRIGORIN. Perhaps I should now go and make my salutes to him.

LEWIS (*going back to piano*). Better not. I doubt if he'll see anyone just now. He's ill!

TRIGORIN. Ill! But I had not heard. What –

LEWIS. Drink.

TRIGORIN. Ach so! (*Staring thoughtfully at* LEWIS, *who is writing at the piano.*) Then to whom shall I salute myself?

LEWIS. Wait till I've finished this. Then I'll call Kate. (*Playing a few chords.*) She's the eldest; she runs the house. (*Playing.*) Nice girl, Kate! (*Humming.*) 'On this maid . . . untimely slain' –

TRIGORIN. What is it, this composition?

LEWIS. Just a little charade I'm writing for the children to act on Sanger's birthday. We call it 'Breakfast with the Borgias'. Anything more you'd like to know?

CHILDREN (*calling off*). Lewis! Lewis!

LEWIS. Here are some of them.

(TERESA *and* PAULINA *run in from the mountain.* TERESA *is nearly seventeen.* PAULINA *is fifteen.*)

TRIGORIN. Please?

LEWIS. Two of Sanger's children.

TERESA. Oh, Lewis! Haven't you finished it yet?

PAULINA. Let me see. Let me see.

LEWIS. How can I finish anything in this menagerie? I've got enough done for rehearsal after supper.

TERESA (*at piano, reading off melody with one finger*). It's nice! A very nice little tune. Clever Lewis!

PAULINA (*in a loud whisper, pointing to* TRIGORIN). Who's that?

(TRIGORIN *makes a low bow.*)

LEWIS. *That* is a visitor.

TERESA. I know. Sanger got a letter to say he was coming. And you should hear how he goes on about it. He says he never –

LEWIS. Come and be introduced! Mr Trigorin – Miss Teresa Sanger. Miss Paulina Sanger. (*To* TERESA, *who is hopping about on one leg.*) Make your curtsey, my cherished one! (*To* TRIGORIN.) She's the pick of the bunch, though she doesn't look it.

TRIGORIN (*who has been bowing all the time*). I am most delight –

PAULINA. You've brought a lot of luggage. Are you staying long?

TRIGORIN. It is permitted?

PAULINA. No. It isn't unless you can eat bacon. That's all there is in the house. Are you a Jew?

TRIGORIN (*offended for the first time*). No, I am from Russia.

PAULINA. Well, there are Jews in Russia, aren't there?

TRIGORIN. They are not as I.

PAULINA. Really? How dreadful for them, poor things. But you shouldn't despise Jews. Our sister Antonia has a great friend who's a Jew. His name's Jacob Birnbaum, but we call him Ikey-Mo. He owns fifteen theatres.

LEWIS (*who has been going over the music with* TERESA *at the piano*). He's an art patron, so you'll like him, Trigorin.

TERESA. But Lewis! We can't rehearse tonight without Tony.

PAULINA. My sister Antonia has run away. (*To* TRIGORIN.) She's been gone for nearly a week.

TERESA. Sanger's quite annoyed about it. He says he'll belt her soundly when she gets back.

PAULINA. And Linda says –

LEWIS. Linda is – er – madame.

PAULINA. – if Tony gets into the habit of going off like this, it's odds she'll be bringing him home a grandchild one of these days.

TERESA. Sanger says that she can take herself off for good if she does, for there's too many to keep in our family as it is.

LEWIS. He doesn't mean half he says.

TERESA. That's true. He's always saying he's going to send Lina and me to school. But nothing ever comes of it.

LEWIS (*lighting a very disreputable clay pipe*). He'll send you one day, as a matter of fact.

TERESA. }
PAULINA. } No, he won't.

LEWIS. He will. I've been talking to him. I told him that the house will be ever so much quieter when you are safely under hatches.

TERESA. Lewis. You dirty dog!

PAULINA. We're much too old.

LEWIS. Not at all. All nice little girls are shut up till they're thirty-five.

TERESA. We aren't nice little girls. And it's too late to turn us into it. What about this rehearsal? It's only three days to Sanger's birthday, and he'll hate it unless it's properly done.

PAULINA. Tony is a wretch to run away.

LEWIS. We can do a good deal without her. Mr Trigorin can help. He dances in a ballet.

PAULINA (*laughing*). Well, I've heard of dancing elephants.

TRIGORIN. Ah, no! I imagine – I make steps for the ballet.

LEWIS. Well then, you'll have to sing.

TRIGORIN. Ach, I cannot sing.

LEWIS. Oh, but you must. Everybody here has to sing. (Playing a note on the piano.) Sing that!

TRIGORIN. Please to excuse. I cannot.

LEWIS. Sanger expects all his guests to sing.

(TRIGORIN *produces so reedy a voice that* TERESA *and* PAULINA *roll on the ground with laughter.* LINDA *comes in from the verandah.*)

LINDA. For the love of heaven, stop that noise. That's the second time you've woke me up. Where's supper!

LEWIS. Mr Trigorin – Mrs Sanger!

LINDA. How do you do, Mr Trigorin. We knew you were coming. Kate's been getting a room ready.

TRIGORIN (*kissing her hand*). Please! You are too kind to me.

LINDA. Not at all, Mr Trigorin. I'm sorry Albert's so poorly.
(*To* LEWIS.) He's been working himself up into a state about Tony.
Says it's all my fault. I tell him if he wants those girls of his minded
properly he should put 'em to school somewhere.

TERESA. Just let him try. That's all.

LINDA. Nobody spoke to you. S'matter of fact, no decent school
would keep you for a week.

PAULINA (*looking out of window*). Here's Ikey-Mo, looking as if he'd
lost a shilling and found a smell. (*Leaning out.*) Hallo, Ike! Are you
escaping from a Pogrom?

(JACOB BIRNBAUM *comes in, looking rather sheepish.*)

LINDA. Why, *Mister* Birnbaum! You are a stranger. Where've you
been all this long time?

JACOB. In München. How is Sanger? Is he better?

LINDA. Much the same. Mr Birnbaum – Mr Trigorin! You don't
know where Tony is, I suppose!

JACOB (*confused*). Tony? She is not here then?

LINDA. She's been on the tiles for a week. We thought perhaps you'd
know something about it.

JACOB. I? I? How should I?

TRIGORIN (*bewildered*). A young lady is lost?

LINDA. No child of mine, I'd have you to know. One of Albert's.

TERESA. We're none of us her children, *Gott sei dank!*

(TERESA *and* PAULINA *are sitting on the step combing their hair with a
very dirty and broken comb.*)

LEWIS. Tony will turn up, you see. These children always fall on their
feet.

LINDA (*muttering*). Not so much a child, either. Going on eighteen, the
dirty little cat!

LEWIS. You sleeping here tonight, Jacob? It looks as if there's going to
be a crush. I'm going to see Kate and bag my bedroom.

(LEWIS *goes out into the kitchen calling for* KATE.)

LINDA. D'you like the Tyrol, Monsieur Trigorin? What do you think
of this view?

TRIGORIN. For me, madame, you make it perfect. (*He bows.*)

LINDA (*flirtatiously*). Flatterer! Let me show it to you from the
meadow.

TRIGORIN. Enchanted – *gnädige Frau.*

TERESA. The last person who went star-gazing with Linda found himself on the mat next morning. Sanger is jealous of views.

LINDA. Tessa! Go and wash your face. And you might find your little sister and wash hers, too.

TERESA. Where is my little sister?

LINDA. I'm sure I don't know. Find her. (*Archly.*) Now I shall put you to the test, Monsieur Trigorin, or have you changed your mind?

TRIGORIN. *Mais non.* Mr Sanger? Perhaps he would see me now? Yes?

LINDA. I shouldn't disturb him now. You'll only get your head bitten off. Perhaps he'll come down for supper.

(LINDA *and* TRIGORIN *stroll out on to the mountain.*)

JACOB (*who has been trying through* LEWIS's *MS. at the piano*). Sanger will see me, I think. I have a little present that may be welcome. (*Producing a bottle.*) Cognac!

(JACOB *goes upstairs and knocks at* SANGER's *door. A roar inside bids him enter. He goes in.*)

(LEWIS *and* KATE *come out of kitchen talking.*)

LEWIS. He looks for all the world like a trainer of performing fleas. And that's what he is, practically. A ballet master! Linda seems to admire the cut of his coat.

KATE. But he must sleep somewhere. Of course the spare room has two beds –

LEWIS. No, Kate. I'll sleep on the doorstep, but not with the flea-trainer.

KATE. The house is so full! There's the big cowshed. But it's never been disinfected since Tessa had scarlet fever there last autumn.

LEWIS. Tessa's germs will never hurt me. I'll sleep there.

KATE (*looking at suitcases*). Are these his? (*Picking one up and staggering towards staircase.*) O-oh, what a weight!

LEWIS. He's got all his lounge suits and whatnots.

TERESA. Lewis! Lazybones! Take them for her.

LEWIS. What? Carry the flea-trainer's bags? Not I?

TERESA (*to* PAULINA). What a little ray of sunshine he is! Such an example for us, Lina. We don't need to go to school to learn manners.

LEWIS (*pulling* TERESA's *ears*). You lop-eared rabbit.

KATE. Never mind. I'll call Roberto.

LEWIS (*grasping bags*). Oh, I'll take them (*Staggering.*) My God, what's he got in here – cobblestones?

(LEWIS *exits upstairs, carrying suitcases, followed by* KATE.)

PAULINA. Oddsbodikins, Tessa! You turn that man round your little finger, so you do!

TERESA (*complacently*). That's what's called womanly tact.

PAULINA. O-oh! *Kirschen!* Let's stuff.

(TERESA *takes a little basket of cherries from the windowseat. She and* PAULINA *sit on the dais step, eating.* ANTONIA *sidles in and sits down between them. She snatches a cherry.*)

TERESA. Tony! You back! Wherever have you been?

ANTONIA (*mumbling her cherry*). Oh – in München.

PAULINA. München!

TERESA. Where on earth did you stop? Not – not with Ikey-Mo?

TERESA.  
PAULINA. } *Himmel!*

(ANTONIA *nods and spits out her stone.* SUSAN *is seen peeping through the window.*)

PAULINA. Did you have a nice time?

ANTONIA (*with a swaggering, jerky defiance*). O-oh yes! A lovely time. Anything I wanted, Ike got for me. Last night we had a vol-au-vent, and lobsters, and an iced bombe, and Ike had a saddle of mutton as well. And we had champagne. I was drunk every night.

TERESA. No wonder he's so fat if he eats all that.

ANTONIA. So I told him. I said so in a restaurant once, at the top of my voice, in seven languages, so that all the people heard.

PAULINA. Why did he ask you to stay with him if you were so rude?

TERESA. Yes. What – (*Catching sight of her sister's face.*) Tony! You'd never let him be your lover! (*Distressed.*) Oh, Tony, you didn't!

ANTONIA. Yes, I did. And do you know, he says I sing much better than Kate.

TERESA. Then he's mad. Because no sane man, even if he was your lover, could think that you sing better than Kate. And you're mad too, Tony. However could you? He's so fat!

ANTONIA. What of it? There's no law that I know of that the first lover anybody takes has to be thin.

TERESA. No – no. (*Pause.*) What on earth will you say to Sanger?

ANTONIA. Nothing. Sanger never asks questions. Unless he thinks he's going to like the answer. It'll be all right. He'll be in a good temper because Ike's brought him a present, of some cognac. That was my bright idea.

TERESA. That'll be no use. Sanger's on the water-wagon. The doctor says he'll die if he doesn't take care. So if you start him drinking again, you'll be a murderess. Did Ike give you that hat?

ANTONIA. Certainly not. I bought it with my birthday money. Do you like it?

TERESA. It's rather vulgar, but it suits you.

PAULINA. You'll have a hell of a time with Sanger.

TERESA (*crushingly*). Did you go walking all about München with that enormous hole in your stocking?

ANTONIA. Ike gave me stockings. He gave me twelve pairs; silk, and all different colours.

TERESA. Fancy taking clothes from Ike!

ANTONIA. I didn't! I said, 'If I'm not grand enough for you in these clothes, I'll go home.' So I threw his old stockings out of the window. They got caught in the telegraph wires and waved about like little flags. I laughed till I nearly fell out of the window.

PAULINA. Liar!

ANTONIA. It's true. Ike pretended he wouldn't mind if I threw all my clothes out of the window. He said I should look wonderful with nothing on.

TERESA. Well, so you do.

ANTONIA. All the same, he was quite annoyed. He couldn't bear to see his wonderful money wasted, the dirty pig of a Jew.

TERESA. But Tony, if you hate him so, why –

PAULINA. Yes, why –

ANTONIA (*collapsing into sudden tears*). Oh, I don't know. I don't know.

(KATE *and* LEWIS *return down the stairs.* ANTONIA, *at the sight of them, checks her tears and turns her back.*)

KATE. Tony! There you are! Where have you been?

ANTONIA. Just visiting. *Grüss Gott*, Lewis.

LEWIS. *Grüss Gott*, Tony.

KATE. Father's very angry. He'll want to know – Hadn't you better tell me? (*She looks searchingly at her sister, and sighs deeply.*) Oh well, I'll get supper.

(*Exits into the kitchen.*)

LEWIS. Hope I shan't have to assist at the spanking. Where's Ike? Has he gone up to Sanger? I want him to act in 'Breakfast with the Borgias'. (*Going to piano and playing.*)

(ROBERTO *comes in with hot plates, vegetables, etc., followed a second later by* KATE *with dish.*)

LEWIS. Roberto, you sing, don't you? (*Bringing score down in his hand.*)

ROBERTO. *Scusi?*

TERESA. You should hear him lay breakfast in the mornings.

PAULINA. He's a tenor.

LEWIS. Good. Then he's Caesar Borgia. (*Giving* ROBERTO *the score.*)

ROBERTO. *Pronto!*

LEWIS. Directly after supper, I'll give you your tunes, and you must learn the words.

KATE. Come along! Supper's ready.

LEWIS. Is Sanger coming down?

KATE. I don't think so. I wish I knew what to do about him. He gets queer giddy turns, like Tessa used to get, and he says it's because he's thirsty. I'm sure he's iller than he thinks. Ring the bell, Tony!

ANTONIA (*ringing a large cow-bell*). Can't Ike be Pope? He'll look so like it.

KATE (*serving out food while* TERESA *cuts up bread*). Where's Linda?

LEWIS. With her new fancy man, the flea-trainer.

KATE. Ssh!

TERESA. Lewis has such a nice way of putting things.

LEWIS. He'll do for the Pope. We'll make him sing again. Fetch him in, Tessa.

TERESA (*goes to door, sees something distasteful, and turns back to speak with a changed voice*). They are coming up the path now.

(*Enter* LINDA *and* TRIGORIN *rather guilty.*)

LINDA. You don't mean to say that supper is actually ready? Whatever happened, Kate? You sit beside me, Mr Trigorin. Oh! (*To* ANTONIA.) So you've come back?

ANTONIA. Yes. I've come back. Soup please, Kate!

LINDA. We mayn't ask where you've been, I suppose?

ANTONIA. On a visit.

LINDA. Oh, really! Enjoyed yourself?

ANTONIA. Very much, thank you.

LINDA. You never know. Sometimes girls don't enjoy themselves as much as they expect. Sometimes they come back quite – changed!

LEWIS. Hurry up, girls. I want to get on with this rehearsal. If only we had anyone to play for us!

TRIGORIN.  I can play.

LEWIS.  You? I doubt it! It's most vilely written.

TRIGORIN.  Believe me, I can play. So often I must read manuscript.

LEWIS.  Kate! You're Lucrezia. This is your first air. (*Goes across to piano and plays it with his mouth full of food.*)

ANTONIA.  Oh, Lewis! Let me be Lucrezia. Kate can't act.

LEWIS.  She can sing. I won't have my music spoilt.

LINDA (*speaking at the same time*). Where's my baby? Where's Susan? Find her, you, Lina.

ANTONIA.  Kate's got no temperament.

PAULINA (*shouting at the same time*). Soo-zanne!

LEWIS.  Temperament is like vinegar in a salad, Tony. A little goes a long way.

PAULINA.  Soo-zanne!

(SUSAN *comes in from the kitchen, sucking her fingers.*)

KATE.  Susie! You've been at the jam again! You'll be sick!

LINDA.  Will you stop chipping at my child, Kate? It's none of your business.

ANTONIA (*speaking at the same time*). And I hope Kate spoils your play! Standing stuck in the middle of the stage like a sofa cushion! Kate as Lucrezia is the funniest thing I ever heard.

LEWIS.  Trigorin as Pope will be funnier.

TERESA.  A darling little temperamental Pope!

KATE.  Has everyone got coffee?

SUSAN.  Me, please.

LINDA.  You're eating nothing, Mr Trigorin!

TRIGORIN.  I listen. It is entrancing. Such youth! Such vitality! It is exquisite! (*Uncomfortable pause.*)

PAULINA.  Pass the pickles, Lewis. Don't eat 'em all yourself.

TERESA.  Is Sanger never coming? Let's chant him.

(*They call for* SANGER *to the tune of the 'Volga Boat Song'.* ROBERTO *changes the plates.* JACOB *appears at the head of the stairs with hand raised for silence.*)

JACOB.  He is not coming. He says he is not hungry. He wishes to finish the first act of his new Opera.

ANTONIA.  Also the new bottle of cognac.

LINDA.  Hold your tongue, Mrs Impudence. You wait till your father lays hands on you! We'll see.

(*A roar of* 'Shut that door!' *from* SANGER'S *room.* JACOB *shuts door and comes downstairs. He sits down beside* ANTONIA, *who moves to the other side of the table.*)

TRIGORIN. There is no privilege which I have more desired than to be a guest in this house. Alas! That I should not already greet my lovely, distinguished host.

LINDA (*on the warpath*). Tony came back same time you did, Jacob. Did you by any chance travel together?

SUSAN. She's been stopping with 'im. I heard her telling Tessa and Lina. Ah-ooh! Mummy! Tessa pinched me!

LINDA (*boxing* TERESA's *ears*). Will you leave the child alone? Come here, duckie, and tell your mother all you heard.

SUSAN. I was listening in the verandah.

KATE (*to* TRIGORIN). Have they told you about the dreadful landslide we had here last year – ?

LEWIS (*at the same time*). Now that Tony's back we can have a full rehearsal tonight –

LINDA. Be quiet, Lewis, please. Kate! I wonder at you interrupting like that! Go on, dearie. What next?

SUSAN. I heard Tony say she'd been stopping at Ike's flat.

TERESA. Schinken, please, Lewis. A nice piece of lean.

LINDA. Will you be quiet, Tessa? (*To* SUSAN.) Yes, darling?

SUSAN. And she said Jacob said she looked best with nothing on.

ANTONIA. She's a filthy little liar. I said nothing of the sort. Did I, girls?

TERESA.
PAULINA. } No!

LINDA. We'll see. I always said you were a slut by nature. (*To* ANTONIA.) Your father shall hear every word of this. Every word!

JACOB (*rising angrily*). Look here – Linda –

LINDA. You can't get round me, Jacob. It's disgusting. (JACOB *sits*.) If Sanger has any self-respect he'll turn you off the place. Coming here as a friend, and then getting his girls into trouble. Why don't you clear off?

JACOB. I cannot explain to you.

LINDA. Explain!

SUSAN. Mummy, can I go and stay with Uncle Jacob too?

TRIGORIN (*going over to piano*). I shall perhaps play now.

TERESA. Come along.

LEWIS (*to* LINDA). It's what I'm always telling Sanger. What else can be expected if he won't send them to school? Why don't you do something?

LINDA (*turning on him*). You're a nice one to talk. I don't know what's turned you so strict for, all of a sudden. You don't generally mind what you do, or other people either, for the matter of that. You're not fit to be let into any respectable house!

(TRIGORIN *begins to play*.)

LEWIS. That's quite right. I'm not. Bravo, Trigorin. That's very good. But don't play as if it was Chopin.

(TRIGORIN *plays much louder*. ROBERTO *approaches* LEWIS.)

That's right. Yes, Roberto?

ROBERTO. Please. (*Showing score*.) No words?

LEWIS. We'll make 'em up later. Let me see – you've just poisoned Ludovico, because you think he's your rival – yes – You'd better sing the word 'Vittoria' over and over again. *Capire?* Vittoria! Vittoria! Vittoria!

ROBERTO. *Si, si! Ho capito!*

LEWIS. Now line up for your parts. Lucrezia! (*Throwing score at* KATE, *who is going out into the kitchen with soup tureen*.) And two couples of lovers, Giulietta, Ludovico. (*Pointing to himself and* TERESA.) Scaramello and Ianca! (*Handing scores to* JACOB *and* ANTONIA.)

ANTONIA. Have I got to be in love with Ike? That's a tall order.

LEWIS. Shut your eyes and don't look at him.

ANTONIA. As long as I don't have to touch him –

LEWIS. You'll play Bianca or you won't play at all. Now I want two Pages. Lina can be one, but the other –

LINDA. What about my baby? She can sing in tune. I don't see why she should be passed over.

(*While this altercation is going on,* TRIGORIN *is playing all the time,* ROBERTO *is clearing away,* KATE *has begun to make an omelette, and the rest are studying their parts in a fury of concentration*.)

LEWIS. You can't sing, Sue, surely!

SUSAN. Yes, I can.

LEWIS. Oh, very well. Hop up on the stage with Paulina, and sing that opening duet. Let's see what you can do.

(PAULINA *and* SUSAN *run up on to the dais and begin to lay the small table with any china they can catch up*.)

PAULINA (*singing*). Coffee – sugar – butter – jam! (*Laying table*.)

(TERESA *gives her a letter.*)

SUSAN (*singing dolefully*). Dies Irae! Dies Illa. Solvet saeclum cum favilla.

PAULINA. Bacon, kidneys, haddock, ham!

SUSAN. Teste David cum Sybilla.

PAULINA. Now cheer thee, my brother, why art thou depressed?

SUSAN. I'm saying a prayer for –

LEWIS (*interrupting*). That'll do, monkey. Before I have that confounded little pipe in my Opera, I'll rewrite the whole thing.

ROBERTO (*with great zeal, breaking out suddenly*). Vittoria! Vittoria! Vittoria!

LEWIS. Oh, damn you, Roberto! It's not time for that yet. Nobody's dead yet. Kate! Come and poison the sausage rolls. Get a move on.

KATE. I can't. Father's omelette is just on the turn. (*She scrapes round the pan with a knife.*)

LEWIS (*tearing his hair*). I ask you? Can anybody be expected to rehearse in this household?

KATE. Can't you skip my song and go on?

LEWIS. We'll have to. (*Moving up on dais.*) Here, Trigorin! You're the Pope. Come and sing this.

TRIGORIN. I have said I cannot sing.

LEWIS. Well say it, then. (*Passing* TRIGORIN *in front of him.*)

(*Pushes* TRIGORIN *off the piano stool, and plays a few flourishes.* TRIGORIN *looks much bewildered.* ANTONIA *and* PAULINA *jump up and put three hats on his head, with* ANTONIA'*s large one last on top of the others, as a Papal crown. He sings in a quavering voice which breaks into a sort of falsetto at times.*)

TRIGORIN. Thrice-crowned pontiff of the Church, I say
        I *won't* have any murdered guests today.
        Sforza shall live, and fair Bianca too.
        The neighbours say we go too far. We do.
        Some poison's here. (*Sniffing food.*)
        Now can it be jam?
        No, 'tis the rolls. (*Changing plates.*)
        Aha! How brave I am!

PAULINA } (*who are now hiding under the table, poke*
SUSAN   } *their heads out and sing*).
        Oh, gentle Pope! Oh, heart devout!
        He'll catch it, when they find him out.

(KATE *takes* SANGER'*s omelette upstairs.* TRIGORIN *goes back to the piano.* JACOB *and* TERESA *come up and break into rapid Mozartian recitative.*)

ROBERTO. Vittoria! Vittoria!

TERESA. Oh, Scaramello! Hast heard the news?

JACOB. Some of it.

TERESA. The lady Bianca is to be poisoned this morning.

JACOB. Ah, misery! I love her.

TERESA. Cheer up! She scorns thee!

JACOB. I like to be scorned.

TERESA. Then thou deservest all that is coming to thee.

ANTONIA (*interrupting*). Hear, hear!

LEWIS. Be quiet, or I'll wring your neck.

JACOB. Oh, hardhearted maiden, hast thou no pity! Two souls today must die.

TERESA. Two?

JACOB. Signor Ludovico is also to be poisoned this morning.

TERESA. It shall not be. I love him.

JACOB. All help is vain. Prepare to see thy lover die.

TERESA. It shall not be. I'll save him. (*Snatching roll from the plate and eating it.*)

JACOB. Hold, rash one!

TERESA. Too late.

JACOB. Then I'll go with thee. (*Beginning to eat the other roll.*)

TERESA. Ludovico!

JACOB. Bianca!

(*They fall to the ground and writhe.* LEWIS *and* ANTONIA *rush in and wring their hands.*)

TERESA  
JACOB  } (*singing*). Long I loved in secret and in vain,

       Long I wept her coldness, her disdain;  
       Now by death our constancy we prove,  
       Oh, live remembering our hopeless love.

LEWIS (*singing, as he hangs over* TERESA). Oh, sight of woe! What ails my dear?

TERESA (*feebly*). I die for thee, so drop a tear.

ANTONIA (*rather rudely to* JACOB). Oh, speak some comfort, Scaramel!

JACOB (*trying to take her hand, which she will not give him*). There is no comfort! Fare thee well!

LEWIS (*singing suddenly with so much fervour that they all startled*). Unsay
that doom, oh faithful heart!
What's life to me, if she depart?

SUSAN. Mummy, can I have some jam with this cake?

PAULINA. Ssh!

LEWIS. When thou art dead, the birds will stop their singing,
    When thou art cold, no sun will ever rise.
    No more, no more the joyful day's upspringing
    Shall bless these eyes.
    When thou art in thy grave, the flowers blowing
    Shall hang their heads and sicken in the grove,
    Beauty will fade and wither at thy going,
    My only love.

TERESA (*sings*). Ah, say not so! Another love will cheer thee,
    The sun will rise as bright tomorrow morn,
    The birds will sing, though I no longer near thee
    Must lie forlorn.
    When I am in my grave, the flowers blowing
    Shall make thee garlands twenty times as sweet,
    Beauty will live though I must sleep, unknowing,
    Beneath thy feet.

(*There is a little pause when this is over. Everybody is impressed.*)

KATE (*who has been listening from the gallery, and now leans over*). That's
good.

LINDA. Too good, if you ask me.

PAULINA (*putting her head out from under the table*). Do we come out
now, Lewis? (*He does not reply. He kneels, looking at* TERESA, *who is
zestfully pretending to be dead on the floor. A first shadow of horror has
flitted over his face.*) When do we sing our bit and say it wasn't
poison after all?

KATE (*as he still doesn't answer*). Lewis!

LEWIS (*coming to himself with a start*). Oh, what! (*To* PAULINA.) Your
bit? No. Not yet. We've got Tony and Ike's duet now. What are
you dawdling for, you two? You must raise him a little, Tony.

ANTONIA. I couldn't. It would need a steam crane.

JACOB (*begins to sing*). Say a hapless death I die –

(ANTONIA, *who has been supporting him, suddenly lets him fall with a
bump, so that he knocks his head on the door. Jumping up in a wild
fury.*)

*Der lieber almächtiger Gott!* But you shall pay for this!

ANTONIA. I couldn't hold you up for ever.

JACOB. I am not insulted so easily. You shall pay. You shall remember
that you are no more than a beggar, the child of a man who owes
me –

ANTONIA. That's right, Mr Made-of-Money. Boast about it. I would if
I were you. It's only your money that gets you any friends ever.

JACOB. It has brought me some things that I desired.

ANTONIA. *Ach, schweinhund!* (*Slapping his face.*)

(ANTONIA *runs out, sobbing.*)

JACOB. She shall pay. She shall kneel to me. In the dirt! In the dust!
Tony – Tony – (*Pursuing her.*)

TERESA. ⎫
PAULINA. ⎭ Tony! Tony! Ike! We've not finished. Come back!

(*They also run out.*)

LEWIS (*flinging down the score*). That's torn it!

LINDA. Such a fuss about a little singing.

KATE. Tessa sang hers very nicely.

LINDA. Oh yes, sweetly pretty, I'm sure. We shall see her slapping
somebody's face one of these days. You'd better be careful, Lewis.

LEWIS. I'll follow your example.

LINDA. What d'you – This moonlight is quite remarkable. Come, Mr
Trigorin, let's get some fresh air.

(ROBERTO *goes into kitchen.* SUSAN *trots after* LINDA.)

It's time you were in bed, duckie. Trot along. See to her, Kate.

KATE. Very well. Go to bed, Susan. I'll come by and by.

TRIGORIN (*to* LEWIS). Perhaps you still need me.

LEWIS. No, go along. (*To himself.*) The moon is busy tonight.

TRIGORIN. Pardon?

LINDA (*sweetly*). Shall we? The valley under moonlight is –

LEWIS. – quite remarkable.

(LINDA *stalks out furiously.* TRIGORIN *follows sheepishly.* SUSAN *goes
upstairs.*)

LEWIS (*to* KATE). That's a brute of a woman! I wonder you put up
with her!

KATE (*clearing table*). What can I do? I can't turn her out.

LEWIS. It's awfully stupid, the whole thing.

KATE. How?

LEWIS. All this mess, and Linda, and the children not going to school; and now, Tony! I must speak to Sanger again. It can't go on. Something dreadful will happen.

KATE. I can't think there's worse that could happen.

LEWIS. Why! It might be Tessa next! (*Hastily.*) Or Lina or Soozanne! Awful!

KATE. I do my best.

LEWIS. Of course you do. Why won't Sanger face things? He's brave enough in music.

KATE. Perhaps their grand relations in England would help.

LEWIS. Have they relations in England?

KATE. They have a uncle, I think. A schoolmaster or something at Cambridge College.

LEWIS (*smiling*). Yes. Have you got his address?

KATE. Father has.

LEWIS. Then *I* shall write.

(KATE *goes out with tray.* LEWIS *wanders about, dreaming.* TERESA *steals downstairs and tries to get out on to the mountain unnoticed. There is bright moonlight outside, and the room is half in darkness, for* KATE *has taken the lamp.*)

LEWIS (*catching sight of* TERESA). Hallo! Where are you off to?

TERESA. To look at the moon.

LEWIS. What are you creeping about like that for?

TERESA. I don't like disturbing you when you look like a broody hen.

LEWIS. You ought to be in your bed.

TERESA. Tony's crying in our bedroom. She often cries. It's no use my trying to go to bed till she's finished.

LEWIS. What is she crying for?

TERESA. That's a secret.

LEWIS. H'm! A pretty open secret.

TERESA. I suppose so. (*Pause.*) What do you think of it, Lewis? Are you shocked?

LEWIS. Don't you think one ought to be?

TERESA. He is rather fat, but Tony says –

LEWIS. My dear Tessa! –

TERESA. What?

LEWIS. Nothing! Only I think it's a pity. It's – it's beginning too soon. I don't like to see babes I've practically rocked in the cradle growing up this pace.

TERESA. Growing up isn't very nice.

LEWIS. It isn't. God help us.

TERESA. You believe in God, then?

LEWIS. I suppose I do. Though I'm blest if I know what I mean when I say it.

TERESA. You don't mean – that God up there? (*Pointing upwards.*)

LEWIS. I don't. Do you?

TERESA. I wish I wasn't so ignorant.

LEWIS (*casually*). At school now, you'd learn such a lot –

TERESA. That old story! I've seen girls in schools. They have faces like suet puddings and they have to walk two and two. You don't really want me to have a face like a pudding, darling Lewis?

LEWIS. You couldn't have a face like a pudding, darling Tessa.

TERESA. Suppose I took a fancy to look at the moon and found myself shut up in a dormitory full of pudding faces?

LEWIS. Exactly. My theory is that it's a pity to go moon-gazing at your age. I suppose it's a symptom.

TERESA. What of?

LEWIS. The green sickness.

TERESA. That sounds very disagreeable!

LEWIS. Anything sentimental is disagreeable.

TERESA. Will they cure me of the green sickness at school?

LEWIS. But there's no saying what school mightn't do for you.

TERESA. But what would happen to me when I come out again? I shan't stay there all my life, I suppose.

LEWIS. You'll come out – a perfect lady.

TERESA. Will that be nice?

LEWIS (*with a grimace*). Very.

TERESA. Shall you like me when I'm a perfect lady?

LEWIS. When you come out, my girl, you'll turn up your nose at me and Ike and poor old Trigorin.

TERESA. Oh, no! Indeed I won't!

LEWIS. But you will. And a good thing too. I know. You'll live in a lovely house with a front door and a back door and all the usual offices. And you'll have it hot on Sundays, cold on Mondays, hashed on Tuesday, minced on –

TERESA. Have what?

LEWIS. Mutton, my cherished one. You can be sure of getting that. Lots and lots of it. Ladies do.

TERESA. Lewis! Don't tease. I shan't like it a bit.

LEWIS. Yes, she will. You'll say: 'Thank Heaven I've escaped the low

haunts of my youth. Do I remember a rapscallion fellow called
Dodd who actually, actually laughed at really serious things like
mutton?'

TERESA. Idiot! Now listen. I may go to school. I'm beginning to see
points in it. But if I do, I shall always, always be thinking of you.
And when I come out, I shall come straight back to you. So there!

LEWIS. Lord save us! You mustn't do that! A sheer waste of a
beautiful education! I've given you up, Tessa. See? (*Holding her
away from him.*) You must learn to disapprove of me as quickly as
possible, or you'll never prosper. (*Rising and moving up Centre.*)

TERESA. It's unkind of you to say that when you know how much I
love you. (*Passionately.*) Promise you won't forget us. I – we shall
be so lonely, when we come out. We haven't any friends, you
know, except you and Ike.

LEWIS. Do you call Ike a friend?

TERESA. He's very fond of Tony really. He doesn't know himself how
much – oh, Lewis, it's dreadful, when people make a mistake over
a thing like that. When they don't see – when they don't see all
that's waiting for them.

LEWIS (*restlessly*). It's a confounded mistake ever to get fond of
anyone, Tessa. Before one knows where one is one begins to get
unselfish, and considerate, and all those tiresome things.

TERESA. Oh well, I hope you'll remember that and not – go getting
fond of any unnecessary people while Lina and I are away. Be as
fond of us as you like, but don't –

LEWIS. Don't what?

TERESA. Get married, or be put in prison or die or anything.

LEWIS. I'll try not to.

TERESA. Say 'Cross-my-heart-hope-I-may-die-if-I-don't'.

LEWIS. Cross-my-heart-hope-I-may-die-if-I-don't.

TERESA. Bless me! I wish I could take you to school with me.
However!

LEWIS. It's no use making plans, Tessa. You enjoy yourself and grow
fat, and I'll try to keep out of mischief. That's a bargain. (*Making
as though to kiss her and then drawing back.*) Good night, my dear.
(*Patting her head, exits.*)

(TERESA *hums*, 'Ah, say not so, another love will cheer thee' – *hears
voices and hides behind piano.* LINDA and TRIGORIN *steal in from the
moonlight.* TRIGORIN *seizes her hand and covers it with kisses.*)

TRIGORIN (*seizing her hands and kissing them*). – *Je t'adore* –

LINDA (*with a heavy smile at him*). Bless you! Now we must go to bed. Good night! (*He looks at her, and then kisses her.*) Ssh! Not here! Wait!

TRIGORIN. *Restez! Restez donc, mon ange!*

(LINDA *glides out of his arms and upstairs, and pauses on the landing.*)

LINDA. Good night, Mr Trigorin.

(*She goes into room, leaving door slightly ajar.* TRIGORIN *sighs deeply and follows her. The door shuts.*)

TERESA (*emerging and talking to herself*). Beasts! Beasts! (*Turning back and noticing* LEWIS's *yellow muffler lying on the piano. Taking it in her hands and folding it round her neck lovingly. Then looking after* LEWIS, *overcome with sadness. Suddenly she buries her head in the end of it and speaks.*) I wish I could die! Oh, I wish I could die! (*Just then there are sounds of heavy stertorous breathing from* SANGER's *room. She stops, petrified with terror.*) *Himmel!* What's that? (*There is a groan, and the sound of a dog whining at* SANGER's *door.*) Lewis! (*She runs upstairs, calling.*) Lina! Tony! Tony! Lina!

(ANTONIA *and* PAULINA *comes on in their nightgowns at top of landing.*)

ANTONIA. What is it?

TERESA. There's a funny noise in Sanger's room. He must be ill.

(*The groaning continues.*)

PAULINA. I'm frightened.

ANTONIA . It's nothing. He's just snoring.

TERESA. Ssh! Keep quiet! Listen. (*Pause.*) We ought to go in.

PAULINA. He'll beat us if we do.

ANTONIA. Why not get Linda? She doesn't mind annoying him.

TERESA. No, no, we can't. She – she's got somebody in there.

(*All the children stare with frightened eyes at* LINDA's *door.*)

ANTONIA. That's Wotan howling. Why doesn't Sanger tell him to shut up?

TERESA. Hush! It's stopped. I'm going in. I don't care if there is a row. Will you come, Tony? (ANTONIA *draws back.* TERESA *goes in – she reappears very soon.*) He's fallen. Wotan won't let me go near him. (*The children stir.*) It's no use. I think he's dead. (*The children begin to cry loudly.*)

(LINDA *appears in her doorway with a candle.*)

(*Putting her arm round the others.*) Go away. Go away. He's dead!
(*She stands guard over the door and won't let* LINDA *in. Screaming
hysterically.*) Lewis! Lewis! Please come quickly!

*Quick* CURTAIN.


## SCENE 2

SCENE: *The Karindehütte, a summer morning some weeks later.*

FLORENCE *is arranging flowers in a jug on the table.* LEWIS *is holding a basket and handing her flowers one by one.* TERESA *and* PAULINA *are sitting on
the stairs, gloomily watching them.*

LEWIS. And what will you do with this pretty thing? (*Holding up a
     gentian.*)
FLORENCE . Oh, that? Put it on one side. We'll have all the tall flowers
     in a jug, and the little ones in a dish. And the primula shall go in
     the middle of the table, don't you think, Mr Dodd?

     (LINDA, *half-dressed, comes out in the gallery.* FLORENCE *does not see
     her, and* LEWIS *waves her back with a fierce gesture. She shrugs her
     shoulders and goes.*)

LEWIS. I do indeed. Tessa! Why did we never have a primula in the
     middle of the table before?
TERESA (*coldly*). Because we never wanted one.
FLORENCE. And we need a large, low dish for the gentians. Do you
     think these infants can find us one?
LEWIS. Girls! Find a large, low dish.
TERESA. Lina! Find a large, low dish.
PAULINA. Find one yourself.
LEWIS. You can both of you find one. Skip along and look lively.
TERESA (*getting up*). Come, Lina! What sort of dish, Florence?
FLORENCE. Anything! A pie dish! Perhaps I'd better show you. Will
     you be sorting out the gentians, Mr Dodd?

     (*She goes out with* TERESA *and* PAULINA *into the kitchen.* SUSAN *comes
     out of* LINDA'*s room and downstairs.*)

SUSAN. Kate! Ka-ate!
LEWIS (*turning basket upside down on table*). Damn it all! Which are
     gentians?

(KATE *comes in from outside.*)

KATE. Yes, what is it? Don't make that noise.

SUSAN. Mammy's getting up, and she wants 'er breakfast.

KATE. Well then, take it up to her. It's all ready in the kitchen. And you can tell her to fetch her own meals after this. I'm through. The sooner she takes herself off, and you too, the better pleased we shall be.

LEWIS. That's my baby, Kate.

SUSAN. I'll tell 'er every word you say. (*She goes upstairs.*)

LEWIS. Round 'em up, Kate!

KATE. Well, it's high time she went. She upsets the whole place. And that Trigorin always in and out of her room.

LEWIS. Put him in Linda's room for good and all.

KATE. Oh, I couldn't do that, could I? It'd hardly be decent, and poor father not dead a month.

LEWIS. It'd keep him out of the other rooms, anyway.

KATE. The house is simply upside down. What with the visitors, and then Tessa and Lina: you know they've been sick off and on ever since that awful night.

LEWIS. Nobody could live in this house and not know how sick Tessa and Lina have been off and on.

KATE. I wish Jacob would come back.

LEWIS. Just now you wanted to be rid of us.

KATE. I'm so horribly worried about Tony's future.

LEWIS. Her future is perfectly obvious. Ike might have thought of that before.

KATE. Oh, Lewis! As if you men ever did. (*Going into the kitchen.*) Well, I suppose you all expect *déjeuner*?

LEWIS. Please, dear Kate!

(JACOB *comes in from the mountain.*)

Hallo, Ike! Talk of the devil. I thought you'd fled to Vienna.

JACOB. Only a few days' business. I return as soon as possible. I wish to see the English uncle who has come. The Herr Doktor. Churchill von Cambridge. I have already written to him. I have offered (*impressively*) money, for these poor children.

LEWIS. Why?

JACOB (*hesitating*). I have loved their father.

LEWIS (*drily*). I see.

JACOB (*breaking out*). You will say that I have also loved the daughter?

But what can I do? She detests me. I have offered marriage to her,
and she will not listen.

LEWIS. Marriage! Ike! You're drunk. Nobody ought to get married.

JACOB. I wish that I were drunk. I have loved this beautiful child. I
have made a great mistake. She came to München trusting to me.
Too late I have discovered that love cannot be bought. I have been
mad. Since she will not love me, I must be sure that she is in good
hands.

LEWIS. That'll be all right. They're going to take her to England with
her sisters.

JACOB (*with a sigh*). And she will be happy there?

LEWIS. Miss Churchill says so. The daughter of the English uncle.
She's here too, you know.

JACOB. The daughter? Ach so! And she will be good to my Tonya?
What is she like?

LEWIS (*with a grimace*). Most – distractingly – beautiful.

JACOB. Beautiful? (*Staring at* LEWIS.) I think it is a pity you stay here,
then. With beautiful women, you are not always wise.

(*A loud yell upstairs.*)

LEWIS. I've been trying to go all the week. Ever since she came.

(SUSAN *comes downstairs again, screaming and crying.*)

What's the matter now?

SUSAN. Ah – ooo – mammy – hoo – hoo – boxed my – hoo – hoo –
'cos I told 'er – hoo – hoo – what Kate said – hoo – ho – hooo!

(SUSAN *goes howling into the kitchen as* CHARLES CHURCHILL,
*distracted, bursts out of the music room.*)

CHARLES. What? What? Who's hurt? Oh! (*Seeing* SUSAN *going out.*)
That child again! Good heavens! How much longer is this going
on?

JACOB (*clicking heels and bowing*). *Bitte sehr!*

CHARLES. Who's this? Another of Sanger's friends called for payment,
I suppose?

LEWIS. Mr Birnbaum, Dr Churchill!

CHARLES (*a little more cordially*). Oh, how d'ye do! You wrote to me,
didn't you? And offered to help. Glad to see you.

LINDA (*bawling off stage*). Ka-ate! Roberto!

CHARLES. There she goes again! Look here – Dodd, it's time we got
rid of this creature – this Linda. How does one shake women off?

LEWIS.  She won't go till she's thrown out.

JACOB.  She will not go?

CHARLES.  She had a nervous breakdown the day we arrived, and she's kept her bed ever since.

LEWIS.  And poor old Trigorin has to act as nurse.

CHARLES.  It hasn't occurred to him to go away either. I never saw such people.

JACOB.  I have the idea. You send Trigorin away and she will go too. He is her only hope.

LEWIS.  Now, why did I let Ike think of that first?

JACOB.  Tell him quite plainly that he must go. He will not mind. He is very amiable. Tell him now.

(TRIGORIN *enters rather sheepishly, carrying a breakfast tray up to* LINDA.)

*Auf wiedersehen, Trigorin!*

TRIGORIN.  Please?

JACOB.  Goodbye!

TRIGORIN.  But I am not going!

LEWIS.  I'm afraid you are!

TRIGORIN (*looking from one to the other*). *Quel dommage!*

LEWIS.  There's too much of a crowd. Now Birnbaum's arrived, the English lady has to sleep in your room. It's true there are two beds, but she mightn't like the idea of sharing it with you.

TRIGORIN (*bewildered*).  You wish that I should go?

JACOB.  We are all going, Trigorin. The house must be sold. The Herr Doktor wishes to take his nieces to England.

TRIGORIN.  I understand. It is better that I go. But first I will wish to give £500 to you, sir (*to* CHARLES), for the eatings and clothings of these so helpless orphans. (*Taking out a pen and chequebook.*)

CHARLES.  Really – bless my soul – that's very good of you.

(LINDA *comes on to the balcony, half dressed.*)

LINDA.  Where's that Kate?

LEWIS.  Busy doing your work. What do you want?

LINDA.  I'll teach her to send saucy messages by my own daughter, the double-faced hussy. Where's Roberto? Isn't he ever going to bring me anything to eat?

LEWIS.  I should think he is.

LINDA.  Nobody spoke to you! Kiril! That you, my precious? Linda's hungry!

TRIGORIN (*still busy writing cheque*). In a moment, *chérie*. I make
    arrangements for my departing.

LINDA. Your departing? What d'you mean?

TRIGORIN (*nervously, as he writes*). I go to Vienna – a telegram has
    come – I arrange a new ballet –

LINDA. You're going?

LEWIS. In a very few minutes, dear Linda. He's got to catch the
    midday express to Vienna.

LINDA (*with instant determination*). So have I.

LEWIS }
JACOB } (*in feigned astonishment*). You?

LINDA. Yes! Me! Think I don't know when I'm not wanted? Oh, I've
    seen how you've all been scheming to turn me out of the place ever
    since the night poor Albert was taken. I'm not the sort to demean
    themselves by staying after those sort of insinuendoes. 'Smatter-er-
    fact, I've had my boxes ready packed for some days. Roberto can
    fetch 'em down. (*Bawling.*) Roberto! Roberto! Kate!

LEWIS. Been awaiting her marching orders?

(ROBERTO *runs in from kitchen.*)

ROBERTO. *Si, Signora – si, si, si, si, si!*

LINDA. Come up here!

(*She disappears and* ROBERTO *goes up.*)

LEWIS (*triumphantly*). And that's that!

(FLORFNCE, KATE, TERESA *and* PAULINA *come in from the kitchen.*
    TERESA *and* PAULINA *are slightly ahead of the others;* TERESA *has the
    pie-dish.*)

TERESA. Here's your large, low dish. It was full of gooseberries. Took
    us some time to empty it.

PAULINA. Tessa did most of the emptying.

FLORENCE. What is it? Who was shouting, just now?

LEWIS. Linda is going.

TERESA. Loud cheers!

PAULINA. Let's all hang out flags!

TERESA (*capering*). O day of joy! O day of gladness!

KATE (*going upstairs*). If she really is, I'll pack for her.

PAULINA. Let's go and see for ourselves!

(*They stampede upstairs and follow* KATE *to* LINDA's *room.*)

TRIGORIN (*crossing to* CHARLES *and giving him cheque*). Sir, it is to me the greatest privilege that I have stayed in this house. I pray to give you this little sum. I go now to make my trunks. I will no longer encumberate the bedroom of this gracious lady.

(*He kisses* FLORENCE's *hand, then hurries out.*)

LEWIS. Come, Ike! We'll make his trunks for him! We'll see he doesn't miss his train.

(*They follow* TRIGORIN *in hoots of laughter.*)

CHARLES (*looking after them*). What a set!

FLORENCE. I think it's all rather amusing!

CHARLES. When is that rapscallion Dodd going to take himself off?

FLORENCE. Now, sir. Don't be philistine. He has genius.

CHARLES. Maybe. So have a number of unpleasant people. He looks no better than all the rest of the ragtag and bobtail we found here. He looks like a scarecrow.

(ROBERTO *comes downstairs with an enormous trunk on his back. He takes it outside; he is seen to fetch a wheelbarrow and to load it on to it.*)

Your poor aunt! What a life she must have led.

FLORENCE. Why should we assume that she was so very miserable? Personally I can't imagine a better fate than to marry a really great man. To – to help him in his work.

CHARLES. Great Heavens, *you're* not falling in love with Dodd, are you?

FLORENCE. I'm tired of meeting clever young men.

CHARLES. You wouldn't find these Dodds and Guggenheims amusing if you met them in your own home. You mustn't be misled by the fact that they live on the top of a mountain.

(TERESA *and* PAULINA *run downstairs with long black veils on. They twirl about, greatly pleased with themselves.*)

TERESA. Don't we look lovely?

PAULINA. We thought we'd better go into mourning for Sanger. It'll look more decent down in the village.

FLORENCE. It looks quite absurd. Take those rags off at once. At once! I mean it.

(*Crestfallen, they remove their veils.*)

(ROBERTO *comes in, and goes up again to* LINDA's *room.*)

Where did you get them?

PAULINA. They're what Kate had when our mother died.

(ROBERTO *comes down with a hatbox and a birdcage.*)

(ANTONIA *comes in from garden, looking very pleased with life.*)

ANTONIA. Thank Heaven. I shan't have to go to school anyway. I'm going to be married.

CHARLES.
FLORENCE. } Married?

ANTONIA. I'm going to marry Ike. I've just told him so. And wasn't he surprised! (*Bursts out laughing.*)

FLORENCE. *Who* are you going to marry?

ANTONIA. Jacob Birnbaum! We call him Ike. That funny fat man you saw just now.

FLORENCE (*to* CHARLES). What does she mean?

PAULINA. I thought you said you hated him.

ANTONIA. No, I never hated him. But I was dreadfully annoyed with him. In Munich he was so stupid.

TERESA. They're all stupid.

ANTONIA. He would keep boasting about all the grand things he was going to give me. I might have been Linda. He didn't seem to think that I could give him anything.

TERESA. They're all as blind as bats. Ike's not the only one.

ANTONIA. It's awful when two friends turn into enemies.

TERESA. But you were right to forgive him.

ANTONIA. That's what I felt. And I couldn't bear to see him going about looking as if he had toothache. We've had it all out and forgiven each other. And now we'll be married.

TERESA. You're lucky – you are. Some people see, and know – and – can't do anything.

(CHARLES *and* FLORENCE, *who have been holding a dismayed parley in the background, now descend upon* ANTONIA.)

FLORENCE. But, Antonia. Please be more explicit. What is this man to you?

CHARLES. Do I understand that you've – er – lived with this fellow?

ANTONIA (*apologetically*). Only for a week.

(KATE *comes out on gallery above, then comes down and goes out.*)

FLORENCE. This is like a nightmare.

TERESA. It's all right now. Really it is.

FLORENCE. Father! She mustn't be allowed to marry this man. He must be an incredible brute.

CHARLES. We must see! We must see!

FLORENCE. Poor little girl! We'll take you back to England and you must forget all about it.

ANTONIA. No, no. I don't want to go away. I want to stay with Ike. I love him. Poor Ike!

FLORENCE. Love! That's not love, you poor little gipsy.

TERESA (*fiercely*). Yes, it is.

FLORENCE. You're too young to know what you are talking about.

(ROBERTO *goes up again to* LINDA's *room. The wheelbarrow is getting crazily full.*)

TERESA. No, I'm not. I'm not. We may be ignorant. But we can feel. We can feel as much as anybody.

FLORENCE (*helplessly*). Father!

CHARLES. Now! Now! Now! We must go into the whole matter very carefully. (*To* ANTONIA.) Can this fellow support you?

ANTONIA (*vaguely*). Oh yes, I expect so. He's rich.

(JACOB *comes in.* FLORENCE *draws back from him in horror.*)

Oh, Ike! I've been telling them.

JACOB. *Ach* so! (*Meeting the stern eye of* CHARLES *and stiffening a little.*) It is true, sir. I ask for the honour of marrying your niece.

CHARLES. We must go into it.

JACOB. She shall live like a princess – clothes – jewels – you shall see. I own fifteen thea –

ANTONIA. Draw it mild, Ike. If you want to boast, say you knew Sanger.

CHARLES. Can't we discuss this in private?

JACOB. *Ja, gewiss!* In here.

(JACOB *and* CHARLES *go towards music-room.*)

FLORENCE. Do you want me, Father?

CHARLES. No, my dear.

(*He goes out with* JACOB. KATE *hurries upstairs.*)

FLORENCE. I think I'll go out a little.

PAULINA. Shall we take you for a walk?

FLORENCE. No, no. I would rather walk by myself. (*She goes out on to the mountain.*)

TERESA. Our stock's gone down. She doesn't like us nearly so well as she did at first. When she came I heard her telling her father we were delicious imps, but now –

PAULINA. I think it's an excellent idea you getting married, Tony. Couldn't we all marry someone? I'll marry Roberto. I'm sure he'll be quite pleased. He's very obliging.

ANTONIA. Pooh! You're too young.

PAULINA. Juliet was younger than me when she married Romeo.

ANTONIA. She was Italian.

PAULINA. So would I be Italian if I married Roberto. People always take their husband's nationalities.

ANTONIA. Idiot! That's got nothing to do with it.

PAULINA. Tessa can ask Lewis. What's the matter, Tessa? I'd ask him myself, but he likes you best.

TERESA (*slowly*). I'm too young.

PAULINA. You could ask him, anyhow.

TERESA. No, I couldn't. I'm too old.

PAULINA. Too old! I thought you said you were too young.

TERESA. I did. Dear me. I'm both. I'm at a perfectly horrid age. I'm too young for some things and too old for others.

PAULINA. Why should you be too young for Lewis? You'd suit him better than any ordinary tiresome woman that would always be bothering him.

TERESA. Would I? Look.

PAULINA. Cousin Florence walking by herself!

(FLORENCE *and* LEWIS *wander past, absorbed in one another, picking flowers.*)

FLORENCE. Tell me! Why is that cow bell sometimes A and sometimes A flat?

LEWIS. It's a different c-cow!

(*They pass on.*)

PAULINA (*strutting up and down*). Oh, really! Fancy that! A different cow! Looking for its calf! (*Stopping anxiously.*) Do you think he wants her?

(*The three sisters draw round the chair.*)

TERESA. We might have known, when first she came, that she was a serpent in sheep's clothing.

ANTONIA. It started the very minute she got into the house.

TERESA. He's stammering. He always stammers when he's in love.

PAULINA. But he wouldn't marry her. Think of all the others. He never married any of them.

TERESA. Yes, But she's a lady. If it's a lady they have to marry them. Look at Sanger and our mother.

ANTONIA. Perhaps he'll go away before he has time to do anything silly.

TERESA. I do hope he will. Just think what she can do to him. She'll want to take him to England, to one of her sort of places. (*With a little cry.*) Oh – and he'll never get any work done!

PAULINA. She can't have seen him drunk.

ANTONIA. Nor in a temper.

PAULINA. Do you think we ought to tell her?

TERESA. Tell her? What?

PAULINA. That he's not a suitable person to be her friend. There are heaps of things we could tell her.

TERESA. I can't.

PAULINA. Why not? If she knew –

TERESA. I don't know why not. I couldn't.

PAULINA. He belongs to us and she doesn't.

(FLORENCE *and* LEWIS *come into view. They stand absorbed, their heads close together, looking at some special flower they have picked.*)

TERESA. Perhaps she'll find out – in time. Everybody finds out, when it's too late. (*Crying.*)

PAULINA. There's no use crying about it. (*Crying too.*)

ANTONIA (*sobbing*). Have you got a hanky?

TERESA. Let's water this primula with our tears. It might change its colour or something.

(*They all bend sobbing over the primula on the table.*)

PAULINA. No use! My tears have stopped.

TERESA. They always do when you've got a use for them.

(TRIGORIN *staggers downstairs with a couple of suitcases.*)

TRIGORIN. I come to go. But first I must make my farewell to the good Doktor. Greatly have I appreciate the privilege to meet this so learned man.

ANTONIA. H'm.

TERESA (*examining*). It hasn't made a bit of difference to the primula.

(TRIGORIN *knocks on the music-room door, opens it, and stands bowing.*)

TRIGORIN (*talking into the room*). Sir! There has come to an end the most distinguished visit of my life.

(LINDA, *in deep mourning, appears in the gallery with* SUSAN, *who is also in black.* LINDA *holds* SUSAN's *hand, and carries a battered old dressing-case.* ROBERTO, *behind, carries some miscellaneous luggage.* KATE, *also in attendance, has her hands full.*)

PAULINA (*squealing*). Oh! Oh! Oh, look!

TERESA. Oh! Lewis! Ike! Come and look! Did you ever?

(FLORENCE *and* LEWIS *come in from the mountain.* CHARLES *and* JACOB *come out of the music-room.*)

LINDA. Come along, my pet! If we're turned out, we're turned out, and there's an end of it.

(SUSAN *sniffs loudly.* TRIGORIN *stands petrified.*)

(*To nobody in particular.*) She's crying for her daddy, poor little mite! You wouldn't think the way she's treated now that she was Sanger's favourite child! Come, dearie. You're going to a lovely new home with Uncle Kiki!

TRIGORIN (*in horrified amazement*). *Himmel!*

LINDA (*firmly*). Will you take my dressing-case, please, Kiril?

ANTONIA (*darting forward*). You mustn't take that. It's mine.

LINDA. What's yours? Yours? You give it here if you please! It's mine. I've had it these five years.

ANTONIA (*snatching it and dodging behind* JACOB). It ought to be mine. It belonged to my mother.

LINDA. What's that got to do with it? It's mine now. Your dad gave it to me. You give it back di-rectly.

ANTONIA. I won't. You're a thief! He never gave you my darling mother's things. You stole them.

KATE. Hush, my dear!

ANTONIA. I won't hush.

(*They all try to hush and restrain her.*)

JACOB. Tony! Tony! Let her have it! I will give you a better one. I will give you –

ANTONIA. Thank you for nothing, Mr Made-of-Money! (*Holding up bag.*) Look! Those are my mother's initials. Evelyn Napier Churchill.

CHARLES. Yes, yes. It was hers. I remember.

LINDA (*screaming*). I don't leave this house without it. You call me a thief! What are you, I should like to know? You turn me out. You treat me as if I was a tart. What better are you? Tell me that! What better was your mother?

FLORENCE (*holding* ANTONIA *back*). Don't listen to her. Don't answer!

LINDA. Don't you worry with her, miss. She's not fit for you to touch, not be a long chalk. She's an artful little slut and no better than what she should be. You ask *Mister* Jacob Birnbaum here if –

LEWIS. Here! Take your bag and go! You'll miss your train!

CHARLES (*watch in hand*). Yes, madam. You'd really better go.

LINDA. Go? I should think I am going! I wouldn't stay here for anything in the world, not with all I've seen going on. Come along, mother's own. But if you're so particular I wonder at you for bringing the young lady here. It's nothing better than a dirty case house and never was.

(*She goes.* TRIGORIN, *shamefacedly, follows her, dropping luggage about.* ROBERTO *brings up her rear with the overladen wheelbarrow. The whole party rush up after her to watch the exit – leaving* LEWIS, CHARLES *and* FLORENCE *alone.*)

FLORENCE. How devastating!

CHARLES (*grumblingly*). Now perhaps I can get on with Sanger's bills. He seems to have vowed himself to poverty but not to chastity. Is there any ink about the place? My fountain pen's dry.

FLORENCE (*producing a dirty bottle with cork of blotting paper and turning it upside down*). Not a drop.

CHARLES. Then I'll have to go to the village too. The sooner we finish up and depart for a less rarefied atmosphere, the better.

(*He goes out.*)

LEWIS. You mustn't, please, blame the children for all this. They're very young. She – er – they need someone to look after them.

FLORENCE. Don't apologise for them. I think they're dears, especially Paulina.

LEWIS. I hope they will like school. Some people can't do with that sort of life. I couldn't myself. I ran away from *my* school. And if they –

FLORENCE (*amused*). How old were you?

LEWIS. Sixteen.

FLORENCE. Not really! Where did you go?

LEWIS. Spain. I played the cornet in a circus band.

FLORENCE. How delicious!

LEWIS. Afterwards I wrote pieces for them to play. It's good training. Sanger says my style bears traces of the circus yet. (*Pause.*) He used to say it, I mean. I keep on forgetting Sanger's dead.

FLORENCE. I adore circuses. They're so vital, aren't they?

LEWIS. Well! That's one way of putting it.

FLORENCE. I wonder if you know my friend Peveril Leyburn's Songs of the Circus? They're rather attractive.

LEWIS. Never heard of 'em.

FLORENCE. Oh, but surely –

LEWIS. Nobody in England knows anything about music. *When* are you going back? Very soon?

FLORENCE. As soon as the debts are paid up. How peaceful it is! One can just hear the waterfall. Isn't running water the most enchanting sound in the world?

LEWIS. No. Wings are. When I was a boy I used to sleep on some cliffs in Cornwall. Once I woke up when it was quite dark. (*Low – almost to himself.*) I could see – nothing! But the air was full of wings.

FLORENCE. Did you live in Cornwall then?

LEWIS. No. B-Bayswater. (*Pause.*)

FLORENCE. What are you working at now?

LEWIS. Nothing since you came. It hasn't been possible.

FLORENCE. I should have thought that you were one of those people who allow nothing to interfere with work.

LEWIS. I am. (*Pause.*) I'd have left here a week ago, if I had been sure –

FLORENCE. Sure of what?

LEWIS (*coming towards her*). That I hadn't a chance – with you.

FLORENCE (*backing away a little*). What do you mean?

LEWIS (*smiling*). I can't make you out. That's what is so tantalizing. I don't quite understand you.

FLORENCE (*rather pathetically*). I should have thought I was a very easy person to understand.

LEWIS (*shaking his head*). You're not quite like any other woman.

FLORENCE. Oh, well. (*With an attempt at lightness.*) No two women are alike, are they?

LEWIS. They're all alike. If you were any other woman I'd have said you wanted me to make love to you, but for all that I'm afraid of you. I don't know how to begin.

FLORENCE. Mr Dodd! Really –

LEWIS (*with bitter mockery*). This is so sudden.

(*Enter* ROBERTO.)

Oh, go to hell, Roberto. Go away!

(LEWIS *pushes* ROBERTO *out*.)

FLORENCE (*distressed*). I don't like this way of talking. I though we
were friends.

LEWIS. Did you?

FLORENCE. Didn't you?

LEWIS. No. I have no friends.

FLORENCE. But that's a dreadful thing to say.

LEWIS. I had one. He's dead.

FLORENCE. Sanger?

LEWIS. Yes! Sanger. Now he's gone the world's so cold – there's
nothing left.

FLORENCE. I'm your friend if you want a friend.

LEWIS (*turning on her*). I don't. I want more.

FLORENCE. No, no –

LEWIS. Well, shouldn't I be a fool if I didn't want more? That's why
I've stayed. On the chance of getting more.

FLORENCE. Oh, don't talk like that.

LEWIS. Wasn't I right? You're never going back to England.

FLORENCE. I – don't – know –

LEWIS. You're coming with me – aren't you?

FLORENCE. Where?

LEWIS. Oh, anywhere. I'm not particular.

FLORENCE. Please don't talk in that way.

LEWIS. Why not?

FLORENCE (*weakly*). You – you take too much for granted.

LEWIS. I always do. (*Intercepting her as she tries to get out of the
room.*) No, don't go away! We may not get a chance to be alone
again.

FLORENCE. Perhaps that would be as well.

LEWIS. And afterwards, when you get back to England, you'll be
sorry. You'll wish that you hadn't run away from me.

FLORENCE. Let me go, please. I – I'm disappointed in you. I thought
you were – that you liked me too well to talk in this way.

LEWIS. Like! I love you!

(*They embrace passionately.* ROBERTO *comes in and begins to clear the
table without taking any notice of them.*)

Damn you, Roberto! Can't you keep your ugly mug out of here.

ROBERTO (grinning). *Si, Signor!*

(*He goes out.*)

LEWIS (*kissing her rather roughly. She starts back, frightened*). What is it? What's the matter?

FLORENCE. Nothing! Nothing! Oh, Lewis! I love you! I loved you from the very first minute I saw you. (*Hiding her face in his shoulder.*) I'll go with you – anywhere.

LEWIS (*touched*). You're only a child really, and I thought you so grand. You're like my poor little Tessa. Don't cry, sweet one.

FLORENCE. I can't help it. I feel so weak.

LEWIS. No one shall hurt you. (*With resolution.*) We'll be married. I'll look after you, Florence. When shall we be married?

FLORENCE (*laughing, her face still hidden*). Whenever you like.

LEWIS. Why are you laughing?

FLORENCE (*holding him away from her*). Now, tell the truth! It had only just occurred to you, hadn't it?

LEWIS (*guiltily*). Oh, no. Not at all. But I ought to have mentioned it before! We'll be married as soon as possible.

FLORENCE. Oh, I'm so happy! (*Gaily.*) Now! Let's make plans!

LEWIS. Plans! What plans? We've made 'em. We'll be married at once.

FLORENCE. Yes. But after? Where shall we live? In England?

LEWIS. I'd sooner live anywhere else.

FLORENCE. Oh, but Lewis! I know just exactly the house for us. I've had my eye on it for ages and I know it's going to be sold this summer. Listen! It's at Strand-on-the-Green, just under Kew Bridge, and it dates from Charles II, and –

LEWIS. You're delicious when you chatter like a little starling.

FLORENCE. Now be serious! Why won't you live in England? Is it because your people live there?

LEWIS. My – Oh yes!

FLORENCE. And you've quarelled?

LEWIS. My family are very disagreeable.

FLORENCE. Yes, dear?

LEWIS. That's all?

FLORENCE. How many are there?

LEWIS. A father and a sister there used to be. My father writes books. Two a year. Little textbooks and outlines of things for working men. You know. Half-hours with the Great Poets; the Starry Heavens in Ten Chapters; that sort of tripe.

FLORENCE. He sounds exactly like a man my father is always

complaining of. He calls him Fulsome Felix, and sits on
Committees with him – Sir Felix Dodd.

LEWIS. That's him. He is Sir Felix Dodd.

FLORENCE. W – what?

LEWIS. He is Sir Felix Dodd. Know him?

FLORENCE. I – I've met him.

LEWIS. You have my sympathy.

FLORENCE. Good heavens! How very strange! I never knew that he
had a son.

LEWIS. Alas!

FLORENCE. At least I did hear that he had a son who was an awful
so –

LEWIS. Don't mention it.

FLORENCE. But then I must know your sister quite well. She married –
someone in the Foreign Office. She sings, doesn't she?

LEWIS. She may. She never had much sense of humour.

FLORENCE. Oh, Lewis. This is extraordinary. Oh, I am happy!

LEWIS. Why?

(ROBERTO *comes in again to clear away. This time she gives it up and
continues, trying not to notice him.*)

FLORENCE. I'd have married you if your father had been a crossing
sweeper.

LEWIS. That's a compliment, anyhow. (*Trying to kiss her, but she edges
away, with a jerk of the head at* ROBERTO.) Oh, don't mind him.
He's used to it.

FLORENCE. I'm not.

LEWIS. You soon will be. Roberto!

ROBERTO. *Si, Signor.*

LEWIS. *Son' promessisposi!* (*Pointing to himself and* FLORENCE.)

ROBERTO. *Ah basta!*

FLORENCE. Poor old Roberto. He doesn't quite deserve that. But why
did you think my father was a crossing sweeper?

FLORENCE. I didn't. I merely said I'd have married you if he had been.
But it will be so much easier for me if my people know something
of your people.

LEWIS. Well, if it makes you happy, I expect it's all right.

FLORENCE. Because some day one hopes –

LEWIS. What does one hope?

FLORENCE. That you may forget it all – and make it up.

LEWIS. Make it up? Not on your life.

FLORENCE (*archly*). We'll see.

LEWIS. No, no, Florence. I'm serious about this.

FLORENCE. So am I.

LEWIS. I ran away from home because I couldn't bear it.

FLORENCE. Probably there were faults on both sides.

LEWIS. I've no doubt that all the faults were on my side. But you must promise that you won't make me go back there, ever.

FLORENCE. I won't promise.

(TERESA *and* PAULINA *appear in the doorway.*)

LEWIS. Then I won't – (*Seeing the girls and becoming silent.*)

TERESA. You won't what, Lewis?

FLORENCE (*turning*). Why children! You're back soon.

LEWIS. A shade long you've been, if anything.

FLORENCE. Did you see them off?

PAULINA. Yes.

FLORENCE. Where's Antonia?

PAULINA. Trying to buy another suitcase with Ike.

TERESA (*turning to* LEWIS). What won't you, Lewis?

LEWIS. Oh, nothing!

PAULINA. You look as if you'd been getting into mischief, doesn't he, Teresa?

TERESA. He does.

PAULINA. Out with it, Lewis. What have you done now?

TERESA (*eyeing him carefully*). I think I'm going to be sick again.

PAULINA. Not here! Not now! You can't now.

LEWIS (*swallowing twice*). Er – girls!

FLORENCE (*in an undertone*). Oh, Lewis! Must you? Now?

TERESA. Let us know the worst.

LEWIS. Girls! I'm going to be married.

(TERESA *gives a little cry of pain and leans against the door.* ROBERTO *lays the plates for lunch.*)

PAULINA . You won't – you won't marry Florence?

LEWIS. Oh, yes, I shall. Shan't I, Florence?

FLORENCE (*smiling*). It looks like it.

PAULINA. But are you sure it isn't a mistake? All right, Tessa. You needn't pinch me. I won't say anything. All I mean is, hadn't you better wait a bit? Don't do it in a hurry.

(TERESA *collapses.*)

LEWIS. Tessa! What's the matter?

FLORENCE. You ran up the hill too fast.

TERESA. Too – many – green gooseberries.

PAULINA. She often faints like that. It's nothing.

FLORENCE. Poor child! Where's the pain? In the chest? Would you like to go to bed?

TERESA (*pushing her away*). – have – to – die – on this chair.

PAULINA. She gobbles them so. I told her she'd be sorry.

FLORENCE. She's very blue. Has she had a shock at any time? Is her heart strong?

(TERESA *faints*.)

LEWIS. She's fainted. Tessa! Don't be so alarming! My dear!

FLORENCE. That won't do much good, Lewis. Get some brandy. Roberto! *L'acqua fredda e asciugamani!*

(LEWIS *and* ROBERTO *run out*.)

PAULINA. You mustn't! You mustn't! You can't have him!

FLORENCE. What on earth are you talking about?

PAULINA. He's Tessa's. He belongs to Tessa.

FLORENCE. Are you mad? You don't know what you are saying.

PAULINA. I do. I do. He loves Tessa better than he loves you. She's too young, but he can wait.

FLORENCE. Ssh!

PAULINA. He ought to marry Tessa, not you. You're just an outside person that's come butting in. We don't want you! Go away! Go away! (*She flings her arms round her sister's neck, sobbing.*)

CURTAIN.

# ACT II

## SCENE 1

SCENE: *The drawing-room at Strand-on-the-Green. At the back three tall, narrow French windows giving on to small balconies with curved iron railings before each. Beyond, a view of the River Thames. The room is very sparsely furnished. The walls are a soft cream or lemon yellow. The floor is polished wood, covered by a square, light carpet, with a circular rug of a darker shade, with one rug by the fireplace and one by each of the doors up and down Right. The grand piano stands in top left-hand corner of room, keys facing towards river, so that a singer standing by accompanist faces the audience. In front of the centre window is a large divan, piled with bright-coloured cushions. There is an oblong table between the doors Right, arranged as a buffet for refreshments. A few etchings and sketches in narrow-beaded frames adorn the walls. Some bright lustre jugs relieve the appearance of the mantelpiece. Quite a bright tasteful room, but somehow lacking in the easy charm of an artist's surroundings. A bluish dusk is falling.*

FLORENCE, *in a chintz overall, is arranging flowers. The room is all ready for a party.* LEWIS *sprawls on the divan, smoking and watching her in some amusement.*

FLORENCE.  You might give those divan cushions a shake-up, Lewis.

LEWIS.  What's the use? They'll get squashed again as soon as people sit on them.

FLORENCE (*violently pommelling every cushion in the room*). Lazybones! Our Italian honeymoon has quite spoilt your *morale*. These southern countries! They're poppy and mandragora, you know.

LEWIS.  They're what?

FLORENCE.  They tend to make one sluttish. It was high time we came back to England.

(ROBERTO, *very fine in a clean white linen suit, brings in a tray of glasses.*)

On this table. The drinks you will bring in at ten o'clock. Supper in the dining-room at a quarter past eleven, and then you will serve the Zabaglione. Bring now the cigarettes and the cigars.

(ROBERTO *goes out.*)

(*Looking around the room complacently.*) I must say, I do think it looks rather nice. (*Pause. Moving down Centre and facing up, looking round the room.*) Do you like your home, dear?

LEWIS (*also staring round*). It's – it's an Ideal Home. I saw on an omnibus today, there's a whole exhibition of 'em somewhere.

FLORENCE. Do you remember when first I told you about this house and you didn't want to come, and I said we simply must?

LEWIS. I remember.

FLORENCE. And now – here we are!

LEWIS. Here we, in a manner of speaking, are.

FLORENCE. I'm going to dress now. Are you coming, or can I have the bathroom first?

LEWIS. I'm not coming yet. There's hours of time. Don't go. I want to talk to you. I've had a letter.

FLORENCE. Oh yes, that reminds me. So have I. Your sister is coming tonight after all.

LEWIS. What? I've told you once I won't have her here.

FLORENCE. My dear Lewis! It's childish, this keeping up of an old feud. Millicent is quite ready to make it up.

LEWIS. Then she wants something.

FLORENCE. Couldn't it be genuine good feeling?

LEWIS. She never had an ounce of it in her life. She's up to no good. Why can't she leave us alone?

FLORENCE. I don't want to offend her. She carries a good deal of weight in some quarters. She could easily put a spoke in your wheel.

LEWIS (*sulkily.*) I haven't got a wheel.

FLORENCE. And she's very musical.

LEWIS. Musical! My God!

FLORENCE. There is no need to be so violent.

LEWIS. She's a damned musical snob, and she's got a tongue like a horseradish. Nothing else.

(ROBERTO *comes in with the cigarettes and cigars.*)

FLORENCE. Ssh!

LEWIS. I won't ssh. Why the hell can't I say what I like in my own house?

FLORENCE. You're perfectly impossible.
(*To* ROBERTO.) Thank you, that will do.

(ROBERTO *goes out.*)

I wish you wouldn't talk like that in front of Roberto.

LEWIS. Why ever not? Roberto is used to bad language, thank God.

FLORENCE (*plaintively*). Can't you see how disastrous it is when I'm trying to train him properly.

LEWIS. Sorry! Who else is coming to this party of yours? Half London?

FLORENCE (*smiling to herself*). I've got the very cream to begin with. If it's known that they come to our house, the rest of the world won't wait to be asked. For one thing, I've actually persuaded Sir Bartlemy Pugh. It's a great honour; he hardly ever goes out nowadays.

LEWIS. That distinguished old pussycat? But, of course, I remember! He wrote the most bee-ootiful hymn tunes!

FLORENCE (*keeping her temper*). You never heard any of them, dear. He's a charming old man, and my godfather. Then I've asked Dr Dawson – you know! The Amalgamated Symphony Orchestra –

LEWIS. He's sound enough. I like him.

FLORENCE. So do I. I've known him since I was that high.

LEWIS. All the distinguished old men in England seem to have rocked your cradle, my dear. Who else?

FLORENCE. Oh! The Leyburns. They run the Guild of Beauty, you know.

LEWIS. What in thunder is the Guild of Beauty?

FLORENCE. They give concerts in the slums. Really good music. They've done some splendid work in bringing music to the people.

LEWIS. What do they want to do that for?

(*He goes across to the piano and begins to pick out notes in a vague way which shows how nervous and impatient he is getting.*)

FLORENCE. My dear Lewis! Why do you write music?

LEWIS. God knows.

FLORENCE. You want to give pleasure to people.

LEWIS. NO!

FLORENCE. That's a pose. Oh, do stop that strumming!

LEWIS (*jumping up and banging down the lid of the keyboard*). It's not. I swear it's not. The sight of a lot of human beings, listening with their mouths open, makes me sick and ashamed of my work. Sanger felt the same way about it.

FLORENCE. I shall want you to play to my guests tonight, so you must try to get the better of that feeling.

LEWIS (*his momentary vehemence a little calmed*). You'd better write down what I have to say and I'll learn it off. (*Casually.*) I've asked Ike and Tony, by the way.

FLORENCE. What? Tonight? Of course, as you know, I'm always delighted to see your friends, but in a party like this, where everyone is so influential –

LEWIS. Ike is as influential as the whole of your party put together. He's very nearly made up his mind to finance the production of my 'Symphony in Three Keys', at Queen's Hall, this spring.

FLORENCE. What! Lewis! Your Symphony at the Queen's Hall? How perfectly thrilling! Why didn't you tell me before?

LEWIS. It isn't settled yet. I want to talk it over with Ike tonight.

FLORENCE. Of course, if I'd known – I'll call on Tony tomorrow.

LEWIS (*acidly*). You needn't trouble.

FLORENCE. You know, my dear – Mr Birnbaum is – isn't a gentleman, and one must face the fact –

LEWIS. Thank God he's not.

FLORENCE. That's quite the wrong attitude! You put the wrong things first. Music – all art – has no justification unless –

LEWIS. It doesn't need a justification –

FLORENCE. You can't put it on a pedestal above decency and humanity and civilization as your precious Sanger seems to have done. Human life is more important.

LEWIS. I know! I know! You want to use it like electric light. Like the saucepans you buy for your kitchen. I know! I've seen it. In my father's house. That's why I ran away! It's plague, pestilence and famine – bloody nonsense.

FLORENCE. Lewis, I will not have it. Is it quite impossible to discuss things without swearing?

(ROBERTO *comes in with a basket of logs.*)

LEWIS. Isn't it, Roberto? All this (*indicating room*) – damn bloody nonsense?

ROBERTO (*not understanding*). *Si! Si!* Damnbloodi nonsense!

(LEWIS *collapses into a roar of laughter, and so does* ROBERTO.)

FLORENCE (*angrily*). That is enough. Go away at once!

ROBERTO (*crestfallen*). *Scusi!* (*Puts the basket of logs by the fire and goes out.*)

FLORENCE. I think you must be crazy, Lewis. (*Crossing to Right Centre.*) I'm going to dress.

LEWIS (*barring her way*). You haven't inquired about my letter yet.

FLORENCE (*impatiently*). Oh, who is it?

LEWIS. Tessa and Lina. They're not happy.

FLORENCE. Little monkeys! Fancy writing to you! May I see?

LEWIS (*taking letters out of his pocket*). Paulina threatens suicide. She says (*reading*): 'I shall hang myself. But Tessa says I'm to say she won't. It's not so bad for her, as she has not got to play this hellish hockey because she has a valvular lesson that they found at the medical inspection, so she has to go walks instead.' (*Anxiously.*) What's a valvular lesson?

FLORENCE. A valvular lesion, I suppose she means. Her housemistress wrote to me about it.

LEWIS. Is Tessa ill?

FLORENCE. No, no. She'll outgrow it. May I see Tessa's letter, please?

LEWIS. She says the same as Lina.

FLORENCE. I'd like to see it, please.

LEWIS (*reluctantly giving it*). As Teresa puts it: she has to be in some place on a timetable at every minute of the day. And no allowance is made for transit.

FLORENCE (*reading*). H'm! Not entirely sincere, is it?

LEWIS. Tessa is always sincere. (*Taking the letter back.*)

FLORENCE. If I were you I shouldn't answer them.

LEWIS. Indeed I shall. I shall advise them to run away if they don't like it.

FLORENCE. Don't be absurd. I must ask you not to do anything so silly.

LEWIS. Well then, take them away at the end of the term.

FLORENCE. I shall do no such thing.

LEWIS. At least take Tessa away. It's worse for Tessa. She was very nearly perfect before she went there –

FLORENCE. Teresa was very nearly perfect! What do you mean?

LEWIS. I don't know what's the matter with me today. The prospect of this party makes me feel like Tessa on what she calls one of her dog days.

FLORENCE. It's only done to get you on.

LEWIS. I know. But I can't stomach it somehow. Only, if I learn off my little piece and say it like a gentleman, will you do something for me in return?

FLORENCE. What thing?

LEWIS. Take those girls away from that tiresome school.

FLORENCE. That I can't do. It's for their good.

LEWIS. But Tessa says –

FLORENCE. Oh, stop reading that nonsense! A schoolgirl's *schwarmerei*.

LEWIS. What do you mean? Give that thing back!

FLORENCE. Why should I?

LEWIS. Because I tell you to. It's mine. Give it me!

FLORENCE. I won't. Tessa's correspondence is my affair. (*Putting letter behind her back.*) As her guardian, I've a right to supervise it. She's nothing to you.

LEWIS (*seizing her wrists and twisting her round*). Give it back or you'll be sorry.

FLORENCE. Lewis! How dare you! You're hurting me!

LEWIS. I mean to. (*Getting possession of the letter.*)

(*They stand glaring at one another.*)

FLORENCE. You beast! You're as bad as Sanger!

LEWIS. Sanger wouldn't have put up with half the nonsense I've stood for.

(*He rushes from the room and falls over* ROBERTO, *who is listening at the keyhole. Curses him in Italian outside.*)

FLORENCE (*standing quite dazed for a minute and then smiling faintly and smoothing her hair*). Dear me! What a hullabaloo! Talk about nerves! (*Calling.*) Roberto!

ROBERTO (*appearing*). *Si*, madame?

FLORENCE. What were you doing out there?

ROBERTO. Please – I watcha you fight viz Lewis.

FLORENCE. I am very much displeased. Has the master gone out?

ROBERTO. No, *signora*.

FLORENCE. Very well. I'm going to dress now.

(*She goes out, switching off the lights, followed by* ROBERTO. *The firelight and the blue wintry dusk fill the room. Presently* LEWIS *pokes his head round the door, sees the coast is clear, and slips in to the piano. He plays the first few bars of the Overture to 'The Magic Flute'; stops, picks out the theme of 'Infelice Sconsolata', and then begins very softly to play* TERESA's *duet. The door is opened a little way as he plays, and there is a great whispering outside.* PAULINA *pokes her head round.*)

LEWIS (*playing*). Who's there?

PAULINA. It's Lewis! (*Giggling.*)

LEWIS (*jumping up*). How! Who! Why! Paulina? How on earth did you get here?

(PAULINA *rushes to him and kisses him.*)

PAULINA. Oh, Lewis! We've run away. We had to.

(*He sees that* TERESA *is lurking in the shadows.*)

LEWIS (*still holding* PAULINA). Tessa! Is that Tessa? (*Seizing* TERESA, *who has come to him, in his arms.*) Let me look at you.

TERESA.  Yes. It's me. I've come to lay my bones among you.

LEWIS.  Oh, Tessa! Dear Tessa! This is splendid! How long it's been!

TERESA.  Longer than the longest book.

LEWIS.  Look up! Lift your head up and kiss me. (*They kiss.*) Well, well!

PAULINA.  Why have you got such a dark house, Lewis?

LEWIS (*switching on the light by fireplace*). It's not my house. It's my wife's. She bought it.

TERESA (*handing him a telegram*). Roberto was on the doorstep taking this when we got here. He paid for our taxi as we had only fivepence-halfpenny left. We've brought as many things as we could. We don't intend to go back; and I thought I would continue my studies here. *Pourquoi pas?*

LEWIS.  'Sanger sisters disappeared. Last seen nine a.m. Are they with you? Butterfield.'

TERESA.  Sanger sisters! Sounds like a music-hall.

LEWIS.  Who's Butterfield?

PAULINA.  The headmistress. We rather liked her, but we didn't see enough of her.

TERESA (*eagerly.*) She had a nice voice and lovely clothes. She nearly made me believe that a person can be highly educated without being as ugly as the devil.

LEWIS.  I don't know that I quite like the sound of Miss Butterfield. It was high time you ran away. (*Staring – firmly, as he looks again at the telegram.*) We'll say that you aren't coming back.

(TERESA *and* PAULINA *jump for joy.*)

PAULINA.  We can't possibly go back. We bore it in silence –

TERESA.  No, Lina! Not in silence!

LEWIS.  What made you run in the end?

PAULINA.  An awful row in church yesterday. We'd forgotten to take

any money to put in that bag, and I had to put in a button that I
pulled off my –

TERESA. Ssh! You mustn't! Do you know, Lewis, they said you
mustn't talk about them.

LEWIS. What?

TERESA. The things that Lina pulled the button off. The girls said
we'd disgraced the school, so nobody would speak to us – what did
they call it? – Sending us to Covent Garden?

PAULINA. No. Coventry!

TERESA. Coventry for a week. Then in the afternoon a girl in the next
cubicle played the 'Sonata Pathétique' over and over. She was
putting in the expression.

LEWIS (*laughing*). Oh, I see.

TERESA. We suddenly got tired of being taught how to behave by two
hundred people all at once, so we up and hooked it. And that's
that. Is this your best room, Lewis?

LEWIS. Yes.

TERESA (*looking round*). It's very pretty.

PAULINA (*with a little shiver*). Is it always as – as tidy?

LEWIS. Always. You mustn't touch anything.

TERESA. Very right and proper, I'm sure.

(*They range round, examining.* TERESA *crosses up to and touches a note
on the piano, and grunts approval.*)

LEWIS (*humming*). I'll build for thee a silver sty, Honey! said she.

PAULINA. Have you any bedrooms?

LEWIS. Three. And my dressing-room.

TERESA. What! A special room to dress in! How unsociable! When
you're washing and dressing, that's just the time you want
somebody to talk to. Is she cross when she wakes up in the
morning, Lewis?

LEWIS. Not as cross as I am. (*Humming.*)
          And in it nobly thou shalt lie!
          Hunks! said he.

Funny! I must have heard that song when I was in petticoats. I've
only just remembered it. It's most appropriate. (*Humming.*)

PAULINA. Why?

LEWIS. Oh, just because – there was a lady loved a swine –

TERESA. Well, I think it's lovely. You wouldn't expect Florence to
have a lot of heavy sofas and things.

PAULINA. But still, she's married. Married ladies always have sofas; I don't call that a sofa. (*Pointing to divan.*)

TERESA. But it's pretty, Lina.

PAULINA. Drawing-rooms ought to be rich and grand. This isn't grand enough.

LEWIS. Our best things are in the parlour. I'll show you the whole concern later.

PAULINA (*espying the buffet*). O-oh! Eatables! May we? We've had nothing all day.

LEWIS. Poor dears! You must be starving. Let's bring them over to the fire.

(*They bring plates, and* LEWIS *the cushions, and sit on the floor. Between them they carry about half a dozen plates of sandwiches, etc., over to the fire. They strew them over the floor in a half-circle round the fire.*)

TERESA (*seeing pair of candlesticks on mantel*). Are those real?

LEWIS. Imitation.

TERESA. Ah, well. It's the sincerest form of flattery.

PAULINA. O-oh! Cream trifle.

LEWIS. Don't overeat yourselves; you'll spoil your appetites for the party.

PAULINA. Are you giving a party?

LEWIS. Florence is giving a party. A musical soirée.

TERESA. What's that?

LEWIS. You'll see.

PAULINA. Shall we have to behave very nicely?

TERESA. We've had lessons in social life and custom from Miss Butterfield.

LEWIS. Ike and Tony are coming.

PAULINA. Fancy coming in for a party the very first night. Aren't you glad now, Tessa, that we ran away? She didn't want to come, you know, Lewis.

(ROBERTO *brings in the kitchen coffeepot, steaming.*)

PAULINA. My! Tessa, look at Roberto.

TERESA. Goodness! Isn't it lo-ovely? What's it for, Roberto?

ROBERTO. Roberto ver' clean, now, not so comfortable.

LEWIS. Looks like a second communion.

PAULINA. Why didn't you answer our letters, Lewis?

LEWIS. I suppose I forgot.

PAULINA. Tessa said you wouldn't answer.

LEWIS. Did you, Tessa? Why?

TERESA. Because you have a forgetful nature.

LEWIS. No, I haven't.

TERESA. Yes, you have. I pity poor Florence.

LEWIS. Oh, hunks! (*Humming as he goes towards the piano.*)

TERESA. Play that tune you were playing when we came in.

LEWIS. What? Our duet?

TERESA. Ikey used always to say musicians who could write good
tunes were very few, and you were one of them.

LEWIS. Street musicians!

TERESA. That's what Sanger would say. But Jacob's right.

LEWIS (*beginning to play*). You're growing very smug, my girl. I don't
like it. With your Miss Clutterbucks and all. I don't like it a bit. A
regular miss!

TERESA. You said I would.

LEWIS. When?

TERESA. When you made me go to school. You said I'd turn into a
lady.

LEWIS. I've been a fool.

(FLORENCE, *beautifully dressed, hurries in.*)

FLORENCE. Lewis! Aren't you ever going to dress! It's nearly – Good
heavens! (*Staring bewildered at the children and the disordered room.*)
What! What is the meaning of this?

PAULINA (*kissing her*). Dear Florence! Don't be angry.

TERESA (*kissing her*). We thought we'd like to pay you a little visit.
We – we've run away.

FLORENCE. Oh! You have, have you? Then you've been exceedingly
naughty. I'm very vexed. And you'll go back at once.

LEWIS. There's no time tonight.

FLORENCE. No, but the very first thing tomorrow –

LEWIS. ⎫
TERESA. ⎬ Oh, Florence!
PAULINA. ⎭

FLORENCE. I won't stand any nonsense of this kind.

(*A loud bell is heard ringing.*)

Good heavens! People are coming! And the room in this mess!
Take these cups into the kitchen someone! (*Crossing, picking up and*

*putting cushions back.*) Go! Go and dress, Lewis! Oh, give me patience!

(*They all tidy the room hastily.* ROBERTO *enters, chattering.*)

TERESA. Shall we put on our party frocks, Florence? We've got them with us.

FLORENCE. No. You'll go straight to bed. Roberto, you get the spare room ready. Do go, Lewis!

PAULINA. But aren't we coming to your party?

FLORENCE. Certainly not! You neither of you know how to behave.

TERESA. Oh, we do! We do! We've learnt a lot of politeness at school. Please let us!

PAULINA. We promise we'll sit as mum as two statues the whole evening. Florence! Please!

(*Another ring is heard.*)

LEWIS. If they don't come, I don't. So choose.

FLORENCE. Oh well, let them come. Only do go now!

(LEWIS *and the children dance gaily off arm in arm, just as* ROBERTO *shows in the first guests.*)

ROBERTO. Missis Gregory! Sair Bartlemy Pugh!

(MILLICENT GREGORY *runs in and kisses* FLORENCE *warmly, staring about her inquisitively as she does so.* SIR BARTLEMY PUGH *ambles in behind her.*)

MILLICENT. Florence dear! What an enchanting house! It's too terribly nice! Lewis is really a very lucky creature.

FLORENCE. I'm so glad you like it. How do you do, Sir Bartlemy? It's so good of you to come.

SIR BARTLEMY (*who knows that it is*). Delightful, my dear child! Delightful! You're very snug here in your little Chiswick home.

FLORENCE. I'm so sorry Lewis isn't down. The wretch went on working till the last minute and I'm afraid he's only just gone to change.

MILLICENT. How like Lewis! Just the same as ever! But then the idea of Lewis as a host at all is so marvellous, somehow. Tell me, who is coming? I heard a rumour that we were going to meet *the* Birnbaum.

FLORENCE. Mr and Mrs Jacob Birnbaum are coming, but –

MILLICENT. My dear, you're wonderful! How did you get hold of him?

SIR BARTLEMY (*disgustedly*). They tell me he wears emerald shirt studs
and owns fifteen opera houses. How do such people exist?

MILLICENT. I don't suppose Lewis minds that. After all, you're made
if you can get in with that man.

ROBERTO (*announcing*). Mister and Missis Leyburn!

(*The* LEYBURNS *come in. She is a dowdy, pretty woman in a Liberty
tea gown.*)

MRS LEYBURN. Florence! My *dear*! What a delicious place!

FLORENCE. So glad!

MRS LEYBURN (*gushing, waving her Liberty scarf about*). Oh, but I can't
*tell* you what I feel about it. It's – it's – Oh, my dear!

MR LEYBURN (*with a squeaky voice*). Such an atmosphere! (*To*
FLORENCE.) How do you do? It's incredibly good! There's a *tenue* –
a feel about it all.

MRS LEYBURN (*to* MILLICENT). How do you do, Mrs Gregory? I
thought I caught sight of you at the Stravinsky thing this
afternoon.

MILLICENT. Oh, really.

MR LEYBURN. Yes, you've quite captured the essence of beauty
without the usual vulgarities of an artistic *milieu*.

MRS LEYBURN (*to* MILLICENT). Very second-rate, I thought, didn't
you?

MILLICENT. Personally I liked it.

MRS LEYBURN. Sir Bartlemy – how too lovely! I told Peveril we were in
for a delicious thing tonight.

MILLICENT (*talking her down*). I always thought Jacob Birnbaum was a
myth.

MR LEYBURN (*squeaking*). Birnbaum! Oh, a dreadful man. A dreadful
man! Don't talk about him. He holds us all in the hollow of his
hand. He is to decide the opera programme this season – Too
fearful!

MRS LEYBURN (*in a loud whisper*). He's coming here tonight, dear.

MR LEYBURN. Oh, excellent, excellent! We'll give him a few hints
about Covent Garden .

ROBERTO (*announcing*). *Il dottore* Dossonne.

(DR DAWSON, *a large, shabby, elderly man, looks a little dazed by the
babel which is going on.*)

FLORENCE. Ah, Dr Dawson. This is nice of you.

DAWSON (*gruffly but good-humouredly*). How d'ye do, Florence Dodd?

No, don't make eyes at me. I've come to talk to this husband of
yours. Where is he?

FLORENCE. He'll be here in a minute. He went up late to dress.

DAWSON. I see. And now he's afraid to come down? I don't wonder.

MRS LEYBURN. Florence, we must ask the great Birnbaum to give us
one of the Sanger operas this year.

MILLICENT. Isn't that a trifle *vieux jeu*?

MRS LEYBURN (*acidly*). Oh, do you think so?

MR LEYBURN. Surely not! The man was dynamic.

DAWSON. How de do, Pugh?

SIR BARTLEMY. Flourishingly well, thank you. And you?

MR LEYBURN (*to* MRS LEYBURN *and* MILLICENT). He had the *Zeitgeist*, a
sort of virginal brutality –

DAWSON. Beg pardon? I'm sorry. I thought you were addressing me.

MRS LEYBURN (*simpering*). No, no! We're talking of Sanger, Dr
Dawson.

DAWSON. What about him?

MRS LEYBURN. Personally, I found his *Akbar* incredibly moving. You
remember, Peveril, in Milan.

SIR BARTLEMY. Ugh! I may be old-fashioned, but I don't think it's
music.

MR LEYBURN. Of course the great point about Sanger is his
chiaroscuro of orchestration. Those plangent values –

DAWSON. Plangent grandmother!

FLORENCE.⎫
MILLICENT.⎪
              ⎬ (*simultaneously*). Sanger – I beg your pardon!
MR LEYBURN.⎪
MRS LEYBURN.⎭

(*They all murmur* 'Not at all,' *and there is a pause.*)

ROBERTO (*announcing with pride*). Miss Antonia Sanger – ah, no! La
Famiglia Birnbaum.

(ANTONIA *and* JACOB *appear.* ANTONIA *is very beautifully dressed, like
a little peacock, in a Chinese coat with amazing jewels.*)

ANTONIA. Oh, Florence, this is fun. Where's Lewis?

FLORENCE. How are you, Antonia? I'm glad to see you. D'you know –
(*Beginning to introduce her.*)

MILLICENT (*pouncing upon* JACOB). How d'you do, Mr Birnbaum? I've
heard so much about you from my brother Lewis.

JACOB (*beaming at her*). *Ach*, so! You are the sister of Lewis? I am so
pleased to know you. Tonya, here is the sister of *unser* Lewis.

MILLICENT. Ah, Mrs Birnbaum! Just the person I want to meet. I've
made such a wonderful discovery. Quite a remarkable contralto.
Would you and your husband go on my list of patrons for her
first – (*Drawing* ANTONIA *aside*.)

FLORENCE (*to* JACOB). May I introduce Mr and Mrs Leyburn?

JACOB (*clicking his heels*). *Bitte sehr*.

FLORENCE. They sing such jolly things, madrigals and chanties and so
forth. Charming duets.

JACOB. So! (*Bowing*.) That must be nice for you.

FLORENCE. Why not break the ice for us, my dear? It's no use waiting
for Lewis.

JACOB (*courteously*). *Bitte! Volksliede! Ach! Ich habe sie sehr gern*.

MRS LEYBURN. Oh, my dear, you are so unexpected. Really we've
brought nothing suitable. Did you, Peveril?

MR LEYBURN. Well, I did bring a few little things in case. (*Producing a
bulky portfolio*.)

FLORENCE. There now!

MRS LEYBURN. No, really. Somebody else had much better begin. You
see, I'd no idea of such a distinguished audience.

FLORENCE. Oh, please. One of your well-known ones.

MR LEYBURN (*jocose*). Come along, Erda. Evidently we shan't get away
without.

MRS LEYBURN. Well, just a short one then.

FLORENCE. That is nice of you. Now, is the piano as you'd like it?
(*Raising her voice*.) Please! Erda and Peveril Leyburn are going to
be kind to us.

(*General murmurs*.)

SIR BARTLEMY. Ah, charming! Charming!

FLORENCE. Sir Bartlemy, won't you sit her?

DAWSON (*to* MILLICENT). Pretty decent view from these windows.

MILLICENT. Quite pleasant.

FLORENCE. Dr Dawson?

DAWSON (*swinging round*). Eh? (*To* MILLICENT.) Somebody's going to
sing. We'd better sit down.

FLORENCE. Can you manage? That lamp is rather tiresome.

MR LEYBURN (*disentangling yards of flex from his feet*). It's quite all right.
(*Setting the lamp on the piano, which begins to flicker*.)

FLORENCE. That switch is a little loose, I think. Can I help you?

MR LEYBURN. Where's the –
FLORENCE. It's underneath.
MR. LEYBURN. I see. Don't trouble. Ah, that's right.

(*The light comes on again.*)

MRS LEYBURN. This one, Peveril?
FLORENCE (*softly, to where* MILLICENT *is whispering to* DAWSON). – Ssh!

(*They begin to sing a ballad with appropriate gestures and expression.
The moment the piano keys are struck, the light recommences flickering.*
FLORENCE *creeps across and gingerly removes lamp to table below
piano, where it remains still.*)

ROBERTO. Mr and Missis Manninga!
FLORENCE (*loudly*). Ssh!

(*The* MAINWARINGS *consist of a large healthy-looking conventional
husband, rather frightened by present company, and a small wife
with a determined but faded intellectual manner and horn-rimmed
spectacles.* FLORENCE *gives them elaborate smiles and indicates seats.*
LEWIS, TERESA *and* PAULINA *poke their noses round the door up
Right.*)

TERESA (*whispering to* PAULINA). Putting in the expression!

(*As the duet finishes they all rush in.* LEWIS *is in untidy dress clothes
with a rather dirty white tie. The two girls are in rather crushed white
muslin frocks, but they have forgotten to change their outdoor shoes.
Their hair has obviously been slapped down with a damp brush. They
rush at* ANTONIA. *Their greetings are mixed with the applause of the
guests.* MR *and* MRS LEYBURN *rather baffled and a little disappointed.*)

TERESA. Tonnikins! How lovely to see you! How are you?
ANTONIA. Tessa! Lina! What are you doing here?
TERESA. We're paying a little visit to Lewis and Florence.
ANTONIA. What a lovely surprise!
FLORENCE (*to* MR *and* MRS LEYBURN). That was charming of you.
   Thank you so much. Can we have some more later?
MRS LEYBURN. Afraid I'm not in very good voice tonight.

(FLORENCE *gathers* MR *and* MRS MAINWARING *into a group beside the
fireplace.*)

MR MAINWARING (*shaking hands*). Good evening. Mrs Dodd.
FLORENCE. D'you know the Leyburns?
MR MAINWARING. How de do? You sang delightfully. There's nothing

to beat Gilbert and Sullivan. (*With a guffaw.*) As a matter of fact, it's the only music I can stand.

MRS MAINWARING (*nudging him*). Robert!

MR MAINWARING. Yes, dear?

MRS MAINWARING (*whispering*). Don't be stupid.

MR MAINWARING. Eh?

LEWIS. Hallo, Ike.

ANTONIA. Lewis, I'm so excited about your concert. But you mustn't have it in March.

LEWIS. Why not?

ANTONIA. Because I shan't be able to come. (*Exchanging glances with* JACOB.) It's a secret. (*Whispering to* LEWIS.)

LEWIS. No! Congratulations.

ANTONIA. You'd much better congratulate Ike. It's more his doing than mine.

FLORENCE (*desperately*). Lewis! Your other guests.

(LEWIS *vaguely and monotonously greets the* LEYBURNS, *the* MAINWARINGS, SIR BARTLEMY *and* MILLICENT, *and then falls upon* DAWSON.)

LEWIS. Hallo, Dawson! I wanted to see you. Do you know Birnbaum? Ike! Come here! We want your orchestra for my concert, don't we, Ike?

(LEWIS, DAWSON *and* JACOB *retire to the drink table and plunge into a discussion over whiskies and sodas.*)

FLORENCE (*detaching the children, who are whispering with* ANTONIA). I don't think you know my small cousins, do you, Millicent? They're here just for the halfterm.

TERESA (*surprised*). Why, Florence –

MILLICENT. Small cousins! Why, I thought they were much younger than that!

FLORENCE. Over there you'd better sit, Teresa. No. Shake hands with people first.

(TERESA *and* PAULINA *go round the circle saying 'How do you do?' exactly as* LEWIS *has done, and then sit down side by side.*)

(*After an earnest conversation with* MRS MAINWARING.)

Now we're going to have some Debussy.

(MRS MAINWARING *marches firmly to the piano and screws up the seat, and wipes her hands on her handkerchief.*)

SIR BARTLEMY (*moving slightly*). Allow me.
MRS MAINWARING (*finally*). It's quite all right.
LEWIS. Have a whisky and soda, Dawson.
DAWSON. Thanks.
MRS MAINWARING (*commandingly*). Robert!

(MR MAINWARING *had been furtively making for the buffet. He turns round and places the music for her, and prepares to turn over.*)

FLORENCE. Can you see?
MRS MAINWARING (*looking expectantly at distant lamp*). I think I can manage.

(MR MAINWARING *goes towards lamp.*)

FLORENCE (*hurriedly*). Don't touch that.

(*Too late. He lifts it up. It goes out. He puts it down hurriedly. Preparatory chord.*)

LEWIS (*in a whisper*). Say when.
DAWSON (*as quietly as a gruff voice allows*). When!

(*With a glare* MRS MAINWARING *plays a rather tiresome, indefinite piece.* LEWIS *beckons to* TERESA *to operate the soda. It explodes, squirting all over the buffet.*)

ANTONIA. Ssh!

(*The piece is played to a running accompaniment of tiny noises as* LEWIS *passes plates of sandwiches, etc., amongst the Sanger family. He indicates various drinks in dumb show to* MR MAINWARING *at the piano. Latter nods and winks back, and creeps away from the piano to take the desired drink from* LEWIS *just when he should have turned over.* MRS MAINWARING *fumbles for a moment, and* FLORENCE, SIR BARTLEMY *and* MR LEYBURN *all make movements to rise and assist her.* MR MAINWARING *goes back hurriedly, but is too late. His wife has turned over for herself. As the piano piece concludes,* LEWIS *is struggling to draw the cork of a cider bottle amidst whispered directions and giggles from the Sanger girls. Amidst much interest from them, he draws it with a loud pop just in the quiet concluding passage of the music. General handclapping and applause.*)

FLORENCE. That was kind of you. Thank you. You played it beautifully.
MRS MAINWARING (*furious*). It wasn't at all good. (*With a glare at the*

*group round the buffet.*) One needs a good deal of concentration for Debussy.

(*There is a burst of laughter from the buffet.*)

DAWSON (*laughing heartily*). I heard a better one last week.

FLORENCE (*struggling bravely to keep things going*). Lewis, dear!

LEWIS. Hallo!

FLORENCE. There are lots of very thirsty people over here, too.

LEWIS. Sorry! Large supplies will arrive by special convoy immediately.

(*The group round the buffet breaks up and invades the other side of the room,* TERESA, PAULINA *and* LEWIS *carrying drinks and sandwiches. General buzz of talk.*)

ANTONIA (*to* JACOB). I'm afraid that lady is really annoyed.

JACOB. I do not wonder. It was not pretty, this accompaniment that Lewis has provided.

ANTONIA. But it's awful for poor Florence. Do let's suggest something to cheer them all up.

JACOB (*moving down Centre to* LEWIS, *who is handing round sandwiches, genially*). It is time, I think, that you shall play us something of your own, Lewis.

(*Everyone turns hopefully to* LEWIS. *Chorus of* 'Yes! Yes!' FLORENCE, *glad of the suggestion, brightens up.*)

FLORENCE. Yes, yes. Will you play now, Lewis?

MRS LEYBURN (*clapping her hands*). Yes, do play.

DAWSON. Something long and loud, Lewis.

MR LEYBURN. The longer and louder the better.

LEWIS. Very well.

(*Playing a few faint notes, thoughtfully, while they sit expectant.*)

I'll sing. (*Begins the prelude of his duet with* TERESA.)

Tessa!

TESSA. Yes? Must I sing now?

FLORENCE (*quietly to* LEWIS). You can't. It would be absurd. Tessa can't sing when we have trained singers here.

LEWIS. Trained singers?

FLORENCE (*to* TERESA). Don't put yourself forward like that again.

(TERESA *goes back to her armchair.*)

DAWSON. Come, come, Dodd! Don't be so coy! You ought as host to have opened the concert, you know.

LEWIS. Since you will have it.

(*Sitting down at the piano again and playing a grand flourish. They compose themselves to listen. Singing.*)

> There was a lady loved a swine,
>> Honey! said she,
> Pig-hog, she cried, wilt thou be mine?
>> Hunks! said he.

(*General discomfort. He sings, not to the old tune, but to a sort of operatic improvised recitative. They look puzzled.*)

MR MAINWARING (*amidst a horrified silence from everyone*). Sounds like an Irish thing. These songs about pigs, you know. You generally find they're Irish! (*Gets a look from* MRS MAINWARING *and subsides.*)

LEWIS (*beginning second verse*):
> I'll build for thee a silver sty,
>> Honey! said she.
> And in it nobly thou shalt lie.
>> Hunks! said he.

MRS LEYBURN. Is that – er – translated from the Russian?

LEWIS (*solemnly*). English traditional, madam. (*Singing the third verse.*)
> Then stay, good swine, oh, stay with me!
>> Honey, said she.
> And all my friends shall howl for thee.
>> Hunks! Hunks! Hunks! said he.

(*There is an awful pause.*)

ROBERTO. Supper *con zabaglione*.

FLORENCE (*rising austerely*). Shall we go? Millicent, will you lead the way?

(*In solemn procession the entire company stalks out silently.* LEWIS *begins very softly to play the 'Dead March'.* DAWSON *pauses at door to shake his head disapprovingly at* LEWIS. *As he swells the music louder,* TERESA *reappears in doorway.*)

TERESA. Lewis! Shut up! It's horrible.

LEWIS (*ceasing to play*). Tessa!

TERESA. Go away. You're drunk – or mad – or both.

LEWIS. Tessa!

(*She exists and closes the door behind her.* LEWIS *bangs the piano viciously.* SIR BARTLEMY, *who has remained half asleep by the fire, wakes up with a start and applauds vigorously.*)

SIR BARTLEMY. Bravo! Debussy! Charming! Charming! (*He looks round at the empty room.*) Good gad! 'Straordinary thing! Most extraordinary!

LEWIS (*from behind piano*). Not at all. It's what you all expected.

CURTAIN.


## SCENE 2

SCENE: *The drawing-room at Strand-on-the-Green. An afternoon four months later.*

TERESA *is sitting in the armchair above the fire, surrounded by school books.*

TERESA. Two minuses make a plus. But then, would two pluses make a minus? Vulgar fractions – what makes a fraction vulgar, I'd like to know? Oh dear!

(CHARLES *peeps round the door and she starts up.*)

Charles! My only uncle. What a sight for sore eyes!

CHARLES. Well, baggage? And how are you? (*Kissing her.*) Didn't you expect me? I couldn't possibly miss the great event. (*Sits in armchair.*)

TERESA (*sitting on the arm of his chair*). Of course we were expecting you. But not quite so soon. Florence is out, and Lewis is lurking in the studio like a bear with a sore head. Ikey-Mo is with him.

CHARLES. Is he jumpy about tonight?

TERESA. Not more than they usually are. He says he's either going to Brussels or Brazil as soon as it's over, to get the taste out of his mouth. Do you want to talk to him, or will you have tea with your only niece?

CHARLES. Tea.

TERESA (*after launching a shrill flood of Italian through the kitchen door*). I am your only niece, in a manner of speaking, now that Lina's gone to Paris.

CHARLES. Is she happy?

TERESA. Very. She always wanted to go on the stage – in France – because she can speak Racine.

CHARLES. I see. And you, my dear? How long are we keeping you at
Strand-on-the-Green?

TERESA. Well, I'm going to a finishing school at Harrogate in May.
But if it doesn't quite finish me I suppose I'll be back here, off and
on, for holidays, till I die.

CHARLES. Oh! Then you're relying on my daughter to house you?

TERESA. You mean – she doesn't want me here?

CHARLES. I never heard her say so. Still, as a guest, you must be a
little anxious not to overstay your welcome.

TERESA. A guest?

CHARLES. What is a guest, do you think?

TERESA. A person who's invited.

(ROBERTO *brings in a large tray with kitchen teapot, big cups, a cottage
loaf and jam in the jar. He puts it on the little table by the fire and goes
out.*)

TERESA. I said the big cups. Men like them. But Charles! Children are
forced to be somebody's guests if they have no home of their own.
It's part of the undignified state of being a child. (*Giving him some
tea.*)

CHARLES. Do you call yourself a child, young woman?

TERESA. I don't. But your daughter, Florence, does.

CHARLES. I see. (*Holding out his cup for sugar.*) Three lumps, if you
please, my dear.

TERESA. We mustn't eat too much because we're going to have dinner
early, up in town, at a restaurant near the Queen's Hall. Florence
said we'd better, so as to be sure not to be late. She's all of a
twitter, is Florence.

CHARLES. I don't wonder. It's a very great occasion. So the famous
concert has come at last. Tomorrow Lewis will be a great
conductor.

TERESA. And he will be a great composer one day. Tell me; when you
said about guests, did you mean that I ought to go away?

CHARLES. Well, what's to be done with you, my child?

TERESA. I've no vocation for anything, it seems to me. I love music.
But that's not enough. I love apples, but I don't want to be a
greengrocer. It's got to be something more than that. Something
that comes quite first, so that there isn't any question of a second.

CHARLES. And there's nothing that comes quite first with you?

TERESA. Sometimes it's a person who comes first, not a thing. That
leads to complications. (*Pause.*)

CHARLES. Oh, come! (*Holding out his cup.*) Don't tell me *you're* tragic so soon.

TERESA (*standing up and filling his cup*). Most people think I'm comic.

CHARLES. You've wit, my dear, you've intelligence, and the power of making people fond of you. I think your capacity for giving happiness must be enormous.

TERESA. Who am I to give it to?

CHARLES (*stirring his tea*). Education is a good investment.

TERESA. Are you educated?

CHARLES. Comparatively speaking – yes!

TERESA. And are you happy? Happier than an uneducated person?

(CHARLES *hesitates. He takes his spectacles off and twirls them round in a manner he has when lecturing. He has almost forgotten that she is a child.*)

CHARLES (*thoughtfully*). I can honestly say – that in such troubles as have come my way – a philosophic outlook – which is the fruit of a liberal education – has been a consolation to me.

TERESA. Could I have a philosophic outlook?

CHARLES (*remembering that she is not an undergraduate*). My dear, a certain amount of unhappiness is bound to come to all of us. But we can fortify ourselves against it by widening our interests. That is the point of education. It enlarges the resources of our minds.

TERESA. I see. Putting your eggs into several baskets instead of only one. More tea?

CHARLES. Thank you. Do you know, my dear, you're going to grow up into a very charming woman?

TERESA. Yes? And which do you prefer? A charming woman, or one who knows a lot?

CHARLES. Of course the world would stop if women weren't charming, but please God they always will be, however we educate 'em.

TERESA. Oh, I see!

CHARLES. And my dear, the most charming woman I ever knew came to grief, as it seemed to me, simply for want of a wider education – a better – regulated mind – (*Sighing.*)

TERESA (*quietly*). Was that my mother?

CHARLES. Yes, my dear.

TERESA. Were you very fond of her?

CHARLES. Very. And proud of her too.

TERESA. Did she go to a finishing school?

CHARLES. Not she!

TERESA. There you are then!

(LEWIS *and* JACOB *come in, talking eagerly.*)

JACOB. And if this concert is a success, we shall, in three weeks, give another? *Nicht Wahr?* That is a promise?

LEWIS (*genially*). I promise nothing. I never was a man to tie myself. (*To* CHARLES.) How do you do, sir? Got any tea, Tess?

TERESA. I'll send out for fresh. And Lewis, hadn't you better have something solid now? You know you'll eat nothing at dinner. You never do.

LEWIS. Not a bad idea.

(TERESA *takes teapot to the door and gives an order to* ROBERTO, *while* CHARLES *and* JACOB *shake hands.*)

CHARLES. Excellent baggage! You study your husband's stomach. I mean (*hastily*) you will study it when you have a husband.

(ROBERTO *brings in corned beef and a fresh brew of tea, and slaps them down on the table.*)

TERESA (*cutting the beef*). You think this concert's going to be a success, Ike? I don't.

JACOB. *Ach!* I tremble! And why not?

TERESA. Because the people in this country won't like the 'Symphony in Three Keys'. They'll say it hasn't any tune. I'll tell you what you ought to do, if you want Lewis to be a success. You should produce that charade we did at the Karindehütte.

JACOB. I agree. In that charade he permitted himself to write melody. It is so rare a gift. Perhaps one in ten million has got it. But he is that one.

LEWIS. If they don't like what I write they can lump it.

JACOB. Na, na! That is what Sanger has said. And (*shrugging his shoulders*) his friends must pay his debts.

LEWIS (*laughing*). That's what friends are for!

JACOB. You will write some tunes, Lewis, and then I will give you many concerts; also, perhaps, pay your debts.

LEWIS. I don't want 'em. You can't raise an orchestra over here fit for a cat to conduct.

TERESA. We've had to rescore half the Symphony as it is. Just look at what we've had to do.

(*Hands a big conductor's score off the piano to* JACOB *just as* FLORENCE *comes in dressed for the concert.*)

FLORENCE.  Why, father! I didn't know you'd come. I went straight up to dress (*kissing* CHARLES.) I hope; they've given you some tea. I've tried six shops for that Brausmann edition, Lewis. I'm afraid we must send to Germany for it.

LEWIS.  That's very good of you, my dear. I hope you haven't tired yourself out. Sit down and have some tea.

FLORENCE.  My dear! Just before dinner? I couldn't possibly.

(FLORENCE *waits till* TERESA *has vacated the place behind the teapot, then she takes it.*)

FLORENCE (*coldly to* TERESA). Thank you. (*To* JACOB.) And how is Tony?

JACOB.  Very well, thank you Mrs Dodd. She is most disappointed that she cannot come to the concert tonight. But I point out to her it will terribly disturb Lewis if our son is born in the middle of his Symphony.

FLORENCE (*hastily*). Oh, I'm sure you're wise.

TERESA.  How do you know it's going to be a son, Ike?

LEWIS.  A boy with Sanger's brains and Ike's money might set the Thames on fire.

TERESA.  Tony's afraid she'll have a daughter with Ike's face and Sanger's habits.

LEWIS.  Morbid! Very morbid! But natural to her condition. (*Waving his teacup.*) Health to the *bübchen*, Ike!

FLORENCE (*remotely to* CHARLES). They've put Lewis's Symphony last on the programme tonight. I'm not sure if it's wise.

JACOB (*rapidly turning the pages of the score which he has got on his knee*). I advised it, Mrs Dodd. My experience – *ach*, Lewis! What have you done here?

(LEWIS *looks at the score over his shoulder.*)

TERESA.  Ah, I said so. One harp won't do there, will it, Ike? He should score it for three or four.

JACOB.  But certainly! Here you have a double orchestra –

LEWIS.  You can score for forty harps, but where can I get them? I told Dawson I wanted three tonight –

FLORENCE (*trying to join in*). Dr Dawson told me he didn't think more than one was needed.

LEWIS (*ignoring her*). I said the bassoons at the end of the scherzo –

TERESA. Sanger said –

LEWIS. Quite overpowered the strings. What, Tessa?

TERESA. Sanger said the bassoons in that scherzo were like channel steamers in a fog.

(LEWIS *and* JACOB *laugh.*)

JACOB. For your next concert you shall have four harps. That I promise you.

LEWIS. You seem mighty hopeful about another concert, Ike. I expect Tessa's right. They'll howl me down.

FLORENCE. Oh, nonsense, Lewis. There's no more broad-minded public in the world than –

JACOB. *Ach,* yes! They will howl you down. But consider that in England it is a success to be howled down. Tonight they will howl, and to the next concert will come all those who have not howled to see what it is like. Every seat will be sold.

CHARLES. You call that a success?

JACOB (*simply*). For me, it will be a success.

LEWIS. You're inimitable, Ike. But tonight will be enough for me.

TERESA. Yes. If we ever get through tonight –

FLORENCE (*breaking in, in a high strained voice*). Need we go on talking about tonight? Aren't we nervous enough already?

JACOB. You are not so used to it as we, Mrs Dodd.

FLORENCE. Stop blowing on your tea, Tessa. It's vulgar.

TERESA. Sorry.

FLORENCE. And why must you drag your hair back in that way? It's terribly unbecoming. Your forehead is quite high enough as it is. Why don't you cover it?

TERESA. If I did I'd look like one of those little girls in shops, called Cash. Wouldn't I, gentlemen?

CHARLES. Personally I like the way she does her hair.

LEWIS. So do I.

JACOB. I also.

TERESA (*complacently*). My admirers are mostly of the opposite sex.

LEWIS. How many are there, Tessa?

FLORENCE. Well, there's the man who winds the clocks, and the piano tuner – and wasn't there a young man who used to follow you in the street?

TERESA. That was horrid.

FLORENCE. My dear child. You don't mind being teased, surely? Funny infant! She's got quite pink.

LEWIS. Let's see how pink she is.

TERESA (*pushing him away*). Go to hell!

LEWIS. Will she have to play hockey at Harrogate, Florence?

CHARLES. Not unless she's fit for it.

JACOB (*looking up from the score which he is still reading*). In England one must always be running about after a ball! I think the football is better than the golf ball only because it is larger.

TERESA. I think England is a detestable country. (*She goes up to the window and stands there, staring out.*)

LEWIS. So do I. I'm leaving it as soon as this concert is over, and I've a good mind never to come back.

FLORENCE. What nonsense, Lewis!

JACOB. If the concert is a success, I shall not allow you to go.

LEWIS (*to* CHARLES). Didn't Florence tell you that we had almost agreed to part?

CHARLES. It is fortunate that you can agree upon so delicate a point.

FLORENCE. Don't listen to him, Father. He's talking nonsense,.

LEWIS. I'm talking sound sense. And everyone sees it but you. You won't live permanently out of England and I won't live permanently in it.

JACOB. To live permanently anywhere must, I think, be difficult for Lewis.

FLORENCE. This is a profitless discussion. Tessa! Is that entrance paper finished?

TERESA (*without turning round*). Not yet.

FLORENCE. Then go and do it. It has to be sent in tomorrow. Go into the dining-room. And remember that you can't go out tonight unless it's finished. How much have you still left?

TERESA. Arithmetic, Scripture, and English literature.

FLORENCE. My good child! Then you'll miss the concert tonight.

LEWIS.
CHARLES. } Florence!

FLORENCE. I gave her those papers a week ago.

JACOB. But, Mrs Dodd! This concert! It is a unique occasion.

FLORENCE. It's her own fault. She wastes her time. Go along, Tessa.

TERESA. She doesn't really mean it. Her bark is worse than her bite.

FLORENCE. Yes. I do mean it. Please don't make any mistake about that.

(*She speaks so sharply that* TERESA *backs away from her frightened.*

*Everybody looks uncomfortable.* TERESA, *crestfallen, turns to go out of the room Right.*)

TERESA (*to* LEWIS *in a low voice as she goes past*). Well, if I'm not there I'll hold my thumbs for you all the time.

LEWIS (*pulling her hair*). Cheer up, Cinderella.

CHARLES. What does he mean by that?

TERESA (*darkly*). He's too clever. That's what's the matter with him. *Lieber Herr?*

CHARLES. Yes, baggage?

TERESA. May one ask how long you are staying with us?

CHARLES. About twenty hours.

TERESA. Dear me! That's uncommonly short. I'd hoped you'd stay long enough to give me a philosophic outlook.

CHARLES. You come and stay with me in Cambridge. And then – who knows?

TERESA (*nodding at him*). Who knows?

CHARLES. My housekeeper can't make tea like yours.

TERESA. Sack her. (*She runs about singing* 'Ah, say not so!')

FLORENCE. When are you going to begin that paper, Tessa?

TERESA. This very instant!

JACOB. I think you must let her come to the concert tonight Mrs Dodd. We shall all miss her so much.

FLORENCE. It rests with her. If she has finished her paper, she will come.

JACOB. Ah well! I must now go, or Tony will be impatient. *Auf Wiedersehen*, until tonight.

FLORENCE. If you want to get off before the rest of us, Lewis, you'd better dress now.

LEWIS. I'll go.

(LEWIS *gets up and goes out with* JACOB.)

CHARLES (*turning on* FLORENCE). My dear! You are heading straight for disaster. I'd no idea things were as bad as this.

FLORENCE. What do you mean?

CHARLES. Your manner to that little girl! Nothing can justify it.

FLORENCE. I think it's a pity that you encourage her, father. That pert manner may be very amusing, but it will get her into trouble later on.

CHARLES. You would get on much better if only you would treat her as if she was a reasonable person.

FLORENCE. How can I, when she behaves like a young hooligan? (*Pause.*) I don't like her.

CHARLES (*sternly*). That's the trouble. And you show it. Is that just?

FLORENCE. I've tried. But she has such a disagreeable nature. So forward – so flippant –

CHARLES. Try to see things a little from her point of view. She has only her affections and her quick wits to guide her. Fortunately these are singularly uncorrupted.

FLORENCE. You think I'm unfair?

CHARLES. I think you are, my love. And it distresses me, when I think of the generous-minded woman you used to be.

FLORENCE. Lewis thinks I'm unfair too.

CHARLES. I think he is very fond of her.

FLORENCE. He's fond of anything that is Sanger.

CHARLES. He is concerned for her happiness. You should respect that concern, Florence. He is not, I imagine, a man who feels affection easily.

FLORENCE. Thank you. I know all about Lewis and his feelings. (*Pause.*) I never thought you'd take their part against me.

CHARLES. My dear!

FLORENCE. She's the kind of girl that men always defend. The kind that's called 'a good sort'.

CHARLES. And she is a good sort.

FLORENCE. She's not. She's not to be trusted. You can't trust any of those girls. They've got bad blood in them. She'll go wrong as fast as ever she can, unless she's watched. Sometimes I wonder if already –

CHARLES. You're mad! You're letting yourself go to pieces. Don't let Lewis hear you speak like that.

FLORENCE. Why not?

CHARLES. Because, if you don't take care, you'll bully those two into making a bolt of it.

FLORENCE (*warding off the suggestion with her hand as if it was a blow*). Oh, no, no! You're quite mistaken.

CHARLES. Very well! I've warned you.

FLORENCE. He couldn't – he wouldn't –

(TERESA *comes in, clutching a pile of school books.*)

What do you want? I thought I told you to go to the dining-room.

TERESA. There's no fire there. I'm cold. Can't work here?

FLORENCE (*to* CHARLES). Hadn't you better go and dress now, Father? We'll be starting very soon.

CHARLES. Perhaps I had. I'll hurl my clothes on and then I'll come and do your sums for you, my dear.

(CHARLES *exits*.)

(ROBERTO *comes in to clear away tea*.)

FLORENCE. Lay out cold supper before you go, Roberto?

TERESA. Are you going to the concert, Roberto. Lucky hound.

FLORENCE (*in Italian*). And leave everything as usual.

ROBERTO. *Si*, madame!

(ROBERTO *goes out*.)

TERESA. Florence! I can't stay all by myself in the house.

FLORENCE. I think it's better in any case that you should stay quietly at home. You're not looking well. You'd only have palpitations at the concert.

TERESA. Really I'm quite well.

FLORENCE. And another time perhaps you'll stick to your work better.

TERESA. Oh! (*With a little sob*.) There won't be another time. Florence! Listen! I must go!

FLORENCE (*coldly*). I shan't take you.

TERESA. Then I shall go by myself. I've got money. I shall go the minute you've left the house.

FLORENCE. You will not – either at this or at any other time.

(*Re-enter* CHARLES *in a dressing-gown*.)

CHARLES. Florence, I have forgotten my dress studs.

FLORENCE (*smiling*). Have you ever remembered them on any visit you ever paid, Father?

CHARLES. These public functions are most detestable things.

FLORENCE. I think I know where Lewis has some. I'll look.

(FLORENCE *exits with* CHARLES. TERESA, *left alone, puts her head down on the table and sobs. Hearing someone coming, she pulls herself together, and bends over her sums.* LEWIS, *with his clothes flung on anyhow and his hair on end, rushes in waving a tie*.)

LEWIS. Florence! This tie – Oh, it's you, Tess! Tie it for me, there's a good girl!

TERESA (*dealing with it*). Do you remember that concert in Paris when we had to make you a tie out of my hair ribbon?

LEWIS. Where are the snows of yesteryear?

TERESA (*patting tie and standing back*). There!

LEWIS. Am I neat?

TERESA. You look like a calf going garlanded to the sacrifice. Never mind! It'll soon be over.

LEWIS. Very soon. Where shall we be this time tomorrow?

TERESA. You'll be in Brussels or Brazil, unless you're an almighty liar. By the way, you might pass your eye over this sum of mine. I've papered this room nine times and –

LEWIS. Why do it at all?

TERESA. The answer comes out that it would take five million yards of paper to paper a room twenty foot square. Is that right?

LEWIS. Let me look at it. My good girl! You've papered it absolutely solid. You needn't find the cubic contents of the room. (*Doing the sum.*) Of course you'll run away, I suppose?

TERESA. I've nowhere to run.

LEWIS (*picking up another exercise book*). What's this?

TERESA. Leave that alone! That's my diary.

LEWIS. Let me, Tessa!

(TERESA *snatches book away.*)

I was reading something about myself! Am I often mentioned?

TERESA. Sometimes. (*Sitting on it.*) Let's get on with these sums. 'Two trains are passing one another at equal rates' – Oh dear! Oh dear! What shall I do? What shall I do? I can't! I can't bear it!

LEWIS. Come with me! Dearest, dearest Tessa! Don't cry! Don't let them make you cry! Come with me!

TERESA (*tearfully*). Come with you? Where?

LEWIS. Anywhere. Brussels! When I go after the concert.

TERESA. Florence would never allow it.

LEWIS (*taken aback*). No. You'd have to do it without leave.

TERESA. You mean, really, that we should run away?

LEWIS. Yes. I shall catch the night boat. Couldn't you get away and come too?

TERESA. Well! There are points in it. (*Pause.*) It's nice of you to be so concerned about me.

LEWIS. No. Not very nice of me. It's for my own sake that I want you to come.

TERESA. Couldn't you let me have it in plain English?

LEWIS. In plain English, I love you. You're too dear to leave behind.

TERESA. Love me? What do you mean by that? There's a song: *Away,*

*false man, I know thou lov'st! I know thou lov'st too many.* Why did
you marry Florence?

LEWIS. You know why.

TERESA. Yes, I do know. If you loved me, it was unfair to both of us.
That's why I'm complaining.

LEWIS. It's done now.

TERESA. And you want it undone. Why couldn't you have thought of
all this before? You were so mad to get her that you forgot all about
me. If you'd waited a bit –

LEWIS. If I'd waited – then – then – Oh, Tessa, say it!

TERESA. I loved you. Of course I did. I promised myself to you ever so
long ago, when first I ever began to think about love. I thought
then that I wouldn't ever love any man but you. And I don't think I
ever will. But it's too late now.

LEWIS. No. It's not too late if you still love me.

TERESA. What's that got to do with it? I can't, now. Because of
Florence. You belong to her. I'd feel mean. She's been very good
to me, though lately she's been a bit snappy, and I don't wonder,
with you going on the way you do.

LEWIS. She's treated you abominably.

TERESA. Still, I'd feel very mean if I ran off with her husband.
(*Grandly, holding her diary.*) The pangs of unappeased remorse
would gnaw my vitals.

LEWIS. I should think it was obvious to anyone that Florence and I
can't get on together. We must part. I expect she'll be very glad to
get rid of me.

TERESA. I expect she will. But that's not my affair. I'm not saying you
hadn't better go. And if you go I expect you'll want another wife.
But she can't be me. Everybody would say we'd been carrying on
here behind poor Florence's back. Really I couldn't. I don't want
to be a viper in anybody's bosom.

LEWIS. Will you stop talking in that strain?

TERESA. It's a very good strain. A person must do what they think
right, mustn't they?

LEWIS. You have changed, these last months!

TERESA. I suppose I have. It's not my fault. Nobody can help
changing. Things are done to us and we change. I'm sorry I ever
came to England and this life. But as I'm here I'd better stay and
see it through. I shall stay until I have a philosophic outlook.

LEWIS. What's the good of that if you're unhappy?

TERESA (*in the voice of* CHARLES). A certain amount of unhappiness is bound to come to every one of us. (*Softly.*) I don't believe we'd escape it, Lewis, in one another's company.

LEWIS. Nor do I. But I want your company.

TERESA. Then want must be your master. I've said my say.

LEWIS. There's been plenty of it.

TERESA. Well, you want to know such a lot.

LEWIS. Only one thing. And I don't know it yet. Do you still love me?

TERESA (*provocatively*). M'm.

LEWIS. Say 'Cross-my-heart-hope-I-may-die-if-I-don't.'

TERESA. Cross-my-heart – he thought I should, yes, but I shan't! (*Edging away to the door, whisks out before he has time to catch her.*)

(*He finds her diary, however, left on stool, and takes it up to the window to read. Stands there, reading and looking out at the river.* FLORENCE, *in an opera cloak, comes in.*)

FLORENCE. Lewis! I thought you'd gone.

LEWIS (*absently, still reading diary*). Not yet.

FLORENCE. Lewis – are you going away tonight? If – if you feel you want a little holiday alone, I shall understand. This concert – I know it's a strain.

LEWIS (*looking at her in surprise. Then, throwing the diary on the divan and crossing to her*). Yes. I am going. It's generous of you to understand. (*Putting out his hand abruptly. She places her hand in his.*) Florence! I'm afraid – you've had a poor time of it with me.

FLORENCE (*gently*). I've made mistakes, perhaps.

LEWIS (*excitedly*). Florence! When I'm gone I wish you could be better friends with her.

FLORENCE (*shrinking*). With Tessa?

LEWIS (*eagerly*). Everybody loves her, I think, who really knows her. If you knew how she speaks and thinks of you, then you'd love her too. I don't think you quite understand how – how good she is.

FLORENCE. No, I don't quite understand.

LEWIS. But try! Do try! This marriage of ours has been a wretched business. I'd better go away. I've only made you unhappy and I should go on making you unhappy. But the worst of it is that somehow I've put you and Tessa against each other.

FLORENCE. Oh, Lewis! Lewis! What does Tessa matter just now? This is the great moment in your career. And you will go on harping about Tessa, who doesn't really concern you at all.

LEWIS. She does concern me enormously. I love her so much! I want

to be sure she'll be happy when I've gone away. What can I say?
You're so much better fitted to love each other, you two, than
I am to have anything to do with either of you. Oh, Florence! If
only I could be sure of this, I'd go away and say God bless you
both.

FLORENCE. Since when have you loved her so terribly?

LEWIS. I can't remember. Always, I suppose.

FLORENCE. Why, then, did you marry me?

LEWIS. I was a fool.

FLORENCE. Does she know?

LEWIS. Yes. She knows. And you knew it too? Didn't you? Didn't
you? You've known it for a long time. And you were angry because
I didn't speak the truth about it, weren't you?

FLORENCE. You may as well tell me the whole story. What exactly has
there been between you?

LEWIS. I've told you. I love her.

FLORENCE. What do you mean by that? Is she your mistress?

LEWIS. Florence! No! she's not. She won't have anything to do with
me, because of you. I've told you.

FLORENCE (*deliberately*). I don't believe you.

LEWIS. It's true. She would never be so unjust to you.

FLORENCE (*her voice rising*). I've seen enough of the whole pack of you
to know that you can't be trusted.

LEWIS. You're making a wicked mistake.

FLORENCE (*suddenly losing control and turning on him*). I think she's
too – too contemptible! She's no better than Tony. Yet I don't
blame her. She's just an unfortunate little animal. It's you I'll never
forgive.

LEWIS. Oh, yes, you would, my dear. You'd forgive me anything.

FLORENCE. Never again after this! Never again!

LEWIS. Oh, yes! As often as I want. (*Seizing her by the shoulders.*) You
would. You would. I needn't have married you. You'd have taken
me without.

FLORENCE. I hate you! I loathe you!

LEWIS. Women like you are fond of saying that. It means nothing. I
know your sort. You've pretty ways. You go about as if the earth
wasn't good enough for you. But you'll eat dirt to get the man you
want. There's nothing you won't stoop to.

FLORENCE (*hoarsely*). Get away! Get out!

LEWIS. And when you've got him you want to make him as low as

yourselves. You want to shut him up. Like a caged beast. In a sty.
A silver sty.

FLORENCE. I hope you treat her like this. I hope you make her suffer
like this.

LEWIS. Tessa? (*Flinging her from him.*) She's not like the rest of you.
She has some pride. If I tried my fascinating ways on her, she'd
give me a black eye.

FLORENCE. Go! Go! I've done with you!

(TERESA *taps on the door and appears, looking rather frightened. A dull
pause.*)

LEWIS. Hallo, Tessa.

TERESA. Who won the Battle of Waterloo?

LEWIS. That I'll never know. Shakespeare when he crossed the Alps.

(LEWIS *exits.* FLORENCE *crosses to the glass over the mantelpiece and
stares at herself.*)

TERESA (*hesitating a moment*). Florence! The taxi is here. Charles is
waiting. (FLORENCE *stares at her silently.*) Florence! Why are you so
cruel to me? You don't mean that I mustn't come to the concert?
Not really?

FLORENCE (*still partially stunned*). What?

TERESA (*both hands pressed over her heart*). I won't have palpitations. I
won't give any trouble. But Lewis would be so disappointed if –

(*The front door is heard to bang.*)

FLORENCE. Lewis is gone.

TERESA. Gone? Oh! (*Bursts into tears.*) And he's never coming back! I
never even said goodbye!

FLORENCE What's that to you? Aren't you ashamed of yourself?

TERESA (*in surprise*). Ashamed?

FLORENCE (*quick and low*). Yes! Ashamed! Do you think I haven't
seen – what's been going on all these months?

TERESA. What's been going on?

FLORENCE. I'll speak this once and then we'll never mention this
again. Teresa, you must know that among decent people, the
woman who openly pursues a man, especially a man who doesn't
particularly care for her, is despised by everybody.

TERESA. I haven't been pursuing a man who doesn't particularly care
for me. I agree with you. It's a mug's game.

FLORENCE. It's obvious that I should have to take you to task for your
   manner to my husband –

TERESA. I'll have to take you to task for your manner to me. I don't
   think you really mean it, but I won't have these things said to me.
   It's not my fault that I love Lewis. I did long before you came to
   the Tyrol. It isn't a happy thing at all. It's brought nothing but
   sadness into my life. But it's so much all of me that I couldn't want
   it to be different any more than I could want to be changed into
   another person. And I've come to understand lately that, now he's
   your husband, I'd better not see him any more. That's why I've
   agreed to go away.

FLORENCE. Agreed! You're going because I mean to put an end to
   this – this disgraceful intrigue.

TERESA (*alarmed*). I don't understand! Intrigue! (*Backing away.*)
   You're making a mistake. Something terrible has happened! You
   don't mean all this. Because I love him –

FLORENCE (*taking a step towards her*). Don't you dare to speak of love.
   You don't know what it means.

TERESA (*with a sigh*). I know all about it.

FLORENCE (*her voice rising*). What do you mean by that? (*Seizes*
   TERESA'*s wrists and pushes her back.*) What do you mean?

TERESA Don't! Don't! What's the matter with you, Florence?

FLORENCE. What do you mean?

TERESA. Don't look at me like that! I've done you no harm.

FLORENCE (*almost screaming*). I knew it. I've always known it. You've
   betrayed me, the pair of you – under my very roof – all these
   nights – when I thought he was working. In my house – my own
   house!

TERESA. Well, then, let me get out of your home.

FLORENCE (*beside herself*). How often has he – ? D'you know the name
   for girls like you?

TERESA (*terrified*). Florence! Stop! I'm not! I'm not!

FLORENCE. Yes, you are! You're a harlot! A harlot! Just a common
   little tart, and nothing else!

(CHARLES *is heard calling for* FLORENCE *outside.* FLORENCE *exits
locking the door.* TERESA *crosses and bangs on the door, then runs from
the door to the window in frantic distress.*)

TERESA. Let me out! Oh, let me out! (*Staggering up to window clutching
her heart and gasping; she is just going to jump from the window when a
key clicks in the door.*)

(ROBERTO *appears in his best clothes and a bowler, carrying an umbrella.*)

ROBERTO. *Scusi!* She forgetta to locka me in too!

(*He grins broadly and holds out her party frock. With a sobbing laugh she falls on his neck.*)

TERESA. Roberto! Dear Roberto!

CURTAIN.


# ACT III

## SCENE 1

SCENE: *The Artistes' Room at Queen's Hall, London. A somewhat cheerless room, although brightly lighted by wall brackets by the fireplace Right. It is possible to hear music and applause whenever the door is opened. Door down Left leads to gentlemen's dressing-rooms.*

*An* USHER *sitting at the table is pricking off winners in the racing column of a newspaper. The* HALL FIREMAN *comes in through doors. A strain of music is wafted in with him.*

FIREMAN. Just finishing, mate!

USHER. Right oh! (*Folding up paper in a leisurely manner.*)

FIREMAN. They seem to like this one.

USHER. Looks like it. These young fellers are all alike to me. They used to 'ave long names and long 'air; an' now they 'ave short names and short 'air. That's about all.

FIREMAN. Ah! These young artists! They don't know what work is. Why, I can remember Sousa – What's yer fancy for the National? They tell me a good double –

USHER. I never give tips. I got my own troubles.

FIREMAN. I suppose we shall 'ave the usual crowd 'ere in a minute.

USHER. Funny thing! All the years I bin 'ere, I never hear anyone say anything new.

FIREMAN. Ah! There's a queer fish 'ere. Found 'im trying to get down the gallery emergency. Didn't seem to understand when I told 'im it was locked. Eye-talian by the looks of 'im.

USHER. What's he want?

USHER. That's the conductor.

FIREMAN (*indifferently*). Oh, 'im! Come in, Jacko.

(ROBERTO *comes in, excited and mysterious*.)

ROBERTO. *Scusi!* When concerto 'e finish, I musta see Mr Dodd. Yes. It is ver' important.

USHER. You give me the message. I'll see he gets it.

ROBERTO. No! No! It is ver' important. I have-a da young lady for 'im. She wait 'ere? Yes?

USHER. Who are you?

ROBERTO. *Scusi?* I am da butler. I ver' important.

(TERESA, *looking pale and ill, appears at back. She carries a brown paper parcel, already half burst open*.)

(*Grandly*.) Dis is da Signorina!

TERESA. Ssh! Roberto! Don't make such a noise. It isn't over yet. Listen! (*She stands enraptured, showing on her face that she knows every bar of* LEWIS's *Symphony. Nodding her head sagely*.) He's doing it very nicely.

USHER. Look 'ere, miss! You've no business –

TERESA (*imperiously*). Ssh! Now the last four bars! (*In a moment the Symphony ceases*.) Oh, grand! Bravo, Lewis! (*In her excitement she drops her parcel, clasping her hands together*.)

ROBERTO. *Magnifico! Magnifico!*

TERESA. Shut up! Listen! Don't they like it?

(*An anxious moment, and then a perfectly deafening burst of applause*.)

FIREMAN. Look out! Here they come! (*He disappears down the corridor*.)

TERESA (*suddenly panic-stricken*). I must wait! I must wait till they've all gone! It'd only upset everybody.

ROBERTO (*watching at door of corridor*). Kvick! He comes. Others comes too.

TERESA. Where can I go? Quick?

USHER. You'll 'ave me in the Divorce and Probate before you've done. 'Ere you are. Pop in the 'Gents cloaks'. Nobody'll look for you there.

TERESA. Give him this, Roberto. (*Giving* ROBERTO *a little note and disappearing through door down Left*.)

(LEWIS, *moving like a man in a dream, charges into the room and pulls up at the sight of* ROBERTO.)

LEWIS. Roberto! Do you have to be here?

ROBERTO. *Magnifico*, Lewis! *Magnifico!* Ah! I wish so much that
Sanger was here.

LEWIS. You heard it, then?

ROBERTO. *Si, si.* In Balcone. Alla your friends here tonight, I tink.

LEWIS (*with a sudden look of grief*). One wasn't.

ROBERTO (*gleefully*). No, no! You make-a mistake. *Ecco!* (*Holding up
the note.*)

LEWIS. From Tessa?

ROBERTO. *Si!*

LEWIS. Did she come after all? I wish I'd known. (*Tearing open note
and reading.*) Oh, bring her down. As fast as ever you can. Quick!

(ROBERTO *bursts into laughter.*)

USHER (*touching* LEWIS *on the shoulder*). Going on, sir? They're
shouting yer.

LEWIS. Let 'em. I've a train to catch.

USHER. But, sir!

LEWIS. Go on yourself.

USHER. Work before play. Ain't that right, Jacko?

LEWIS. Oh, all right. Look here! There's a young lady I'm expecting.

USHER (*with a knowing smile*). Oh, yes, sir?

LEWIS. Shut up! You don't understand. Look after her till I come
back.

USHER. Well, it's not my business to –

LEWIS. Here! Take this! (*Gives* USHER *coin.*)

USHER (*looking at it*). Excuse me, sir! That's a na'a'penny!

LEWIS. Lord! Lord! (*Gives him half a crown and hurries to double doors.*)
When you've got her, mount guard at the door, Roberto, and don't
budge.

(*Exit.*)

USHER (*looking after him*). Mad! Mad as a Natter.

(TERESA'*s head appears round the cloakroom door. The* USHER *waves
her back.* ROBERTO *firmly plants himself in the very middle of the
doorway.*)

USHER. 'Ere, Jacko! Shift a bit. Nobody can't git past you.

ROBERTO (*very excited*). I will notta go. I will stay 'ere alla da night. I
have been told to stay, and I will stay.

USHER. Oh, Lord! Come 'ere! Wait 'ere! *Restez là!*

ROBERTO. You spik French?

USHER. When it's wanted. (*Loftily.*)

(*A crowd of excited people are talking in the passage outside and pushing into the room, including* DAWSON, SIR BARTLEMY, MILLICENT, *the* LEYBURNS *and* MAINWARINGS. *Applause goes on, off stage, throughout the scene.*)

DAWSON. Well, Pugh? Never heard such a filthy hullabaloo in your life, did you?

SIR BARTLEMY. Every young man writes one symphony as bad as that. Our friend Dodd is no exception.

DAWSON. So that's your line?

SIR BARTLEMY. He'll get over it. I wrote something very like that myself once.

DAWSON (*derisively*). I don't believe you!

MILLICENT. Personally I feel as if I'd fallen down three flights of stairs. It's not like any music I ever heard.

DAWSON. No, madam. But it's like music that you will hear.

SIR BARTLEMY. My dear Dawson!

DAWSON. I'm not yer dear Dawson.

SIR BARTLEMY. Beauty and violence cannot exist together.

DAWSON. They're inseparable.

(MRS LEYBURN *claps her hands at this pronouncement, trying to look like a Bacchante, in spite of a Liberty scarf.*)

MRS LEYBURN. But surely, Sir Bartlemy, you'll admit that he's a magnificent conductor.

(MILLICENT *moves up with* MRS MAINWARING.)

SIR BARTLEMY. Able! Very able!

DAWSON. Finest conducting we've seen here since Richter retired. (*Going to look out.*) Have those fellows in there eaten him? Oh, no –

(*Makes way for* LEWIS, *who drifts back into the room, quite bewildered to find so many people there. The whole company fall upon him. A babel ensues, people saying their lines together.*)

MILLICENT ⎫ (*together*) ⎧ Congratulations, Lewis! You've set 'em all by the ears.
MR LEYBURN ⎭          ⎩ Bravo! Bravo! The most marvellous thing that ever happened!

LEWIS (*politely and absently*). Thank you!

MRS MAINWARING. I'm so proud to think that I've been at your first English concert.

MR MAINWARING. Jolly good I call it. Jolly fine. Afraid I don't know much about it, you know, but it knocked 'em all right.

LEWIS. Thank you.

MRS LEYBURN. It's a great moment in our lives.

SIR BARTLEMY. Most interesting. It's been most interesting.

LEWIS. Thank you. (*Catching the eye of* DAWSON *and coming to the surface for a moment.*) Dawson! That first fiddle of yours is a fool. You ought to sack him.

MR LEYBURN (*squeaking*). It was amazing! It's gone to my head like –

MRS MAINWARING. Like champagne!

SIR BARTLEMY. H'm! Raw spirit!

MR LEYBURN. I want to shout! I want to sing! I want to throw my hat in the air. I want to run into Oxford Street and knock policemen on the head! He is the one god, and I am his prophet.

DAWSON (*in an audible undertone*). Can nothing be done to stop that fellow? (*Going to* LEWIS.) What's that? From an admirer, signed 'Lover of Good Music'. You mustn't start that game. (*Indicating note, which is still in* LEWIS'*s hand.*)

LEWIS (*crushing up note in hand*). I'm not starting anything. Are they going to stop here all night, Dawson?

DAWSON (*catching sight of* LEWIS'*s face*). Lord, man! Have you come into a legacy?

LEWIS (*in a low voice*). Something like it.

(JACOB, CHARLES *and* FLORENCE *come in.*)

JACOB (*shouting*). A thousand million bravoes. It is a great beginning! Not one of them know what to think, what to say. You will, tomorrow, be famous.

LEWIS (*in a gale of high spirits, parodying* JACOB'*s manner*). *Ach mein lieb würdig Birnbaum! Wunderbar! Erstaunlich! Ach! ich bin so glücklich! Ach, wie glücklich bin ich!*

JACOB. *Ja, ja!* But listen to them, how they are shouting!

CHARLES. A thousand congratulations, Lewis! I don't know one note from another, but I can see that you've succeeded in frightening the farmyard.

LEWIS (*radiant, nearly shaking his arm off*). Thank you, sir! Thank you!

(FLORENCE *comes to* LEWIS *a little shyly, and trying to seem casual. She is mortally afraid that he will make a scene, and she wants to secure an immediate retreat if he does.*)

FLORENCE. I had to come, Lewis, to tell you how very good it was.

LEWIS (*in his polite, sleepwalker's tone*). Thank you! (*He suddenly disentangles her from the mass of people who are harassing him, and looks astonished.*) Florence! You here?

FLORENCE (*very brightly and nervously*). Yes! Me here!

USHER (*moving down between* FLORENCE *and* LEWIS). You'll have to take another call, sir. They're shouting the place down.

LEWIS. What? Again? Oh, all right.

(LEWIS *goes off again.*)

FLORENCE (*to* MILLICENT). He doesn't approve of relations coming round, you know. I really came because I want to make up a little party.

MR LEYBURN. Bravo! Let's celebrate! By all means!

FLORENCE. I've collected some people already – they're waiting in the foyer. Dr Dawson! You'll come, won't you.

DAWSON. I'll go anywhere where I can get a drink.

MRS LEYBURN. Let's be really Bohemian for once and go to the Eiffel Tower!

FLORENCE. Oh, yes! Let's! And you must all be my guests, please! Lydia! You'll come? And Roberto? And you, Mr Birnbaum?

MILLICENT (*maliciously*). Will Lewis come?

FLORENCE. I think we must persuade him.

(LEWIS *comes back, his tie more crooked than ever.*)

JACOB (*again falling upon him*). *Ach!* It is as I have said! They will all scream at you, and the next concert will be packed. Now I arrange it. The next concert –

LEWIS. There won't be a next concert, Ike. I'm going away.

ALL. Going away?

JACOB. *Ach*, you must not go away! Listen! In three weeks, another concert here. And then to Hamburg for the festival –

LEWIS (*looking again at the letter, which he still holds in his hand, and smiling a little*). No, no. No more concerts here. I'm not coming back here any more. I have to go. At once.

(*Throughout the ensuing contest he is never violent, but he speaks with the absolute determination of a man who is under the influence of a completely dominating passion.* TERESA *and music have become identified in his mind, and both are drawing him away. The conflict is over, and these people, including* FLORENCE, *are so unimportant that he has no need to fight them.*)

MR LEYBURN. You mustn't go, Dodd! You must stay here with us. We are your people now.

LEWIS (*shaking his head*). No. You're not my people.

JACOB. Your fate must keep you here! You cannot fight it.

LEWIS. My fate must take me away, and I'm in a hurry.

DAWSON. Don't be a jackass.

SIR BARTLEMY (*unable to help joining in*). Really, Dodd! Don't you think this is very unwise?

LEWIS. I've never been wise before.

JACOB. But it is madness! It is raving madness! You will lose all that you have gained.

CHARLES. Is this a good moment to discuss this question? I should have thought tomorrow –

JACOB. Yes, yes. This is not the time. Tomorrow we will speak of this again.

LEWIS. I'm sorry, Ike. I'm afraid I must go tonight.

MILLICENT. How like Lewis! He always upsets his own apple-cart. When he was six weeks old he was sick all over his rich godfather. And that's been his line ever since.

JACOB. Can you do nothing, Mrs Dodd? Can you not reason with him?

FLORENCE. I think, perhaps if you'd all go on, up into the foyer, and wait for me, I could do better with him alone.

MR LEYBURN. Florence! You're a woman in a thousand! That's what we'll do. We'll leave him to his wife!

(*They all hurry out, speaking as they go.*)

MRS LEYBURN. It will make a very bad impression if he goes now.
MR LEYBURN. Fatal! Absolutely fatal! } (*The first couple to go out.*)

MRS MAINWARING. He can't really mean it.
SIR BARTLEMY. When I was young we didn't make hay of our best opportunities like this. } (*Second couple to go passing* DAWSON.)

DAWSON. You never were young, my friend.

MR MAINWARING. It's what they  
  call temperament, I suppose. ⎫  
MILLICENT (*spitefully*). Then we'll   ⎬ (*The third couple to go.*)  
  expect you both to join   ⎭  
  us in a *very* few minutes?

DAWSON (*going*). If all else fails, put him into handcuffs! (*Exits with*  
  JACOB.)

(*They leave* CHARLES *and* FLORENCE *alone.*)

CHARLES. My dear, my dear! Is this wise?

FLORENCE. Father! I must. (*Very much excited.*) You don't  
  understand. Go on with the others. Please!

CHARLES. You'll do no good now. Wait till he's calmed down a bit.

(LEWIS *comes back with his baton in his hand.*)

FLORENCE. If I wait I shall be too late. (*Sitting chair Right of table.*)  
  Father! I entreat you! If you ever loved me –

(CHARLES *exits.*)

Lewis!

LEWIS (*again in his dream*). Yes?

FLORENCE. I've arranged a little party, all our friends. Won't you  
  come?

LEWIS (*staring round*). Where are they all?

FLORENCE. Listen. I – I – I've been in the wrong. I want to say I'm  
  sorry. (*Pause.*) I came to the concert tonight, full of bitterness  
  and hatred. I felt that the whole of our life together has been a  
  failure.

LEWIS. So it has.

FLORENCE. It's been largely my fault. I'd forgotten – why I married  
  you. But when I heard your Symphony tonight – I remembered.  
  It's been – it's been so wonderful. Lewis! I'm ready to try again, if  
  you will.

LEWIS. Try again?

FLORENCE. This great success! This wonderful moment in your life.  
  Don't throw it all away, just because a few bitter words passed  
  between us this evening.

LEWIS (*with an effort*). What are you talking about? (*Remembering.*)  
  This evening! Oh, that!

FLORENCE. It does seem a long time ago, doesn't it?

LEWIS. Too long ago to remember.

FLORENCE (*stumbling a little over the difficult words*). I – I expect I was unjust to Tessa.

LEWIS. That doesn't matter now. I'm sorry, Florence. We can't talk about this. All that's over.

FLORENCE. What can I say to you?

LEWIS. Nothing.

FLORENCE. It's like talking to someone on another planet. My aunt stuck to Sanger – through everything. What she could bear, I can bear. But for your own sake, don't leave England just now.

LEWIS. It's too late now.

FLORENCE. Oh, don't hate me so!

LEWIS. I don't hate you, Florence. (*A little wildly.*) But we must save ourselves, mustn't we?

FLORENCE. For God's sake, wait till tomorrow. Till we can talk of this more calmly. I haven't loved you enough; that's been the trouble. But if we can love enough, if we can hold on to what's best in us, as you do – as you do in your music – perhaps we could come through to something that wasn't hatred. Wait till tomorrow.

LEWIS (*hesitating*). What do you mean? How can I wait –

FLORENCE. Oh! (*Stretching out her arms to him, transfigured, as her great moment comes to her.*) Love her! Love her if you must, but love her enough!

(*A small pale-faced clerk sidles in with a book and a fountain pen.*)

CLERK. Mr Dodd?

LEWIS. Hallo?

CLERK. Might I have your autograph, please?

USHER (*entering*). Now then! What's all this? 'Ow did you get in? You must know it ain't allowed.

CLERK. I didn't know. I've been waiting in the corridor. I've been there an hour.

USHER. Serves you right. No business there at all.

LEWIS. He's all right. Here you are. (*Bending over and signing the book.*)

FLORENCE. Lewis!

CHARLES. Florence! Your guests are all waiting in the foyer. Shall I tell them to go on without you?

FLORENCE (*distractedly*). Oh, tell them to wait – to go – No, I'll come and explain. Wait for me, Lewis! I won't go on without you.

(*Going out with* CHARLES, *turning and looking back reluctantly from the doorway.*)

LEWIS (*signing*). There! (*Turning pages.*) What's this?

CLERK. That's George Robey. Here's Lloyd George. I've got two of him. Hobbs, Steve Donoghue, Melba, Trotsky, du Maurier, Delysia. I waited three hours to get that.

USHER. Here! Come on! 'Op it!

> (*The* CLERK *exits,* USHER *following him up.*)

LEWIS (*seeing* ROBERTO). Quick, Roberto! Where is she?

(ROBERTO *flinging open the door proudly,* TERESA *enters.*)

TERESA. Lewis!

LEWIS. Tessa!

> (*They fly into one another's arms.* ROBERTO *and* USHER *exchange glances, and slip out.*)

TERESA. I thought they'd never go!

LEWIS. Oh, Tessa, Tessa! That's over! Thank God, that's over.

TERESA (*drawing his head to her breast, and soothing him as if he had been a child*). Yes, yes, it's all over now. You needn't worry with them any more.

LEWIS. How was it, Tessa? Was it all right?

TERESA. Magnificent! Sanger ought to have been here.

LEWIS. Really?

TERESA. Oh, my darling, my baby, my funny little child, my lover –

LEWIS. I'm dreaming.

TERESA. No, you're not. I'm yours. I love you. Oh, if you knew how much I love you! And all these months, when I've been finding out what I could give you. It was all crushed down and wasted. But now we'll go away and never, never, never come back.

LEWIS (*anxiously*). Can we! Can we ever get away?

TERESA. Of course we can. By the Ostend boat. If we're quick.

LEWIS. As easily as that.

> (*The* USHER *comes in again, coughing discreetly, followed by the* FIREMAN.)

USHER. Excuse me, sir. You'd better not go by the artists' entrance. If you want to get away quietly you'd better use the Royal entrance.

LEWIS. Right! The Royal entrance, Tessa! Just a minute.

> (*Going into the cloakroom for hat and suitcase.* TERESA *sinks exhausted for a moment into chair by the table.*)

USHER (*looking at her*). Looks blue, don't she? (*To* FIREMAN.) Got anything, Alf?

FIREMAN. 'Ere, missie! You 'ave a drop o' my good hot cocoa. (*Produces it from a peg behind the door, where also hangs his night lantern.*)

(LEWIS *comes back with suitcase.*)

LEWIS. Yes, drink it, Tessa. It'll buck you up.

TERESA. Is there time? The boat train goes at eleven-thirty.

USHER. Boat! Why, you're never going on a boat tonight!

FIREMAN. You run back to your ma, missie, and get her to tuck you in bed. You'll be safe there.

TERESA (*drinking*). I haven't got a ma.

USHER. Dear me!

TERESA (*bravely*). I'm quite used to this sort of thing. I was born in a room like this.

USHER. You don't say.

TERESA. Oh, well! Not quite, but nearly. I was born in the middle of a first performance of one of my father's operas.

FIREMAN. Very uncomfortable for your ma, that must have been.

(ROBERTO *runs in very excited.*)

ROBERTO. Lewis! Tessa! Kvick! Madame! She come back. She stop you eef you don't go.

LEWIS. How did you know we were going?

ROBERTO. By da heart. It tella me everything. Besides, I listen. Always I listen. All da time!

LEWIS. I see. Here! (*Taking baton from table and giving it to him.*) You can use this to stir the puddings with.

ROBERTO. Excuse! Please! Madame would not allow –

LEWIS. Wouldn't she! Well, then she'd better have it herself. Come, Tessa –

USHER. This way, then.

FIREMAN. Them lights are all out by now. Here! Where's my glim? I'll show yer royal 'ighness the way.

ROBERTO. Lewis! Teresa! I wish you ver' happy, ver' rich, and many many *bambini*. Some day I shall come to serve you. Teresa! Da gift for *la sposa!* (*Producing an old shoe.*) It belong to Sanger. (*Flinging it over* TERESA's *head with a shout of laughter.*)

LEWIS (*sardonically*). Aha! I knew there was a slipper in this story somewhere.

TERESA (*flinging her arms round* ROBERTO). Goodbye, darling Roberto!

(LEWIS *and* TERESA *move up to door, followed by* ROBERTO.)

USHER. Goodbye, missie. Good luck!

FIREMAN (*who has been quietly tearing up the* USHER'*s newspaper*).
We're out of weddin' bells (*chuckling*), but here's the confetti.
(*Suddenly throws pieces of the newspaper over them.*)

LEWIS. Goodbye, Roberto.

TERESA. The train! The train!

THE MEN. Goodbye! Goodbye!

(*In a whirl of laughter and goodbyes* LEWIS, TERESA *and the* USHER
*disappear down the corridor. The lights flicker in and out several times as
a signal of closing.* FLORENCE *appears from the end of the corridor.*
ROBERTO *handing her the baton. She turns and walks out slowly,
between* FIREMAN *and* ROBERTO, *just as the lights give one more flicker
and then go out entirely, leaving only the* FIREMAN'*s lantern.*)

CURTAIN.


## SCENE 2

SCENE: *A dingy top-floor bedroom in a boarding-house in Brussels. It has a
sash window on Left with a broken roller blind and some dirty lace curtains.
The panes of glass are so dirty that they obscure the view, which, in any event,
would only be of rooftops and church spires. There is a simple iron bedstead in
the middle of the room, end-on to the audience. The coverings are not attractive. The door is up Right. Between door and bedstead is chest of drawers. A
box-couch at the foot of the bed; a chair or two.*

*The door is flung open.* MADAME MARXSE, *an enormous, coarse Belgian
woman, enters, ushering in* LEWIS *and* TERESA. TERESA *is very exhausted;
she clutches in her hands a brown paper parcel, burst open at one end, and in
the other the exercise book containing her diary.* LEWIS *supports her with one
hand; in the other he carries a small, much-battered suitcase, well plastered
with hotel labels. He leads* TERESA *to the box-couch, where she sinks
exhausted, while* MADAME MARXSE *goes on talking.* MADAME *should speak
with a thick Flemish accent.*

MADAME MARXSE. Ah! Ah! Here we are, my turtledoves. That will
do, I think? If you wish, you may sleep well. Me, I find that a good
bed is wasted on a pair of lovers. It is all one to them. But she

looks fatigued, *la gosse!* Tired and pale. You have been ill, *petite ange?*

LEWIS. Only on the boat, madame.

MADAME MARXSE. The boat? Ah! Ah! One understands! When the ship walks, it is not good, *voyons!* But you remember this house? This place? *Chérie?*

TERESA. A little. We were all here once, long ago, weren't we?

MADAME MARXSE. Yes, yes! For three months. (*Holding up three fingers.*) I lodge Sanger and his family. Ah, that man! That man! So many children he had. It is unknown how many. Here we have one also. The little Paul. My grandson.

LEWIS. I'd forgotten Paul. How is he, madame?

MADAME MARXSE. *Mais malade!* He will not live long, that one! He is at school with the Jesuits now. And he coughs! *Effrayant!* Many days he is too ill to learn. But still he wins all the prizes, yes!

LEWIS. Takes after his father. They all do. They're all too clever to live. (TERESA *gives him a quick look, which he does not see.*)

TERESA. My sister Antonia is going to have a baby.

MADAME MARXSE. Aha! The little Tony? I recollect her very well. *Bichette bien jolie!* And to be a mother already! That one expected.

TERESA (*primly*). The child will be born in wedlock.

MADAME MARXSE. *C'est gentil! Mais – toi aussi, n'est-ce-pas?* You also have a lover? Monsieur Dodd? Aha! You shall learn much. For he is the first, I think, yes?

LEWIS (*irritably*). Bawdy old thing, isn't she?

MADAME MARXSE. Bawdee? What is bawdee? I think it is something – not very ni-ice. For me, I am entirely *comme-il-faut, voyons!*

(*A bell clangs noisily downstairs.*)

Ah! Ah! One rings! My bell, it never stop ringing. Lovers are impatient. Let me embrace you, *chérie.* Good luck! *Bonne fortune à présent.* Do not be too kind to him. It is not wise. Food is downstairs if you wish. (*The bell rings again.*) I must go. (*As she waddles out, she shakes a finger at* LEWIS.) Aha! *Même jeu toujours? C'est bien rigolo, voyons!*

(*She exits.*)

LEWIS (*helping* TERESA *to take off her hat*). Lord! What a hag! Fancy! We used to call her the Fairy Queen!

TERESA. Light the gas, will you? And open the window. It's stuffy!

(LEWIS *lights gas and is just crossing to open window when she calls out.*)

Lewis – I do feel so very ill.

LEWIS (*embracing her tenderly*). Ah, my dear one! That's not surprising, with the crossing we had. And you've had no food for nearly twenty-four hours. You'll be all right when you've had supper and a good night's rest. (*Pause – a little anxiously.*) Won't you?

TERESA. I suppose so.

LEWIS. Of course you will.

TERESA (*getting up*). Though I doubt the good night's rest. (*Feeling the bed.*) I wonder if this is really madame's idea of a good bed!

LEWIS. It'll be our bridal bed, I suppose. So it's a pity it shouldn't be comfortable. Let me feel it. Oh! Tessa, it's not so bad. I've slept on worse.

TERESA. Feels to me more like a stone quarry. But this is a very odd place altogether. I'm surprised at you for bringing me here.

LEWIS. I'm a little surprised at myself. I've been living in a silver sty for so long that I'd almost forgotten what this was like. It isn't very nice, is it?

TERESA. Will you look at that indecent little ornament next door to a statue of the Sacred Heart? How Uncle Charles would laugh at it!

LEWIS. Would he?

TERESA. Of course he would. That's why I do. A year ago I wouldn't have thought this a funny room. I'd have taken it for granted. Oh dear! Oh dear! You never can get quite back. Life goes on and little bits of us get lost.

LEWIS (*lighting his pipe*). I liked your Uncle Charles.

TERESA. So did I. I loved him. I wonder if I should have liked living with him in Cambridge.

LEWIS. Were you going to live with him in Cambridge?

TERESA. When I'd left school. Next year. We'd arranged it. His housekeeper can't make tea. I must remember to send him a picture postcard tomorrow.

LEWIS (*opening his suitcase and beginning his unpacking by turning it upside down on the floor*). But do you really think you might have liked living with him in Cambridge?

TERESA. Perhaps. I'd rather be with you.

LEWIS. I see. (*Extracting a pair of boots from the pile on the floor and standing uncertainly, staring round him.*) I'm a fool! (*Puts boots on mantelpiece.*) We'll go away tomorrow.

TERESA (*lying on the bed*). Dear heart! Why? Are we the Wandering Jew?

LEWIS. Filthy place!

TERESA. It can't hurt us as long as we're together.

LEWIS. Can't it, my blessing? I'm not so sure. There must be other places –

TERESA. I think you'll find they all look pretty much the same. (*Raising herself on one elbow and looking round with a smile.*) All our rooms will have music on the floor and boots on the mantelpiece.

LEWIS. I ought to have thought – It took me so much by surprise when you changed your mind in that sudden way, I couldn't think of anywhere to go – Tessa!

TERESA. Um?

LEWIS. You haven't told me yet why you did change at the last.

TERESA. No. And I shan't ever tell you.

LEWIS. Why not?

TERESA. It isn't a suitable subject to talk about.

LEWIS. Dear me! (*Sitting on bed beside her.*) Tell me!

TERESA. Blest if I do.

LEWIS. Tessa, you must. You must let me have everything now.

TERESA. You have everything, my heart, except that. You can keep on guessing till the cows come home, but I won't tell you.

LEWIS. Something frightened you.

TERESA. Aren't you clever!

LEWIS. I always know when you're frightened. There are two funny little lamps in your eyes, right in the very middle of your eyes, and they always light up when you're afraid. I can see them now. You're frightened still. Tessa! Don't hide away from me! Tell me what it is. Are you ashamed of anything?

TERESA (*hiding her face*). Leave me alone. I feel so ill.

LEWIS. Look at me, my girl. (*Pulling her round, lifting her up and staring at her.*) Dear love! Was it something that Florence said?

TERESA. I shan't tell you.

LEWIS. She said something that made you run away. It's an ill wind – What was it? Why can't you tell me?

TERESA. Because – women oughtn't to tell men – about each other.

LEWIS. I see. (*Pause.*) You're an astounding creature! You listen to that old hag's conversation without turning a hair, and yet a genteel person like Florence –

TERESA. Please! I want to forget all that.

LEWIS. You're the most innocent creature in the world really!

(*Stroking her hair with a sort of shy kindness.*) I don't believe you understood half that old devil said.

TERESA. Perhaps not. But I know one thing she thinks. She thinks I'm your fancy lady.

LEWIS. So does Florence, as a matter of fact.

TERESA. Does she? (*Sitting up.*) Darling Lewis, I've a hard thing to ask you. If I'm not – what they think – what am I?

LEWIS. You mean, what would I call you if I wasn't your lover?

TERESA. I've heard you say hard things of other women.

LEWIS (*after a long pause*). Listen, beloved. Will this do? I wouldn't – I couldn't ever again, in all my life, call any woman by a name that sounded too hard for you. I shall try to think every woman can be to some man what you are to me.

TERESA. That sounds all right. (*Pulling him to her and kissing him.*) Don't worry. I only wanted to know. Put your arms round me. Hold me. (*They sit with clasped arms, looking out towards the window.*) Do you know, I never realized before that we live on a star.

LEWIS. It's an ill star.

TERESA. I can feel it tonight, going flaming round and round in space. And you and I the only real live people on it, just clinging on to it, clinging together for a minute or two, before we get lost again. Do you have a feeling that this moment is all – everything? Nothing is behind us, and nothing in front of us. Just only now. I wish it could be now for ever.

LEWIS. So do I.

TERESA. It's getting quite dark. Never mind! (*With a little laugh.*) Another sun will shine tomorrow morn – (*Singing.*)

'Ah, say not so! Another love will cheer thee,
The sun will shine as bright tomorrow morn.'

Do you remember? Shall we see the sunrise through this window, Lewis?

LEWIS. We shall see the stars. (*A pause.*) What's the book you're clutching? You don't mean to say you've brought that silly old diary away with you?

TERESA. You mustn't laugh at my most cherished possession. It's all my past life, this book.

LEWIS (*turning the pages*). It's very short.

TERESA. I haven't been alive so very long. I've put instructions in the beginning for it to be laid in the grave with me.

LEWIS. I know. I've read it.

TERESA. When?

LEWIS. Yesterday. You left it behind you in the music-room.

TERESA. You must try not to be so ungentlemanly.

LEWIS. Must I? Well, well! (*Pause.*) My darling! You're shivering! (*Peering at her.*) You really do look very mouldy. Come down to supper.

TERESA. I couldn't really. I don't want anything. I'm too tired.

LEWIS. Well then, I'll get them to send something up. I shan't be long.

(*Exits.*)

(TERESA *rises and tries to sort out the music on the floor, but is evidently too ill to do much. Unpacks her own parcel and takes out her party frock and her nightgown, and hangs party frock. Begins to try to take off her frock.* LEWIS *comes back.*)

LEWIS. Tessa! Let's get out of here. We'll go away at once.

TERESA (*in dismay*). At once, Oh, Lewis! Why?

LEWIS. It's a filthy place. The reek of it seemed to rise up and hit me in the face the moment I got outside the door. You shan't stay here a single night. We'll have something to eat and go.

TERESA. Go? Where?

LEWIS. Back to England.

TERESA. Back to England?

LEWIS. I shall take you back to your uncle.

TERESA. Tonight? Oh, Lewis, I couldn't.

LEWIS. A convent will put you up for the night.

TERESA. A convent?

LEWIS. Yes, the largest we can find.

TERESA. Never! You won't take me out of this house alive. So you needn't think it.

LEWIS. Do listen to reason.

TERESA. I've come away with you because I think it's right. Because I think it's best. And I shall stay with you.

LEWIS. But I'm not sure if *I* think it's right.

TERESA. What you think doesn't matter.

LEWIS. I should have thought it did.

TERESA. You've thought a lot of silly things in your life.

LEWIS. All the more reason for trying to be sensible now.

TERESA. I'm the deciding person.

LEWIS. Even you have been known to change your mind?

TERESA. It's made up now. I won't leave you.

LEWIS. But, Tessa –

TERESA. We've run away and we've got to go on running away.

LEWIS. God knows, it's not for myself –

TERESA. You don't suppose it's for me?

LEWIS. But –

TERESA. I've been through so much for you. Don't always go on dithering and losing everything. Will you never understand?

LEWIS. Understand what?

TERESA. It would be living our life all over again – to give you up a second time. Remember before?

LEWIS. Before?

TERESA. The night Sanger died. I told you then. But you never understand anything until it's too late.

LEWIS. I'm not too late now, anyway.

TERESA. Oh, you are so blind, my love. Are you quite sure you won't be too late again? (*Suddenly flinging herself into his arms and sobbing bitterly.*) Oh, my cruel, cruel love. I couldn't bear it.

LEWIS. My darling.

TERESA. I can't ever leave you. I won't. I won't.

LEWIS. All right. You shan't. You shan't. Only stop crying now. I don't know you like this.

TERESA. Kiss me. Kiss me. (*He does so.*) Again – again – as if it were never no more.

(*They embrace.* TERESA *struggles with her dress.*)

Damn these buttons! (*Her dress half off.*) Oh, Lewis!

LEWIS. Here, let me help you. (*Lifting the dress over her face.*)

TERESA. Now will you please to go and sit down out of the way and wait for me.

(*She falls back quite exhausted on the bed.*)

LEWIS. At all events let me write to your uncle.

TERESA. Oh, what's the good of that?

LEWIS. I want him to know where you are. Suppose anything happened to me? Suppose I got run over by a train?

TERESA. You are apt to lose your head in traffic.

LEWIS. We can't have you stranded.

TERESA. I can look after myself.

LEWIS. No, you can't. I'm going to write. (*Taking writing-pad and pencil from floor near the box-couch where he flung them.*)

TERESA. Write if you like. But I – won't – give you up – any more.

LEWIS. You shan't. But I'll just tell him where you are. (*Starting to write.*) I'll post it tonight. I'll explain everything. (*Stopping, confronted by a difficulty.*) Though it's not so easy to know how to begin.

TERESA (*gasping for air*). It's very stuffy in here.

LEWIS. Well then, open the window. (*Writing without looking at her.*)

(TERESA *staggers across to the window and tries to do so. She is evidently in great pain.*)

TERESA. I can't open it. It's stiff.

LEWIS. Try at the top. How will this do? (*Reading.*) 'Dear Charles, I love your niece, and as soon as things can be arranged we are to be married. Meanwhile this is our address.' That's not much. But it's really all there is to it.

(TERESA, *after another attempt at the window, sinks down on the floor with a little sigh.* LEWIS *goes over letter again.*)

'Dear Charles, I love your niece enough.' (*Looking up.*) Who was it now that said, 'love her enough' –

(*It is very silent.*)

Tessa! (*Rushing to her.*) Have you fainted? Tessa! Darling! (*Carrying her to the bed.*) Don't frighten me so! (*Hanging over* TERESA.) Tessa! She's dying! Dear Christ, help me!

(TERESA *stirs and sighs.*)

Tessa! Look at me. Speak to me.

TERESA. Light the light.

LEWIS (*frightened*). It is lighted.

TERESA. I can't see. Oh, Lewis, I can't breathe – The gas – It's dark – another sun – tomorrow – Lewis – tomorrow – (*Dies in his arms.*)

(*He rushes to the window, sees a wedge at the top, pulls it out and throws up the sash. The wind blows all the music about.* MADAME MARXSE, *carrying a tray, kicks open the door and moves down to foot of the bed.*)

MADAME MARXSE. *Eh bien? Qu'est ce que tu faites là?*

LEWIS (*standing by the window*). Tessa's got away. She's safe. She's dead.

CURTAIN.

# THE WARTIME REVUES

## Hermione Gingold
## Nina Warner Hooke
## Diana Morgan

*Hermione Gingold in* The Bacchante

# About Revues

A now unfashionable theatrical form, a revue consisted of a number of short sketches, monologues and songs, usually satirical in content and acerbic in style. These shows were performed by small groups of actors and singers in arts theatres and small West End venues.

Descended from the English music hall and American burlesque, the revue was an enormously popular theatrical phenomenon of the twenties, thirties and forties. In the 1960s after the success of *Beyond the Fringe*, a sort of anti-revue, performed and devised by Peter Cook, Dudley Moore, Alan Bennett and Jonathan Miller, it all but died out in the British theatre, although elements of it remain in TV variety and satire programmes from *The Black and White Minstrel Show*, through Les Dawson and Benny Hill, to Victoria Wood and French and Saunders.

The sketches featured here are from seven revues:

*The Gate Revue* – The Gate Theatre & The Ambassadors Theatre, 1939 (449 performances);
*Swinging the Gate* – The Ambassadors Theatre, May 1940 (126 performances);
*Revuedeville* – The Windmill Theatre, 1940 (programme constantly changing – the theatre's motto: 'We never closed');
*New Ambassadors Revue* – The Ambassadors Theatre, 1941;
*Rise Above It* – The Comedy Theatre, 1941 (380 performances);
*Sky High* – The Phoenix Theatre, 1943 (149 performances);
*Sweet and Low* – The Ambassadors Theatre, 1943 (264 performances).

# Hermione Gingold

*1897–1987*

'I don't try to be funny, dear. It's just that I have a certain slant on life,' Hermione Gingold once said. At the height of her powers, critics' flattery – 'the queen of the stage harpies', 'less of a comedienne, more of a paroxysm' – often obscured the fact that she was a brilliantly creative actress. Towards the end of her career she became a cult figure, almost a send-up of herself.

Daughter of James Ferdinanda, an Austrian stockbroker in London, and his wife Kate Walter, Hermione Gingold was born on 9 December (she declined to mention the year, but evidently it was 1897). She was educated by governesses in France, and at private schools before going to the Rosina Filippi School of Theatre.

Her first stage appearance was as the Herald in *Pinkie and Fairies* at Her Majesties in 1908. Ellen Terry played the lead. She followed this up playing Cassandra in William Poel's *Troilus and Cressida* (Edith Evans as Cressida) in 1912, and Jessica in Shakespeare's *Merchant of Venice* (Edith Evans as Portia) at the Old Vic in 1914.

She went through a fallow period in the 1920s, but gradually, during the '30s, she built up a reputation in intimate London theatres, playing in revue. During the war she became a star.

In 1949 she played opposite Hermione Baddeley (who had appeared in many revues with her, although they did not care for each other at all) in Coward's play *Fallen Angels*. In the drunken second act, both actresses made the most of their famous rivalry at the expense of the play, and although Coward was appalled, the public was enthralled.

In the 1950s Hermione Gingold moved to America, where she appeared in the films *Gigi*, *The Music Man*, *Bell, Book and Candle*, and *Around the World in Eighty Days*. After this she again struggled to keep up a profile, working mainly on television chat-shows, returning to England for a time in the late 60s.

When Harold Prince was casting *A Little Night Music* in 1975, Hermione Gingold turned up at the auditions, without an appointment, to be told she shouldn't bother to play a woman of 74. 'But Mr Prince,' she replied, 'I am 74.' She got the part.

She married twice. First the publisher Michael Joseph, by whom she had two sons, Leslie and Stephen. Stephen, who died young, was the leading advocate of theatre-in-the-round in England, and founder of the Scarborough Theatre which bears his name and is now run by Alan Ayckbourn. Her second husband was Eric Maschwitz, the writer and director.

Gingold wrote two autobiographies: *The World is Square* (1946) and *How to Grow Old Disgracefully* (1987). She also wrote a play, *Abracadabra*, which she describes as 'an insane, wildly funny, brilliant play that I wrote myself' (1966), many revue sketches for herself and others, the books *My Own Unaided Works* (1952), *Sirens Should Be Seen and Not Heard*, and articles in magazines including a column in *Books of Today* entitled 'These I Have Loathed'.

She won various awards including a Golden Globe, a Grammy, the Jan Mitchel Award for Exceptional Devotion to Dogs and an award from the United Nations for 'furthering Anglo-American relations'. She is responsible for the now over-quoted remark that, whereas 'Olivier had been a *tour de force*, Wolfit was forced to tour', and various other *bon mots*.

She died in New York in May 1987.

# What Shall I Wear?

*Performed by Hermione Gingold at The Ambassadors Theatre in 1943. From the* Sweet and Low *revue (264 performances).*

What shall I wear? What shall I wear? Which of us has not at some time or other, during these trying days, been faced with this difficult problem?

You rush to your wardrobe – and what do you find? Your last year's flank musquash has been all but eaten by a moth – your beige crepe-de-soie has a large tear just below the inverted pleat, which gives fullness and swing to an otherwise plain tailored skirt.

Ah, a thought strikes you – what about my *marron* two-piece with the sweet-pea reverse? You detach it delicately from its hanger – what do you see? Horror, devastation! For on the third tuck from the right, just where the bishop sleeve cleverly meets the blouse, you see a large stain – it resembles in shape the isle of Ceylon. (Ceylon is a pear-shaped island at the foot of India, population 3,000, chief export tea – that is by the way.) What can it be, you ask yourself? Tea, coffee, cocoa, custard (made with dried eggs), fruit (tinned of course) or austerity trifle, for until you know what sort of stain it is, you cannot remove it. You raise it to your lips – umm . . . . mulligatawny soup, delicious . . .! Regretfully you put it aside and look at the skirt – except for the back, which is seated and shiny, it looks as good as new. Why not wear the skirt with your bridge coat? Why not? I will tell you why not, because even if we are at war, there is no reason why any self-respecting Englishwoman should wear a bridge coat unless she is definitely going to play bridge. Put it back, put it back, and you will feel you have done something to keep alive the spirit that went to build our empire.

Ah, but what is this? Your turquoise-blue knitted three-piece. You slip it on – ah, but what is that? On the very front a large triangular stain surrounded by four or five smaller ones.

Undaunted, you turn it back to front – it gives a most peculiar effect. No, you must remove the offending stains. Looking at them closely, you find tiny dried segments of . . . what? You raise the offending garment to your lips, a taste leaves no further doubt – fish cake, your favourite dish, but perhaps a little tasteless without some kind of savoury sauce, be it piquant or tartare. Hastily you hunt through your wardrobe and there, on the bust of your white satin evening dress, is a generous patch of anchovy sauce! Ah, but that makes all the difference in the world. But it leaves us with the clothing problem still unsolved, though you find the hard work has give you quite an appetite. Still, we mustn't give in, must we? That's not the spirit that got us out of the Black Hole of Calcutta, no! So we go on, blouse after blouse, dress after dress, stain after stain . . . salmon mayonnaise, ice cream, lobster salad, hock, jam sponge *à la crème*, jugged hare, *coupe marron*, smoked haddock and egg, banana royal, potted shrimps, plum pudding with brandy butter. At last, at last, the garments are carefully sorted out for cleaning.

You may think regretfully as you look at them that you still have nothing to wear – but cheer up, for you must admit you've had a very good lunch!

# I'm Only A
# Medium Medium
## (with Eric Maschwitz)

*Performed by Hermione Gingold at the Gate Theatre and the Ambassadors Theatre 1939. From* The Gate Revue *(449 performances)*.

[Banned section in square brackets]

> I was sitting in the window of my house in Leinster
>         Gardens,
> I was feeling just as lonely as a cloud
> When a knock came at the door, like I'd never heard
>         before,
> So mysterious I really felt quite cowed.
> 'Who is that?' I loudly cried.
> Came reply: 'Your spirit guide.'
> 'But how nice of you to call! Hang your aura in the
>         hall!'
> 'Twas a charming Indian brave who'd come hotfoot
>         from the grave
> Come to cheer my lonely spirit,
> Cheer it with his kindly laughter,
> Tell me in his simple language
> Of the life that cometh after
> And his cousin Hiawatha
> Spirit guide to Hannen Swaffer,
> Told me I should be a medium
> For it would relieve my tedium.
>
> I'm only a medium medium
> But good heavens the men I have known!
> What with giving séances and falling in trances
> I don't spend a night on my own.

I can't say the life's full of tedium,
With the famous I'm always in touch.
[No spirit is barred
Though the Marquis de Sade
Gets occasionally rather too much.
I shall always remember the time I got off
With a lady called Sappho from Greece!
She played on my trumpet,
Said like it or lump it,
I cried 'Stop it', and called for the police.

I'm only a medium medium,
But with Nero I once had a turn.
He remarked with a glance, 'Shall we sit out this
          trance?'
Then just fiddled and left me to burn.]
I'm only a medium medium,
With the famous I'm always in touch;
Still I make certain rules and though ghouls will be
          ghouls
I won't have them behaving as such.
I shall always remember the day I went down
To the country to spend a weekend.
It was on the south coast and my host was a ghost
Who was haunting my room for a friend.
I'm only a medium medium,
But the memory stays with me yet
He remarked with a glance, 'Shall we sit out this
          trance?'
Then proceeded to pinch my planchette.

I'm only a medium medium
But my fees are remarkably small.
Though my husband (deceased) left me nothing, (the
          beast!)
But his ouija and one crystal ball.
At times I am quite a comedienne, the life and the soul
          of the group,
I produced Louis Three from a hot cup of tea,
And Dracula out of clear soup.

And there's Frankestein too, such a well-spoken spook,
But I dread it each time he appears.
I don't like to object but my carpet gets wrecked,
For he will bring his monster, my dears.
I'm only a medium medium,
But I give myself plenty of rope,
What with Byron to go for, and gay Casanova,
While there's h'ectoplasm, there's hope.

# Conversation Piece:
# The Stars Look Down

*Performed by Hermione Gingold and Clive Desmond at the Amabassadors Theatre 1939. From* The Gate Revue *(449 performances).*

COMPÈRE. And now, ladies and gentlemen, we are taking you over to the countryside. I want you to imagine a quiet lane.

(*Enter* AGNES PULLPLEASURE.)

There is the village inn. (*He points out into the audience.*)

AGNES. Where is the village inn?

COMPÈRE. There is no village inn.

AGNES. Oh, so it is. I can't see very well without my specs. I wonder, have you seen my lady friend?

COMPÈRE. What does she look like?

AGNES. Well, she looks like me. And then again she doesn't.

COMPÈRE. That's not very helpful, is it?

AGNES. Where are you going?

COMPÈRE. I am going for a nice walk down a country lane.

AGNES. Well, if you see a lady who looks like a lady looking for a lady who looks like me, will you tell her I am looking for her, sitting on that bench?

COMPÈRE. All right, I will.

(*He exits. She goes and sits on the bench.*)

AGNES. Maud's very late. Did she say Sunday? Or 'ave I been misleading myself? Let me see what me diary says. (*She looks at her diary.*) Yes . . . that's right . . . Passion Sunday – meet Maud Fishbother in the lane between high tide and blackout time. It's half-past high tide now.

(*Enter* MAUD. *She carries a copy of the 'Sunday Express' and the 'Weekly Stargazer.'*)

MAUD. 'Allo, dear.

AGNES. Oh, 'ere you are.

MAUD. I'm sorry I'm late, Agnes . . . oooh, dear.

AGNES. What 'eld you up?

MAUD. I 'ad to walk.

AGNES. Why?

MAUD. Well I mustn't travel in a mechanically propelled vehicle today.

AGNES. Why?

MAUD. It's me 'oroscope.

AGNES. Oh, I see – 'ave you tried inhaling?

MAUD. On, you don't understand. My 'oroscope is my life according to the stars.

AGNES. Oh, of course – that's what it is.

MAUD. I never move without Mr Naylor.

AGNES. Is he the gentleman you have been evacuated with?

MAUD. No, he's a famous seer.

AGNES. Oh, I see. A seer. I'm evacuated in a Manor.

MAUD. In a manner of what?

AGNES. Just in a Manor.

MAUD. Are you all right? I tell you what, come round and have tea at the Manor next Sunday.

AGNES. I'm very booked up. I'll have to look in my diary. Sunday. Anniversary of the death of Nelson. No, I couldn't come that day, I wouldn't enjoy it. Thursday's a gay day. The Relief of Ladysmith. I don't know Her Ladyship personally, but we might celebrate.

MAUD. I must see what Mr Naylor says. (*She reads from the 'Sunday Express'.*) 'Ere we are . . . 'Thursday . . . Your planetary positions denote that you would make a very good swimmer . . . Act warily – a close associate may be involved in a quarrel.' No, I don't think I'd better risk it on Thursday.

AGNES. Well, 'ow about Tuesday? Oh yes, that'll be lovely. It's my birthday and the anniversary of the abolition of slavery in America.

MAUD (*she looks at the 'Stargazer'*). Really. That'll be the what?

AGNES. The twenty-fifth.

MAUD. Yes . . . 'ere we are. Those born between August the twenty-second and September the twenty-first . . . Why, that makes you a Virgo.

AGNES. Does it? That's clever of it . . . Oh, look at that child . . . what's it doin'?

MAUD. It'll ruin them geraniums . . .(*She reads the 'Sunday Express.'*) Now, let's see what Mr Naylor says about me. Aquarius, Taurus, Leo . . . Oh, 'ere I am – Pisces. 'The sun was in Pisces when you were born, and Mars being in conjunction with Mercury, it makes for awkwardness.'

AGNES. Makes for rudeness, I should think. What 'ave you got there?

MAUD. 'The Weekly Stargazer.' I wouldn't move without it.

AGNES. 'There will be trouble in Germany as the eclipse on October 28th falls uncomfortably close to Hitler's Uranus and shakes his prestige.'

MAUD. Marvellous 'ow they can tell isn't it? Read out what it says about my Maisie.

AGNES. What is she?

MAUD. She's Lunar.

AGNES. Oh . . . Where is it . . .? Lunar . . . let's see now . . . Lazy for Leo . . . Capricious for Capricorn . . . Sad Sagittarius . . . Ah, 'ere it is – Lucky Lunar.

MAUD. Well . . .?

AGNES. 'Lunar people are confirmed lovers . . . of home life.'

MAUD. That's all right. Where's the answers to correspondents?

AGNES. You didn't write in, did you?

MAUD. Yes, I wanted to know whether I ought to let my top front to that Indian chap.

AGNES. What shall I look under?

MAUD. Curry – Clapham.

AGNES. All right. Where is it? Ah – readers' problems solved by the stars . . . Oh, here we are – Curry.

MAUD. Let me see it. 'The anxieties to which you refer are due to the fact that Neptune is in Scorpio. At the present moment you have Saturn going over your Mars in Pisces. They are chafing you very much, but they are part of your Karma, as you probably know.'

AGNES. That makes things pretty clear, doesn't it? Does it say when the war will end? 'Ere let's have a see. 'Hitler having Saturn on his sun, Venus squared by Jupiter is bound to culminate.' Then we shall be back in London on Thursday.

MAUD. Come on, dear, let's get a bus and go down to the village.

AGNES.  Orl right, dear.

MAUD.  We can walk down slowly. We'll just get there when they open.

AGNES.  Maud, are you sure our journey is really necessary?

MAUD.  Of course, dear

(*Ad lib chatter till they both exit.*)

# *Madame La Palma*
## (with Robert MacDermot)

*Performed by Hermione Gingold at the Ambassadors Theatre in 1939. From* The Gate Revue *(449 performances).*

I was touring once with *Chu Chin Chow* in India,
When a very well-known Rajah saw the show.
He came and asked me back to his zenana
For a little cup of tea and a banana.
We disposed of the banana, and were settling down to
    tea,
When he gave a sudden cry of joy and turned and said
    to me:
'You are wasted in the chorus;
Won't you please do something for us?
For your fortune you would make
If you'd stay and train our snake.'

I'm Madame La Palma, the lady snake charmer,
I've been in the business for years.
The snakes, who adore me,
Do everything for me,
I make them come out of my ears.
In the theatre my oriental science
Really fascinates my simple-minded clients,
With crystals and trances and strange Eastern dances
To which I can waggle my tum.
Then I undo my clasp and show them my asp,
And then there's a roll on the drum.

But the Rajah had to go and see a durbar,
And I was left once more upon my own.

I couldn't find a friend among his Gurkhas
So I though I'd take my snake act at a circus.
I got an introduction from a Ringmaster, so kind.
He had a lovely black moustache, he was ever so
    refined.
'What you want,' he said, 'just ask it.
Would you like a little basket?'
'Thanks,' said I, 'I never use 'em,
All my snakes sleep in my bosom.'

I'm Madame La Palma, the lady snake charmer,
A gambler once asked for my aid,
So I lent him my adders to play snakes and ladders
And, my, what a packet he made!
At the cinema, when watching Robert Taylor,
I found that I was sitting next to a sailor
He got very bold, said, 'My, aren't you cold?'
I replied, in the iciest way,
'You've made a mistake, you've been stroking my
    snake,
Move your left hand, the right one's OK.'

These medals I wear on my chest:
That's for winning a race,
That's for knowing my place,
And these are to hold up my vest.
For a kindness I once did to a Rajah
I got this, although it should have been much larger.
And this is for daring,
And that's for not caring,
And these are to cover a stain,
And these I wear on my bust I wear 'cos I must,
To cover one purl and one plain.

# *Beauty Beauty*

*Performed by Hermione Gingold at the Ambassadors Theatre in 1939. From* The Gate Revue *(449 performances).*

'Uproariously received' – *Financial Times*

> If you want to have a real good time,
> If you want to have a figure just like mine,
> You must do
> What I tell you to.
> If you want to exercise your bust
> Pay attention, friends, to me, you really must.
> Take my tips,
> For those Rubens hips.
> You may cry, 'What is it I lack?
> Is it fame or fortune?'
> 'No!', I answer back.
>
> Beauty Beauty,
> To have it is everyone's duty.
> Every girl can get good looks,
> With the aid of one of our sixpenny books,
> Beauty Beauty,
> Just try a diet that's fruity,
> Full many a man has wooed a maid
> On radishes and orangeade,
> With nuts to help him make the grade.
> Three cheers for beauty.

Healthy healthy!
I'd sooner be healthy than wealthy.
What is the good of pearls in rows
If you're quite unable to touch your toes?
Healthy healthy!
Really my footwork is filthy!
That's not the way to catch a man.
Remember that our two-year plan
Turns weak Miss Can't into strong Miss Can.
Three cheers for beauty.

Four years ago when I walked down the street, nobody looked at me.
Now they all stare. 'To what', I hear you all eagerly asking yourselves,
'do I attribute my great strength and virility?' (*She coughs.*) I will tell
you in a word – exercise. Exercise has made me what I am today,
virile and strong. I should like to see any man try to take advantage of
me – I should love it. And now I am going to throw something in the
nature of a bombshell among you. I have had several letters from
people in the audience who have asked me to answer their personal
problems, and standing here on this very stage I will answer their
personal problems as if they were *my* personal problems. (*She pulls a
letter out of her blouse.*)

Now first of all, the lady in the second row is suffering from goose
flesh. Well, you should wash the affected parts in a weak solution of
vitriol. This will remove first the goose and then the flesh, leaving the
skin daisy-petal clean underneath.

The sergeant in the fourth row is suffering from a red nose. You
should soak your face in Rinso overnight. Won't the other sergeants
be envious when you arrive in the Mess next morning with your lovely
white nose!

A lady in the fifth row wants to know how to avoid chaps. Well,
most girls prefer to encourage them. A lady in the eighth row wants to
know how to get rid of superfluous hair. From what? Afterwards . . .!
And now, girls, for my final beauty hint:

A lady in the ninth row asks how to put out an incendiary bomb. If
a bomb should fall on the room in which you are sitting, do not rush
to remove it. You may laughingly say – 'Oh! what a whopper! Let me
give you a hand with it.' Then, if he is an old friend, he will laugh and
say 'OK,' but if he is a new acquaintance your teasing will help to
break the ice.

Now fill a bucket about three-quarters full of water and place the bomb in it. Be careful not to fill the bucket too full or the water will spill and make a mess on the carpet.

Now telephone your ARP warden. Tell him from where you are speaking and say quite calmly that you have a bomb in a bucket, and he will tell you where to put it.

> Dainty dainty!
> Don't go all swoony and fainty.
> To fall on your back is simply grand
> If you fall on the proper word of command.
> Dainty dainty!
> A man's only human now, ain't he?
> Take my advice, you'll find it wise,
> He's made like that, so realize
> He likes a girl who takes exercise.
> Three cheers for beauty.
> Hearty hearty
> The life and soul of the party.
> You'll never long for a prune or a fig
> If you join the health and beauty league.
> Hearty hearty!
> I'd rather be hearty than tarty.
> For virtue brings its own reward
> And many a girl who's not been pawed
> Has ended up with a real live Lord!
> Three cheers for beauty.

# Bicycling

*Performed by Hermione Gingold at the Phoenix Theatre, 1943. From the* Sky High Revue *(149 performances).*

Have you thought how you are going to get to work if transport becomes more difficult? I bet you haven't though of a bicycle. And why not? A horse may be the friend of man. The bicycle is everybody's pal.

> (*She produces a postcard from her pocket.*)

Look at this picture of one. Isn't it pretty? Why, it is as pretty as a picture.

> (*She puts the card back.*)

Look at my blazer. Is not that pretty too? And I am proud to say that I am a bicycling blue and race for my college of shorthand.

Now I want you to try and make up your minds as to whether you would like the single-seater roadster or the tandem model. The single-seater roadster has one saddle and two pedals attached to a crank. The tandem model has two saddles and two cranks, usually attached to each other. On the tandem model the rider in front faces the same way as the rider behind, which is gay. The rider behind faces the behind of the rider in front, which is not so gay. But to business.

Of course you will find it difficult to buy a bicycle in wartime, but if you follow my instructions you will be able to make one for yourself.

First of all you will want some wire for the wheels. Any sort of strong wire will do, but I advise you not to get touching the telegraph wire or you will get into trouble.

Next you will want a bell and a lamp, but I advise you to get these ready-made.

Now remove some wheels off an old pram, or it will save you trouble if you remove some wheels off an old bike; and why not remove the handles off it at the same time? You will be silly if you don't.

Now perhaps some of you young ladies have a boyfriend. Don't be too shy to ask him to come round some night and help you to adjust your mudguard. And perhaps he will put a spoke in your wheel at the same time.

The peddler can supply you with pedals. Or you can wrench some off an old piano. Won't someone be surprised the next time they sit down? And if they're cross at first, never you mind. Just laugh and tell them that they can play the piano without pedals but you can't ride a bicycle without, and then they will laugh too – I hope. Be unconventional, don't bother about brakes.

And now for the chain, which is to the bicycle what the engine is to the motor. You can either pull one off of something – (*she makes a gesture of pulling down the chain with her hand*) – or you can crochet one for yourself. Use a chain-stitch, and if you find it hurts you casting on cast iron, cast off and cast round for something else.

The bicycle as we know it today was invented in eighteen-forty by a Scotchman who was attracted by the idea of a freewheel. And the freewheel gives you this great advantage – you can ride downhill without pedalling. You can also ride uphill without pedalling, by simply getting off and pushing. And that is why the bicycle is sometimes known as the push-bike.

Oh yes, you thought I had forgotten the seat – or saddle as we bicyclers call it. Well, I had not. And I advise you to get a good one, for, as Hamlet says, 'Aye, there's the rub.' And oh, how I wish I could show you my seat, for I think it is the only one in the world that is stuffed with feathers and covered with chintz.

Well, now your machine is almost finished and you are nearly ready to go on the streets. I hope you will all go home tonight determined to make yourselves bicycles, and maybe we shall bump into each other one fine day soon. I hope so. – Ta-ta.

# Talk on Music

*Performed by Hermione Gingold at the Comedy Theatre in 1941. From* Rise Above It *revue (380 performances).*

Good evening.

I have been asked to provide a little intellectual interlude.

I want to talk to you about music. Now music is very important in these troublesome times, for it is the common ground on which we can all meet, and the common language we can all comprehend. Please don't misunderstand my use of the word 'common'. (*She giggles.*)

The music I am going to help you to appreciate tonight is that of the composer Bucalossi.

Now Bucalossi is one of those composers whom you never know where you are with – with, and that is all I intend to say about him. Were I to go on I should say he is the tease of music – he says 'Don't take me seriously' with his flute, and immediately after that he says 'I'm sad' with his wind. And are we cross with him? – Not a bit of it; we are transported wherever he like to take us.

Now our obvious choice of Bucalossi's music falls on that saucy romp of his, 'The Grasshoppers' Dance'.

Now it would be wrong to say Bucalossi has  no style – he has too much style.

Take his allegro – what can we say about that? – nothing. Take his andante – what can we say about that? again – nothing.

Take his presto – what can we say about that? – ah! you are wrong – it is one long musical wink – in a word, c'est gai – or, as we should say in English, it is gay.

Now, without another word, I'm going to ask the piano to play 'The Grasshoppers' Dance'

(*The pianos play . . .*)

I think that is one of the most supremely satisfying openings I know: it is supremely triumphant, and tells of the fortitude of those frail insects, though I think I may say, in a way, it is almost brutal.

(*Piano . . .*)

Listen, listen to the dialogue between the right and the left piano, before I slip into the D Major. What a pity we haven't room for that clever Sir Adrian Boult and his boys. Ah! I'm afraid at this point we sadly miss the grunts of delight from the basses and the pizzicato voices of the violins; a diabolically clever device, typical of Bucalossi.

(*Piano again . . .*)

As you hear, the theme is repeated and the whole of the first movement makes us think of Death. Yes, Death in conflict with the life-giving joy of the Grasshopper (if you will forgive me the abandon of the phrase) – I was educated abroad.

(*Piano . . .*)

Shut your eyes while you listen to this and you can see Bucalossi's Grasshoppers dancing a stately minuet, and does it remind us just a little bit of Mozart?

No, it does not.

And sometimes you can see them hopping from flower to flower, breathlessly happy; surely this is musical genius before which we must all bow.

By the way, I want to correct an idea many of you seem to have. It was not Bucalossi, but another musician, called Beethoven, who was deaf.

(*Piano . . .*)

Doesn't that make you laugh? It does me. (*Piano.*) Doesn't that make you want to dance? It does me.

And now for my big surprise. I'm going to turn myself into a grasshopper and dance. Ah! The magic power of music.

(*The pianos take up the tune. Dance. After the dance:*)

Wasn't that a lovely illusion? I hope you used your imagination. After all, seeing is not always believing. And if I have helped you to understand Bucalossi's music, and if for a while you have lost yourselves in a world of beautiful sounds – I shall not have wasted my time and yours. – Good evening.

# No Laughing Matter

*Performed by Madge Elliott, Betty Ann Davies, Charles Hawtrey, Frith Banbury, Rowan Milne, Heather Boys and Constance Hungate at the Ambassadors Theatre in 1939. From* The Gate Revue *(449 performances).*

SCENE: *A smart salône in the West End.*

ASSISTANT (*on the phone*). No, Madam, I'm sorry, we can't take any more orders now; no, Moddom; yes, Moddom, we will send you a card for our show. Good afternoon.

(*Enter* GIRL *and* MAN.)

ALL. Good afternoon. – Good afternoon. – Good afternoon.

ASSISTANT. Won't you sit down? Can I help you at all?

MAN. My fiancée and I are going to be married this month.

ASSISTANT. Charming.

GIRL. Oh, Jack, must you tell the whole world?

MAN. We have been lucky enough to get a house in the country.

GIRL. It's really little more than a cottage.

ASSISTANT. Most interesting. People are living anywhere these days.

MAN. The dining-room is oak-panelled.

GIRL. The panelling goes nearly to the ceiling, then it stops suddenly – and there is a foot of bright yellow paint.

ASSISTANT. I couldn't be more surprised.

MAN. We have rather a nice oak sideboard.

ASSISTANT. I'm sure you'll be very happy. I always say there's nothing like a nice oak sideboard, especially with some nice oak panelling.

GIRL. How funny you should always say that – it's just what I always say.

MAN. And we were thinking of buying an orange to put on the sideboard.

ASSISTANT. An orange – an orange?

MAN. Yes, a *real* orange.

GIRL. Yes, we thought with all that panelling and the oak sideboard – it would be just perfect.

ASSISTANT. Yes, I see what you mean. (*She goes to the phone.*) We have a demand for an orange, Mr de Lopez. Will you come down? Thank you. Mr de Lopez will attend to you; he handles all our oranges.

(*Enter* DE LOPEZ.)

DE LOPEZ. Someone enquiring for me? I understand we have an enquiry for an orange.

GIRL. Yes, we have some oak panelling that goes almost to the ceiling and then stops.

ASSISTANT. They are going to be married.

DE LOPEZ. Then we must do our best for them, and as it happens they are lucky – I know a little man in South America who –

GIRL. It's terribly hot in South America, isn't it?

ASSISTANT. Shall I show them the orange?

DE LOPEZ. Yes, do.

(*The* ASSISTANT *claps her hands. Enter* GIRL *with an orange in her hand. She walks round like a mannequin showing off a frock.*)

Isn't it lovely?

MAN. It's rather big –

(*The* GIRL *crosses round, back off.*)

We don't want anything too ostentatious.

GIRL. No. Could you show us something more suitable to a small house?

(*Enter another* GIRL)

I think this is awfully good.

ASSISTANT. It give the feeling of fruit without your being swamped by it.

GIRL. It's rather small, but perhaps with a grape on each side –

DE LOPEZ. You'll kill it if you use grapes.

ASSISTANT. Now this is quite an exclusive model; Moddom won't see another like it anywhere.

GIRL. It's rather like one I had six years ago, don't you think so, darling?

MAN. Yes, perhaps it is – no, perhaps it isn't.

ASSISTANT. Of course it looks nothing in the hand; would Madame like to see it on a dish? (*She calls off.*) A dish, Fleurette!

GIRL 
MAN } (*together*). That would help tremendously.

(*A dish is brought in.* DE LOPEZ *puts the orange on the dish.*)

DE LOPEZ. There!

ASSISTANT. Of course the sideboard will lift the whole thing tremendously.

DE LOPEZ. I'm not sure about an oak sideboard, it's a bit heavy.

ASSISTANT. But with Moddom's figure and colouring that orange on an oak sideboard with the oak panelling – the effect will be shattering.

GIRL. Perhaps you're right.

(*Enter another* GIRL.)

DE LOPEZ. Would Moddom like to hold it?

GIRL. Oh, thanks.

MAN. You look lovely with it. How much is it?

DE LOPEZ. Well, as you are going to be married we must make you a special price. We are going to let you have it at the ridiculous price of a hundred guineas.

MAN. A hundred guineas! I say – I could get a banana for that.

DE LOPEZ. I doubt it.

(*He takes the orange and gives it to the* ASSISTANT, *who passes it to the other* GIRL.)

GIRL. Oh, I did want an orange.

ASSISTANT. We could arrange hire-purchase terms if your references are satisfactory.

DE LOPEZ. How much were you thinking of giving?

GIRL. We couldn't give a penny more –

MAN. Than forty pounds.

ASSISTANT. For a real orange!

DE LOPEZ. In that case I can be of no further use to you. Show Madame to the artificial orange department.

BLACKOUT.

# Nina Warner Hooke

*1907–*

Born in 1907, Nina Warner Hooke studied at Oxford University, and became a professional writer at the age of 19. In December 1940 she married the writer Gilbert Thomas. Her books include *Darkness I Leave You* (1937), *The Striplings* (a trilogy, 1934–8), *Home is Where You Make It* (1953), *The Deadly Record* (1961), *The Seal Summer* (1964), *White Christmas* (1967), *The Starveling* (1968), *Moon on the Water* (1975) and, with her husband, a biography of the physician, Marshall Hall.

Apart from her contributions to wartime revue, she also wrote the play *No Man's Land* (1958), and her novels *Darkness I Leave You* and *The Deadly Record* were made into films.

Fluent in French, Spanish and Italian, she has written articles for *Good Housekeeping* and *Cosmopolitan*. Her *Who's Who* entry declares her 'Politics: radical. Religion: Atheist.'

She lives in Tunbridge Wells.

# Reprieve

*Performed by Hermione Baddeley at the Phoenix Theatre in 1942. From* Sky High *revue (149 performances).*

*A neat little middle-aged spinster stands irresolutely clutching a cat-basket. Backstage is a door marked:* ANIMAL DISPENSARY – CASES FOR PAINLESS DESTRUCTION RECEIVED HERE. *Nearby is a bench. She approaches the door, then retreats and sinks down on the seat, the basket on her lap.*

*Now*, you mustn't struggle! I know you don't like being shut up in there, but we shan't be long now . . . We'll just rest a little while before we go in. It's not as if there's any hurry.

We aren't trying to postpone it again, are we, Sooty? Now that we've made up our minds, it's simply a case of going through with it and getting it over. Because, of course, we know it's the only thing to do. The vet said so . . . Such a *nice* young man, so gentle and patient – and we know he did the best he could. But, you see, it's the same with us humans, Sooty – we don't get over these things so easily when we're getting old. And it hurts us every time we move where that nasty bit of shrapnel hit us, in the air raid.

We're both getting old now, Sooty. We've had nine years together, keeping each other company through good times and bad. Such a pretty little kitten you were, just a black ball of fluff! And always getting into scrapes, from the first moment Mrs Littlefield brought you to me on my birthday. I shall always remember that. The first thing you did was to climb up the chimney! Tch, tch, the job we had getting hold of you – and the *soot* that came down with you! Yes, and you hated the taste of it so much that you refused to lick yourself clean, and we had to put you in the bathtub. Dear, dear, what an adventure . . . And that was how you got your name!

There, there – it's nothing to be frightened of. All they do is to put
you in a box with a saucer of milk, and while you're lapping it up they
turn on the gas – and it's all over in a moment. You won't feel
anything at all . . .

No, I won't open the basket again. We said goodbye when we left
home, and if we go on behaving like this, we shall never get anywhere.
We shall – never get anywhere . . . Come along, Sooty.

(*She gets up, goes to the door and rings the bell.*)

Oh, good afternoon, I – I've brought my cat. The vet said there was
nothing else for it, so I – but perhaps after all there might be a chance
of a cure. Oh, I know that's what I said before, and I don't want to be
a nuisance, but I'm afraid I've changed my mind again. Yes, that's
right, a *reprieve* – that's the word! You do understand, don't you? I've
had him such a long time . . . Yes. Good afternoon.

(*She sits down again, hugging the basket, and breaks into tears.*)

Oh dear, oh dear, what a silly old woman I am! Now I've got to go
through it all over again. I'm so bad at taking decisions. It's a good
thing poor dear Mr Churchill isn't like me, or we should all be in a
pretty pickle. Now, if you had been run over and the whole thing
taken right out of my hands, I'm sure I wouldn't have minded quite so
much. It's having to *sentence* you myself . . .

What was it the vet said? My head's going round so that I can't think
properly. Something about – Ah yes: 'The only true reprieve is release
from suffering.' Only true reprieve . . . That was it. I can see now that
I've been selfish and unkind. Thinking of myself all the time. I've got
to stop imagining what it'll be like without you – opening my front
door and not seeing you running to meet me, sniffing at my shopping
bag to see if there's a little bit of fish. And later no Sooty purring by
the fire, having such a game with my knitting . . .

Well there, now that I've offered to stay late at the WVS instead of
Miss Simmons, I shan't have so many evenings at home. And what
with milk rationed and fish so scarce, perhaps it's all for the best.
Everything is difficult these days, Sooty. Life isn't much fun for
anybody any more . . . Besides, when you think what this war has
taken from other people – some having lost their homes, their loved
ones, their *children* – and all I've lost is a cat, it doesn't seem such a
great deal to bear in the general scheme of things, as they say. But
then, I never had any children . . .

Ah, you're quieter now. I believe you've curled up and gone to sleep
in that nice cosy basket. You're well off in there, you know. It's such a
cold dismal afternoon, and coming on to rain again. It always hurts
more when there's rain about, doesn't it? *I* know. But don't you
fret . . . You shall have your *reprieve*.

(*She gets up, rings the bell again and hands in her basket without saying
a word. The door closes. For a moment she stands motionless, her hand
to her mouth – then walks quickly away.*)

# Front Door Steps

*Performed by Hermione Baddeley at the Comedy Theatre in 1941. From the* Rise Above It *revue (380 performances).*

*An old woman sits on a flight of steps – all that is left of her house after an air raid.*

Well, that's that – as they say. Nothin' left but the old front steps. No point in scrubbin' them this mornin'! First time I'll have missed for nineteen hears . . . Not that they need it, anyway. Funny how they've kept so clean and bright in the middle of all the rubbish. It takes more than Hitler to make a mess of my steps!

It must have bin a fair-sized bomb, and no mistake . . .

Mind you, I always expected it. Always knew that one morning I'd come up out of the Tube shelter and find the old house knocked flat. It's flat, all right. Nothing left of it but rubbish. Never was anything like them Nasties for making a muck and mess wherever they go. No respect for anythink, they haven't. Look what they done to the old church on the corner. Fair makes yer blood boil, don't it? That church was what they calls 'istoric. Beautiful, them coloured windows was, of a Sunday morning, with the sun streaming through . . .

Not that you could compare the two. There wasn't any partikler beauty about this old house; but it was mine. And a rare good friend it's been to me, since Jim was took. Don't know how I'd have managed but for letting out the two front rooms . . .

Oh, hallo, Mrs Rawlings – yes, you can come and 'ave a look, though there isn't anythink left to look at but the front steps . . . Not *you*, though – yer silly things! Standing there staring all in a row, just as if you 'adn't never seen bricks and mortar before. What do you think

I'm supposed to be – a penny peepshow? Clear off, the pop-eyed lot of yer, and leave me alone!

No, I'm all right, thank you, ducks. Just a bit dazed, like. Feel as though I've been knocked all of a heap myself. No, I'd – I'd rather stay here a bit. What d'you mean – they won't let me? There may be nothing left but a flight of steps, but they're me *own* steps, and I'll sit on them as long as I like . . .

Yes, them few things was all I could find. A few curtains and a rug and the dog's basket. Seems funny the basket wasn't touched, and there isn't any trace of poor old Smiler. No. You see, they don't let you take dogs into the shelters . . . Oh well, he was getting old – like the rest of us; and a bit smelly, and I dare say it was the best way out. He'd never have took to fresh quarters now. Still, I wish they could have found the old chap . . .

That kind, the men were – took no end of trouble searching for 'im. 'Don't you fret, ma,' they says to me. 'His end must've come quick. There's a ton or two of bricks in the passage where he used to sleep. Lucky for you that you wasn't here yerself.' 'Oh, I dunno,' I says. 'I dunno. Maybe it is, and maybe it isn't . . .'

Oh no, I'm not going to tell Will. He's a good son to me, is Will. He'd worrit something fearful. Oh no. He's got enough to think about as it is, out there in the North Sea in that submarine. He's all I've got left now, is my Will.

Made a rare mess of the old place, haven't they? Them *Nasties* – I'd like to make a mess of them, for a change!

Just after I'd had the front repainted, and all . . .

Mind you, I never really like it – not really. What with the *damp* – and as for that stove, you wouldn't 'ardly credit the tricks it used to get up to. And the stairs used to tire me legs a bit. No, I can't say as I ever really *liked* it. But when you've lived in a place all those years and raised yer family in it, and lost yer old man in it – well, it don't seem right to think of moving, if you see what I mean . . .

I wish they could've found the old dog.

What say? Oh, it's you sergeant. Yes, I'm all right. Well, and why shouldn't I be sitting on me own front steps? No, I'm not going to no rest centre. I never lived anywhere but here for nineteen years, and I'm not going to start 'ouse-'unting all over again at my age. All

right – let 'em start their dynamiting. It don't make a ha'porth of
difference to me. You leave me alone . . .

What's that you're saying now? Oh. Oh yes. That's right. There's got
to be a home for my Will to come back to. I didn't think of it that
way. Yes, you're right there. It's what my boy's fighting for, when you
come to think of it. Them Nasties aren't going to stop us living clean
and decent in our own way, like we always done. We'll show 'em . . .

Yes, a nice cup o' tea would go down a treat, and no mistake. All
right, sergeant, I'm comin' . . . Better just say ta-ta to the old place.
Not that I ever really *liked* it, you know. Funny how the steps have
kept bright and nice. It takes more than Hitler to make a mess of my
steps . . .

# The Amazons

*Performed by Ernest Thesiger and Charles Hawtrey at the Ambassadors Theatre in 1941. From the* New Ambassadors Revue.

EDITH *is expecting a friend to tea. An elderly cultured woman, she sits knitting by the fire, at her side a loaded tea-table. Enter* MARY, *rather young and hearty.*

EDITH. Oh, there you are, dear, at last.

MARY. Sorry I'm so late.

EDITH. It doesn't matter. The tea's only just made.

MARY. I got held up at the rifle range.

EDITH. Shall I pour out now?

MARY. Do. I'm simply parched. I brought my own sugar.

EDITH. You needn't have bothered. I've got plenty. Did you make a good score to-day?

MARY. Top-hole. Beat my own record. Nine bulls out of ten shots.

EDITH. How splendid! That's the stuff.

MARY. Yes, but it's a sickening waste of lead. Just think – it might have been nine Huns! And why ever won't they have us in the Home Guard – when they accept the most pathetic little men, even Eric, who'd faint at the thought of handling a bayonet?

EDITH. I quite agree. They should give the weapons to those who'd make best use of them. Men are so ridiculously softhearted about hurting things. Look how they pampered Hess when they captured him!

MARY. I know. Too sickening. Well, if any parachutists land near here, they'll get a far more fitting reception.

EDITH. Which reminds me. I've something to show you later. I've constructed a new booby trap.

MARY. A nice painful one?

EDITH. Agonizingly. And so *simple*.

MARY. You're a marvel, Edith. Can I have another scone?

EDITH. Oh, not one of *those*, dear. You haven't already eaten one, have you?

MARY. Yes, I think so – oh no, it was off the other dish.

EDITH. That's all right, then. These are full of strychnine for the parachutists. Seen the paper? Our boys seem to have had a field-day yesterday. Five Dorniers, eleven Messerschmitts and an E-boat. Splendid bag.

MARY. Pretty fair. But they ought to have got more than one E-boat.

EDITH. Never mind. I don't suppose they rescued any survivors.

MARY. I should think not, indeed! You know, I'm thinking of writing to the Admiralty suggesting that our sailors should be equipped with long poles, curved at the ends like billhooks; so that whenever they saw any Germans swimming about in the water, the could simply poke them under, till they drowned.

EDITH. Not a bad idea. But why not make them *real* billhooks, razor-sharp? – And then they could save time by neatly decapitating them. *Such* fun!

MARY. Marvellous, Edith. I'll write that letter tomorrow. Why, you've left the poker in the fire. Did you know?

EDITH. Of course. It's part of my defence programme. I like to have it ready at hand, white-hot and sizzling. But to revert to today's paper. I see that that nasty little Laval has been up to his tricks again. Ought to have had his eyes gouged out long ago.

MARY. Too true. And as for Darlan, he should be hanged, drawn and quartered.

EDITH. Or torn asunder by wild horses. You know, I feel convinced that in order to win this war we shall have to instil a little of the *medieval* spirit into our fighting forces.

MARY. If only they'd have us in the Home Guard!

EDITH. Never mind, dear. Our own little organization is coming on well. Simply because the men won't have us, is no reason why we shouldn't bag a few Boches on our own account.

MARY. You're *so* right. Oh, I'm longing for the invasion to start! It's going to be thrilling – all the women in the village enrolled in a sort of secret legion. I can just see us creeping ahead of the troops with our daggers in our teeth –

EDITH. Couldn't we carry them in our hands, dear? I doubt if my denture will stand up to it.

MARY. Our hands will be full of grenades. Which reminds me. I hope
you're keeping in training? Mustn't get slack.

EDITH. Of course not.

(*Rising, they go through the movements of hurling a grenade.*)

One, two, *three*! . . . *One, two THREE!*

MARY. Phew! Warm work. Do you mind if I open a window?

EDITH. Oh, not that one, dear. Be careful!

(*Before* EDITH *can stop her,* MARY *throws up the window – and is
immediately clamped round the neck by a wooden contrivance which
descends with a clang from above the frame.*)

That's the booby trap I was going to show you. Isn't it effective?

MARY. Oh, gorgeously . . . Here, let me out of this, for God's sake.

EDITH. You see, I though that if my parachutist escaped the
strychnine buns, he might go to the window to summon his
companions. And then I should catch him in my booby trap; and
when I had him completely at my mercy, I should use the poker.
Just *think* – I could apply it wherever I liked!

MARY. You're a genius, Edith. But there's one thing we've overlooked,
and that's a possible miscarriage of our plans. It may not be so easy
for us to get hold of rifles when the time comes. I hardly think the
soldiers will be likely to leave many of them lying around.

EDITH. Doesn't matter in the least, my dear. When it comes to close
fighting, there are plenty of weapons equally good. What could be
better than a meat-chopper, for instance? Didn't they use them at
Agincourt?

MARY. Those were halberds.

EDITH. The same thing, with longer handles. And again, if you're out
in the fields when you spot a Hun parachutist coming down, what
could be more effective than an ordinary pitchfork? All you have to
do is to place it in position and wait till it contacts his
undercarriage.

MARY. That's all very will. But I prefer a bit more action myself.

EDITH. Well then, what about that other good old English method –
pouring boiling oil on them from the ramparts?

MARY. We haven't any ramparts on our roof. But now I come to think
of it, there *is* a flat bit between the gables; and we could take up the
preserving pan filled with oil or pitch, and tip it over them at the
right moment. Delicious buns, dear.

EDITH. Another thing we have to decide is what we're going to do with the ones we capture alive. By means of a little judicious torture, we might extract all sorts of military secrets. Father used to have a splendid little book on the Spanish Inquisition – fully illustrated. I must see if I can find it again.

MARY. It shouldn't be difficult to rig up a fairly satisfactory thumbscrew.

EDITH. And if you'd lend me your mangle, I believe I could make a sort of makeshift *rack*. The very stubborn ones we could suspend upside down over a slow fire . . .

(*The doorbell rings.*)

EDITH. Ah, that'll be the fishmonger.

(*She opens the door, revealing an errand boy with a parcel.*)

BOY. Your lobster, mum.

EDITH. That's good. (*She takes the parcel, and drops it in alarm.*) Oh, *oh* – it's alive!

BOY. Yes'm. You said you wanted it extra fresh.

EDITH. Yes, so I did – but I never thought you'd bring it here alive. What on earth am I to do with it?

BOY. Just drop it in the pot and cook it.

EDITH. Whatever do you mean? *Boil it alive?*

BOY. Yes'm.

MARY. Oh, the poor, poor thing!

EDITH. Whatever does he take me for? – The *cruel little* BEAST!!!

# Such a Ferocious Bell

*Performed by Betty Ann Davies at the Ambassadors Theatre in 1941. From the* New Ambassadors Revue.

*A pawnshop.*

Good afternoon . . . *Oh!* Oh, of course, the bell doesn't stop till the door shuts, does it? Aren't I an idiot? I thought I'd sprung the burglar alarm. Such a ferocious bell, isn't it? I expect quite a few people get scared and pop outside again when they hear it. I nearly did myself. At least, I mean, I sort of *imagined* myself reacting like that, once I'd opened the fatal door. You get thinking of all sorts of things while you're standing outside screwing up your courage.

You probably think I'm feeling nervous, not having been in a pawnshop before. But I wouldn't be so silly. After all, it's nothing to be ashamed of. We all come to it eventually, don't we? 'Here today and hocked tomorrow,' as my sister-in-law says whenever she gets a new dress!

Besides, once you've definitely made up your mind, it's quite easy. You know there's no alternative, and so you don't mind. Oh, no – it was that bell that threw me off balance a bit. Certainly is a ferocious bell.

Oh, I'm so sorry. Of course, you're waiting to see the – the ring I want to pawn. A beauty, isn't it? My engagement ring. A much grander one than I expected to have. I didn't know whether to laugh or cry when Tom gave it to me. I mean, it must have cost such a lot. All he had, and more. In fact, I wouldn't be surprised if he'd had to borrow a bit – and maybe that explains the row he had with Fred Horrocks. He was always very secretive about that. Naturally he'd have hated me to know . . .

I never realized diamonds were so *terribly* expensive till I looked at those in your window. Goodness, they must be the most precious things in the world. *And* the most beautiful. American gangsters call them 'ice', don't they? At least, on the films. And it's so true. They're exactly like bits of ice, with a sort of fiery heart . . .

Tom used to get embarrassed at the way I gloated over mine and brandished it about on buses – even after we'd been married for a year. What? Oh, everybody says that. But I'm older than I look. It's just the way I do my hair.

I suppose I'd better take it off, so that you can have a better look at it. I dare say you think it's pretty awful, wanting to pawn one's engagement ring . . . But it's the only valuable thing I have. Of course, I shouldn't have dreamed of – this way out, if the emergency hadn't been so pressing. Such an *unromantic* emergency, too. The gas bill. They're coming to cut it off tomorrow, unless . . . That's a cute little spy glass you're using. Just like half a pair of binoculars. Cute, the way it screws into your eye . . .

No, of course I don't mind waiting. That is, provided you're not too long. In case I change my mind! . . . It isn't easy, having to part with it. It's the only present Tom's ever been able to give me. He's had pretty bad luck since we were married. Lost his job soon afterwards. He's had others since, but they were too hard for him. His heart's weak, you see. They turned him down for the army because of that. So it's pretty rotten of my sister-in-law to say he's just lazy. A man can't help having a weak heart, can he?

I'm glad he won't be called up. I don't mind having to work overtime at the factory – I don't mind anything – so long as we can be together! You couldn't imagine how nice it is, coming home to him at night, finding he's got supper ready, and the kettle on . . .

When he's *not* there, it seems as though all the light had gone out of the sky, and it's grey and cold. I do try not to mind, because it's only natural for a man to want a night out with his pals sometimes. And he's not like Fred. He doesn't get drunk – often . . .

Have you decided yet how much you're going to give me? It'll have to be a lot, you know!

What? Oh no, Tom doesn't know I've come. When he misses the ring from my finger, I'll tell him I dropped it down the bath plug, or something . . . Have you decided yet what it's worth?

What did you say? It isn't worth anything? It's only *paste*? Oh! But why are you so sorry? It's wonderful! I can keep it, after all! Give it back to me quickly! . . .

Never mind the emergency. When you're in love, there are other ways of keeping warm, without gas! Goodbye – sorry to have bothered you. Oh, I've started that bell off again. Such a ferocious bell, isn't it? Makes such a noise. Goodbye – and thank you, *thank you* . . .

# Park Meeting

*Performed by Hermione Baddeley and Hermione Gingold at the Phoenix Theatre in 1942. From the* Sky High *revue (149 performances).*

'At their best in a sketch which has more of pathos than burlesque' – *The Times*

*St James's Park, on a summer evening.*

*A middle-aged governess is sitting on a bench, watching her charge at play.*

GOVERNESS. Rosalind, if you talk to that ragged little boy again, I'll have to take you home!

(*Enter a* STREETWALKER, *hot and tired, who sits down on the other end of the bench.*)

STREETWALKER (*rummaging in a handbag for a cigarette*). Got a match? (*Silence.*) I said, got a match?

GOVERNESS. I don't smoke.

STREETWALKER. Mighta known that. Nice evenin' . . . Bit too warm though. Makes my feet swell something cruel.

GOVERNESS. Why don't you wear more sensible shoes? . . . Rosalind, don't pick the flowers, dear!

STREETWALKER. Oh, go on – let her pick some! The keeper ain't looking.

GOVERNESS. My charge will take orders from *me*, thank you.

STREETWALKER. So you're a governess, are you? Mighta known that, too. Dunno why it is, but your kind look alike the world over.

GOVERNESS. And so, if I may say so, do *your* kind.

STREETWALKER. Sarky, aren't you? Well, I can give as good as I get –

GOVERNESS. Please don't shout so. I apologize. I didn't mean to be rude.

STREETWALKER. Oh, that's all right. I begun it, as you might say. Wish you had a match . . .

GOVERNESS. I must be getting along. Rosalind! *Rosalind* – heavens, wherever has she got to?

STREETWALKER. There, behind them trees. Sitting on the grass, too. Shouldn't let her do that, if I was you.

GOVERNESS. My goodness, no. Get up at once, dear! The grass is damp . . . Thank you for telling me.

STREETWALKER. Oh, I'm an old hand at keeping an eye on a brat. Got one of me own, you know. Seven, she is now.

GOVERNESS. Indeed?

STREETWALKER. Haven't seen her for six months, though. Put her with a family in the country. Real class. None of yer government billets for my kid. I pay out thirty bob a week for her. Takes a bit of finding sometimes.

GOVERNESS. I expect it does.

STREETWALKER. They ought to send that one of yours away, too. What do you call her – *Rosalind*? Pretty name . . . Sounds like it came from one of them Shakespeare plays.

GOVERNESS. It does.

STREETWALKER. I seen a Shakespeare play once. Far-fetched sort of a thing. Didn't make much sense, but it was real comical. Hamlet, it was called . . . Quiet here, ain't it? Ever so peaceful . . .

GOVERNESS. It *was*.

STREETWALKER. You know, I often used to think my kid was a blasted nuisance – but when I sent her away, I missed her like hell.

GOVERNESS. I'm sure she's much better off where she is.

STREETWALKER. They just sent me a snap of her. (*She produces a photo from her pocket.*) Here, have a look.

GOVERNESS (*giving it a brief glance*). Hm. Underdeveloped. What a pity.

STREETWALKER. No, she ain't then. She's a strapping little kid.

GOVERNESS. The photograph I meant.

STREETWALKER. Oh, sorry! My mistake . . . Looks cute, doesn't she – rolling in the hay? Name's Ivy. (*Silence.*) This your paper?

GOVERNESS. No. It was left here.

STREETWALKER (*picking up a dingy newspaper*). Tch, same old war . . . Hallo – 'Italians driven out of Bardia.' . . . Never do anything but get chased all over the shop, poor little baskets!

GOVERNESS (*with unexpected venom*). And a good thing too.

STREETWALKER. Oh, I dunno. I mean, you can't reely work yourself
up against *them* like you do against the Germans. They wasn't
meant to be fighters. Give 'em a guitar to twang, and they do fine.
Not that I'm a fair judge, though. You see, I married one.

GOVERNESS. You – married an Italian?

STREETWALKER. Yes, what's wrong with that? It was years ago. He left
me soon after the kid arrived. Went back to his own country. I
didn't have no hard feelings. The foggy winters made his chest bad.

GOVERNESS. Was he – a Neapolitan?

STREETWALKER. Bless you, no – he didn't have no politics!

GOVERNESS. I mean, did he come from Naples?

STREETWALKER. Believe he *did*, come to think of it . . . Rare good
company, he was. Of a moonlight night we'd sit out in the yard,
him strumming away and singing songs in his own lingo. My, but
some of them was pretty! *Folk songs*, he called them . . . Said the
fishermen used to sing them in their little boats with the red sails,
so that you could hear 'em far away over the sea –

GOVERNESS. Yes, that's right . . .

STREETWALKER. And sometimes he'd push the table back and do a
dance – oh, he was a *turn* – like a sort of a jig. He called it a –
tarantella.

GOVERNESS. Oh – don't!

STREETWALKER. Why, what's up? I haven't said anything to upset
you, have I?

GOVERNESS. No, no – nothing.

STREETWALKER. Come orf it! What's the matter, dearie?

GOVERNESS. The way you spoke brought it all back to me so clearly.
I – I almost felt I was there again, in Naples – looking out over the
blue bay from my little terrace, with him beside me –

STREETWALKER. *Who?*

GOVERNESS. My – my gentleman friend.

STREETWALKER. A wop, eh?

GOVERNESS. Oh, but a very nice young man. His father was a count,
he said.

STREETWALKER. Whatever was you doing out there?

GOVERNESS. I was in the employ of an English family who took a villa
out there for the winter.

STREETWALKER. Go on. Sounds ever so romantic.

GOVERNESS. I don't know why I should be telling you about it. I never
told anyone before. It's such a long time ago now . . . But there

seems to be a sort of link between us. I met my – my gentleman friend while I was bathing with the children. He was so handsome – so polite.

STREETWALKER. They got a way with 'em, wops have, and no mistake!

GOVERNESS. I was very young at the time. No one had ever paid me any attention before. Oh, it was all like a dream – the flowers, the music, the dancing! . . . And then –

STREETWALKER. Yes?

GOVERNESS. When the family heard about it, there was a terrible scandal. They sent me home. He promised to follow, and marry me. But he never came. I waited and waited . . . There wasn't even a letter. I never was able to save enough money to go back. Gradually it began to hurt less . . .

STREETWALKER. Was you very struck on him?

GOVERNESS. I loved and hated him, both at the same time.

STREETWALKER. You got a raw deal, and no mistake. Wops is all right once you nail 'em down. Mine made an honest woman of me, all right!

GOVERNESS. I suppose I ought to be ashamed of myself.

STREETWALKER. Don't talk soft. Ain't nothing to be ashamed of in loving a man that lets you down. Don't you fret, dearie. All you can do with this life is to take it as you find it.

GOVERNESS. Yes, that's true. Now I must be getting back, to give Rosalind her supper.

STREETWALKER. Better get going myself . . . Feel all the better for the rest. Gee, but this weather's hard on your feet!

GOVERNESS. Try bathing them with a little salt in the water. Rosalind – come away from that little boy at once! The *idea*! Goodbye, Miss – Mrs –

STREETWALKER. So long, dearie. Never mind the handle . . . Blimey, look what's coming! One of them Free French generals. I always had an eye for a foreigner . . .

(*Exit in the opposite directions, the* GOVERNESS *prim and disapproving again, clasping her charge firmly by the hand; the* STREETWALKER *mincing in pursuit of her quarry.*)

# I Wonder How It Feels

*Performed by Lesley Osmond at the Windmill Theatre in 1940. From the* Revuedeville.

*The fitting-room of a fashionable dress shop.*
MISS BROWN *is discovered, making alterations to an elaborate model.*

Though poets have impressed on us that ignorance is bliss,
I wonder how it really feels to wear a dress like this?
To know the taste of glamour and prove it sweet or bitter;
To be a 'valued client', instead of just the fitter.
To rise sometimes quite early – but of your own accord –
And take a morning canter, while escorted by a lord;
To saunter down St James's with a poodle at your heels –
I wonder what it's really like? I wonder how it feels?

A cavalier immaculate with top hat and cigar
To kiss your lacquered fingertips and hand you to his car.
'Darling, you're divine tonight,' softly he would say.
'Exotic as the orchids I sent to you today . . .'
For lunch a plate of oysters, (head waiter bowing low)
Some caviare to toy with, a partridge wing or so . . .
Plovers' eggs for breakfast – champagne with *all* your meals!
I wonder what it's really like? I wonder how it feels? . . .

I think I'll have the Rolls today, the Daimler's rather muddy.
James, tell His Grace it's time  to start. He's dozing in the
    study . . .
He knows it's Gold Cup day today. We're running Dibble-
    dabble!

It's such a bore to get held up by charabancs and rabble.
Oh, there you are, dear. *Do* get in. Why must you take so long?
Now don't squash little Fifi, for you know her heart's not
          strong.
Well, James, you'll have to 'step on it', to use a coarse
          expression.
Oh dear, I do loathe Ascot so, it fills me with depression.

The same old crowd are here again. There's Dora Wilberforce!
Poor thing, she's growing day by day to look more like her
          horse.
This frock looks simply terrible. Just wait till I get back –
I'll see that wretched girl at Madame Chloë's gets the sack.
We'll lunch in the Pavilion before the second race . . .
What? Dibble-dabble's won again? James, do wake up His
          Grace.
It's been a rather lucky day. I like a little flutter.
Don't bother with that five-pound note; just leave it in the
          gutter.

I wonder how it really feels to wear against your skin
Underwear like gossamer, chiffon thin as thin?
To take a bath (green marble, perfumed with bergamot)
'Louise, turn on the shower – and mind it's not too hot!'
Bond Street in the morning, just to fix your face and hair,
Then a stroll round Asprey's to spend a tenner there.
A jade and silver compact, diamond-studded heels –
I wonder what it's really like? I wonder how it feels?

Cocktails at the Berkeley, luncheon at the Ritz.
Then to Madame Chloë's – (let's hope the new frock fits) . . .
Why can't we *all* live lives of ease, with wealth enough to burn,
And no more silly stitches and no more hems to turn?
But p'raps we'd feel uneasy, common folk like us,
Riding in a Daimler instead of in a bus.
A black and silver Daimler, with silent, cushioned wheels –
I'd rather like to try it . . . Oh, I wonder how it feels?

# Diana Morgan

## 1910–

An actress, playwright and broadcaster, Diana Morgan was born in Cardiff on 29 May 1910, the daughter of Charles Morgan and Diana Jane Gwynne-Thomas. Educated at Howell's School, Llandaff, and the Central School of Speech and Drama, she later married Robert MacDermot-Barbour of the BBC, her co-writer on many of the revue sketches.

Her first stage appearance was in a matinee of her own play *Cindelectra* at the Arts. In 1931 she played in Coward's extravaganza *Cavalcade* at Drury Lane. Subsequently she appeared in repertory productions at Newcastle and Cambridge. In the West End she appeared in *The Country Wife*, *Hippolytus*, *Lysistrata* and *Parnell*.

Diana Morgan wrote the comedy *Bats in the Belfry* which ran at the Ambassadors theatre for 178 performances in 1937. Her other plays (some co-written with her husband Robert MacDermot) include *This World of Ours* (1935), *The House in the Square* (1940), *Three Waltzes* (1945), *The White Eagles* (1950), *After My Fashion* (in which she played the role of Chloe Gwynn; in New York produced as *The Starcross Story*, 1952), and *The Little Evenings* (in which she played Mrs Pritchard; for the Welsh National Theatre, 1970).

She was a contract writer for Ealing Studios, and her films include *Run For Your Money* (1949), a comic study of two Welsh miners on a spree in London, which starred Donald Houston, Moira Lister, Hugh Griffith, Joyce Grenfell and Alec Guinness, and the sentimental children's film *Hand in Hand*, which starred John Gregson and Sybil Thorndike and won fourteen international awards. She later wrote for television, including scripts for *Emergency Ward 10* and was also, for a time, theatre critic for BBC radio's Woman's Hour.

She contributed sketches to many wartime revues including *The Gate Revue, Let's Face It, Swinging the Gate, All Clear, The New Ambassadors Revue* and *Big Top*.

She now lives in a residential home for members of the theatrical profession.

# The Bacchante

## (With Robert MacDermot, with additional dialogue from Hermione Gingold)

*Performed by Hermione Gingold and Guy Verney at the Ambassadors Theatre in 1940. From the* Swinging the Gate *revue (126 performances).*

'A clever number' – *Bystander*

HERMIONE. Excuse me, sir, does the bus stop here for Chorley Wood?

GUY. Who is Chorley Wood?

HERMIONE. Sir Henry Wood's brother, I think! No, I mean Chorley Wood – the wood you can't see for the trees.

GUY. Oh, I see.

HERMIONE. I'm looking for a wood to spend the night in.

GUY. It's only a tuppenny ride to Shepherds Bush.

HERMIONE. Bush? I'm afraid that wouldn't quite do.

GUY. Why do you want to spend the night in a wood? If it isn't a rude answer.

HERMIONE. Well, you see, I'm a Bacchante.

GUY. Good heavens, a real Bacchante? I say, how are you?

HERMIONE. I'm very well, thank you. How are you?

GUY. Pretty well.

HERMIONE. Nothing serious, I hope.

GUY. Just a touch of spring fever.

HERMIONE. Have a grape.

GUY. No, I'm afraid my friend wouldn't like me to. Can I lend you a comb?

HERMIONE. I'm sorry my hair's in such a mess. It's being out in all winds and weathers. And the birds! The eagles are flying very low this summer, don't you think?

GUY. Well, I . . .

HERMIONE. I suppose you're not troubled much with birds?

GUY. Well, no. That's an awfully jolly outfit you're wearing.

HERMIONE. Do you like it? I made it myself with a pattern out of *Homers' Chat*.

GUY. I say, do you have orgies? I'd love to go to one.

HERMIONE. As a matter of fact, we're having one in Battersea Park next Tuesday. And I was told I could bring a friend. Would you like to come?

GUY. In fancy dress?

HERMIONE. Optional.

GUY. I've got a lovely Pierrot costume I wore at the Vic-Wells ball.

HERMIONE. Will you call for me?

GUY. Well, I'd rather meet you there. I don't think my friend would like me to be seen out with a Bacchante.

HERMIONE. Why not?

GUY. Well, they do go about 360 times too far, don't they?

HERMIONE. I see.

GUY. Well, I must be getting along. I'm frightfully glad to have met you.

HERMIONE. Goodbye.

GUY. Goodbye. By the way, what's your name?

HERMIONE. I'm Bessie Bacchante.

GUY. See you next Tuesday, Bessie.

HERMIONE. It's always the same! No really nice young man ever wants to take me home and introduce me to his mother

Oh why was I born a Bacchante?
I find all-night orgies a bore.
I feel such a sick dilettante
In the morning after every night before.
I'm tired of the taste of Chianti,
Falernian makes me feel queer,
And as for that Asti Spumante
Well, I'd rather have some Alka Seltzer, dear.

We lead the strangest life on tour with Bacchus,
You never know what's going to happen next.
Those fauns are always waiting to attack us
And nobody could call them undersexed.
The other girls just think that nothing matters
And never seem to know WHO crushed their grapes,

But I must say I have no use for satyrs
From whom I've had the narrowest escapes.

Oh why was I born a Bacchante?
I never had much of a head.
The clothes are a great deal too scanty,
And it's always three before you get to bed.
I think that it must have been Dante
Who said, 'If you need an excuse,
When caught *in delicto flagrante*,
You can always tell your mother it was Zeus!'

I'm always spilling claret on my chiton,
I really hate to have to show my knees,
A wood's not very nice to spend a night in,
With all those Hamadryads in the trees.
I've never had a chance to meet Apollo
I'm always getting followed round by Pan,
And he's too much for any girl to swallow,
He's such a very hairy little man.

Oh, why was I born a Bacchante?
I find that my throat's got so hoarse
With shouting 'Eureka Avanti!'
And other things considerably more coarse.
I'd make such a good Corybante,
But I'm in a furious rage,
The censor they say is so Anti
That he won't allow my act on any stage.

# *South Coast Women*
## (with Robert MacDermot)

*Performed by Hermione Gingold, Madge Elliott and Phillida Sewell at the Ambassadors Theatre in 1940. From the* Swinging the Gate *revue (126 performances).*

'The big laugh of the night' – *Bystander*

> ALL: In nice hotels in Eastbourne,
> In Bournemouth, Brighton, Rye,
> We live and have our being,
> And ultimately die.
> We are the South Coast Women
> From whom no flower burgeons,
> Widows of men not quite upper ten,
> And uninteresting virgins,
> South Coast Women, living a life apart,
> How does your story begin?

> 1: I'm Mrs Kingston-Brassey – I'm very dull and mean,
> I read lots of novels and I like 'em just obscene.
> I'm horrid to young people, I make 'em hot and cold,
> And they can't answer back, you see, because I'm very
> old.

> ALL: We're all so old
> 1: Everyone's resigned, dear,
> 2: Pretending they don't mind, dear,
> 3: When we are unkind, dear.
> ALL: We're so old

2: I'm Agatha Smith Tomkins, my father died of drink,
   I've whisky in my wardrobe – it's just a harmless kink.
   I'm rude to all the waiters, swear they don't do as they're
      told
   And they can't answer back because

ALL: We're so old.
1: I live for my tummy
2: I make boys call me Mummy
3: I cheat like hell at rummy
ALL: We're so old.

3: I'm Mrs Albert Lambert, I have a special chair,
   If anyone sits on it there's trouble everywhere.
   My temper is quite famous – people say it's uncontrolled,
   But they can't answer back, you see, because . . .

ALL: We're so old.
1: Everyone respects us
2: Nobody neglects us
3: Our grey hair protects us
ALL: We're so old.

In nice hotels in Worthing,
In Bognor, Rottingdean,
We sit down to our dinner
In old lace, not quite clean.
We are the South Coast Women
Who live on unearned money
Filling our days in most useless ways
We sometimes think it's funny

[*spoken*] Why someone doesn't call our bluff and tell us to go
   straight to hell . . .

# *The Guardsman*
## (with Robert MacDermot)

Banned by the Lord Chamberlain's office, so never performed in the shows.

## SCENE I

SIR RUPERT. Meadows, Lady Dolly sups with me here tonight.

(*Enter* MEADOWS.)

MEADOWS. Ah, we met her at Trouville, did we not, sir?

RUPERT. We did indeed. By gad, what a high-stepping little filly.

MEADOWS. In that case, sir, I suggest oysters, celery *à l'amoureuse* and a bottle of Aphrodisiac '69.

RUPERT. That ought to do the trick – and we will wear our petunia dressing-gown, Meadows.

MEADOWS. No, sir, if you will excuse me, I have laid out the cerise with the tassle and the Eastern motifs; if you remember, sir, we had much success in that with the young ladies of the 'Little Miss Winsome' company.

RUPERT. You are right, Meadows. I will go and put it on at once.

(*Exit.* MEADOWS *ushers in* LADY DOLLY.)

MEADOWS. Your cloak, my lady. Sir Rupert will be here immediately.

(*Withdraws.*)

DOLLY. Ah, Dolly, this is folly. If his Evelyn should hear of this escapade – but impossible. How could Evelyn know?

(*Enter* RUPERT.)

RUPERT (*exultantly*). So you have come!

DOLLY (*shrinking*). Yes, Rupert.

RUPERT. I vow you are more tantalizing than ever, Dolly. A little kiss?

DOLLY (*coy*). No, no.

RUPERT. You are a woman of the world.

DOLLY (*with spirit*). But not of your world, Rupert.

RUPERT. Witty as well as pretty, but no more words. My arms are aching for you. Come, Dolly, do not be shy. Surely you realize what having supper with a man means.

DOLLY. Remember Evelyn!

RUPERT. Can I forget? But this is Jermyn street, Dolly, where men are men. (*Clasping her.*)

DOLLY. Unhand me, sir.

RUPERT. No, you intoxicate me.

DOLLY. Let me go.

RUPERT. Never, you provoking little devil.

DOLLY. Do not forget you are another's.

RUPERT. But for this one night I would be yours. (*Crushes her to him madly. The door burst open and a young woman in evening dress appears.*) Evelyn!

EVELYN. Rupert, how could you?

BLACKOUT.


## SCENE II

DOLLY. Meadows, Sir Rupert is having supper with me tonight.

MEADOWS. Is that the young gentleman we met skiing at Skid?

DOLLY. No, it's the boy from Blot.

MEADOWS. In that case I don't know what to suggest for supper, my lady, now that Benzedrine is on the poison list.

DOLLY. Oh, well, we can always go to a milk bar later on. I think I shall wear my off-white housecoat.

MEADOWS. I'm afraid it's a bit too off-white, my lady, after last night's party, so I've put out your Swan and Edgar *robe de soir*. It used to go down big with the boys from 'Nine Sharp'.

DOLLY. You're quite right, Meadows. I shall go and put it on.

(*Exit.* MEADOWS *ushers in* SIR RUPERT.)

MEADOWS. Your scarf, Sir Rupert. Lady Dolly will be here in a moment. (*Exit.*)

RUPERT. Rupert, this is stupid. Have I counted my money? What if

Evelyn should find out – but no, of course Evelyn could not
possibly know.

(*Enter* DOLLY.)

DOLLY (*passionately*). So you've come at last.

RUPERT. Yes, dolly.

DOLLY. You're more glamorous than ever. Kiss me.

RUPERT (*shy*). No, no.

DOLLY. Don't be coy. You're a man, aren't you?

RUPERT. Yes, I suppose so.

DOLLY. I'm mad about you, Rupert. Don't be so dreary. Surely you
realize what I meant by supper.

RUPERT. Remember Evelyn.

DOLLY. Can I forget? But this is Dolphin Square, Rupert, where
women are . . . desperate. (*Clasping him.*)

RUPERT. Don't do it, Dolly.

DOLLY. I can't help it.

RUPERT. Let me go.

DOLLY. Never, you lovely thing.

RUPERT. Don't forget I'm another's.

DOLLY. But tonight you shall be mine.

(*She crushes him to her madly. The door bursts open and a young
guardsman appears, brandishing a cane.*)

RUPERT. Evelyn!

EVELYN. How could you, Rupert?

BLACKOUT.

# – And Friend
## (with Robert MacDermot)

*Performed at the Ambassadors Theatre in 1939. From* The Gate Revue *(449 performances).*

I have a grudge against the illustrated papers,
Those glossy chronicles of social life.
You know the ones I mean, they scan the weekly
    scene,
With pictures of MFH, and wife
At some obscure hunt ball.
They snap them in the hall
With Bunjy Blackerton,
Who is of course the son
AND heir
Of Viscount Tyre, the rubber millionaire.
They label them by name,
But what I think's a shame,
I really can't deny
At any party I attend
The most I get is so-and-so and friend.

I go to exhibitions,
I'm there at all first nights,
I talk to great musicians,
I see the better fights,
I'm always in the papers, but I cannot comprehend
Why others have their proper names
When I am just 'and friend'.
I'm always seen at Ascot,
With Anne or Lady Jane,
My lovely luncheon basket

Is brimming with champagne.
But though I was at Eton, still, however much I spend,
It's Princess Sarsaparilla, Lord Eagertread and friend.
It isn't as if I was nobody much,
But the way that I'm always ignored
Would lead you to think that the press didn't know
That my twenty-fifth cousin's a Lord.
But still I'm growing tougher
Through playing gooseberry
I'll really hardly suffer,
Though I know how it will be:
When they publish my last picture
I guess how it will end
A snapshot of St Peter, St Cecilia, and friend.

# All Smart Women Must
## (with Robert MacDermot)

The Lord Chamberlain's notes claim that 'this was sung by two effeminate men and a lesbian'.

*Performed by Hermione Gingold, Walter Crisham and Michael Wilding at the Ambassadors Theatre in 1939. From* The Gate Revue *(449 performances).*

ALL: Three dress designers who influence the mode
    And tell you what you've simply got to wear.
1: Make yourself a sight
    In red cellophane at night
    And pin a ripe tomato in your hair.
2: My dress of purple crepe
    Is cruel to your shape
    But you've got to wear it if you'd be well dressed.
3: You must obey our rules
    All you silly little fools, or other women will not be
      impressed.

ALL: Why do we bother to make you plain?
    Listen then to our refrain.
    We don't want women to be beautiful
    Beauty, we say, is through.
1: We make you all go choosing hats that are amusing
    And made of billiard balls and glue,
2: We are monstrously unkind to each feminine behind,
    We like to make you look like the ma of ten.
3: Our clothes are madly witty
    And we'll see you don't look pretty.
ALL: Oh we'll see you don't attract the men.

Three dress designers who simply laugh like hell
And get the greatest kick of all their life.

1: When, resulting from a suit
   Made of canvas and waxed fruit,
   A husband gets fed up and leaves his wife,

2: Oh screw your hair right back, and look your age in
      black,
   Vogue says you must stick sequins on your nose.

3: And women say, 'My dear,
   You look divinely queer,
   Where do you get your quite demented clothes?'

ALL: Why do we bother to make you wear
     Things that a queen could not bear?
     We don't want women to be beautiful
     We don't *want* women to allure.

1: When out shopping in your Rolls,
   Wear a shoe with inch-thick soles,
   If a man's infatuated that's the cure.

2: Paint on lips, oh modern miss,
   That the boldest dare not kiss,
   With pain tweak out your eyebrows, hair by hair.

3: Like a dummy in a shop you will be before we stop,

ALL: Oh we'll soon see that men will cease to care.
     We don't want women to be beautiful; It's really an easy
        task.

1: We say your skin is bad
   Then your husbands may get mad
   You'll go to bed each evening in a mask.

2: And our rubber corsets too
   Will soon leave their mark on you
   But you've got to wear them or you'll soon be stout.

3: For you see, dear Jane or Mary
   Dame Fashion is a fairy
   And fairies get you if you don't watch out.

# Kensington Girls
## (with Robert MacDermot)

*Performed by Joan Swinstead, Gabrielle Brune and Kay Young at the Ambassadors Theatre in 1939. From* The Gate Revue *(449 performances).*

'Fresh treatment . . . sung with bored nonchalance' – *Tatler*

> We're Kensington girls from Kensington Gore,
> Honest and decent and clean to the core,
> Hoping to marry as soon as we can,
> For the sake of the race and the sake of a man.
>
> My name is Celia, my father's a Major,
> My mother's great-uncle's a Lord,
> I've just been presented, I thought it was heaven,
> But had to pretend I was bored.
> I worship my dog and though usually mild,
> Cruelty to animals just drives me wild,
> It's so much more fun to be cruel to a child.
> Girls of Kensington Gore.
>
> My name is Cora, my father's a Colonel,
> I've got a young man in Shanghai.
> He's rolling in money, with two lovely cars,
> So I do hope the darling won't die.
> I go to Miss Fogerty's school every day,
> They're frightfully nice, as they know I can pay.
> I couldn't face Rep, but the West End's OK.
> Girls of Kensington Gore.
>
> My name's Belinda, my father's a General,
> In case he may go to the Front.

I'm socially better than these other two,
For you see, in the winter I hunt.
And I tell you straight if I had Hitler here,
I'd give him a jolly good sock on the ear,
Then throw him to hounds of the West
     Worcestershire.
Girls of Kensington Gore.

Oh ye of lesser breed,
Listen to our creed:
There is one place to live and that is Kensington,
Including parts of Chelsea or a Brompton Square.
There is one uniform to wear:
A good fur coat, a string of pearls,
And a black dress for English girls.
There is one shop, and that is Harrods, where
We've lots of time to stand and stare.
There are no plays but those that run a hundred
     nights,
And have lots of names in lights.
There are no men except those in the Army, Navy or
     RAF,
All others make us laff.
We are the backbone of the country,
The really nice girls
Of quite good family,
Who get married about twenty-four
And go to India, China,
South Africa and Burma,
That's what God made us for.
We're the girls from Kensington Gore,
Not very rich and not very poor,
Hoping to marry as soon as we can,
Just for saving our face and a man
We're girls of Kensington Gore.

# *Folk Songs*
## (with Robert MacDermot)

*Performed by Joan Swinstead and Ernest Thesiger at the Ambassadors Theatre in 1941. From the* New Ambassadors Revue.

ANNOUNCER. And now we have with us here in the studio Professor and Mrs Cartwheel, who are going to give you a little talk on the unknown folklore with some jolly little unknown songs. Professor and Mrs Cartwheel.

PROFESSOR. Good evening. How many of you, I wonder, know anything about the curious superstitions still existent in the furthest corners of our countryside? How many of you have heard the curious song sung by sheep-dippers in the Mendips – the odd verses chanted by beet-growers in the Cotswolds – the little limericks intoned by wool-gatherers in the Chilterns? My wife and I have made a study of their fascinating rhythms, and with myself at the minipiano, my wife will sing the song sung by hop-pickers in the Beconshire Beacons. Ready, Gertrude?

GERTRUDE. How many of you have heard the little tune sung on Michaelmas day at Willow-in-the-Wold? Or the song they say is heard on Candlemas Day at Willow-the-Marsh, or . . .

PROFESSOR. Ready, Gertrude?

GERTRUDE. Do you know the words of the song the children sang on Fridays in Leamington Spa? Or the words old men use on Saturday nights in Walthamstow?

PROFESSOR. My wife will now sing a very old song. It is so old that only five people yet alive know it. My wife and I know it, a poor hop-picker and his crippled brother know it, and I have also told a friend of mine, a Mrs Jones, who lives in Maida Vale. How many of you know how few know these unknown folk songs of your island? How many of you . . .

GERTRUDE. I'm ready, Humphrey.

(*Chord. Bursting into song.*)

> As I was going to meet a man
> Fol de rol
> Fol de rol
> Fol de rol . . .

PROFESSOR. That's just a fragment. But what a fragment! It comes
from deepest Dorset. The spinsters and the knitters in the sun hum
it continually. No one has any idea how it happened. My wife will
now sing the hop-pickers' song. (*Chord.*) Ready, Gertrude?

GERTRUDE. How many of you know the song of the water-diviners?
The chant of the oakum-pickers?

PROFESSOR. Ready, Gertrude?

GERTRUDE. Humphrey, I don't know the song of the hop-pickers!

PROFESSOR. Gertrude, after all our tours, after all my teaching!

GERTRUDE. Forgive me, Humphrey.

PROFESSOR. Sometimes, Gertrude, I don't believe you care!

(*He strikes a few chords and they sing.*)

> In any hotel the guidebooks recommend
> You'll find us if you have an hour to spend,
> Self-consciously drinking a pint at the local
> And learning some earthy old song from a yokel.

GERTRUDE. Each evening at seven I powder my face
> And come down to dinner in bugles and lace;
> We copy out notes for a book we may write
> Then hey for hot milk and a real early night!

BOTH. We're very keen on folklore
> On anything that's quaint
> We like a pretty fable
> Of elfin or a saint.
> We like lots of local colour
> And pretty local rhymes
> And nothing could be duller
> Than our letters to the *Times*.

GERTRUDE. We're interested in goblins
> And pixies on the hearth.

PROFESSOR. We're certain there are fairies
> Down the garden path.

GERTRUDE. I like everything that's Tudor
> To me Tudors can't be wrong.

PROFESSOR. And nothing could be ruder
   Than a little Tudor song.
GERTRUDE. We like to hear of witches
   We're interested in sprites.
PROFESSOR. We like to know what happens
   On warm midsummer nights.
GERTRUDE. Our knowledge we are storing
   Though unpleasant people say
   We couldn't be more boring.
BOTH. How many of you know the old song they sing in Wimbledon
Park on Sundays? Or what the nightingales chant in Berkeley
Square? Or what camp-followers in Worcestershire and pub-
crawlers in Gloucestershire . . .

# Daphne du Maurier

*1907–1989*

The world-famous novelist was born on 13 May 1907, daughter of the matinee idol Sir Gerald du Maurier, and granddaughter of the novelist George du Maurier (author of the novel, *Trilby*). Educated privately in London and Paris, she began writing in 1928 and published many novels and short stories, including *Rebecca, Frenchman's Creek, Jamaica Inn, My Cousin Rachel, The King's General, The Birds* and *The Scapegoat* (all of which were made into films). She also wrote biographies of her father, *Gerald: A Portrait* (1934), and the rest of her family, *The Du Mauriers* (1937).

Her own adaptation of *Rebecca* played at the Queen's Theatre in 1940. She wrote another play, *September Tide* (starring Gertrude Lawrence), which played at the Aldwych in 1948. The play *The Years Between*, originally entitled *The Return of the Soldier*, is evidently semi-autobiographical. It deals with her own reaction to the return of her husband from the war, after she had had an affair with a neighbour in his absence.

She was married to Lt Gen Sir Frederick Browning (known as 'Boy' Browning), chancellor of the exchequer to Princess Elizabeth and later to the Duke of Edinburgh. They had three children. She lived in Cornwall which features in many of her powerful novels.

# About *The Years Between*

The critics were divided over this play. While the *Evening Standard* were disappointed the author 'abandoned the play for the message', the *Observer* wrote that she seized 'a huge and harassing topic of the time, and generally treats the playgoer as an adult, showing him, with serious fidelity, one aspect of modern love.' The public however flocked to Irene Hentschel's production, which starred Nora Swinburne and Clive Brook and played for 617 performances at Wyndham's in 1945.

A film was made in 1946 with Valerie Hobson as Diana, and Michael Redgrave as her husband. Flora Robson played the nanny.

It is a well-constructed domestic drama, with a strong leading character who reflects a problem faced by many women when the war (during which they had assumed much responsibility and power at home) came to an end. The play has a very dark side to it too, for although the heroine does welcome her husband's return, it is not done with unquestioning romance, and clearly the character of the husband is a cold and difficult person. To me this uneasiness, which clouds the 'happy' ending, brings an unexpected depth to a play on this familiar subject.

# The Years Between

## Daphne du Maurier

*Nora Swinburne and Ronald Ward*

First acted at the Opera House, Manchester, on 20 November 1944, and subsequently transferred to Wyndham's Theatre, London, on 10 January 1945, with the following cast:

| | |
|---|---|
| ROBIN | *John Gilpin* |
| NANNY | *Henrietta Watson* |
| RICHARD LLEWELLYN | *Ronald Ward* |
| DIANA WENTWORTH | *Nora Swinburne* |
| THE VICAR | *Geoffrey Morris* |
| SIR ERNEST FOSTER | *Allan Jeayes* |
| THE VICAR'S WIFE | *Lilian Christine* |
| VENNING | *Arthur Chesney* |
| MICHAEL WENTWORTH | *Clive Brook* |
| MISS JAMESON | *Betty Sparkes* |

# ACT I

SCENE 1

*The Library of The Old Manor. A lovely old room, musty with books, and at the back, Centre are long windows leading on to a terrace or garden. There is a door to the hall left. Books line the walls to Left. A large open fireplace Right, a sofa, chairs and table Centre. The room must suggest rest, repose – a place to browse in. There are fishing rods and things in the background. We feel that a man has lived here. It is his room.*

*There are five people that matter in the play.*

*The first we see is* ROBIN, *aged about ten. He is a nice, rather original little boy. It is a misty afternoon in autumn, and rain has been falling all day. There are leaves outside on the terrace.* ROBIN *is alone. Presently* NANNY *comes in. She is any age, plain and thin, and very capable. She has been with the family ever since* ROBIN *was born, and has stayed on since he went to school.*

*The other people, whom we shall see later, are* DIANA, RICHARD, *and* MICHAEL. DIANA *is* ROBIN'*s mother, aged about thirty-five. When we first see her, she is quiet and subdued, because of recent sorrow, but she will become different as the play proceeds, with a strength and efficiency that her good looks belie.* RICHARD *is the quiet, steady, pipe-smoking fellow that every woman depends on, and quite often ends by marrying. We must feel an affection for* RICHARD *at the start.*

MICHAEL, DIANA'*s husband and* ROBIN'*s father, has a tenseness about him that gives us uneasiness and pain directly we know he has come home. Not the repose that* RICHARD *has. Whenever* MICHAEL *is present, there must be an atmosphere of strain, something must surely happen, and we are afraid.*

*The* CURTAIN *rises with* ROBIN *lying on the floor, a large atlas spread in front of him.* NANNY *enters from the hall with a tray of tea things. She puts the tray down on the table and then glances at* ROBIN. *After a moment she speaks.*

NANNY. You'll strain your eyes in that dark corner, Robin. Put away your book, there's a good boy, and do the blackout, while I lay the tea. (*She speaks gently, as though she does not wish to show authority.*)
ROBIN. It's too early to do the blackout yet. (*He still looks at his atlas, but moves to a crouching position.*) Nan?

NANNY. Yes, Robin?

ROBIN. Is the Mediterranean really as big as it looks on the map?

NANNY. I don't know. You're still at school. You should know better than me. (*She glances at him furtively, and goes on laying tea things.*)

ROBIN. It looks so frightfully big here. I don't see that an aeroplane would have much chance of being found, once it was forced down. Has the post been?

NANNY (*quietly*). Not yet. (*Fussily.*) You know the postman doesn't get here until nearly six. Come on, Robin, you'll get your clothes all dirty on the floor.

(ROBIN *gets up and in doing so knocks down fishing rod.*)

Careful now, Robin – Daddy's fishing rod.

(*She speaks sharply.* ROBIN *looks scared. He waits a moment, and then picks it up quickly.*)

ROBIN (*relieved*). It's not broken. Nan. (NANNY s*tares a moment, then glances away. Slowly – rather nervously.*) Nanny, what is it? It wouldn't have mattered actually, if it had been broken, would it, Nan? (*He has the queer callousness of childhood still.*) Not any more?

NANNY (*upset*). That's not the way to talk, Robin. You wouldn't like Mummy to hear you. Come on now, help me set the tea. I've managed to get some honey for a treat. Careful of the scones, the plate's hot.

(RICHARD's *voice, off, saying:* No, Sandy, go off, old boy, not indoors with all that mud on you. Lie down . . . lie down . . . lie down. Good boy.)

ROBIN (*smiling*). There's Uncle Richard.

(*He darts to the long window and runs into* RICHARD, *wearing a raincoat.*)

Hallo, Uncle Richard.

RICHARD. Hallo, Robin. What've you been doing?

ROBIN. I've had a cold.

RICHARD. Hallo, Nanny.

NANNY. Good evening, Mr Llewellyn.

ROBIN. Nanny wouldn't let me go out, otherwise I'd have come and looked you up. Have you come to tea?

RICHARD. Yes, if Nanny has any to spare.

NANNY (*smiling; she is fond of* RICHARD). Of course, Mr Llewellyn. Go along, Robin, and wash your hands.

(ROBIN *makes a face but exits.*)

RICHARD. Mrs Wentworth not back yet?

NANNY. No, sir. She said she would catch the 3.10 and trust to getting a taxi at the station.

RICHARD. No news, I suppose?

NANNY. No, sir.

RICHARD. Did she expect to hear anything in London?

NANNY. I don't know, sir. She has said so little to me. You know how she has been all along, so quiet, and shut up in herself. When I think how she lived for the Colonel, all these years! He came first in everything, sir, and now – sometimes I think it would be better if she broke down.

(NANNY'*s voice breaks. She grabs for a handkerchief.*)

RICHARD (*pats her shoulder*). Yes, I know exactly how you feel, Nanny, but you mustn't be the one to give way. Why, the house would fall to pieces but for you.

(NANNY *smiles through her tears, and blows her nose.*)

NANNY. It's the way it happened that made it seem so dreadful – just the plane crashing and no trace found. I remember when my father died, somehow we all felt better after the funeral – that sounds a queer heartless thing to say, but now . . . the shock has been such a strain on Mrs Wentworth and the boy's a bundle of nerves.

RICHARD. I wish to heaven I could do more to help.

NANNY. Oh, but you do help, sir. Just to know you are so close means a lot to Mrs Wentworth. She was saying so the day before she went to London.

RICHARD. Was she?

NANNY. You'll forgive me – it sounds forward of me, perhaps, but you are a gentleman that is always the same. People know where they are with you. And that makes for confidence, you know.

RICHARD (*smiling*). Thank you, Nanny.

NANNY. When you first came down here to live, and bought up old Mr Rawlin's farm, I remember thinking, 'He won't stay long,' even though you were a friend of the family.

RICHARD. Just another idler come down to play at farming, eh?

NANNY (*admitting*). Well – I suppose so. But I soon learnt different. And so did the village. I must get your tea, sir.

RICHARD. Nanny.

NANNY (*turning*). Yes?

RICHARD. I want you to feel that – if you are ever worried about Mrs
Wentworth, or the boy, you can come to me. Just that.

NANNY. Thank you, Mr Llewellyn. Do you know, the Colonel never
spoke to me that way all the time I'd been with them. (*She adds
slowly.*) But being so clever and all that – he was a gentleman of
moods.

(RICHARD *does not answer, and at that moment* ROBIN *comes in. He
glances at them suspiciously.*)

ROBIN. What are you two talking about?

RICHARD. Nanny was telling me what a packet of trouble you are.

(ROBIN *crosses below the sofa to* RICHARD.)

Let's have a look at your hands. (*He examines them jokingly.*) I
thought so. They haven't used up much of the soap ration.

NANNY (*reproachfully*). Oh, Robin.

ROBIN (*imperiously*). Don't be such an old fusspot, Nan. Go along and
get the tea. Uncle Richard is starving.

(NANNY *and* RICHARD *smile.*)

(NANNY *exits.*)

(RICHARD *sits on the chair left and* ROBIN *on the sofa.*)

ROBIN. Was Nanny crying?

RICHARD. I don't think so.

ROBIN. I believe she was, all the same.

(*There is a silence for a moment.* ROBIN *kicks the leg of the table.*)

Uncle Richard, there's a chap called Dawson at school. *His* father
was killed last term.

RICHARD. Bad luck . . . I say, it's getting a bit dark, isn't it? What
about the blackout? You do that one and I'll do this one here.

(ROBIN *jumps up and pulls the curtains.* NANNY *brings in the tea things.*)

NANNY. I can easily make fresh when Mrs Wentworth gets back.
Here's a raisin cake. I know you'll like that.

RICHARD. One of these days, Nanny, I shall have to report you to
Lord Woolton.

ROBIN. Pooh, that's nothing. You ought to see the store cupboard,
Uncle Richard, it's positively groaning.

NANNY. Never mind my store cupboard. You enjoy your tea.

(NANNY *shakes her head and exits.*)

ROBIN (*with importance*). I shall pour out. I'm host.

RICHARD. All right.

ROBIN. Funny, isn't it?

RICHARD. What's funny?

ROBIN. I've never been host in this house before.

(RICHARD *glances up, but* ROBIN *does not notice, and copes with the tea.*)

You know, Uncle Richard, I've decided not to go into the Army, after all.

RICHARD. Oh, really? How's that?

ROBIN. Well, you see – actually I never did want to much. But Daddy being in the Regiment was so keen that I felt I had to. Now of course I can do as I like.

RICHARD. There's plenty of time to decide these things. Better wait and see how the war goes first. Have a scone?

ROBIN. Thank you. I don't suppose Mummy would mind what I did. Of course she used to agree with Daddy. She had to. Have some honey? There's heaps of things I'd like to do. I've never had a chance to up till now – fishing, for instance. Can I have some more tea, please?

RICHARD. I thought you were gong to be host? Where's your saucer?

ROBIN. All things considered, I think I'll probably farm like you. It's very convenient that you live so close, because you'll be handy for showing me the ropes.

(*He is rather superior.* RICHARD *is amused.*)

RICHARD. Delighted, at any time.

ROBIN. Daddy wasn't very interested in farming, was he? I suppose, when a person writes books, and is a Member of Parliament, and a soldier as well, he hasn't much time for cows, and pigs and things.

RICHARD. No, I don't suppose he has.

ROBIN. I'm glad your leg kept you out of the Army, Uncle Richard.

RICHARD (*doubtfully*). Thanks. Jolly good scones, these.

ROBIN. Yes. (*Patronisingly.*) Nanny says you do a very good job of work with your farming, and every bit as useful to the country as being in one of the services.

RICHARD. Nanny is very kind.

ROBIN. Of course, you'll probably feel a bit flat when it's all over. If you ever marry and have children, it would be rather dull telling them you just had a farm in the war, wouldn't it?

RICHARD. Yes, Robin. I think it would. Can I have a piece of Nanny's
cake?

ROBIN. Yes, do. (*Quickly, afraid he has hurt* RICHARD's *feelings.*) Mind
you, I don't suppose they'd really care, because you're a jolly good
farmer.

RICHARD. Thank you.

ROBIN. But it does make a difference at school if a chap has a father
who's well known. All our masters read Daddy's books, and Mr
Wilmot went up to the House to hear his Maiden speech. Do you
know – (*impressed*) – he said it was supposed to be the best Maiden
speech for years and years.

RICHARD. I'm sure it was.

(ROBIN *gets up.*)

ROBIN (*munching*). The post's awfully late this afternoon. It must
be ages after five. (*He stares once more at the fishing rod and touches
it.*)

RICHARD (*gently*). Better not handle it, Robin. They're fragile things.
If Nanny lets you out tomorrow, you must come over and see my
new tractor. It only arrived this morning, and poor old Jim's scared
stiff of it. 'What did you buy a thing like that for?' he said. 'Haven't
we got enough to do already?'

ROBIN. I don't like tractors. They're much too slow. What's the fastest
you've ever driven in a car, Uncle Richard?

RICHARD. Oh, I don't know. I suppose my old Alvis used to touch
eighty.

ROBIN. Dawson told me their Bentley used to do ninety. (*Pause.*)
Dawson wore a black band on his arm last term when his father
was killed. (*Glances down at his left arm.*) I wonder whether Nanny
would make one for me.

(*There is a pause. Then the sound of voices from the hall.*)

(*Excitedly.*) Here's Mums. Hallo Mums, you're awfully late.

(RICHARD *looks towards the door. His face changes. We know now how
much he loves* DIANA. *The door opens,* DIANA *comes in, looking white
and tired but very lovely.*)

DIANA. Darling. (*She holds him and kisses him.*) Is your old cold a bit
better?

ROBIN. It's absolutely gone, but Nanny doesn't believe me.

RICHARD. Hallo, Diana.

DIANA. Richard, how lovely and thoughtful. I was hoping you would come in. No post?

NANNY. No, no post yet.

DIANA. Just tea, please, Nanny. I don't want anything to eat. Oh dear, how I hate train journeys nowadays.

NANNY (*calling over her shoulder*). Robin, you come along and help me get Mummy's tea. (NANNY *exits*.)

ROBIN. Tell me what you did, Mums! Were there any bombs when you were up in London? Did you see lots of people you knew? Did you go to the House at all and hear any debates? The postman is a great one for politics, you know. He says nothing will ever be the same again, when the war is over. Everyone will have lost so much, and gained so little.

(DIANA *says nothing. She is very still.*)

RICHARD. I say, Robin, old fellow, would you like to take Sandy into the kitchen and give him a rubdown. He's too filthy to bring in here, and he hates sitting outside in the dark.

ROBIN (*rising*). Does he eat raisin cake?

RICHARD. He eats anything.

ROBIN. All right, I'll give him a good feed. And I'll make him as sleek as a panther for you.

RICHARD. Thank you.

(*Exit* ROBIN. *He runs off, glad of something to do.*)

(DIANA *sits up and smiles wistfully at* RICHARD.)

DIANA. I think the postman was right, don't you? Nothing will ever be the same again. (*Pause.*) But he puts it in such a depressing way.

RICHARD. The postman is a depressing sort of chap. It can't be much fun living with a stone-deaf wife!

DIANA (*smiling*). Poor Postman . . . I suppose we shall all get a little harder and more bitter as the war goes on. Already people have altered since last year. There's not the defiant gaiety there used to be, when the bombs were falling every night. Things have become less grim, and yet more grey. We're letting the war become a kind of drab routine.

RICHARD. It's inclined to happen, you know. Danger is a great stimulus.

DIANA. We shouldn't need stimulus. We ought to feel proud and inspired all the time.

RICHARD. Did anything happen while you were in London?

DIANA. Why do you ask?

RICHARD. When you went away last Friday you were lost and helpless.
For the past three months you've been like that, ever since you had
that telegram. And now, tonight, although I know you're dog-tired,
there's a different look about you.

(NANNY *comes in with the tea.*)

NANNY. Tea, Mummy.

DIANA. Thank you, Nan.

NANNY. Drink it while it's hot.

DIANA. Yes, Nan, I will. Thank you.

(NANNY *exits.*)

(DIANA *sits staring in front of her.*)

You're right, Richard. I feel different. (*She looks at him a moment
and then squashes her cigarette.*) I've decided to do something . . .
which I believe to be right; for me, for everyone. But chiefly because I am certain it is what Michael would have wanted me to do.

RICHARD. What is it?

DIANA (*sitting up straight, as though challenged in some way*). I'm going
to stand for North Arlsea . . . in Michael's place. Is that rather a
shock to you?

RICHARD. It is.

DIANA. You don't think I'm capable of doing it, do you? It's so utterly
unlike me, in every way.

RICHARD. Not that, exactly.

DIANA. Ernest Foster and the others are very keen for me to do it.
They say I'm practically certain to be returned unopposed. You
remember Michael's fantastic majority.

RICHARD. I don't think you'll find the slightest difficulty in being
returned. And you'll do it very well, Diana, and be a great success.

DIANA. What is it, then? Why do you look like that? It's not very
encouraging.

RICHARD. Are you sure that Michael would have approved?

(*There is a pause.* DIANA *looks suddenly uncertain, when before she had
been so sure.*)

DIANA. But – of course. That's what decided me. I shall be doing it
for Michael's sake.

RICHARD. I know what he meant to you, Diana, what he will always
mean. I've lived here long enough to know you never thought

about yourself, or even Robin very much, but only of Michael. When he wanted peace, you gave it to him. When he wanted quiet, while he wrote his books, you saw that he had it in this house. When he wanted enthusiasm when he stood for Parliament, you saw that he had that too. In fact, he was the centre of the world you made for him, and now that world has crashed – do you really want to take his place? Isn't that something he might have resented, or possibly – misunderstood?

DIANA. Michael resented nothing and no one. He was the most generous man that ever lived.

RICHARD. I know that.

DIANA. Of course the place revolved round him, he was that sort of person. And I don't grudge one day in all the years we had together, not one hour. I was glad and proud that he needed me. You think I've suddenly become ambitious, don't you? That I want some sort of reflected glory for myself?

RICHARD. Oh no, of course not . . .

DIANA. You're absolutely and entirely wrong, Richard. I've never had any kind of personal ambition. I never wanted to be anything more than a background for Michael, ever. As for taking his place, that would be impossible. I wouldn't even try. But don't you see that what I can do is to follow his views, his ideals, as closely as possible, so that his work won't be forgotten. I've thought of nothing else all this week I've been in London, I've gone over it in my mind a thousand times. It's not the sudden reckless impulse that you imagine it to be – or a kind of dope to stop me from thinking. There! You don't believe me, I can see it in your *face*, you think . . .

(*The telephone rings.*)

Oh, answer it for me, would you?

RICHARD (*his voice very quiet*). Hallo. Yes. Mrs Wentworth is back. Do you want to speak to her? (*He turns to* DIANA.) Who is it, please? . . . Hold on and I'll get her. Ernest Foster.

DIANA (*losing her nerve*). Oh, heavens, what shall I say? Tell me, Richard, quickly. Shall I say I must have longer to think it over? . . . Or I've changed my mind, or what?

RICHARD. It's a big thing, you know. I can't advise you, Diana. It's something you'll have to decide for yourself.

(*She waits a moment, looking at* MICHAEL'*s photograph. Then, lifting the receiver.*)

DIANA (*lifting receiver*). Hallo. Yes, Ernest. Good evening. Er – yes. I
stand by everything we agreed upon yesterday . . . (*nervous laugh.*)
That's very sweet of you . . . Well, I suppose I could come up again
after the weekend . . . Yes, naturally . . . there's a lot of talk about.
But we mustn't count on me being unopposed, must we? . . . You
can say that, if you like . . . The Press – oh dear . . . well, perhaps
you could cope with them for me . . . Yes, I understand . . . Thank
you very much . . . Goodnight.

(*She replaces receiver slowly. Suddenly she begins to cry.*)

RICHARD. Diana, my dear, you're so damned tired.

DIANA. It was true, what you said. I'm not doing *this* for Michael's
sake. I'm doing it for myself.

RICHARD. No, my dear, no.

DIANA. I am . . . I am . . . You were right about Michael, he's been
everything to me. These last weeks have been hell . . . (*Her voice
changes.*) And then, up in London, I suddenly realised my life
doesn't belong to him any more, it's mine, I can do what I like with
it. And oh, Richard, that sudden sense of freedom – almost as
though the years had rolled away and I was young again. (*She is
calmer now.*) Do you think Michael would understand?

RICHARD (*very quietly*). I don't know.

DIANA. You know what he was like. So alive. When he came into a
room nobody else counted. His personality was so strong it seemed
to put out the light in other people. You felt that, didn't you?

RICHARD. I know he thought I was a dull stick, but then he was
probably right.

DIANA. No, Richard, never dull – very, very dear. But Michael, with
his head in the clouds, his vision, his enthusiasm – his queer sort of
childishness at times – he needed so much love, and
understanding.

RICHARD (*with conviction*). You were happy with him, weren't you?

DIANA. Happy! (*She thinks a little, puzzled.*) I don't know. I've never
thought. There wasn't time. What I was feeling, what I was
thinking, never seemed to matter. It was just Michael, Michael, his
needs, his comforts. (*She smiles a little.*) I was thinking, when
Nanny brought in the tea just now, how he would hate our pigsty
way of living. We still had a sort of staff, you remember, when he
went away. And now Nanny cooking, and Robin in to all meals,
and me making the beds – he would think it so incredibly
uncomfortable. He wouldn't understand.

RICHARD. You won't be able to make beds when you're a Member of Parliament.

DIANA. Oh yes, I shall. And if I can't I shall ring up the farm, and ask you to leave your old pigs, and do them for me. You're going to help me a lot, Richard, in the future.

RICHARD (*smiling*). Am I?

DIANA. You know I've no head for business, or anything like that. You must look after all my money affairs, while I make my speeches. And if the toughs throw dead cats, you'll have to rescue me.

RICHARD (*laughing*). What a future!

DIANA. You heard what Ernest Foster said? They want me to go up to London as soon as possible. I shall go up next week and look for a small flat at the same time. Nanny can look after things here, and I shall try and get back for weekends. I'd like to get the car licensed again. She's been laid up since the summer. You could see about that for me, Richard. I suppose I shall be allowed petrol. Oh no, you're not going. There's so much to discuss, and I've no one to turn to, but you. Stay to supper.

RICHARD. Nanny will fuss.

DIANA. Nanny never fusses, where you're concerned. You're so easy. Nan! (*She finishes putting the tea-things together.*)

(NANNY *enters.*)

NANNY. Yes, Mummy?

DIANA. Nan, Mr Llewellyn will be staying for supper. What is there?

NANNY (*grimly*). Spam.

(RICHARD *and* DIANA *laugh.*)

But I believe I can find a tin of sardines.

RICHARD (*urgently*). For the Lord's sake don't do that.

(ROBIN *comes running in.*)

ROBIN. I've given Sandy the grooming of his life, Uncle Richard, and what do you think his lordship is doing now?

RICHARD. I haven't the faintest idea.

ROBIN (*triumphantly*). He's curled up asleep on Nanny's bed!

NANNY. Oh, Robin!

(*Exits with the tray.*)

RICHARD. No hope of sardines now.

DIANA (*not meaning it*). Robin, you're impossible.

ROBIN. I stay up to supper now, you know. It makes the work easier.
I've started doing all sorts of things since – since quite a long time.
(*His voice trails off. He looks uncertainly from one to the other. They
both know what he means.*)

(*There is the sound of the front-door bell. They all listen instinctively.*)

DIANA (*slowly*). There's the post.

(*They can hear* NANNY'*s footsteps in the hall going to the front door.*
ROBIN *waits a moment, watching his mother's face, then runs quickly
out of the room.* RICHARD *and* DIANA *do not look at one another. A
constraint has come upon them.*)

ROBIN (*re-entering with an envelope*). One for you, Mums – a printed
one. It says 'Official Paid.' What does it say? (*He watches her with
anxiety.*)

DIANA (*the strain lifting again, throwing the telephone account aside*). It's
nothing, darling – (*Sighing.*) Look, nothing at all.

(*We feel them all relax once more.*)

CURTAIN.


# SCENE 2

SCENE: *The same. It is now April 1945, nearly three years afterwards. The
time is about six o'clock.*

*The scene is the same, but the library somehow has a different air. It is no
longer a man's room, where he would browse among his books. Furniture has
been moved. The old cabinet has gone that once stood against the wall, the
table has been shifted. The room looks brighter, yet a little lacking in personality. The long windows to the terrace are open, and we can hear applause
coming from the garden.*

DIANA. So you will remember, won't you, that this salvage drive is,
and will continue to be, enormously important. I won't keep you
any longer, except to say thank you very much for coming and
listening to me this afternoon. And to those of you who have sons
and husbands fighting, may you see them soon. And I wish to all of
them a speedy and safe return.

(*Applause off and singing of 'For she's a jolly good fellow'. Sound of
people moving away. Then some laughter and talking.*)

(ROBIN *comes in through the windows, dancing on his toes, followed by* DIANA, THE VICAR, SIR ERNEST FOSTER, *the* VICAR'S WIFE, *and* RICHARD. *They are all talking at once.*)

VICAR. Well done, well done.

DIANA. Thank you. I hope it was better than the first speech I made three years ago.

VICAR. Well, you've got them moving again. And I tell you, Sir Ernest, we take some shifting in this part of the world.

(SIR ERNEST FOSTER *is grey-haired, middle-aged, intellectual, with an air of refinement about him. As a matter of fact he is 'possibly in the Government' but we do not quite know in what capacity. Possibly Minister Without Portfolio, whatever that really means.*)

SIR ERNEST. Diana always strikes the right note, and I know from painful experience that she'll get exactly what she wants out of all of you.

DIANA. Now then, Ernest.

VICAR'S WIFE. I loved the bit early on about the unnecessary railings. I did not dare to look at Mrs Harrison. I'm not looking forward to the Institute tonight.

RICHARD. What about me? Diana's been round my farm with a pickaxe, wanting to break up my second tractor for scrap.

DIANA. Hurry up with the drinks, Richard. Come and sit down, Alice.

VICAR'S WIFE. Well, anyway, Diana's a splendid speaker. I only wish there were more like you in Parliament, Diana. Things might get a move on, then. (*Seeing* SIR ERNEST *and giggling.*) Oh, I beg your pardon.

SIR ERNEST. I couldn't agree more.

ROBIN. For she's a jolly good fellow,
For she's a jolly good fellow.

(DIANA *puts her hands over her ears. Everyone laughs.*)

RICHARD (*good-naturedly*). Dry up, Robin.

DIANA. Cigarettes, Robin.

VICAR. I can recommend the sherry here, Sir Ernest. I don't now how Diana manages it, but I sometimes suspect her of evil dealings. (*He shakes his head in mock reproof.*)

SIR ERNEST. She and I run a black market together, didn't you know?

DIANA. We supply all the sherry to the House of Lords. Hadn't you noticed the Bishops – how sparkling they are lately.

VICAR'S WIFE. I wish you'd sell a case to James.

VICAR. You know Diana preached a sermon for me last week? The church was packed. Just like the cinema on Saturday night.

SIR ERNEST. Matins at eleven, featuring Diana Wentworth!

VICAR. The trouble is that she's gone and spoilt the form for me. No one will ever listen to a word I say again.

ROBIN. That's just what the postman said to Nanny.

(*Everyone laughs.*)

VICAR. Out of the mouths of babes . . . Come on, Alice. I've a choir practice in exactly ten minutes' time.

(*Finishes his drink, movement of departure.*)

VICAR'S WIFE. And I've got to cook the supper and bicycle down to the Institute all within the hour. Still without help, I suppose, Diana?

DIANA (*gaily*). Oh, heavens, yes. Nanny does everything; we couldn't exist without her.

ROBIN. And Uncle Richard and I bring in the coals and chop the wood.

RICHARD. When we remember!

(RICHARD *escorts the* VICAR *and his* WIFE *out of the room into the hall.* ROBIN *stands looking out of the window.*)

ROBIN. I bet the trout are rising.

SIR ERNEST. Are you a fisherman, young man?

ROBIN. Rather!

DIANA. He's become so keen. Richard has been very patient with him.

ROBIN. I think I shall run down now, Mums, and try my luck.

DIANA. All right, darling.

ROBIN. Goodbye, sir.

SIR ERNEST. Goodbye.

(ROBIN darts out of the window.)

They grow up fast, don't they?

DIANA. Terrible. Thirteen last month.

SIR ERNEST. Amazing to think you have a son of thirteen. I suppose that's why you put in so much work on the Education Bill – pangs of conscience.

DIANA. I'd hoped you hadn't guessed. Help yourself to another glass of sherry.

SIR ERNEST. Thank you. The Vicar is perfectly right, you know, I wish there were one or two more as decorative as you at Westminster.

When I think of some of the other attractions . . .

DIANA (*smiling*). Now, now, Ernest . . .

SIR ERNEST. No, I'm serious, but when old Gresham gets up and makes one of his really boring speeches, it would be so much pleasanter for all of us if there were several counter-attractions.

DIANA. I am shocked.

SIR ERNEST. No more meetings for a month, eh?

DIANA. If you are sure you can manage without me.

SIR ERNEST. We can't, but we shall have to. That Richard Llewellyn of yours is a lucky man. What exactly are the plans?

DIANA. We're going to be married very quietly in London, and then just have a fortnight up in Scotland. Richard can't leave the farm any longer, and I must be back for the conference on the 29th.

SIR ERNEST. I do congratulate you both so much, Diana, and all my very best wishes for the future.

DIANA. Thank you, Ernest.

SIR ERNEST. Is Robin happy about it?

DIANA. We haven't really told anyone until today, but he knows there's something in the air. He adores Richard.

(*Telephone rings.*)

SIR ERNEST (*laughing*). No escape for the famous. Will Mrs Wentworth open the new hostel for Paralytic Parsons the day after tomorrow?

DIANA. Mrs Wentworth will not. (*Lifts receiver, smiling at him.*) Hallo? Yes . . . I'll find out. (*Laughing, puts her hand over the receiver.*) So much for your backchat. Will Sir Ernest Foster take a personal call?

SIR ERNEST (*playing up*). I've told that damn woman not to ring me up in business hours.

DIANA. It's a man. Go on Ernest, you'd better speak on the extension in the study. I don't want to listen to your guilty secrets!

SIR ERNEST. If every Cabinet Minister led as blameless a life as I do . . . (*at door.*) Which way do I go?

DIANA. First on right.

(SIR ERNEST *exits*)

(*Calling after him*). Shut your door!

(RICHARD *enters. He smiles, suddenly remembering something, and puts his hand in his pocket.*)

RICHARD (*looking around*). Where's Sir Ernest?

DIANA. Someone wanted him on the telephone! Pour me out a tiny drop more sherry.

RICHARD. Shut your eyes first.

DIANA. What for?

RICHARD. You'll see. (*He fastens a chain around her neck.*) Present for a clever girl.

(DIANA *opens her eyes, and gives a cry of pleasure.*)

DIANA. Oh, Rikky, how lovely! But how naughty of you. Where did you find it?

RICHARD. Little shop – you know.

DIANA. Why do you spoil me so?

RICHARD (*lightly*). Because I happen to be rather fond of you.

DIANA. Thank you.

(T*hey hold each other and rock backwards and forwards.*)

Oh, it will be heavenly to get to Scotland. (*She sits.*) But I give you fair warning: none of your five-mile walks before breakfast.

RICHARD. You shall have your breakfast in bed every morning, I promise you. I'll even spread the butter on your toast! You're not going to write a single letter for a month, or open any either. Give 'em to me. What's the use of paying a fat salary to that secretary of yours? I'll see she deals with this lot.

DIANA. How did it really go this afternoon? Do you think the locals were bored stiff?

RICHARD. Bored? They lapped it up, like strawberries and cream. You've got the knack, darling.

DIANA. It's funny. It all comes so easily these days. Do you remember the first time I spoke, and you had to give me a nip from your flask?

RICHARD. Yes, and your hat got cockeyed, and you called old General Bradshaw General Brandy by mistake.

DIANA (*laughing*). Oh, Rikky, I didn't!

RICHARD. You did!

ROBIN. Uncle Richard . . . Uncle Richard!

RICHARD. What's that brat of yours hollering for?

DIANA. He went down to the river.

RICHARD. What's the matter?

ROBIN (*from the river*). I've hooked a whopper! Come quickly!

RICHARD. Why did I teach that boy to fish?

DIANA. He's adored you ever since, anyway.

RICHARD. I suppose I'd better go and see what he's up to.

DIANA. Ernest's a long time. I ought to go and cope with my packing.

RICHARD. Won't Nanny do that for you?

DIANA. Poor Nan, I couldn't possibly ask her.

RICHARD. Leave it till the morning, darling. No sense in getting worn out. You've had a busy day.

DIANA. Oh, there's not much to do really. I shall live in trousers, you know, and my oldest and most threadbare shirts. No glad rags for you, Richard Llewellyn.

(*They smile at each other with understanding. We feel they are in love.*)

ROBIN (*calling from the river in agony*). Uncle – are you coming?

(DIANA *takes the* VICAR's *glass off the mantelpiece.* SIR ERNEST *enters,* DIANA *doesn't look round at him.*)

DIANA. That you, Ernest? I was getting quite anxious about you. You've had considerably longer than six minutes. (*She looks round and sees his face.*) Why, my dear?

(SIR ERNEST *looks shaken, queer.*)

Has something happened? Not bad news?

SIR ERNEST. It seems they've been trying to get through to us for hours. The telephone must have rung while we were all outside at the fête and nobody heard. My dear, you've got to keep very calm and brave. I'm going to give you a great shock.

DIANA. What do you mean? Is there a Government crisis?

SIR ERNEST. Not a political crisis, Diana. A personal one. I'm afraid you and Richard won't be able to go away.

DIANA. But, Ernest . . .?

SIR ERNEST. Listen, dear . . . You know my brother John, who is in command of the destroyer *Valiant*?

DIANA. Yes.

SIR ERNEST. It was he I spoke to on the telephone. He was speaking from Portsmouth. They docked there about five hours ago. They've just returned from the North Sea, and have with them on board somebody who must see you . . . I will take you down there myself tonight.

DIANA. Oh, but Ernest, I can't possibly . . . what does the man want?

SIR ERNEST. John could not say very much on the telephone except that this – man – was picked up by his ship from an isolated spot, somewhere in Northern waters. He has lived through a series of adventures. John said they are staggering, and almost beyond belief. But they are all quite true. For over three years, he has been making his way through the occupied countries . . . for three years you and I and the world believed him dead . . .

(DIANA *stares at him. We must see realisation on her face.*)

DIANA. Michael . . .
SIR ERNEST (*gently*). Yes.

(DIANA *goes on staring at him.*)

John says he was not hurt, not wounded in any way – just that he was very exhausted, very tired. The only thing in the world he craved was sleep. He was still asleep when they docked at Portsmouth this morning. Later he woke. It was then he asked immediately for you.
DIANA (*still whispering*). Michael.
SIR ERNEST. John has got Michael ashore now, with the C.-in-C. at Portsmouth. Already he seems rested, more himself. He wants us to motor down to him tonight.
DIANA (*still dazed*). Ernest . . .
SIR ERNEST. My dear . . . I wish I knew what to say to you. (*Pause.*) You know I'm a very old friend of you both. (*Pause.*) The thing to cling to at the moment is that Michael is alive and well . . .
DIANA. Yes . . .
SIR ERNEST. You would rather be alone, wouldn't you? Just for these first few minutes?
DIANA. Please.
SIR ERNEST. We'll go quite quietly and take our time. No need to start for an hour or so.

(*They hear laughter and voices outside.* DIANA *looks with sudden horror and realization at* SIR ERNEST.)

(*Understanding*). Do you want me to tell him?
DIANA. No . . . No . . . (*She is very white and shaken now.*)
SIR ERNEST (*realizing there is nothing he can say*). I'll go and see the car's ready by seven o'clock.

(*He exits, closing the door.*)

(RICHARD *and* ROBIN *come in laughing.*)
ROBIN. Come and look what I've caught, Mums.
RICHARD. I say, the young blighter has landed a three-pounder at least. I shouldn't be surprised if . . .

(DIANA *does not move.*)

ROBIN (*anxiously*). What's the matter? What's happened?

RICHARD (*sharply, for the first time*). Go along Robin. Do as I tell you.

(ROBIN *goes away, looking back over his shoulder.*)

(*To her – very quietly*). What is it?

Darling . . . (*She cannot speak.*)

DIANA. It's Michael . . . he's alive . . . he's come back. The telephone . . . It was Ernest's brother . . . the one who commands a
destroyer . . . he's been trying to get through to us all day . . . (*She
can't speak.*) They landed at Portsmouth this morning . . . They
found Michael somewhere near the German coast . . . he's not
wounded or anything. Not hurt. He's come right through Europe
from . . . I don't know . . . I didn't understand . . .

RICHARD. Darling.

DIANA. Oh, Richard, what are we going to do? They want me to go
down to Portsmouth with Ernest tonight.

RICHARD. Yes. Yes, of course.

(*We should see the difference in their minds. On his face, the knowledge
that his world has crashed, for ever; on hers, the inevitable swing back to
the past.*)

DIANA. He will come back, Richard, expecting to find everything the
same. He will want his home again, all the things he loved. He will
want me.

RICHARD (*very softly*). And you . . . you will want him, too.

DIANA. Ernest's brother says he's very exhausted . . . very tired after
all he's been through. He will want peace and quiet. He mustn't be
worried about anything. Richard, we must keep it from him about
you – about us. He must come back and find his home unchanged,
mustn't he?

RICHARD. Yes, if you think that's for the best.

DIANA. I can't go through this alone, you've got to help me. We must
face it together, Rikky, please . . . please . . .

RICHARD. Of course.

(*But* DIANA *doesn't see the hopelessness of it as* RICHARD *does. Already
she makes plans to find a way out.*)

DIANA. You'll have to be at the farm, of course, for the time being,
until – until we can make plans. It's not as though you were a
stranger. He will expect to find you here, about the place. He will

think it natural and neighbourly that you've been helping me. He'll be grateful and pleased. I can explain how wonderful you've been to me – about business things, about everything. How you've helped with Robin . . . (*She breaks off, and looks at him with a new gesture of despair.*) Robin – one of us has got to tell Robin – oh, my God!

(NANNY *enters*).

NANNY (*puzzled*). Is that right? You are motoring up to town, Mummy? I heard Sir Ernest say something to his chauffeur . . . (*She breaks off – seeing their faces.*) I'm sorry . . . I didn't know . . .

(*She moves to leave the room.*)

RICHARD. Nanny. Sir Ernest's brother, Commander Foster, has just rung up with very wonderful news. The Colonel is alive and well. He landed in England this morning.

NANNY. The Colonel? (*Long pause.*) Oh, Madam . . .

(*No one speaks.*)

Will – will he be coming home?

RICHARD. Yes. We expect so. Mrs Wentworth is going down to Portsmouth with Sir Ernest this evening. We understand he is quite all right, but very tired. He has been through a terrible time.

NANNY (*slowly*). Yes, sir.

(*They are all quiet for a moment.*)

DIANA. Nanny, I think you are the best person to tell Robin. I – I don't know how to do it . . . (*Her voice trails off.*)

NANNY: It's – not going to be very easy. But I'll do my best.

DIANA. You must make him understand that Mr Llewellyn and I – that there's no question now . . .

RICHARD. Mrs Wentworth is anxious, Nanny, that the Colonel should come home to find nothing changed. She doesn't want him to be worried about anything.

NANNY. Yes, sir, I understand.

RICHARD. I think Robin is old enough to realize what has happened. I'll try and talk to him myself.

DIANA. Oh, Richard . . . (*She realizes what he is going through.*)

NANNY (*half to herself*). There'll be a lot to do. There'll be the Colonel's room to get ready, and he'll expect everything as it used to be. There'll be several things we shall need . . . (*As she realizes what it will mean to them.*) Oh Mr Llewellyn . . .madam . . .

(*They know what she is trying to tell them.*)

I'll do everything I can to help you, everything.

(*Suddenly the telephone rings. It strikes a jarring note.* NANNY *looks from one to the other. Then she answers it.*)

Hallo . . . Hallo . . . (*Her voice is rather fussy and anxious on the telephone.*) Who is it? Please speak up, I can't hear you. Yes? (*Turns round.*) It's a trunk call, madam.

(DIANA *stares at* RICHARD.)

Hallo . . . yes. (*Pause.*) One moment, sir . . . (*She turns to* DIANA.) It's the Colonel.

(DIANA *stands very still.* NANNY *exits.* RICHARD *goes slowly out of the window into the garden without looking back.* DIANA *goes to the telephone. Her hands are trembling. Then she lifts the receiver.*)

DIANA. Hallo, Michael . . . Michael darling . . .

CURTAIN.


## SCENE 3

SCENE: *The same. The following Monday. About six p.m.*

*The room is empty. There has been an effort to restore the room to its original state as in Scene 1, but this has not been entirely successful. Perhaps* NANNY *and* DIANA *have forgotten where everything stood. The room has neither the leisurely haphazard comfort of Scene 1, nor the methodical brightness of Scene 2. A grandfather clock in the hall strikes six. There is the sound of voices in the hall.*)

DIANA. Thank you, Venning. What else is there in the car?
VENNING. Cigarettes, madam, and the box of groceries, and another large package.

(DIANA *enters carrying a beauty case, and a box of cigarettes. She is followed by* VENNING, *the soldier servant, who carries a case and an overcoat.* DIANA *looks tired and strained. She is in travelling clothes.*)

DIANA. Oh, yes, that's for the kitchen. Cigarettes in here. And I think the other box is wine. That coat can go in the hall, and the suitcase upstairs. First room on the left at the top of the stairs.

(*Exit* VENNING.)

(NANNY *enters.*)

DIANA (*down centre*). Ah, there you are, Nan. Is everything all right? Where's Robin?

NANNY. I think he's over at the farm. (*She looks enquiringly at* DIANA.)

DIANA. We left the Colonel at the gate. He wanted to walk up through the woods, though I tried to persuade him not to. The doctor wanted him to stay but he insisted on coming home, at once.

NANNY. That's natural, isn't it?

(*There is a small restraint between them.*)

DIANA. Oh, Nan . . . He looks so strained and tired. I've brought down some extra groceries and I managed to get some wine.

NANNY. I tried to get the room right, but somehow I'm not quite sure . . . (*She glances, half-frowning, round the room.*)

DIANA. Oh, Nan, how good of you . . . He hasn't asked any questions, Nan, about his home, about us – about anything at all. He has told me nothing about himself. The doctor at Portsmouth said he was suffering terribly from reaction. More than anything he must have peace, and quiet.

NANNY. He won't be worried from the village. I've seen to that. Everyone has been most understanding, and I believe the Vicar said a word in church yesterday. Of course the London people are different. I thought the telephone would never stop yesterday, after the news came on the wireless. I told them all the same. That you were away with the Colonel, and I had no idea when you would be coming back.

DIANA. Poor Nan. I'm sorry to have left you with all this.

NANNY. It's been no trouble. I'm only hoping that you haven't got too tired, two long journeys so quickly.

DIANA. No. I'm all right.

NANNY (*pause, lowers her voice*). Mr Llewellyn was here this morning. He said if there was anything you wanted him for, anything special, he would come over but that he would not be coming otherwise.

DIANA. Thank you, Nan. (*Pause.*) He didn't leave a letter?

NANNY. No'm. Yes, these came this morning. Poor postman could hardly walk up the drive. They're mostly for you, but there's a good few for the Colonel too.

DIANA. Messages of congratulations from all our friends. They'll all have to be answered too.

NANNY. You'll have to have Miss Jameson down from London to do that.

DIANA. Miss Jameson! (*She sounds uncertain and very weary.*) I'd
forgotten for the moment that I had such a thing as a secretary.

(VENNING *re-enters.*)

VENNING. Is this box to go to the kitchen madam?

DIANA. Yes, please. Nanny, this is Venning, the Colonel's new
servant. He joined us today.

NANNY. Good evening.

VENNING. Good evening.

NANNY. We shall be able to manage all right, then. I have Mrs Willis
coming in every morning, and she has promised to come in during
the evening for an hour, to help with the washing-up, but I don't
suppose she will.

DIANA. I dare say Venning will help with that, too?

VENNING. Yes, Madam.

DIANA. Well, come along then. Nanny will show you to your room,
then we can open the groceries and the wine afterwards.

(*She exits, followed by* NANNY *and* VENNING.)

(*Presently we see someone standing at the open window. He has his hand
on the frame, leaning a little, and he looks thin and worn. It is*
MICHAEL. *He stands there looking in upon the room with a queer half-
smile on his face. After a moment he enters the room. We must feel that
to see all this again is a dream he has long had, but difficult at first sight
to absorb. He stares into the corner, where the cabinet once stood, which
is no longer there. He is puzzled at this.*)

(DIANA *enters the room.*)

DIANA (*very gently, in the voice one uses to a sick person*). All right? Not
too tired?

MICHAEL. Where's the old cabinet?

DIANA (*following his glance*). The old cabinet? We had it moved out of
the way, upstairs. It seemed to take up so much space.

MICHAEL. It's altered the room, somehow, Funny . . . and the table
has been shifted too, hasn't it?

DIANA. Has it? I don't think so. (*She frowns – she is not sure.*)

MICHAEL (*still looking about the room*). I used to try and imagine this,
when I was – out there. And it was strange because the picture I
made of it was so distinct and clear. There were always roses in a
white bowl. (*He smiles a little.*) There's the white bowl, but, alas, no
roses.

DIANA. I expect that was all Nanny could find. I'm afraid I've had to let the garden go. Thompson was called up. (*She is worried.*) I'll have the old cabinet moved down again in the morning.

MICHAEL. Good.

DIANA. And now I come to think of it, that table isn't right. We used to have the flap up. (*She is so anxious to please, she puts the heavy flap up herself.*)

MICHAEL. No . . . no . . . don't bother, it doesn't matter.

(*He is rather nervy, and suddenly tired. He sits on the sofa.*)

DIANA. Walking up through the woods was too much for you. You've overdone it. Lie down and relax a little. Would you like your dinner in bed?

MICHAEL. God, no. I'm not a blasted invalid.

DIANA. The doctor said you needed all the rest you could get, remember.

MICHAEL. Doctors are a bunch of hypocrites. They prescribe Rest in Capital Letters, to be taken three times a day after meals. Where's Venning?

DIANA. Unpacking your things. Do you want him?

MICHAEL. I thought he might open the case of drink we brought down with us.

DIANA. Nanny and I can do that.

MICHAEL. Lord, I was forgetting Nanny. I shall have to face up to her. Will she cry on my shoulder?

DIANA. No, of course not. She's been so splendid all along.

MICHAEL (*smiling up at her.*) My poor sweet, you've had a hell of a time, haven't you? I don't understand this servant business. Why don't you pay them more?

DIANA. Alas – it's not a question of money, darling. They've all been called up.

MICHAEL. Well, Venning can do the dirty work. Venning! (*He shouts loudly.*)

NANNY (*opening the door*). Venning is upstairs. Can I do anything?

MICHAEL. Nanny!

NANNY. Good evening, sir. Welcome home. (*She is nervous.*)

MICHAEL. Return of the soldier – and all the trumpets had sounded for him on the other side . . . (*He rises and goes to her.*) How are you, Nanny?

(NANNY *shakes hands with* MICHAEL.)

NANNY. Very well, thank you, sir. He hasn't changed much, has he, madam? A little thinner perhaps, but otherwise – just the same.

DIANA. Yes, just the same. (*Her voice is wistful.*)

MICHAEL. Only rather more difficult than before. You can't be a fugitive for three years, at my age, and get away with it entirely.

NANNY. No, sir.

MICHAEL. Half-starved most of the time, and practically naked.

DIANA. Michael . . . (*She looks at him in great distress.*)

MICHAEL. Don't worry. I'm not going to unfold my lurid tales upon you. I'll keep them for the House of Commons.

(NANNY *and* DIANA *exchange a glance. We realise that* MICHAEL *does not yet know that his wife is now MP in his place.*)

As Colonel Wentworth walked into the Strangers' Gallery, cheers echoed from end to end of the historic building! (*He pauses.*) Or didn't they? (*He looks mischievously at them both, and the look is vaguely disconcerting. Then he leans back on the sofa.*) All right, Nanny. Go and break open that box of booze in the kitchen.

(NANNY *exits.*)

(DIANA *stands uncertainly*). Poor Nanny. She's never been at her ease with me since the day I told her that Robin was the worst-mannered child in the kingdom.

DIANA (*in defence*). She's very devoted to – all of us.

MICHAEL. Fidelity is always *touching*.

(DIANA *turns away to the letters on the table; picks up one or two.*)

You've a hell of a lot of correspondence there. What's it all about? The conquering hero?

DIANA (*lightly*). I expect so.

MICHAEL. You're turning them over with the set, grim expression of the type of woman who sits on committees and runs things with dire efficiency.

DIANA. Perhaps I do.

MICHAEL. You'll have to drop it, then, now I'm home. Come and sit down. (*He pats the sofa beside him.*)

(DIANA *seems restless and on edge.*)

DIANA. I will – directly. I must go and give Nanny a hand with that box first.

(*She exits rather hurriedly.*)

MICHAEL (*calling after her*). Venning can do that. What's the damn
fellow for?

(*But* DIANA *has not heard.*)

(MICHAEL *lies still on the sofa and closes his eyes.* ROBIN *comes to the
garden entrance and looks in. He does not see* MICHAEL *lying on the
sofa. He has the fishing rod in his hand. He has a queer, rather resentful
expression on his face. He goes slowly to the old corner and places the rod
against the wall. Then he stares at it.* MICHAEL *has been watching him
all the time.*)

What are you doing with my rod?

(ROBIN *whips round, guilty and startled. He doesn't know what to say.*)

ROBIN. I – didn't know you were there. I never heard the car.

MICHAEL. Never mind the rod. Let's have a look at you. (*Holds out his
hands to him.*)

(ROBIN *comes forward self-consciously, and kisses* Michael.)

ROBIN. I hope you are quite well.

MICHAEL. That's very considerate of you. I might be worse. And what
of yourself?

ROBIN. Oh, I'm all right, thank, you.

MICHAEL. How's school?

ROBIN. Oh, all *right*, thanks. (*He is very nervous.*)

MICHAEL. Good.

(*There is a long pause.*)

ROBIN. I expect you're feeling jolly tired. You'd like to rest a bit. I'll
go and see what Mummy's doing.

MICHAEL. Don't run away. Come and sit down. We've got a good
many gaps to fill up, haven't we?

(ROBIN *smiles politely. He doesn't know what* MICHAEL *means.*)

You were a little chap in shorts when I went away. You look so
different.

ROBIN. I'm thirteen.

MICHAEL. Are you? Perhaps that's it . . . Do you still take that
golliwog to bed with you?

ROBIN (*insulted*). Good lord, no. Nanny gave it to an evacuee ages
ago.

MICHAEL. Did she? She'd better not try that game on me. (*He feels in*

*an inside pocket, and brings out a tiny teddy bear.*) Do you remember
Ted?

ROBIN (*staring*). It's the one you used to keep in your dressing-room.
I'd forgotten all about it. Do you mean to say you took it to the
war, and didn't lose it?

MICHAEL. He didn't leave my side, did you, Ted? (*Kisses bear solemnly
and puts it back in his pocket.*)

(ROBIN *looks very embarrassed.*)

ROBIN. I suppose – actually – it's a sort of mascot.

MICHAEL. Mascot be blowed. He's my greatest friend.

(ROBIN *stands on one foot. Glances away.*)

ROBIN. The war news is very good, isn't it? We seem to be absolutely
rushing ahead everywhere. And we're bombing the Germans to
blazes.

MICHAEL (*yawning*). Are we? Were the rhododendrons good last year?

ROBIN. The rhododendrons? I didn't notice.

MICHAEL. What's happened to the old iron gates at the entrance to
the woods?

ROBIN. Oh, Mummy gave them for salvage.

MICHAEL. Salvage?

ROBIN. Why, of course. Don't you know? Iron railings were melted
down everywhere and turned into bombs. Mummy made a speech
*about* it, only the day before yesterday.

MICHAEL. Mummy did what?

ROBIN (*disconcerted*). Oh, I forgot. I wasn't to speak about that.

MICHAEL. Why, was the speech such a rotten one?

ROBIN. No, it was jolly good.

MICHAEL. You astound me. Does she often make speeches?

ROBIN. Yes . . . No . . . I don't really know. (*He looks very
uncomfortable.*)

MICHAEL. What's the mystery?

ROBIN. Nothing . . . I – I expect you saw an awful lot of chaps killed
where you've been, didn't you?

MICHAEL. I saw a hell of a lot who would have been happier killed.
But tell me more about the iron gates, that's much more
important.

ROBIN. I don't know any more, except that they went. (*Pause.*) I think
I'll just go and see what Mummy is doing.

MICHAEL (*rather bitterly*). Mummy went to see what Nanny was doing.

ROBIN. I expect they're seeing about supper. It's made a bit extra work, you see, your coming home.

MICHAEL. I'm sorry. (*He looks at* ROBIN *half-sadly, half-amused.*)

(ROBIN *exits.*)

(MICHAEL *gets up slowly, picks up the fishing rod, and, frowning a little, examines it.* VENNING *enters with a tray of drinks, and looks uncertainly at* MICHAEL.)

Oh stick 'em anywhere. Clear all that junk off the table.

(VENNING *lays the tray down on the table, moving all* DIANA's *correspondence to one side.*)

Have you come across an old brown velvet jacket hanging in the wardrobe upstairs?

VENNING. No, sir.

MICHAEL. Wardrobe on the left. As you go into the room?

VENNING. There is nothing hanging in any of the wardrobes, sir.

(MICHAEL *stares for a moment.*)

MICHAEL (*slowly*). No – no, I suppose there wouldn't be. (*Pause.*) You might ask Nanny, Venning, if all my clothes were given away.

VENNING. Yes, sir.

(*He exits.*)

MICHAEL. And Lazarus came forth from the tomb . . .

(MICHAEL *pours himself out a drink – picks up the letters, glances idly through them.*)

Mrs Wentworth, MP. Mrs Wentworth, MP.

(*He stands there staring at the letter his hands. His expression is curious, baffled. He looks over his shoulder.*)

Diana! (*There is no answer.*) Diana!

(DIANA *enters.*)

DIANA. I'm so sorry about your brown jacket . . . Venning has just asked me. You see, we never thought . . . and then all those bombed people . . .

MICHAEL. Never mind the jacket.

DIANA. What is it?

MICHAEL (*holding out the letter*). Is this true?

DIANA (*taking the letter*). Yes . . . Michael.

MICHAEL. That's what Robin meant . . . about your making speeches.

DIANA (*anxiously*). You don't mind?

MICHAEL. I can't tell . . . (*He stares at her.*) You – of all women. You
don't know the first thing about it. It's not your line of country.
(*Suddenly he burst out laughing.*) Oh, my God, how damned funny.

(DIANA *is not quite so amused.*)

How long have you been one of His Majesty's faithful Commons?

DIANA. Ever since you – you went. Oh, don't you see, Michael, that it
was for your sake I did it! And they pressed me to it, Lord
Gresham, Ernest Foster, and the others. It sounds silly and
conceited, I know, but I've worked very hard.

MICHAEL. What was your majority?

DIANA. I was unopposed.

MICHAEL (*looking at her*). Sob stuff, I suppose? Widow's weeds and so
on. That's what got them.

DIANA (*hurt*). Perhaps.

MICHAEL (*mocking*). My husband gave his life for his country sort of
thing. And to those of you who hold his memory dear . . .

DIANA. Michael . . .

MICHAEL. Well, isn't that the line you took? It never fails, you know.

DIANA. You're angry . . . Oh, I didn't want you to feel this way. (*She is
really upset.*)

MICHAEL. Angry? Why should I be angry? It makes me rock with
laughter, that's all. Give me another drink.

(DIANA *pours out a second glass.*)

I told you, when you were glancing at those letters, that you had
the face of a woman who sits on committees, didn't I? What a shot
in the dark!

DIANA. Michael, darling . . . of course, it's a surprise to you. I was
always so much the one at home, wasn't I? Ordering the meals,
arranging flowers; it's been a revelation to me too. I never realised
for a moment I was capable of carrying out the work I do today.

MICHAEL. Thank you. What else have you achieved besides giving
away my gates for salvage?

DIANA (*puzzled*). The gates? Salvage? Oh, that was just a little local
affair. No – real work, I mean, in the House. We got the Education
Bill passed. I was on the Committee and they used one or two of
my suggestions. It will have a tremendous effect in the schools. A
form of National Service for everyone is being considered, too.

Naturally, there is some opposition and bitterness to this, but what
does that matter when it's for the good of the coming generation?

MICHAEL (*raising his glass*). What indeed?

DIANA. We're hoping to get the Housing Bill through during the next
session. I've had a *little* to do with that too, but of course, it's not
really my baby. Heavens – what one has learnt, Michael. We're all
of us to blame for having permitted such living conditions all these
years. And yet we call this a civilized country.

MICHAEL. So it is – compared to the countries I have come from.

DIANA. Ah, but that's different.

MICHAEL. Is it? Go on – tell me more about your Housing Bill.

DIANA. I have the report, somewhere. You shall read it after supper.
There won't be a house after the war, Michael, or a flat, or a tiny
cottage, without a bathroom. That's just one small step.

MICHAEL. Supposing people don't want baths?

DIANA. They won't get away with it. Inspectors will go round to see
that the baths are used.

(MICHAEL *shouts with laughter.* DIANA *looks at him strangely.*)

You don't take it seriously? You think it's a waste of time – what
we've done?

MICHAEL. Not a waste of time if it keeps you all happy in your
monkey house.

DIANA (*really hurt*). Michael . . .

MICHAEL. Forgive me – I've been rude, and unkind. It's only that I've
been living all these months in such a different world.

DIANA. I know. I understand.

MICHAEL. No, that's where you're wrong. (*Puts his glass down.*) You
don't understand. I told you, just now, that when I was out there I
used to make pictures of this house, this room. I saw nothing
changed. And I'm not the only one. Thousands of us. All the
fellows, who, in peacetime, ask nothing better than a pint of beer
on their way home and the pictures on Saturday night. They want
the life they know – the woman they love – they don't want to
come home to conscription bills and Compulsory Baths.

DIANA. I've described it all so badly.

MICHAEL. No . . . too well.

DIANA. But Michael – you wouldn't have us put back the clock, and
return to where we were before?

MICHAEL. Why not?

DIANA. I thought we were fighting for a new world.

MICHAEL. Was the old one so very bad?

DIANA. Well – I don't know . . . but I think we all feel rather differently about it, here at home.

MICHAEL. Safe in an English churchyard snore,
  The businessmen who won the war,
  While by the foreign seas they crossed it
  Happens lie the men who lost it.

DIANA. Bitter twisted words of a generation ago.

MICHAEL. Generations don't change as much as you think. Poets are bitter twisted people. And so are soldiers – sometimes.

DIANA. Michael . . . I wanted your homecoming to be peaceful, happy. And now, on the very first evening, I've spoilt it for you.

MICHAEL. You haven't spilt it for me. I'm to blame. (*Glances round the room.*) I might have known the picture could not come quite true. The iron gates gone – roses gone – Robin a schoolboy in long trousers – let's forget all about it, shall we?

DIANA. Will you also forget that I am a Member of Parliament?

MICHAEL. That's something that I shall never remember. (*Smiles, then looks at her curiously.*) You enjoy it, don't you?

DIANA. Why – yes – I do.

(VENNING *enters.*)

VENNING. The nurse wishes to know about the time for dinner, madam.

DIANA. Do you mind seven o'clock, Michael? It means Nanny can get cleared away and washed up sooner. She has so much to do.

MICHAEL. I don't mind.

DIANA. Perhaps we had better say half-past seven, Venning.

(VENNING *exits.*)

MICHAEL. Do Nanny and Venning have to eat with us in this Brave New World you've been creating?

DIANA. No, of course not.

MICHAEL. Thank God for that! I want so terribly to be alone with you.

DIANA (*gently*). Yes, darling. (*She turns away, a look of strain on her face.*) You won't mind Robin though, will you?

MICHAEL. Not if he goes to bed directly afterwards.

DIANA. He generally stays for the news.

MICHAEL. The news?

(*She doesn't see the gesture which is as much as to say:* 'What about me? I'm the news.')

What have we got for dinner?

DIANA. I think Nanny said there was a chicken from the farm.

MICHAEL. Old Richard still in charge? How is he?

DIANA. Very well.

MICHAEL. Not married or anything?

DIANA. No.

MICHAEL. What does he think about your gadding round the country as a Member of Parliament?

DIANA. Oh, I don't know. I think he's used to it. (*She moves letters, arranges things unnecessarily.*)

MICHAEL. Must you go on flitting round the room tidying everything?

DIANA. Sorry . . . it always did irritate you, didn't it? (*She sits on the sofa beside him.*) Nanny's been extravagant for once and lighted up the boiler. That means we can have baths before dinner.

MICHAEL. Are there restrictions on water too?

DIANA. No, but we have to save fuel.

(MICHAEL *watches her busy hands.*)

MICHAEL. Where's that tapestry work you used to do?

DIANA. I gave that up a long time ago.

MICHAEL. It was quiet and restful.

DIANA. Yes, but it wasn't any use to anyone. This is a Balaclava helmet . . . I have a working party in the village and everything goes up to a Central Depot. Lie back and be comfortable. I wish you'd let me give you your dinner in bed.

MICHAEL. No. I'd rather be down here. With you and Robin.

(*Another pause.*)

What do you think about, as you knit? The Committee stage of the Housing Bill?

DIANA. No . . . No. I was thinking how funny it was, you and I, sitting here together. Just like it used to be. Almost – almost as though nothing had ever happened.

MICHAEL (*dreamily*). Has – anything happened?

DIANA (*sensitive*). No – no, of course not. (*She looks in front of her, still knitting, and then very slowly.*) Only – the war.

CURTAIN.

# ACT II

## SCENE 1

*A month later. Morning, about midday. The room has been restored to its former state. The cabinet is back in the corner.*

MISS JAMESON, *the secretary, sits at the table with her typewriter in front of her.* DIANA *stands by the mantelpiece, her hands behind her back.* MISS JAMESON *is typing as the curtain rises. She looks up enquiringly at* DIANA *as she finishes her page.*

DIANA. That's all, I think. Leave a space in case I should want to add anything. Now the next.

(MISS JAMESON *puts a fresh paper into the machine.*)

This is to the Chairman of the British Women's Council. Dear Madam, I am most grateful for your message of congratulation on the miraculous return of my husband from the Continent. I am, at present, rather uncertain of my movements, and under the circumstances I feel it is best to refuse your very kind invitation to speak at the annual meeting of the Council. Yours sincerely . . . Did you do anything about that luncheon on the 20th?

MISS JAMESON. Yes, Mrs Wentworth. I sent the Secretary a telegram in your name. Here is a copy of it. (*She hands* DIANA *a piece of paper.*) And I also cancelled your engagement to dinner with the Mayor of North Arlsea on that day, giving the same reason, of course.

DIANA (*frowning, trying to think of a hundred things at once*). Was there anything else?

MISS JAMESON. Miss Gower asked you down on Wednesday week, if you remember, to an inspection. I left it open because I thought you might be especially interested.

DIANA (*signing the letters*). I am – but I don't see how I can manage it. (*She stops, because at that moment* MICHAEL *calls her from the garden.*)

(MICHAEL *enters.*)

MICHAEL. Diana? How much longer are you going to be? Look, it's too bad, these books are absolutely green with mildew.

DIANA. Are they?

MICHAEL. Yes. My precious first editions. And where the devil do you think I found them? In an old box in the garage, beside a lot of junk.

DIANA. Darling, I'm terribly sorry. I promise you I'll go through all of them directly. But I must just get through these letters first.

MICHAEL. You say that every morning, and yesterday you weren't through until lunch-time, and then dashed off to some perfectly unnecessary meeting in the afternoon.

DIANA. It wasn't unnecessary, Michael. It was very important.

MICHAEL. Important, my foot. A lot of women yattering about nothing at all.

(MISS JAMESON *looks very disapproving*.)

MISS JAMESON. Your wife is a very busy person, Colonel Wentworth.

MICHAEL. You've said it, Miss Jameson. So damned busy she hasn't time to look after her home, or her husband. Go ahead both of you. Don't mind me. I won't listen to your fireworks. (*He throws himself on the sofa, and lights a cigarette.*)

DIANA. Where were we, Miss Jameson?

MISS JAMESON. About that letter to Miss Gower.

DIANA. I think I'd better ring her up personally.

MISS JAMESON. Then there's only that message to be sent to the big rally of the GTC at Westminster. You remember you were to have spoken, but the date clashed with the meeting of the British Women's Council, and so you promised you would send a message instead.

DIANA. Oh, yes . . . how far had I got?

MISS JAMESON (*picking up the paper and reading*). 'To those of you who are about to enter one of the services, I would say a special word. Your schooldays lie behind you, the stern realities of life are ahead.'

DIANA. Yes . . . (*She bites the end of her pencil, and thinks.*)

(MICHAEL *lies back on the sofa, blowing cigarette smoke in the air.*)

(*Continuing.*) Nothing will matter to you any more now but your duty to your country. Just as once you played for the side in hockey or cricket, and thought only of your school team, so now you will put aside all thought of personal selfishness or individuality, and become one small unit in a magnificent army of women, the great army that is helping in so large a measure to win this war.

(MISS JAMESON *rattles away on typewriter*, MICHAEL *rises, looks at books on the table above the fireplace, puts on the radiogram – Grieg Concerto –*)

The girls today are the women, and the mothers of tomorrow. Much of the responsibility for the future peace of the world will rest upon your shoulders. We none of us want to return to the dreary, slack, go-as-you-please Britain that existed before the war; but side by side with our menfolk . . . (*She breaks off.*) Michael, please, it's impossible to concentrate.

(MICHAEL *turns off the gramophone.*)

(*Very strained.*) Repeat that, Miss Jameson . . .
MISS JAMESON (*reading*). Side by side with out menfolk . . .

(MICHAEL *tiptoes to the sofa and sits.*)

DIANA. We shall build a saner, stronger Britain, where slackness and inefficiency will not be tolerated; where everyone will work for the community, and our children shall be brought up to service, duty and obedience to the State.
MICHAEL. Christ! What an outlook!

(DIANA *and* MISS JAMESON *stare at him with hostility.*)

Who do you say is going to listen to all that tripe?
DIANA. The Westminster Division of the Girls' Training Corps.
MICHAEL. And is that the sort of stuff you're handing out at all your meetings?
DIANA. Yes. Of course.
MICHAEL. Do you mean to tell me that a fastidious fellow like old Gresham, and our old friend Ernest Foster and the rest of the bunch, talk that language too?
DIANA. Why not? What have you against it?
MICHAEL. Before I left this country I remember making a speech in the House of Commons about freedom. The right for every man to think for himself, to choose for himself, to do as he bloody well pleased. I understood that that was what we fellow were fighting for.
DIANA. So it is.
MICHAEL. Then I'm afraid you put it in a very complicated way, likely to be misunderstood by simple soldiers like myself.

(*There is a pause. No one looks at anyone.* MISS JAMESON *sits very stiffly.*)

DIANA. I think, Miss Jameson, we had better leave this until
    tomorrow.

MISS JAMESON. Yes, Mrs Wentworth.

MICHAEL. I've spoilt your train of thought. How very unfeeling of
    me.

DIANA. It doesn't matter

MICHAEL. Oh, but it does! The girls are the women and the mothers
    of tomorrow. You mustn't keep them waiting.

(MISS JAMESON *gathers her papers together, and covers the typewriter.*)

How many words per minute, Miss Jameson?

MISS JAMESON. Sixty-five.

MICHAEL. Admirable efficiency!

(MISS JAMESON *exits.*)

Well, what about your duty to your husband, and cleaning some of
the mildew off his books?

(DIANA *comes forward, and drops on her knees beside the books.*)

DIANA (*her voice flat*). I'm afraid they are spoilt. I'm terribly sorry. (*She
tries to dust them, ineffectively.*)

MICHAEL. Seeing that you are so great on service and efficiency in the
    country, it's a pity you don't exercise it a bit more in your own
    home. Did you put these to moulder in the garage?

DIANA. As I matter of fact, I put them there for salvage, but the first
    editions must have got mixed up with the other books. That was
    Nanny's fault. It's so difficult to see to everything myself. We had
    this Salvage Drive, and the village promised to give five hundred
    books.

MICHAEL. My dear girl, do you honestly believe that if all the books in
    the house were boiled down to pulp, they would help the war effort
    in the very slightest?

DIANA (*unhappy*). Wouldn't they?

(MICHAEL *makes an exasperated face. There is a long pause.* DIANA *is
still on the floor beside the books.*)

Michael . . . What's happened to you?

MICHAEL. Nothing. Why do you ask?

DIANA. You've changed so . . . Three years ago you had so much
    enthusiasm and drive and vision. You believed in this war as a
    crusade, a fight for good against evil. And now, when at last it's

nearly over, and peace seems only a question of days, perhaps of hours – you make a mockery of everything.

MICHAEL. You say I've changed. What about you? Three years ago you were quiet and gentle, you had a quality of stillness that was the thing I loved about you most. Out there – where I lived like a hunted rat, month after month – I would think of that stillness, and long for it. I came home to find you had grown another personality. One of those managing, restless women, always writing letters, going to meetings arguing about ridiculous questions, having interminable conversations on the telephone, and it's no use pretending that patriotism has driven you to it. It's become your life. You are that sort of woman.

DIANA. It's not true.

MICHAEL. It is true. The woman I married died with me when I crashed into the sea in '42.

DIANA (*quietly*). I've tried, very hard, to be the woman you remembered.

MICHAEL. I know that. I've seen you, this last month, day after day, forcing yourself to play a part you had forgotten. Trying to pick up the threads of our old routine. Not only you, but Robin, Nanny, the very house itself, plunging back into a past that none of you wanted, a past that isn't with us any more.

DIANA (*stricken*). Michael . . .

MICHAEL. I'm not blaming you, or anyone. You believed me dead. Now I know that the dead must not return.

DIANA. You can't say that. Oh, Michael, darling, we were happy once.

MICHAEL. And we're not happy now. Are we? Not your fault. Nor mine. The years between.

(*The telephone rings,* MICHAEL *gestures to* DIANA *to answer it.* DIANA *rises, lifts the receiver.*)

DIANA. Hallo. Yes. Yes, speaking. I'm very well, thank you, Ernest. Yes, he's here with me now. He's very much better. Quite himself again. Whenever you like. (*She claps her hand over the receiver.*) Ernest. He wants to come down and see you today.

MICHAEL. Tell him to go to hell.

DIANA (*into the telephone*). He'll be delighted to see you. There must be heaps of things you want to discuss. I want to see you too. I feel my political position at the moment is absolutely unique. No, we haven't talked about it much. As far as I'm concerned there's only one thing to be done. I must stand down for Michael. But surely,

there's no question about it . . . Yes, well, if it's as important as
that, come right away – to lunch. We shall be here . . . The news is
wonderful, isn't it? It seems impossible that it can be really true.
Very well, Ernest . . . See you later. Goodbye. (*She replaces the
receiver.*)

MICHAEL. What exactly were you saying to Ernest?

DIANA. Only something that I feel is right and just. There can't be two
members for North Arlsea, can there? You must go back to the
House where you belong. I shall return to the home that I seem to
have neglected.

MICHAEL. When did you first think about this?

DIANA. Directly you came back. No, I'm lying. Before I went to
Portsmouth. That first evening, when Ernest told me you were
safe.

MICHAEL. This Parliament stuff means a lot to you, doesn't it?

DIANA. I thought it did. I'm not so sure, now.

MICHAEL. I've made you doubtful, haven't I? You were certain of
yourself before I returned. And here I am, like an evil ghost,
peering at you over your shoulder, breaking your new world to
pieces.

DIANA (*wearily*). I don't want a new world. I only want the men and
women who live in it to be happy.

MICHAEL. Compulsory baths – compulsory babies – it that how you
propose to do it?

DIANA. You deliberately misunderstand everything I try to tell
you.

MICHAEL. Perhaps I do. Perhaps I misunderstand because I want you
still and quiet like you were before. I want it to be winter and the
curtains drawn, with you lying there, on that sofa, doing some
tapestry, and Robin a child asleep upstairs. I want the old world
that we knew and loved. The old world for which I fought and –
did not die.

DIANA. I've failed you, Michael, when you needed me most.

MICHAEL. Would you really stand down for me? Chuck politics aside,
and be the one I knew?

DIANA. I would do anything, if it would only make you happy.

MICHAEL. Yes . . . but would it make you happy too?

(*There is a step outside on the terrace.* RICHARD *appears standing by the
window.* MICHAEL *turns his head and sees him.*)

MICHAEL. Greetings, Richard Coeur de Lion. You find us in a

moment of high drama ill-suited to the hour. Why the devil haven't you been to see me before? I'm seriously offended.

RICHARD (*not looking at* DIANA). I've been pretty busy, I'm afraid. The fact is, Robin was over at the farm and feel into the stream. I've made him take a bath and wrap himself in my dressing-gown, and I've come over for a change of clothes. I couldn't find Nanny in the kitchen.

MICHAEL. Your excuses are elaborate and entirely unnecessary. Have a glass of beer. (*He shouts to the servant.*) Don't look so disapproving. Can't the honest farmer have a drink after pulling your son out of the river?

DIANA. Is Robin quite all right?

RICHARD. Oh, completely. He got soaked through, that's all. It wasn't deep.

DIANA. I'll see about his clothes, and I'll tell Venning you want some beer.

(*She exits. We feel she has gone out of the room purposely.*)

MICHAEL. Three weeks I've been back, and not a sign of you, although I've walked to the farm once or twice. I was saying to Diana only yesterday, you were keeping yourself very aloof.

RICHARD. I didn't think you'd want outsiders butting in on your first few weeks at home.

MICHAEL. Who said you were an outsider? You're one of the family to Robin, at any rate. He spends all his time at the farm.

(VENNING *enters with beer. He puts the tray on the table and exits.*)

Richard, Diana tells me you've given her a hand with her money matters, and helped her in a hundred ways. That was good of you. My very grateful thanks.

(RICHARD *looks wretched and uncomfortable. There is a pause. They never did have much to say to each other.*)

You're a fortunate fellow, Richard. I suppose this war hasn't touched you at all?

RICHARD. Only indirectly.

MICHAEL. Like all conscientious chaps you have an inferiority complex, because a game leg kept you from Active Service. But don't let that worry you. We're nearly through now, anyway.

RICHARD. You really think that's true?

MICHAEL. Cigarette?

RICHARD. No, thank you.

MICHAEL. Only a question of hours, my dear fellow . . . we'll be caught napping, of course. Unready for peace, just as we were unready for war. And it's going to take devil of a time clearing up the mess.

RICHARD. I suppose you know more about that part of it than anyone over here. Our people will listen to you, won't they?

MICHAEL. The soldiers have done so already. They're the only ones that matter. I don't care a damn about the politicians. Won't you take a pew?

RICHARD. The thing that impressed me most about the whole business has been the work of the Underground movements. Did you come across many of them? The Resistance chaps, I mean.

MICHAEL (*smiling*). Only lived with them day and night, for the best part of three years.

RICHARD. It must have been pretty difficult evading capture, wasn't it?

MICHAEL. Oh, not so bad when the thing got organised, and I could get my reports through to this country.

RICHARD. Reports?

MICHAEL (*smiling*). Every day by wireless, from my extremely mobile HQ.

RICHARD (*puzzled*). I don't quite follow. You talk as though you'd been on some official job.

MICHAEL. I was. Somebody had to do the spadework, hadn't they? Somebody who knew the countries, spoke the languages, and who was supposed to have gone to glory when his plane crashed in the Mediterranean?

RICHARD (*staring at* MICHAEL). Do you mean – it was all planned from the start, before you left here? The crash – and everything?

MICHAEL. Yes.

RICHARD. You did it deliberately, knowing that Diana, and the world would believe you dead?

MICHAEL. There was no choice, to my mind. One weak link and the scheme would have failed.

(*There is a pause, the two men stare at one another.*)

RICHARD (*slowly*). I suppose you're the most courageous man I've ever known.

MICHAEL. Not courageous, Richard. Only filled with a sublime conceit.

RICHARD. Does – Diana know?

MICHAEL. Not yet.

RICHARD. I don't think I should tell her – if I were you.

MICHAEL. No? you think a woman wouldn't understand?

RICHARD. She might find it difficult – I mean, so many months of unnecessary anguish.

(MICHAEL *looks at him, half-curiously.*)

MICHAEL. I don't know why I told you. Strange. A sort of impulse, when you came into the room. We've never known each other particularly well, have we?

RICHARD. No. (*He takes a drink.*)

MICHAEL. Here's to our closer friendship, then, from this day forward. (*He lifts his tankard.*)

RICHARD. I'm afraid that's not very likely.

MICHAEL. What do you mean? (*He puts down his tankard.*)

RICHARD. I'm going away in a few days.

MICHAEL. Leaving the farm?

RICHARD. Yes, I've taken a smallholding in Wales. I've always had a love for the place. And if this war is really packing up, as you say, there will be plenty of work for me to do in my part of the world.

MICHAEL (*impulsive*). I say, I am sorry. Diana and Robin will miss you so much.

RICHARD. I think not. You see – they've got you home again.

MICHAEL. Yes . . . But Robin spends all his days with you, and Diana dictating letters to her secretary. It's been a funny sort of homecoming, you know.

RICHARD (*quietly*). You took an awful risk, didn't you, when you crashed into the sea?

MICHAEL. Yes. Sometimes – I wondered out there, what I should feel like if I came home and found that Diana had married again. (*Laughs.*) God, it was one of my worst nightmares. And instead of that bogey to haunt me night and day, I return to a blasted politician. Have some more beer?

RICHARD. No thank you. I must get back to the farm.

(DIANA *comes in with Robin's clothes.*)

DIANA. He's so untidy. Things all over the place. Here's a sweater and a pair of shorts.

MICHAEL. This fellow is going to leave us.

DIANA. Leave us? What do you mean?

MICHAEL. Going back to the Land of his Fathers. Taken a farm in
Wales. I think he's crazy, myself.

DIANA (*forgetting caution, a world of fear in her voice*). Richard . . .
(RICHARD *does nothing. He just stands dumbly.* MICHAEL *catches
the inflection in her voice, and looks from one to the other.* DIANA
*recovers.*)

That's a very sudden decision, isn't it?

RICHARD. Not so very sudden.

(MICHAEL *continues to watch them. He whistles to himself.*)

DIANA. When do you propose to go?

RICHARD. In a few days . . . I've been settling things during the
past weeks. The war will be over any time now. I'd like to be in
Wales when the aftermath begins and help straighten the
muddle.

(MICHAEL *switches on the 'Grieg Concerto'.*)

DIANA (*with bitterness*). The aftermath . . . that goes for all of us, I
suppose. It will take us the rest of our lives to straighten out the
muddle that this war has made.

MICHAEL (*softly, leaning over the back of the sofa*). Who's being bitter –
now? (*Turning to* RICHARD.)

Why don't you stay to lunch? Venning can take Robin's clothes
across.

DIANA (*still bitter*). Yes, why not? If we're not going to see much of you
in the future. (*She is overstrained, hurt and bewildered.*)

RICHARD. Thank you. I'd like to very much.

(VENNING *appears at the door.*)

MICHAEL. Venning, Mr Llewellyn will be staying for lunch. Will you
go across to the farm with these clothes for Master Robin?

VENNING. Sir. (*He takes the clothes from* DIANA *and exits.*)

(MICHAEL *goes to the radiogram.* DIANA and RICHARD s*tare at one
another in misery.* MICHAEL *switches off Grieg abruptly.*

MICHAEL. Shall we go forward – to reality? (*He grins like an evil imp,
refusing to suffer, and switches over to the radio. The voice of the
announcer says:*)

ANNOUNCER. Yesterday, at 2.41, Grand Admiral Doenitz, designated
head of the German State, signed an Act of Unconditional

Surrender of all German land, sea and air forces in Europe. Hostilities will end officially at one minute after midnight tonight. His Majesty the King will broadcast to the nation and to the world this evening at nine o'clock.
(MICHAEL *switches off.*)

MICHAEL. Peace finds us ill-prepared.

CURTAIN.

## SCENE 2

*That afternoon.*

*The* WENTWORTHS *and* RICHARD *are still at lunch. We can see* VENNING *carrying a tray from the dining-room. There is the sound of a bell, and* VENNING, *after taking the tray through to the dining-room, calls to* NANNY.

VENNING. There's the front-door bell, Nurse.
NANNY (*from the kitchen*). Well, goodness me, you can answer it, can't you? You can see I'm busy with the coffee.

(VENNING *goes to the door. The voice of* SIR ERNEST, *off.*)

SIR ERNEST (*off*). I'm rather early. I expect the Colonel is still having lunch.
VENNING (*off*). They're just finishing, sir. Perhaps you'd care to go straight into the dining-room?
SIR ERNEST (*off*). No. I'll wait in the library.

(SIR ERNEST *enters, followed by* VENNING.)

VENNING. What name shall I say, sir?
SIR ERNEST. Sir Ernest Foster. They're expecting me. Don't disturb them.
VENNING. I'll tell the Colonel, sir.

(VENNING *exits.* SIR ERNEST *looks about the room in slight curiosity.*)

MICHAEL (*from dining-room*). Why the devil doesn't he come in here? (*He crosses the hall, and enters the room.*) My dear Ernest – why the Gestapo entrance? Come along, and have some cheese and coffee.
SIR ERNEST. Cheese and coffee be damned – don't you know the war's over?

MICHAEL. So I gather – come along and have some cheese and coffee.

SIR ERNEST. No, thank you. Besides, I want to talk to you before seeing Diana.

(MICHAEL *shuts the door and comes slowly back*.)

Well, you're looking better. More like your old self again.

MICHAEL. Perhaps to you. Not to others.

SIR ERNEST. The war has been a strain on all of us, but to you it must have been unbearable.

MICHAEL. On the contrary. Responsibility sat very lightly on my shoulders.

SIR ERNEST. I was only told the whole history of what you did a couple of days ago. At first I did not believe it.

MICHAEL. Very sensible of you. It was a crazy thing to do.

SIR ERNEST. Crazy perhaps – but your work has helped to give us victory six months before we expected it.

MICHAEL. And now, it's only a question of putting out the flags.

SIR ERNEST. But for those who *really* know – the work has only just begun.

MICHAEL. Perhaps. But that doesn't interest me.

SIR ERNEST (*quietly*). Doesn't it? You surprise me.

(*They both smoke. There is a pause.*)

MICHAEL. Well? What do you want to see me about? The reward for my labours? Aren't you going to hand it to me on a silver salver?

SIR ERNEST. You know perfectly well why I've come.

MICHAEL. Yes . . . damn you. It's no use, Ernest, I'm not going back again. I've done what I set myself to do. Now it's the turn of somebody younger.

SIR ERNEST. You know what's needed in Europe, Michael, better than anyone over here. You've had nearly three years of it, living close to the people, looking at the world with their eyes. You're not the man to shrug your shoulders and leave them alone, now that the fighting is over.

MICHAEL. Aren't I? That's where you're wrong. I've lost three years, Ernest, because of the people of Europe. Three years that they can't give back to me. And it hasn't all been funny and amusing. I've had my share of the blood, and sweat, and tears. Now I'm going to make up for the time I lost. I want to get to know my wife and my son, all over again. I want to rebuild my home, just like the destitute, the bombed.

(SIR ERNEST *has been watching him closely.*)

SIR ERNEST (*lightly*). Of course, if you feel as strongly as that, then there's no more to be said. I had hoped – so had we all – that your response would have been different. But God knows, after what you've been through, you have a right to put your family first, before your country. (*Pause.*) How did you find Diana?

MICHAEL. Very much the politician. Full of meetings and good works. I understand she plays her part remarkably well.

SIR ERNEST. Yes. She is a darling. She has worked very hard. (*Another pause, and then, quietly.*) Three years was a long time to lie dead, Michael.

MICHAEL (*softly*). Isn't that just what I've been trying to tell you?

(*Enter* DIANA.)

DIANA. Ernest, why didn't you come into the dining-room? What are you two discussing in secrecy?

SIR ERNEST. As a matter of fact I came on a matter of – national importance. It has been badly received.

DIANA. You sound very solemn. Do I come into it? (*She looks bewildered, and rather hostile.*)

MICHAEL. My beloved wife, Ernest, feels the safe seat of North Arlsea rock from under her. As she observed to you on the telephone this morning, her political position is unique. Who is the legal Member for North Arlsea?

(*Enter* ROBIN *and* RICHARD.)

Colonel Wentworth, believed by the constituents for many months to be lying peacefully under foreign waters – or the charming and able wife who succeeded him? (*Turning to* RICHARD.) What is your opinion, Richard, as one completely unbiased? By the way – do you two know each other?

SIR ERNEST (*rather embarrassed*). Yes. Yes, rather, we have often met.

RICHARD (*stiffly*). How are you?

ROBIN (*precociously*). The last time you were here was when Mummy made the speech at the Salvage Drive, wasn't it? The village did awfully well. We considerably overshot *our* target.

SIR ERNEST. That was clever of you.

ROBIN. And we were runners-up for the Shield, and would have won it, only the judge favoured his own village.

SIR ERNEST (*gravely playing up to* ROBIN.) Local politics are so difficult.

MICHAEL. When I was your age, 'Little boys were seen and not heard.'
(ROBIN *looks offended*.) Richard, you haven't volunteered an opinion
whether Diana or myself should represent North Arlsea?

RICHARD. Surely that's a matter for you and Diana to discuss
together.

MICHAEL. What a model of discretion! No taking of sides. You must
be a very restful companion.

(*There is an uncomfortable pause*.)

Ernest, perhaps we had better continue our unprofitable
conversation in the garden. But you've had my answer.

SIR ERNEST (*moving up Right of the sofa*) I shall see you later, Diana?

DIANA. Yes – of course.

(MICHAEL *and* SIR ERNEST *exit to the garden. Silence*.)

RICHARD. Thank you for lunch. I must be getting back to the farm.

ROBIN (*eagerly*). Can I come with you?

DIANA (*not looking at either*). Robin, I want to talk to Uncle Richard.
Will you leave us for a little while?

ROBIN (*awkward*). Yes, Mum.

(*He hesitates a moment, then runs off*.)

DIANA (*her head turned away*). Do you grudge even five minutes alone
with me?

RICHARD (*in great pain*). Diana . . .

DIANA. You haven't been near me once – not once in the post month.
And when I sink to sending you messages by Robin, you don't
even answer them. And now you're going away. (*Her voice breaks*.)

RICHARD. What else can I do?

DIANA. Don't you love me any more?

RICHARD. Love you? (*He goes towards her*.) Do you want me to tell you
what it's been like for me, these nights and days?

DIANA. Rikky . . . (*They hold one another a moment and break away*.)

ROBIN (off). Daddy, are you going fishing tomorrow?

MICHAEL (*off*). Yes, but bring your own rod.

RICHARD (*quietly*). You see?

(*She moves away*.)

That's why I have to go away, isn't it? (*Pause*) Don't let's pretend
to one another. Do you want me to come to your house secretly
and linger in the woods, and wait for the sound of a car driving
away down the avenue? Do you want me to be that sort of man?

DIANA (*crying*). I can't go on like this any longer. I'm so terribly
unhappy.

RICHARD. My dear one.

DIANA. I've tried so hard to be the same to him, the one he wants, the
one he used to know. But it's no use. I'm not that woman any
more. None of our interests are the same, none of our thoughts.
And it's not his fault or mine, as he said this morning – it's the
years between.

RICHARD (*gently*). He loves you – still.

DIANA. I'm not sure, even of that. He's so different, so bitter, and
twisted, and strange. Oh, I know he's been through hell, and it's
cruel and hard of me to criticise, but any companionship we had
seems to have gone. Our hearts and our minds are not in tune.

(*There is a long pause.*)

RICHARD. Well, what are we going to do? Are you thinking of telling
him everything that's happened?

DIANA. I don't know.

RICHARD. Would you really do that, and come away with me, to
Wales?

DIANA (*torn to pieces*). Oh, Rikky . . .

RICHARD. Shall I tell you what would happen if you did? We'd find a
little happiness together, yes, for a time. We'd build a cottage in
the wilds and think only of ourselves. And then, gradually, his
shadow would come between us, and there'd be no peace in the
mountains any more, darling, only doubt and anxiety. I'm right,
aren't I?

(*She does not answer for a moment. Then:*)

DIANA. And if it's to be the other way, he and I that stay together, and
you that are alone, do you think I shall have peace in my heart?

RICHARD (*softly*). I don't know. But he is your husband. And you have
Robin. There'll always be that bond between you.

DIANA. We were going to be so happy, you and I.

RICHARD. I know.

DIANA. Do you realise, that if Michael had not come back, we should
have been together, now?

RICHARD. Yes . . .

DIANA. It's the little things that I've missed so much. You going
through my speeches with me – correcting the bad grammar; doing
my income tax – mending the wireless; our funny suppers on a

tray. Other people have snatched happiness and found a middle
way. It wouldn't be difficult for us, living so close.

RICHARD. We're not 'other people' . . . We'd find deceit a bitter,
hopeless thing. I love you too well to snatch at happiness. That's
why I'm going away.

(*She knows now that this is final.*)

DIANA. Richard, perhaps this is the last time we shall be alone
together. I want you to kiss me.

(RICHARD *kisses her.*)

RICHARD. You do know how much I love you?

DIANA (*in a whisper*). Yes.

(RICHARD *rises, turns and goes out of the room, into the hall, closing the
door behind him.* DIANA *hears it, and realises the finality. She turns and
see* MICHAEL, *who has just entered, standing looking at her from the
window.*)

MICHAEL. Is anything the matter?

DIANA. No – why should there be?

MICHAEL. You look so white and strange. Where's Richard?

DIANA. He's gone.

MICHAEL. Elusive fellow.

(SIR ERNEST *comes on the terrace behind* MICHAEL. *They enter the
library together.*)

I was just telling Ernest about your tremendous message to the
Girls' Training Corps. He was very much impressed, weren't you,
Ernest?

DIANA. Wouldn't it be kinder if you kept your mockery to yourself?
My sense of humour is rather lacking these days. (*She takes a
cigarette from the box on the mantelpiece.*)

MICHAEL. Amongst other new habits, Ernest, Diana has taken to
smoking like a chimney.

SIR ERNEST. Don't nag the woman. Why shouldn't she smoke? But
you're looking a bit pale, Diana.

MICHAEL. The result of my coming home. It makes so much work, as
Robin informed me the evening I arrived. Here we are, Ernest, the
excellent Miss Jameson has left behind her carbon copy. The
climax of the speech about the stronger, saner Britain – 'Our
children shall be brought up to service, duty and obedience to the
State.'

SIR ERNEST. A damn good thing too.

DIANA. Thank you Ernest.

MICHAEL. Yes, the girls of the GTC will come away bursting with enthusiasm. (*Softly.*) But does Diana really mean it? Are any of us here prepared to sacrifice ourselves to service, duty and obedience?

DIANA. Sometimes – there is no alternative.

MICHAEL. There's always an alternative. We can throw our caps over the mills and run away and say 'To hell with this.' Isn't that so, Diana?

DIANA. I don't know.

MICHAEL. Wouldn't you like to try – just as an experiment?

(*The atmosphere is dangerous.* SIR ERNEST *sees it, looking from one to the other.*)

SIR ERNEST (*Lightly*). For months I've tried to persuade Diana to run away with me. But alas – she will insist that Members of Parliament mustn't do these things.

DIANA. But I don't intend to be a Member of Parliament much longer. Now Michael is home, he will go back to the constituency. I've no right to the seat at all. There'll be a General Election in a few weeks anyway.

MICHAEL. You know, Ernest, her face alone is good for a couple of thousand votes.

DIANA. No, Michael. I'm serious about this. Ernest, you believe me?

SIR ERNEST. My dear, of course I do. But I assure you that the people of North Arlsea would far rather be looked after by you than by this madman. (*He nods in* MICHAEL'*s direction.*) Anyway, he tells me he is going to forsake public life, and take his ease. He turned down my suggestion before I'd even made it.

DIANA. And what was your suggestion?

MICHAEL (*Lightly*). Ernest and his fellow conspirators want me out of the way again. I know their filthy plots. Ernest has come down to offer me a job which I decline to take.

DIANA. What kind of job?

MICHAEL. A sort of benefactor-cum-policeman. Not a very attractive role.

DIANA. Won't you tell me the truth, Ernest? Michael has talked in riddles ever since he came back. You'll hardly believe me. But even now I know nothing of his life these past three years, except what I read in the newspapers. What he did – what he saw – how he lived. He doesn't want to tell me.

MICHAEL (*lightly*). Too many ghosts looking over my shoulder.

DIANA. I know he lay hidden for months in Europe, and made a miraculous escape. But he hasn't added to the story.

MICHAEL. There's nothing to add.

SIR ERNEST (*quietly*). Perhaps Michael wants to spare you the history of his three years, Diana, just as you might want to spare him – yours?

(SIR ERNEST *and* DIANA *look at each other. Both are thinking the same thought.*)

(*Lightly.*) At any rate, you can take it from me that your husband is one of the bravest men alive today.

MICHAEL (*turning*). Oh no, he's not. He's an almighty coward. He's so afraid of being hurt that he would like to walk the world blindfold, with his fingers in his ears.

(*His voice is suddenly savage, and they both stare at him in wonder.*)

DIANA (*suddenly afraid*). Michael . . .

(ROBIN *appears at the window.* MICHAEL *catches sight of him.*)

MICHAEL. There's the poor devil I'm sorry for. He's the one who'll have to pay for all the mistakes we make. Come in here, Robin – you're the chap that matters now.

(ROBIN *enters, looking rather frightened.*)

Ever drunk champagne, Robin?

ROBIN. No, Daddy, I don't think so.

MICHAEL. You're going to drink it now. We've got much to celebrate. Venning! Champagne at three o'clock in the afternoon. That's the proper way to bring in the peace, isn't it?

(*Enter* VENNING.)

VENNING. Sir.

MICHAEL. Venning, I found a bottle of champagne in the cellar, and I stuck it in the study. You'll recognise it by the gold cap and thick layer of dust. Bring glasses for us, and for yourself and Nanny.

VENNING. Thank you, sir.

(*He exits.*)

ROBIN. Why is everybody going to drink champagne?

MICHAEL. Because we've won the war, Robin, and I shan't have to work any more.

SIR ERNEST (*rising*). We're going to drink to the future, Robin, and rejoice that your father is with us again, and your mother as first woman Prime Minister. You'd like that, wouldn't you?

ROBIN (*not certain*). I don't know. (*Turns to* DIANA.) Where's Uncle Richard?

DIANA. He went back to the farm.

ROBIN. He ought to be here, to drink to the future too.

(*No one says anything.* VENNING *enters with the bottle and glasses.*)

VENNING. Is this right, sir? Bollinger '28.

MICHAEL. Thank you, Venning.

SIR ERNEST (*rising*). Lovely sound.

(VENNING *puts the tray on the table.*)

(NANNY *appears from the hall.*)

NANNY. Venning said you asked me to come, sir.

MICHAEL. You heard the news, Nanny?

NANNY. Yes, indeed.

MICHAEL. I know you're a teetotaller, Nanny, but I want you and Venning to join us in a glass of champagne in honour of the occasion.

NANNY. Thank you, sir.

(MICHAEL *pours champagne into the glasses.*)

ROBIN. I've seen this before, it's the stuff people drink at weddings, isn't it, Mums?

DIANA. Yes, darling.

MICHAEL. And occasionally at funerals, Robin – of the rather better sort. When the deceased is really safe beneath the ground. Has everyone got a glass?

(*Murmurs of 'Yes'. The* SERVANTS *are a little embarrassed.* MICHAEL *raised his glass and looks across at his wife, who lifts hers at the same time.*)

To your *brave* new world, Diana.

CURTAIN.

SCENE 3

SCENE: *The Same. – That evening, about eight o'clock. Supper is over.* SIR
ERNEST *and* DIANA *are sitting on the sofa, she is making coffee on the small
table there.* MICHAEL *is halfway up a stepladder with books in his hand, while*
ROBIN *hands more up to him from below.*

MICHAEL. Next – not that one, fathead, we can't have William Butler
    Yeats alongside George Moore. They don't agree.
ROBIN. They've both got red bindings.
MICHAEL (*laughing*). Listen to the rising generation! He only knows
    books by their bindings. That's the result of Diana's Higher
    Education.
DIANA. Do you want any coffee, Michael?
MICHAEL. Not until I've finished this job. Now the big one, Robin.
    The plays of J.M. Barrie. Did you ever see 'Mary Rose', Ernest?
SIR ERNEST. Rather! Cried my eyes out. Had to be supported from the
    theatre.
MICHAEL. She came back after twenty years, didn't she? But she never
    did find what she had lost.
ROBIN. What did she do?
MICHAEL. She died, Robin – and her pale ghost haunted the
    shadows . . . Don't stamp on Bernard Shaw, he wouldn't
    appreciate the compliment.

(ROBIN *hands up more books.*)

    'Man and Superman'. That's the stuff your generation need,
    Robin. There's more flesh and blood to him than to Mary
    Rose.
SIR ERNEST. Where are the writers of today?
MICHAEL. We shan't know for fifty years.
SIR ERNEST. What about yourself?
MICHAEL. Oh, I don't count. I'm only a debunker of bad history, who
    tells you what Charles the Second didn't do to Nell Gwyn. Besides,
    I haven't put pen to paper since 1939.
DIANA. You had better start again, if the war is really over. There
    won't be very much for you to do otherwise.
MICHAEL. What would you have me write?
SIR ERNEST. A history of the Second World War.
DIANA. Your experience of the past three years.
ROBIN. Yes, Daddy, write about all the things you've been doing.

MICHAEL. What did you do in the Great War, Daddy?
>        I hated mine enemy.
>        And what did you hate him for, Daddy?
>        For being as big a fool as me.

DIANA. Oh, come. That's 1918 obviously.

MICHAEL. I have a 1918 mentality. You forget that I fought in that war, too.

DIANA (*suddenly nervy*). I don't know why we're all sitting in here. It's a lovely evening. Let's drink our coffee in the garden, Ernest.

SIR ERNEST (*rising*). You mustn't let me forget the time. I've got to drive back to London before dark.

ROBIN. And all the church bells are going to ring again tonight before the nine o'clock news. Ours are going to ring in the village here. Not like on Sundays. The real genuine peal that we had before the war.

MICHAEL. Do you remember, Diana, when we heard that last?

DIANA. No, Michael, when was it? In '39, I suppose?

MICHAEL. That Sunday in September, when war was declared. We went to church together. You were wearing a blue check suit. Suddenly the siren went. You put out your hand to me. It was in the middle of the Creed.

DIANA (*slowly*). Yes . . . Yes, I remember now.

SIR ERNEST. A long time ago, isn't it? Anyway – you've both come out of it unscathed. You're the lucky ones.

MICHAEL. Yes – we're the lucky ones.

(*There is a pause that all feel.*)

SIR ERNEST (*trying to break it*). Come and show me the blue border, Diana, and let's pretend the war never happened.

DIANA. Alas, the blue border went a long time ago.

MICHAEL. There's a lot of beetroot there now – why not take look at that instead?

(SIR ERNEST *and* DIANA *exit to the garden.*)

ROBIN. Do you want me to go on helping you with the books?

MICHAEL (*suddenly tired*). No – not particularly.

ROBIN. Because, if you don't, I think I shall just slip across to the farm and see what Uncle Richard is doing.

MICHAEL. He talks of going to Wales, doesn't he?

ROBIN. Yes, it's a rotten shame. I'm sure he doesn't really want to go. The farming's not half so good there. I can't think why he's doing it.

MICHAEL. You like him, don't you?

ROBIN. Rather! He's a splendid chap. He's my greatest friend. He taught me to fish.

MICHAEL. With my rod?

ROBIN. Well, you see – we didn't know then that you'd be coming back.

MICHAEL. No. That did make rather a difference.

ROBIN. It will seem awfully queer without him. Though lately, of course, he hasn't been to the house at all. He was always here before.

MICHAEL. Before what?

ROBIN. Before you came home.

MICHAEL. Yours wasn't such a bad war, Robin, was it?

ROBIN. We had a bomb once, half a mile away. There's an enormous crater still.

MICHAEL. Is there? I wasn't thinking about bombs.

(*There is a pause for a moment.*)

Tell me something, Robin. What plans had you and Mummy made about your Easter holidays if I hadn't come home?

ROBIN. Oh, I was going to stay with Dawson – that's a pal of mine at school – for part of the holidays, while Mums and Uncle Richard were in Scotland.

MICHAEL. Scotland? Where were they going, in Scotland?

ROBIN. Some little cottage that Uncle Richard had taken. They were going to picnic, you know, do all the cooking themselves. Uncle Richard's a jolly good cook. Then Mums had to be back by the 29th, because of a meeting in London. We were all three going to the flat to have a week up there, doing theatres and things, before I went back to school.

MICHAEL. I'm sorry I spoilt the plan. Run along to the farm, then. I shan't be putting away more books tonight.

(ROBIN *exits.* MICHAEL *looks up and about him, round the room, as he did the first evening he came home. After a few minutes, he looks over his shoulder towards the door.*)

Venning! Venning!

(VENNING *enters.*)

VENNING. Sir?

MICHAEL. I shall be going up to London this evening with Sir Ernest.

Will you pack a suitcase, with my pyjamas, shaving kit, usual things? And I shall want you to travel up by train in a day or two. I'll let you know what I need by telephone.

VENNING. Sir.

MICHAEL. I may be away for some considerable time. I shan't know full details until I get to London. I may need you with me, where I'm going, or I may not. At any rate, you shall have your forty-eight hours' leave as soon as I can arrange it.

VENNING. Sir.

MICHAEL. All right, Venning.

(VENNING *exits*.)

(SIR ERNEST *and* DIANA *enter at the windows*.)

SIR ERNEST. Of course we'll have a national Government for the next four years. The country won't be prepared for such violent changes, all of a sudden. We shall see some new faces, I suppose, which will be quite a good thing. I'm getting very tired of a lot of the old ones, I don't mind telling you. But no one is going to start a revolution, I can promise you that.

MICHAEL. What about me?

(SIR ERNEST *turns round and smiles*.)

SIR ERNEST. You're not in the running, Michael. You've come back to peace and quiet.

MICHAEL. I've changed my mind.

(*They both look at him*.)

SIR ERNEST. What do you mean?

MICHAEL. The starving millions want a leader, don't they, to take them into the land of promise? Perhaps you are right, after all, and I am suited to the task. Very well, then, Ernest, I take back my refusal. Your offer is accepted.

SIR ERNEST. Are you joking?

MICHAEL. I was never more serious in my life. I shall come up with you to London tonight.

(*He smiles, and exits*.)

DIANA. What's he talking about?

SIR ERNEST (*slowly*). I had a feeling, all the while, that he wouldn't back out of it.

DIANA. You've got to tell me what you are asking Michael to do.

SIR ERNEST. The Government want him in Europe, Diana, but this time in the political field. He will be able to help us, as no one else can do.

DIANA. I still don't understand.

SIR ERNEST. Is it really true that you know nothing of your husband's work all these years?

DIANA. Absolutely. He's been so secretive and strange.

SIR ERNEST. How much *do* you know?

DIANA. Only what I've read in the papers. What else, Ernest, is there for me to know?

SIR ERNEST. A very great deal, Diana. (*A pause.*) Michael was in touch with our people over here from the very first moment that he landed in Greece. Messages came through by wireless, in those early weeks, messages that only ceased when he arrived back in this country last month. Little by little, he built a secret, powerful organization around him. People who watched, and waited, and whispered. The messages came from the Balkans, Holland and Belgium. Those thousands of people in the occupied countries who came to know something of Michael's secret mission, Diana, are the ones who have been helping our armies on the Continent. All owing to his work.

DIANA (*in a whisper*). Michael – did that?

SIR ERNEST. The risk of exposure and death never lifted day or night, all that time. But he never wavered.

DIANA. When did you learn all this?

SIR ERNEST. Only a few days ago. His identity was known only to one or two people, certainly not to an ordinary politician like myself. We knew the plan was progressing but we didn't know who was behind it. Like you, like all his friends, I believed that Michael Wentworth crashed into the sea in '42 and was drowned. I never thought to question whether the crash was genuine or faked.

DIANA (*slowly*). Do you mean the flight to the Middle East was false, was a blind? That deliberately he flew to Greece, and landed there in secret, so that the world, and you, and I, should think him dead?

SIR ERNEST. Yes, Diana.

(*She is very much moved.*)

DIANA (*slowly*). Is it possible that Michael could have been so cruel?

SIR ERNEST. The best soldiers, Diana, have always fought the hardest wars.

DIANA. How could he leave me, as he did, smiling, cheerful, knowing
what he was going to do, without a word or hint of any kind?

SIR ERNEST. He happened to be rather fond of his country, Diana.

DIANA. His country . . . you believe that? You believe that he cares
about his country after the way you've heard him laugh at
efficiency and discipline – all the things we've been trying to do, ·
here at home? Do you think he cared for one moment? Do you
think he cared whether I broke my heart, or married another man?

SIR ERNEST. Oh, my dear . . .

DIANA (*in anguish*). I want to love him as I loved him once. I want so
much to believe in him.

SIR ERNEST. My dear . . . You mustn't mind what I'm going to say,
but I must say it. You're very unhappy, aren't you?

DIANA. Yes.

SIR ERNEST. There's a terrible conflict in your mind, isn't there?
You've given love and loyalty to two men, and you've had to
choose between them.

DIANA. There's never been any question of choice. Michael came
first – always.

SIR ERNEST. Yes. But you want your choice to be justified, don't you?
Richard is a dear, unselfish fellow, I know that – but Michael needs
you more than Richard does. Richard can live without you.
Michael can't.

DIANA. What makes you think that?

SIR ERNEST. Don't you realise that the only thing that kept him sane –
during those three years of hell – was the thought of you and
Robin, of his home?

DIANA. If I could believe that, it would make the months to come
easier to bear. But will he ever tell me, Ernest? Shall I ever
know?

(MICHAEL *comes in from the hall. He has changed. He looks alert,
different somehow.*)

MICHAEL. I tell you what we'll do, Ernest. We'll get roaring drunk
tonight, to celebrate peace. If Diana wasn't such a wet blanket
she'd come up with us. But it wouldn't do for a woman MP to be
seen fighting in the streets; the Girls' Training Corps might get to
hear of it. It doesn't matter for an old stager like myself.

SIR ERNEST. Merely keeping up the traditions of the House of
Commons.

DIANA. I'll come with you, if you really want me to.

MICHAEL. No, not for the world. You'll be happier down here, with
Nanny and Robin.

DIANA. What are your plans? Does Venning know? Have you given
orders about packing?

MICHAEL. Everything's laid on. I'm a quick worker, you know, when I
get going. You can give me a bed tonight, can't you, Ernest?

SIR ERNEST. Yes, of course.

DIANA. Why don't you go to my flat?

MICHAEL (*carelessly*). Your flat? I'd forgotten you had a flat. I've never
seen it, have I?

DIANA. No.

MICHAEL. I don't think I want to. I'd feel wrong there.

DIANA (*gently*). What nonsense.

SIR ERNEST. Why doesn't Diana come up in a few days, and both of
you go to the flat? You won't be off for a while, I suppose.

DIANA. Yes, why not. Where will it be this time?

MICHAEL. Germany, I suppose. To join the fun and frolic with the
boys. Hasn't Ernest been telling you all about it?

DIANA. He's told me what you've done.

MICHAEL. How very indiscreet of you, Ernest, to give away State
secrets.

SIR ERNEST (*lightly*). Isn't it time your own wife knew something about
your life?

MICHAEL. It's always a mistake, my dear fellow, to find out too much
about anybody's life. And the closer you are to someone, the less
you ought to know.

SIR ERNEST. Cynical nonsense.

DIANA (*to* MICHAEL). Do you really mean that?

MICHAEL (*lightly*). Of course, my sweet. (*He opens the door and shouts
'Venning.'*) What about a little drink before we go?

SIR ERNEST. Not for me.

MICHAEL. Actually I haven't the slightest idea what I'm going to do,
nor has Ernest. But I suppose first thing tomorrow morning I shall
be dragged like a reluctant schoolboy before a lot of old gentlemen,
and they will put their heads together and talk me over for a week,
and then decide to send me in a special plane to some God-
forsaken spot, and this time I really shall fall into the sea.

(*Enter* VENNING.)

Tell Sir Ernest's chauffeur we'll be leaving. And stick my bag in the
car, will you?

VENNING. Yes, sir.

SIR ERNEST. I wonder what's happened to that boy of yours. Isn't he going to come and say goodbye? (*He goes on to the terrace, and calls* 'Robin.')

MICHAEL. If you really feel like coming up in a few days – it will be nice to see you.

DIANA. You know I'll come if you really want me, but why is it necessary to dash off with Ernest this evening?

MICHAEL. Once I've made up my mid about a thing, I like to be off and away, you know that. Anything else is anticlimax.

DIANA. There will be anticlimax now, though, won't there? Peace, and –

MICHAEL. And what?

DIANA. Oh, everything.

MICHAEL. Doesn't that rather depend on ourselves?

DIANA. Michael, why are you doing this thing? Is it a sudden wave of patriotism, of blind conviction?

MICHAEL. Not exactly. You came to a decision today, didn't you, that was difficult for you, and hard. Don't ask me how I know – I understand. It gave me a feeling of humility and at the same time a funny sort of pride. If you could win your battle, so could I. I realised suddenly that if we are to make any future for Robin – for ourselves – I've got to help the people over in Europe, just as you're going to help the people here at home. There must be no sitting back yet awhile. Not for our generation.

DIANA. That's the way you used to talk to me five years ago. Michael, I want you to forgive me for these past few weeks. You must have thought me very cold, and dull.

MICHAEL. Not dull.

DIANA. When you come home again I'll be different . . . I promise you.

(MICHAEL *smiles. She is not sure why he smiles.*)

MICHAEL. Will you?

(*They might be going to say much to each other, but at this moment* SIR ERNEST *appears at the window with* ROBIN.)

SIR ERNEST. Here's this fellow. Why don't we take him with us?

MICHAEL. He wouldn't want to come.

ROBIN. Why are you going to London, Daddy?

MICHAEL. The lights and the music were too much for me.

ROBIN. When are you coming back?

MICHAEL. I'm not sure. It depends, as I was telling Mummy, on a lot
of old gentlemen up in London.

ROBIN. Perhaps they are going to give you a medal.

MICHAEL. I shall be enormously offended if they don't.

ROBIN. Perhaps they'll make you President of the new German
Republic.

MICHAEL. That's the most terrifying suggestion anyone has made yet.
Come on, Ernest.

SIR ERNEST. You must come up with Mummy in a few days and join
Daddy in London.

ROBIN. Before I go back to school?

SIR ERNEST. Yes.

ROBIN. Good.

(SIR ERNEST *and* ROBIN *go out.*)

MICHAEL. Don't come out. I hate anyone waving farewell from a
doorstep. It gives one such a feeling of finality.

DIANA. There are so many questions I haven't asked you. After what
Ernest told me I want to know more – much more.

MICHAEL. I wouldn't bother if I were you.

DIANA. Will you promise to tell me next time when you pretend to
plunge into the sea and drown?

MICHAEL. Next time I'll take you with me, and we'll make a proper
job of it.

DIANA. I believe you enjoyed it, Michael, and never thought of me at
all.

MICHAEL (*smiling*). I didn't think of anyone. Do you remember the
Irish airman? I quoted him to my Sergeant pilot before we crash-
dived off the coast of Greece?

'Nor law, nor duty, bade me fight,
Nor public men, nor cheering crowds,
A lonely impulse of delight,
Drove to this tumult in the clouds.'

Good night, darling.

(*He lays two fingers on her cheek, and exits.*)

ROBIN (*off*). Goodbye, Daddy. See you soon.

MICHAEL (*off*). Very soon, old fellow.

(DIANA *is about to light a cigarette when she remembers* MICHAEL'*s*

*remarks on her 'smoking like a chimney', so she puts it back in the box
and picks up the copy of her speech.* ROBIN *comes back and stands
aimlessly. He sees the books on top of the steps.*)

ROBIN. Daddy never finished putting away the books.

(DIANA *does not answer.*)

Perhaps I'd better do it for him. (*He climbs up the stepladder.
Glancing at the titles.*) *Paradise Lost* and *Paradise Regained*. That's
awfully stiff. The seniors have been reading that at school. (*He
places it on the shelf.*) *Grimm's Fairy Tales*. Gosh! Fancy a Colonel
reading Fairy Tales. Daddy's got an awfully queer collection here. I
can't think why he didn't let them go for salvage.

(*He puts the last book on the shelf, and dusts his hands.*)

(DIANA *is looking at her carbon copy of the GTC speech. In the distance,
the church bells begin their peal for victory. It is getting darker.*)

The bells, Mums. (*He descends.*) Do you hear them? (*He runs up to
the windows.*)

(DIANA *lifts her head, and listens.*)

DIANA. Yes, darling.

(ROBIN *looks out of the windows.* DIANA *moves to telephone and lifts the
receiver, the paper still in her hand.*)

ROBIN. Are you going to ring up Uncle Richard?

DIANA. No. 32 please –

ROBIN. I expect he's listening to the bells too. (*He returns to the
windows.*)

(*The bells continue all the while.*)

DIANA. Is that Miss Jameson? Yes, it's Mrs Wentworth speaking. Miss
Jameson, have you got that message to the GTC that we were
working on this morning? That's right . . . because I want to alter
the end . . . And just put instead 'We hope to build a wiser, happier
Britain, where our children and ourselves shall grow in courage,
faith and understanding.' Yes . . . that's all. Thank you so much,
Miss Jameson. Good night.

(NANNY *enters from the hall.*)

NANNY. Aren't the bells wonderful?

DIANA. Aren't they lovely, Nan?

ROBIN. I bet the old sexton is stiff tomorrow.

NANNY. Venning tells me the Colonel will be away for some time. He has to take the rest of his things up in the morning.

DIANA. Yes, Nan. The Government want him for some very important post. He's going up with Sir Ernest this evening.

NANNY. Will it be abroad?

DIANA. I'm afraid so.

ROBIN. Uncle Richard is going away, too. To Wales. Will we be going up to see Daddy before he goes?

DIANA. Would you like to, darling?

ROBIN. Rather.

NANNY. Shall I close the windows?

DIANA. Please, Nan.

(NANNY *shuts the windows. The sound of the bells dies away.*)

NANNY. It's queer, isn't it? I was saying to Venning in the kitchen, all over the country people have been longing and waiting, and praying for this day to come, and now that it's over, it's been quiet and ordinary, just like any other day. The war is over, the peace is to come, and we shall all go back to being just the same as we were before.

DIANA (*slowly*). Shall we?

(*There is a pause.*)

ROBIN. Not quite the same, Nan. You forget I'm five years older. And I'm the chap that matters. Daddy said so. Isn't that right, Mums?

DIANA (*putting out her hand to him*). Yes, darling . . . You're the one that matters.

NANNY. It's just on nine. Shall I turn on the wireless?

DIANA. Yes, Nan.

(NANNY *switches on. We hear the last two notes of Big Ben, and then the voice of the announcer: 'This is London. His Majesty, King George the Sixth.'*)

*Slow* CURTAIN.

# Lesley Storm

## 1903–1975

Born Margaret Cowie in 1903 in Maud, Aberdeenshire, Lesley Storm was the daughter of the Reverend William Cowie and Christian Ewen. She studied at Peterhead Academy and Aberdeen University where she gained an MA. She later married James Doran Clark, a Harley Street surgeon, and the couple had two sons and two daughters.

Her first play *Dark Horizon* (starring Ann Todd and Marda Vanne, 1934), was a prophetic picture of London during wartime bombing. The same year she produced *The Wise Woman* (starring Mary Clare). In 1936 she wrote *Follow Your Saint* (starring Edna Best). Her first great success, *Tony Draws a Horse* (starring Lilian Braithwaite and Diana Churchill) and later filmed, came at the beginning of 1939. The play ran for 364 performances at London's Criterion Theatre.

Other plays followed, including *Heart of a City*, *A Night in Venice* (1944, the book for the Johann Strauss operetta), *Great Day* (1945, about preparations for Mrs Eleanor Roosevelt's visit to an English village, which therefore had to be taken off when Roosevelt suddenly died), *Black Chiffon*, *The Day's Mischief* (1951), *The Long Echo* (starring Joyce Redman and Moira Lister, 1956), *Favonia* and *Roar Like a Dove* (1957, her greatest success; described by critics as 'a wittily developed comedy' and 'a kind of fertility rite', it played at London's Phoenix Theatre and ran for 1007 performances), *Time and Yellow Roses* (starring Flora Robson, 1961), *The Paper Hat* (starring Marie Kean, 1965), *Three Goose Quills and a Knife* (1967) and *Look No Hands* (1970).

Her screenplays include *The Fallen Idol* (starring Ralph Richardson and Sonia Dresdel, 1948 and nominated for an Oscar), *The Golden Salamander* (starring Trevor Howard, 1951), *The Heart of the Matter* (starring Trevor Howard, 1953), *Personal Affair* (starring Gene Tierney and Glynis Johns, 1954), and *The Spanish Gardener* (starring Dirk Bogarde, 1957).

She died on 19 October 1975.

# About *Black Chiffon*

The play opened at the Westminster Theatre on 3 May 1949 and ran for 416 performances, before doing a British and an American tour.

The critics hailed both the play and the return (after three years) of Flora Robson to the London stage: 'The Dialogue is consistently neat and pointed, and tense situations open smoothly into situations yet more tense' – *The Times*; 'This is a most sensitive, heart-searching, adroitly written play' – *Evening News*; 'A Pinero play with a modern setting . . . a compelling triumph' – *Evening Standard*; 'an absorbing play . . . excellently written and brilliantly acted, and is worth going a long way to see' – *Telegraph*; 'exciting theatre . . . a theatrically effective play most movingly acted' – *Tatler*.

Flora Robson, who played Alicia Christie, describes the play's fortunes when it was taken on tour to America. There were cast replacements and most of the rehearsal had to be done on board the liner that transported the company. Held up by fog, they arrived only just in time for the first performance in Boston, in sticky and humid weather. Flora Robson was exhausted and drained as she walked onto the stage. Shortly after, a violent storm shook the theatre. It was the tail-end of a hurricane. The company received mixed reviews in Boston and in New York, a few weeks later: 'a straggling British importation' – *Herald Tribune*; 'the first steadily interesting play of the new season' – *New York Post*; and bad luck dogged the production.

The dressing rooms in the New York theatre were not waterproof, two leading members of the cast developed pneumonia,

and Flora Robson had to be admitted to hospital. In her absence
the show was closed. When she recovered, the first act was
shown on television and the Broadway run continued.
Unfortunately, the break had dissolved the momentum of the
show's initial reception and after four months the notices went
up. During the last performance, the sound of carpenters removing the hoardings and putting up the names for the next show
could be heard on stage, the stage management had forgotten to
light the on-stage fire and electricians had already removed some
essential lamps. The cast were delighted to get aboard the *Queen
Mary* and head home.

Back in England, where the vagaries of the US tour had little
influence, the play soon became a Rep warhorse, playing all over
the country on tour and in rep, with a steadily falling standard of
production until its reputation was tarnished by familiarity. It
could be said that its success was its downfall.

The myth of *Black Chiffon* is better known than the reality.
There are few people in the theatre who have not heard of it, but
few people actually know it.

Written along the same lines as the Hitchcock film *Marnie*, it
delves into the unconscious mind of its heroine, a woman who in
a fit of madness shop-lifts an unsuitable negligee because her son,
who she loved more than she thinks, is getting married. Some
years ago (long after *Black Chiffon* had fallen out of the theatrical
repertoire) there was a famous case of a successful TV personality, Lady Isabel Barnett, who took up shop-lifting as a *cri de
couer*, and who subsequently committed suicide in her shame.
That case demonstrates that the subject matter of the play is not
as banal as a brief potted synopsis might make it sound. The
story-telling is compellingly handled and the dramatic opportunities are all there for a star turn by the leading lady.

# BLACK CHIFFON

## Lesley Storm

*Flora Robson and Anthony Ireland, Act II*

First acted at the Westminster Theatre, London, on 3 May 1949, with the following cast:

| | |
|---|---|
| ALICIA CHRISTIE | *Flora Robson* |
| ROBERT CHRISTIE | *Wyndham Goldie* |
| ROY | *Owen Holder* |
| LOUISE | *Dorothy Gordon* |
| THEA | *Rachel Gurney* |
| BENNETT HAWKINS | *Anthony Ireland* |
| NANNIE | *Janet Barrow* |

# ACT I

SCENE: *The drawing-room of the* CHRISTIES' *house on Chelsea Embankment. It is a large room on the first floor with two long windows looking out on the river with the trees of Battersea Park in the distance.*

*It is a Monday afternoon in October.*

*It is the sort of room that has been lived in a long time (the* CHRISTIES *have been married twenty-four years), it is mellow and a little overcrowded.*

*When the* CURTAIN *rises,* LOUISE *and* ROY *are standing in the centre of the stage in a comfortable sort of embrace. Nothing passionate about it. They are standing cheek to cheek. They stand like that for a moment without speaking.*

LOUISE. I think you're a very nice boy.
ROY. I think you're a very nice girl.

> (*The door opens and* THEA *comes in. She glances at them without interest. They don't move.*)

THEA. Break it up. Break it up.
ROY (*placidly*). Why should we?
LOUISE. Yes, why should we?

> (THEA *sits down. Takes out some knitting.*)

ROY. We like it.
THEA. You've only got about four more days to last out. You look as if you'll scarcely make it.
ROY. So what?
LOUISE. Yes. So what?
THEA. You put me off my knitting.
ROY. Your knitting puts us off. It fills us with gloomy foreboding . . . The moving finger knits and having knit moves on . . . you sit waiting for that infant of yours like a *tricoteuse*. (*Sits sofa.*)
THEA. A shade more grimly.
ROY. All that clicking going on a few inches from its ears . . . suppose it thinks it's a time-bomb?
THEA (*pertly*). Might hurry it along a bit . . . Where's Mother?
ROY. She said she had some letters to answer.
THEA. Why aren't you at work?
LOUISE. He's got three weeks off. Isn't he clever?

ROY. In view of my approaching nuptials they said I could start today.

THEA. Did they give you a present?

ROY. A cheque.

THEA. How much?

ROY. Twenty guineas. (*He clicks his tongue twice.*)

THEA. What's the score now?

LOUISE. Three hundred and eighty-six.

ROY. It's a good racket getting married. I've never had so much money in my life . . . tax-free at that.

THEA. Bill and I got much more.

ROY. We've still a few days to go. We're waiting for the last-minute rush.

THEA. Has Daddy given you anything yet?

ROY. We're hoping for his blessing.

THEA. He'd much sooner give you a cheque.

ROY (*in same tone*). Perhaps . . . for the pleasure of hearing me say thank you.

LOUISE (*gently*). Roy – why must you be so awful about him?

ROY. Darling, don't be the little peacemaker, will you?

LOUISE. I was only thinking how it must hurt your mother.

ROY (*bluntly*). It doesn't.

LOUISE. But Roy it must.

ROY (*abruptly*). She's lived with the situation for twenty-two years.

LOUISE. Well, I think . . .

THEA (*cutting in quickly*). He's getting out of the house in a few days' time, Louise. It doesn't matter any more.

LOUISE. It might be the moment to patch it up.

ROY. As the boy said when he stuck his thumb in the dyke.

LOUISE. It's something I don't understand. It seems unnatural to me.

ROY. Is it? I don't know. You see, I've never known him.

THEA. He was away long spells in South America when we were children. We were here in London with Mother . . . every time he came home he was a stranger who took her away from us.

LOUISE (*smiling*). And you were jealous? He should have spanked you both.

ROY. He was jealous. We were too friendly – the three of us. He would have preferred unruly children in need of masculine discipline. So that he could have thrown his weight about.

LOUISE. Weren't you ever unruly?

ROY. Only with him. There was no need otherwise . . . I took on

responsibility very early – (*Smiling,*) I was the man of the house . . .
He once read me a long lecture before he went, about how I was to
look after Mother and Thea and the house . . . and I took him too
seriously. When he came back he didn't like it.

THEA. There were frightful rows. And Roy ran away.

LOUISE. Did you?

THEA. He was away for two days – Mother was frantic.

LOUISE. How old were you then?

ROY. Eight or nine . . . Why this sudden probing round the family?

THEA. We never really were a family. It was always lopsided. He was
away for a couple of years at a time . . . we used to forget what he
looked like.

LOUISE. And when he came back he was a stranger.

THEA. To us. Not to Mother, of course. He commandeered her – and
resented us intruding on it.

ROY. He didn't resent you.

THEA. No, not so much.

LOUISE. It was you, Roy?

ROY. Oh Lord yes. Always. And I was scared of him. That didn't
help.

THEA. It's Mother who always had the heavy end of the stick – having
to be a wife and mother in face of sabotage from both sides.

LOUISE. I think she's wonderful. That calm she has . . .

THEA. Most women would have thrown their hand in. But she'll stand
beside Daddy in church on Thursday and see Roy married and no
one will know the long war *she's* fought!

(*They sit in silence for a moment, then* ALICIA's *voice is heard off.*)

ALICIA (*off*). Roy!

ROY. Yes, Mother?

ALICIA (*off*). Will you slip across to the pillar-box with those letters?

ROY. Sure.

(ROY *goes out.*)

THEA. The whole trouble, of course, is Roy.

LOUISE. In what way?

THEA. He's so like Mother – in temperament, tastes, everything. Even
in appearance he's the image of Mother's father. In going into
publishing he's following her family. You know her father was John
Meredith.

LOUISE. Yes. Roy told me.

THEA. She knew a lot about her father's business, and all her interest has wakened again since Roy decided that was what he wanted to do. Tho' he made the decision.

LOUISE. I know she lent him money – or gave it him.

THEA. Oh yes. She'd give him her last penny . . .

LOUISE. I realized that when I first met her. I was afraid she wouldn't like me – wouldn't think I was good enough.

THEA. You don't think that now?

LOUISE. No. No one could have been sweeter . . . I like your father too.

THEA. He's all right except for this bee in his bonnet . . . This awful jealousy thing . . . it's something he can't help. It's grown with the years and it's there however much one tries to ignore it. I'm sorry for them all – for Daddy and Mother – *and* Roy. It's like some awful thing that's dogged their footsteps. It keeps cropping up in different shapes, different circumstances. Cut off one head and it grows another.

LOUISE. Perhaps our being married will solve it.

THEA. It will to an extent.

LOUISE. I'm afraid he won't come back here very much.

THEA. No. It will be much more of a break than it ought to have been . . . throw me over that bag on the desk, will you, darling?

(ROY *enters.*)

ROY. How about going to a film, Louise?

LOUISE. Yes, I'd love to.

(ROY *picks up an evening paper and looks down the list.*)

ROY. What would you like to see?

LOUISE. Let's look!

(ALICIA *enters quietly. She is forty-four, but a young forty-four. Smart and attractive. Carries a wrapped magazine.*)

ALICIA. Did they catch the 2.30 post, Roy?

ROY (*looking at the paper*). Yes, darling.

ALICIA. Oh, hallo, Thea, I didn't hear you come in . . . how are you?

THEA. Horribly well, I'm afraid. I saw Dr Stephens this morning – he says he's bored with me, I'm so normal. Says I could probably have it under a hedge and walk home . . . dull, isn't it?

ALICIA. Yes. Too bad, darling. We shall have to find you a nice hedge to test his theories.

ROY. It would certainly make an unusual announcement? 'To Mr and Mrs Hopkins – suddenly – in Battersea Park . . .!

ALICIA (*laughing*). Roy!

ROY (*reading*). Mickey Rooney in 'Fugitive from Quarantine'.

ALICIA. Oh dear! Why don't you go and see the French film at the Academy?

ROY. Who's in it?

ALICIA. Jean-Louis Barrault.

THEA. Mother's crazy about him. Dragged me three times to see 'Les Enfants du Paradis'.

ROY (*to* ALICIA). How dare you have a crush on an actor?

ALICIA (*smiling. Has envelope open*). I shall try to control it – but seriously, you ought to see him.

LOUISE. What we ought to do is to go round to the flat with a tape measure and start measuring things.

ROY (*smiling*). Flat? Our room, you mean.

LOUISE. You can't call a studio just a room. It's an all-purpose flat. You haven't seen it, Thea. It's one large room with a gallery – and a little kitchen and bath.

THEA. What are you going to do with the gallery?

ALICIA (*smiling*). When Louise burns the dinner Roy can always go up there and boo.

(LOUISE *laughs.*)

ROY. Thanks, Mother. Have you any other bright ideas?

LOUISE (*to* ALICIA). What colour should we have it?

ALICIA. I should say white.

LOUISE. That's what I said. Roy says green.

ALICIA. Too cold. It's a north light.

THEA. Have you seen it, Mummy?

ALICIA. Yes.

ROY (*to* ALICIA). Only for a couple of minutes. You blew in and blew out again.

ALICIA. I was in a hurry.

ROY. I don't think you like it.

LOUISE. Did you get some sort of queer feeling about it?

ALICIA. No, darling, what makes you think that?

LOUISE. You know how one sometimes feels about a house . . . as if it was being sort of secretly – hostile.

ALICIA (*smiling*). Did you feel that about it?

LOUISE (*quickly*). No . . . but I wondered if you did.

ROY (*smiling*). Louise is chock-full of superstitions; she's always looking for pegs to hang them on.

THEA. If there had been anything clairvoyant about Mummy we should have sent her out to cash in on it long ago . . . Where is this studio, anyhow?

ROY. Yeoman's Place.

THEA. Quite near. You never get rid of your children, do you, Mummy?

ALICIA (*smiling*). No. It's too bad.

THEA. They marry and set up house a few yards away.

ROY. I shan't come round every afternoon with my knitting, anyhow.

ALICIA. When Thea was a little girl she used to say that when she married she'd build a house next door – with a secret tunnel between . . . and that's just about what she's done. Except for the tunnel.

ROY. She got that idea from me. I had it first when I was about five. How about that movie, Louise?

LOUISE. I wonder if I ought.

ROY. Oh come on –

LOUISE. I've such a lot to do.

ROY. What?

LOUISE (*smiling*). Preparing for this date we have in church. Should I wear gloves?

ALICIA. I shouldn't. They always stick – especially if one is nervous. (*Smiling.*) I wore long white suede gloves, and they were agony – they might have been glued on.

LOUISE. Where were you married?

ALICIA. St Martin's. In 1925 . . . (*Smiling.*) Another era – another world. We took the car over to France and toured Europe, Germany, Austria, Czechoslovakia . . . we went wherever we wanted to.

LOUISE. It must have been wonderful!

ALICIA. It was . . . life was simple and uncomplicated then. We didn't know what was before us . . . (*Hastily.*) I mean Fascism and Communism and all the other horrors.

LOUISE. I wonder what's before *us*?

ALICIA. Well – it isn't within one's own control, I'm afraid . . . Keep your marriage right. It's a great source of strength, they say.

LOUISE. I shall try.

ALICIA (*smiling*). And keep your children in their place.

ROY. What she means is, don't park them on her.

THEA. Because I shall have priority.

ALICIA. Thanks very much. But rearing one family is enough. I should be terrified of a second generation – the gap's too big.

ROY. Not for you. Don't slack. Come on, Louise.

ALICIA. That's wonderful.

LOUISE. I don't think I will come to a movie, Roy.

ROY. Oh!

LOUISE. I've a hundred things to do.

ALICIA. Can I help you with anything, darling? – Any packing?

LOUISE. I'm only taking one suitcase down to Cornwall. I shall leave the rest of my things here, if I may, until we come back to town.

ALICIA. You'll be staying here. Anyhow for a little until your flat is ready?

(*There is a slight pause.*)

ROY. I thought we'd go to an hotel, Mother.

ALICIA. Why? There's plenty of room here.

ROY. I know, darling, but –

ALICIA. Roy!

LOUISE. Roy thinks his father mightn't like it much.

ALICIA (*quietly*). Nonsense.

ROY. Darling, I'd rather go to an hotel. I don't have to tell you why. I don't want to come back.

(ALICIA *is silent for a moment.*)

ALICIA (*defeated*). It seems silly you should have to go elsewhere when this house will be practically empty.

ROY. I'm sorry, Mother . . . But it's a new life, darling.

ALICIA. Yes, of course.

ROY. And you understand?

ALICIA (*with a smile*). Why, yes, Roy . . .

(*The telephone rings.* ROY *answers.*)

ROY. Hallo – who is it speaking? It's someone for you, Louise – a woman – she won't say who she is.

(LOUISE *crosses over and takes the receiver.*)

LOUISE. Hallo . . . (*Uncertainly.*) No, I don't know . . . (*A sudden flash of unbearable excitement crosses her face.*) Mummy! (*Scarcely able to speak.*) Mummy! Are you speaking from India? . . . From London!!! . . . No, darling . . . I can't speak – I'm nearly weeping with excitement – Where are you? Both of you? You flew . . . No, I can't wait. I'm going to hang up. I'll dash out and get a taxi. I'll be with you in a few minutes. (*She hangs up the receiver. Tears are running down her cheeks. Tremulously.*) It's my parents. They've flown over for the wedding – suddenly took it into their heads. (*She cries and laughs. Flings arms round* ALICIA.)

ALICIA. Darling, I'm so pleased!

LOUISE. I haven't seen them for three years. And I'd pictured them thousands of miles away on my wedding day.

ALICIA (*smiling*). It's wonderful for you, darling!

ROY. I'll get a taxi. Where are they staying?

LOUISE (*laughing*). Brown's.

ROY. Well, hold your horses till I get a cab.

(*He goes out quickly.*)

THEA. Well, I call that a pretty nice surprise. No cable. No anything. Just a ring on the phone: 'We're here.'

LOUISE (*excitedly*). And they were so positive they couldn't make it!

ALICIA. I couldn't be more delighted. I didn't say it, but I've felt so sorry for you these last few days. I knew you were missing someone of your own around. You were like a little orphan . . .

LOUISE (*impulsively*). Oh, I hope not! You've been so marvellous – so sweet to me! You've been the absolute reverse of all one ever thought about mother-in-laws.

ALICIA (*smiling*). Mothers-in-law, darling.

LOUISE. Yes.

(*She runs out.*)

ALICIA. She's terribly excited, poor child! No wonder . . .

THEA. Oughtn't we to do something about them?

ALICIA. Oh yes – of course – I'll ask them to dine with us tonight. (*Calling off.*) Louise, ask them to come to dinner tonight, will you? Here.

LOUISE (*off*). They'd love to. I know.

ALICIA. And we'd love to meet them. Half-past seven.

LOUISE (*off*). Lovely! –

THEA. It's funny to think none of us have ever met –

ALICIA. There's Roy with a cab. Now hurry!

LOUISE (*off*). All right!

(*She waves her hand and dashes out.*)

*(The front door bangs off. A taxi door slams.)*

ALICIA. Roy's gone with her.

THEA. He's mad. I'm sure she'd rather have gone alone – and prepared them for the shock.

ALICIA. I'd better think about this dinner . . . we were going to have fish . . . *(Rings bell.)*

THEA. They haven't been in England since before the war. You can't throw a piece of fish at them the moment they arrive.

ALICIA. I don't intend to, darling – I must go out and see what I can find.

THEA. Shall I go for you?

ALICIA. No thanks, dear. I'm a much better shopper than you.

THEA. They've got some pheasants at Mac Fisheries. They're a filthy price.

ALICIA. I can't help it tonight. They're Roy's in-laws, after all – we must make it a bit of an occasion.

*(NANNIE comes in. She is about sixty. She wears an overall.)*

Oh, Nannie – Miss Louise's parents have suddenly arrived from India . . .

ALICIA. Isn't it exciting? ⎫
NANNIE. Well, I never! ⎬ *Overlap.*
            ⎭

ALICIA. They flew, for the wedding. And I've asked them to dinner tonight, to meet us all.

NANNIE. Oh dear, madam . . . we've only got that bit of fish.

ALICIA. I know.

NANNIE. And it isn't all that fresh.

ALICIA. I know. Thea says they've got pheasants at Mac Fisheries.

THEA. I saw them there, Nannie!

ALICIA. If you attend to that, I'll go up to Hartman's and see what else I can find.

THEA. Peaches in brandy . . . *(She clicks her tongue twice.)*

NANNIE. Who taught you that vulgar noise?

*(THEA smiles at her and does it again.)*

ALICIA *(thinking hard)*. Let's see, soup, pheasant . . . and peaches in brandy, or something like that. And they might have smoked salmon . . . I'll go up there now. I shan't be long.

NANNIE. How many will there be, madam?

ALICIA. What? – Oh – You'll come, Thea – you and Bill?

THEA. We can't, darling, I'm sorry. We've got a date.

ALICIA. What a pity! We'll be six, then, Nannie. Is there enough gin?
I'll call in at Mrs Waters on my way and ask her to come and give
you a hand.

NANNIE. She'll come all right!

ALICIA. Better get another bottle.

NANNIE. Five shillings an hour for evening work! When I first went to
your mother's I got five shillings a week.

ALICIA. Never mind, Nannie. You can't do it alone – it's too much.
Mrs Waters can wait table. Oh! Where's my bag! You see, where
they come from, they've servants to pick up a handkerchief if they
drop it. They'll have to get used gradually to us poor natives and
our ways.

(*She goes out.*)

NANNIE. I'll tell you something, Thea – I'll be glad when this
wedding's over and done with.

THEA (*quietly*). Me, too.

NANNIE. And she's got used to the idea that he's not living here any
more. It's just a case of getting used to it.

THEA. Yes.

NANNIE. She's restless. Can't settle to anything. The nearer the day
comes, it gets worse. I'm so afraid she works herself up into a state.

THEA. Now, you've never seen her 'in a state', Nannie – have you?
She's not that kind.

NANNIE. Well I don't know! You'd better hurry up and have that baby
and give her something to occupy her mind.

THEA. It can't be soon enough for me.

(ALICIA *enters in her outdoor clothes, drawing on her gloves.*)

ALICIA (*spoken off*). I'll get some fresh flowers for the table when I'm
out. (*Enters.*) And we'll use the lace mats, Nannie . . .

NANNIE. Very good, madam.

ALICIA. Thea, will you phone Daddy some time, and tell him, in case
he's late.

NANNIE. Very good, madam.

THEA. Yes, darling.

ALICIA (*turns to go out*). I shan't be long. I'll be back by about half-past
four.

(*Goes.*)
(*Quick fade-out to indicate passage of time.*)

(*Fade in again to the room in half-darkness.*)

THEA *is sitting on the couch with her feet up. The curtains are not drawn. The blue of the late evening hangs over the river like a Whistler painting. The low muffled hoot from a passing barge sounds off.*

NANNIE *opens the door and switches the lights on.*

NANNIE. You asleep, Thea?

THEA. No. I'm still waiting. Where on earth can she be, Nannie?

NANNIE. It's nearly half-past six.

THEA. The shops are closed. She said she'd be back by half-past four. And she knows dinner's a bit of a scramble. Where can she be? . . . I rang up Rita's. She isn't there.

NANNIE. Sometimes she goes to a newsreel.

THEA. Not till this hour. And not when she knows there are things to attend to at home . . . I'm worried, Nannie.

NANNIE. Well, if anything had happened to her we'd have known.

THEA. But should we? If anything happened to me, no one would know who I was. Men carry identity things, but not a woman.

NANNIE. They find out just the same. Don't go getting silly ideas in your head.

THEA. If she's all right, why hasn't she telephoned?

NANNIE. She wouldn't think you'd still be here. I should go home if I was you. Mr Bill will be back.

THEA. I can't. I'd be on the phone every five minutes.

NANNIE. I don't know what to do for a sweet.

THEA. Oh! Have you any tins of fruit?

NANNIE. Plums. They're not up to much.

THEA. It doesn't matter. You can trick them out a bit.

NANNIE. I can't even do the table. I know she'd want the best silver, and it's locked up.

THEA (*with renewed anxiety*). Nannie . . . something must have happened! They're due at half-past seven and it's quite an occasion. You know what she's like – she's not careless about these things.

NANNIE. Perhaps she had to see about something for the wedding.

THEA. No, that's all been done.

NANNIE. Don't you go and get yourself into a state.

THEA. Do you think I ought to ring up the police?

NANNIE. Give her another hour. Wait till your father comes back.

THEA (*fearfully, turns*). Suppose she's in some hospital?

NANNIE (*sharply*). It's no use meeting trouble halfway. We'd have heard.

(*The front door slams.*)

There's somebody now.

(*They listen anxiously.* ROY *enters.*)

ROY. Hallo . . . you still here?

THEA. Roy, Mother isn't back yet.

ROY. Back from where?

NANNIE. She went out to get some odds and ends for dinner. She said she'd be back by half-past four.

ROY. She must have gone somewhere – Rita Hedge's, perhaps.

THEA. I rang Rita.

ROY. What are you in such a flap about? Can't she be a couple of hours late if she wants to?

THEA. It's . . . odd, that's all. She's got this dinner tonight . . .

ROY. They're changing.

THEA. Oh Lord! That makes it worse . . . what are they like?

ROY. Not a bit like Louise. Nice, though. Rather hearty.

THEA. Did they want to know all about you?

ROY. That's why they're here.

THEA. Well, you've nothing to worry about. No past – no future, either.

ROY. Thanks. I shot a terrific line about the book trade! I'm working my way up in publishing, then I'm going to start – found – the Christie Press. So I am, too – don't you make any of your cracks about wrapping up parcels in front of them!

THEA. I shan't be here tonight. Where's Louise?

ROY. I left her at the hotel. I thought they might like a natter on their own. I had some shopping to do.

NANNIE. What have you been buying?

ROY. My trousseau.

THEA. Let's see!

NANNIE. Be careful, Thea. She can't keep her hands off anything!

(THEA *pulls out a terrible dressing-gown. Silk. Dazzling. A deadly yellow and red pattern.*)

THEA. Blimey!

ROY (*proudly*). Gay little number, isn't it?

THEA. You going to wear it, or signal with it?

ROY. Pretty nifty, isn't it, Nannie?

NANNIE (*dubiously*). Plenty of colour in it.

ROY. It'll knock the girl for six when she sees it. She'll realise what she's picked.

THEA. You'd have looked better done up in cellophane, with a blue ribbon.

(*The front door bangs.*)

THEA. Listen!

ROY. You're giving us the jitters. Don't be so silly.

NANNIE. It's your father.

(ROY *hastily takes off the dressing-gown, puts it behind cushion.*)

(NANNIE *goes out quickly, takes wrappings with her.*)

THEA. I rang him up and told him about Louise's parents.

ROBERT (*off*). Good evening, Nannie.

NANNIE (*off*). Good evening, sir.

(ROBERT *comes in. He is about fifty – solid, well-dressed. He goes over to a chair and begins to unfold his evening paper. His talk is casual and perfunctory.*)

THEA. Hallo, Daddy.

ROBERT. Hallo. Well, Roy, you're early.

ROY. I'm on three weeks' leave.

ROBERT. Of course. I had forgotten. Where's your mother?

THEA. She's out.

ROBERT. Where?

THEA. She went up to Hartman's to do some shopping.

ROBERT. She's late. Hartman's closed an hour ago.

THEA. Yes.

ROBERT. Anything the matter?

THEA. Nothing. I've just been wondering why she's so late.

ROBERT. What time are these people coming?

ROY. Half-past seven.

THEA. You've got to put on a dinner-jacket.

ROBERT. What a bore! Have you met these future relatives of yours?

ROY. Yes. This afternoon.

ROBERT. They're well, I hope?

ROY. Yes, thank you.

ROBERT. I trust they'll find us to their liking.

THEA. Sounds as if they were cannibals.

ROBERT. Isn't it time you went home?

THEA. I'm just waiting till Mother gets back.

ROBERT. Bill will be back, won't he?

THEA. Well . . . he can put the dinner in the oven.

ROBERT. That's your job, surely.

THEA (*brightly*). Why?

ROBERT. He's the worker . . . the wage-earner.

THEA (*demurely*). I know. I don't like to let it go to his head.

ROBERT. You might get me a drink, Roy, will you?

ROY. What would you like?

ROBERT. Pink gin . . . I hope these people are not going to get me
    involved in a lot of silly arguments about money and settlements
    and nonsense.

ROY. They won't.

ROBERT. Thanks.

THEA. Do you have to keep calling them 'these people', Daddy?

ROBERT. What's the matter with it?

THEA. Their name is Fletcher.

ROBERT. Yes, I know. Forgive me if I don't seem over-enthusiastic.
    But having strange people to dinner is always a little trying at the
    end of a hard day's work.

ROY (*politely*). Of course. Would you prefer me to ring them up and
    ask them out to a restaurant?

ROBERT. That, I'm afraid, would make trouble with your mother.

ROY (*strained*). Would it? It hadn't occurred to me.

ROBERT. One is always aware of the innocence of your intentions,
    Roy. If I have to change, I'd better go and have my bath. What can
    be keeping Alicia . . .? She may have phoned. How long have you
    been here?

THEA. I've been here since she went out, and she hasn't phoned.

ROBERT. Let's hope she's back before these people arrive.

(*He closes the door.*)

ROY. I can't wait to get out of this house!

THEA. He's in one of his moods. I shouldn't take any notice. He'll
    ooze charm when they arrive.

ROY. And I shall find myself closing up like a clam . . . I can see the
    way the evening's going to go! Thank heaven for a wife of my
    own and my own house! I shall be able to simplify my life at
    last!

THEA. I think Mother suddenly saw this afternoon how complete the break would be.

ROY (*quickly*). Not with her.

(THEA *doesn't speak for a moment.*)

Not with her, Thea. She knows that.

THEA. You can't ask her to your house without Daddy. You can't make a point of coming here only when he's out.

ROY. That's exactly what I shall do.

THEA (*painfully*). Oh – Roy! Between you, you tear her apart . . .
(*Angrily.*) I wish I knew where all this began!

ROY. Don't ask me.

THEA (*impatiently*). You must have contributed to it.

ROY. If I did, it was unconsciously.

(*The front door slams.*)

THEA. Is this her?

LOUISE (*off*). Thank you, Nannie!

ROY. It's Louise.

THEA. I don't know what's the matter with me. Roy, as she was going out, she looked tired somehow – sick of everything – I should have gone with her.

(LOUISE *enters.*)

Hallo! Are they very thrilled with you? What do they think of Roy?

LOUISE. I've been exaggerating him, of course . . . All they're worried about is our finances.

ROY. Did you tell them we have the same deadly premonitions?

LOUISE. They know nothing about postwar England. They talk about 'soundness' and 'solidity'.

THEA. They'll be all right after they've met us.

LOUISE. Where's your mother?

THEA. She's not in. We're worried. She should have been back about half-past four.

LOUISE. Could she be with some friends?

THEA. Might be.

LOUISE. Thea . . . I wanted to ask you before . . . does she ever walk in her sleep?

THEA. Mother? What on earth put that into your head?

LOUISE. I just wondered.

ROY. Why?

LOUISE. Because I woke up last night and she was standing at the foot of my bed.

THEA. Did she say anything?

LOUISE. No.

THEA. Did you?

LOUISE. I sat up but before I could speak she went away . . . She walked out slowly as if she was walking in her sleep.

ROY. You must have dreamt it!

LOUISE. I swear I didn't!

THEA. She must have just come in to say goodnight.

LOUISE. But it was three o'clock in the morning.

THEA. You haven't mentioned it to her, have you?

LOUISE. No.

THEA. Well, don't.

LOUISE. Darling, I didn't warn the parents that you and your father don't quite . . . hit it off.

ROY. Are you afraid of a scene tonight? Don't worry. We shall have our party manners on.

THEA. A normal unhappy family giving their imitation of domestic bliss.

LOUISE. They're not very grown-up. They think all family life is happy.

THEA. They're coming to the right house.

ROY (*mildly*). Shut up, Thea. I'll watch it.

THEA. You'd better go and change, Louise. They'll be here before you're ready.

LOUISE. What shall I wear?

THEA. I wish I had that problem. I've got to wear this little maternity number till it disintegrates.

LOUISE. Poor Thea!

(LOUISE *goes out.*)

THEA. Roy, where can she be?

ROY (*seriously*). I don't know . . . One thing you can be sure of, she's all right. I mean, don't start thinking in terms of accidents.

THEA. How do we know?

ROY. If there's anything like that, one hears quickly.

THEA. Well, I can't go home now until I know she's back . . . you'd better go and change.

ROY (*reluctantly*). I suppose I must.

THEA. Do you think I should ring up the police?

ROY. Don't be crazy. She'd be furious . . .

(ROY *dashes to the window, draws a curtain aside, and looks down.*)

There she is! Paying off the taxi-driver! Unscathed and sound in
wind and limb! Silly little fool, you. 'Shall I ring up the police,
Roy?'

THEA. Get out!

(ROY *goes.*)

(ALICIA *comes in.*)

(*Airily.*) Darling, you've miscalculated a bit, haven't you? You
know you've got to change – you've got less than half an hour.

ALICIA (*rather abstractedly*). What time is it?

THEA. A quarter to seven . . . Where are your things?

ALICIA. What things?

THEA. Your shopping.

(ALICIA *looks bewilderedly at* THEA.)

Mother, don't say you've left them in the taxi?

ALICIA. I must have.

THEA. Nannie will slay you . . . *Did* you leave them?

ALICIA. I forgot to get them.

THEA (*slowly*). You look all in, Mummy . . . sit down and I'll get you a
drink.

ALICIA. No. Really, Thea, I don't want one.

THEA. You've got to have it. (THEA *brings her a drink, looks suspiciously
at her.*) You haven't been in an accident or something, have you?

ALICIA (*pulling herself together*). No, darling. Of course not.

THEA. Well – put yourself outside that. Then I'll come and help you
change.

(ROBERT *appears at the door in his dressing-gown.*)

ROBERT. Where on earth have you been, Alicia?

ALICIA. I didn't realize how late it was.

ROBERT. You'll have to hurry. These people are due.

ALICIA. It's all right. I shall be ready.

ROBERT. You're tired. No wonder. Ridiculous trying to entertain
these days without any help and precious little to eat . . . Roy
should have invited them out.

(*He goes.*)

THEA. Drink that up, darling.

(ROBERT *comes back.*)

ROBERT. Shall I run your bath?
ALICIA. Please, Robert.

(*He goes out.*)

THEA. Have a cigarette, darling.
ALICIA. No thank you.
THEA. Relax.

(ALICIA *takes cigarette automatically.* THEA *lights it for her.*)

(NANNIE *appears.*)

NANNIE. Did you get the peaches, madam . . . and the flowers?
THEA. She left them in a taxi, Nannie. Don't worry her. (*Behind*
    ALICIA's *back she motions* NANNIE *to go away.*)
ALICIA. I'm sorry, Nannie.
NANNIE (*puzzled*). That's all right. I'll make do with the plums.

(NANNIE *goes, reluctantly.*)

THEA (*sharply*). Mummy, your hand's trembling. What's upset you?
    (*Softly and anxiously – sits beside* ALICIA.) Tell me. Tell me, darling.
ALICIA (*very quietly*). I've done a terrible thing.
THEA (*trying to be casual*). What could *you* do that would be terrible?
ALICIA. I don't know what . . . I don't know what to say to them.
THEA (*softly*). To whom?
ALICIA. You . . . and . . . the others.
THEA. You're sure you're not imagining things? (*Softly.*) What has
    happened, darling?
ALICIA (*after a pause*). I took something from a shop. (*They look at each
    other without speaking for a moment.*) I told you I'd done a terrible
    thing. I stole it. I put it in my handbag. They found it there.

(LOUISE *looks in, in her dressing-gown.*)

LOUISE. Oh, you *are* in! We've been so worried! Are you all right?
ALICIA (*trying to smile*). Yes, dear, thank you.
LOUISE. The parents are looking forward awfully to meeting you. I
    gave you such a build up.
ALICIA. Oh dear . . . (*Automatically.*) How are they after their long
    journey?
LOUISE. Marvellous! They loved it.

THEA (*rises*). Hurry and get dressed, Louise.

(LOUISE *goes*.)

Mother's just coming up.

LOUISE. Are you staying to meet them, Thea?

THEA (*confused*). I don't know . . . Perhaps.

LOUISE. I hope you do.

(*She closes the door.*)

THEA (*quiet and firm*). Now Mummy, tell me exactly . . . which shop?

ALICIA. Hartman's.

THEA. Does anyone know? Did anyone see you?

ALICIA. Yes. A detective. A woman.

THEA. And then what?

ALICIA. I had to go to the police station.

THEA. You mean – they arrested you?

ALICIA. Yes. I've to appear in court on Wednesday.

THEA. The day before the wedding.

ALICIA (*a whisper*). If I could think . . . how to tell them.

THEA (*sharply*). Don't worry about them . . . (*Quietly.*) What was it you took, mother?

ALICIA (*after a slight pause*). A nightdress.

THEA. But it's so ridiculous! You've got plenty. It's *so* ridiculous! They can't touch you! When it's explained to them, they'll see how ridiculous it is! Mummy, what sort of thing was it? Was it expensive? I mean . . . what attracted you . . what colour was it?

ALICIA (*frowning*). Black. Black chiffon.

THEA (*utterly dismayed*). But darling, it just doesn't make sense! You wouldn't *wear* a thing like that. Nothing would *induce* you to wear it. You know that. Oh, God, they must be made to see how ridiculous it is! (*In agony.*) Darling, I want to laugh! *Really* I want to laugh. How could they think you'd want a thing like that? How dare they treat you as if . . . as if you'd taken it!

ALICIA (*quietly*). But I did take it.

THEA. I know what it is! It's this trousseau fuss! You meant to buy it for Louise!

ALICIA (*a sudden sharp edge in her voice*). No. I didn't.

THEA (*persuasively*). But you meant to pay for it! You saw it, and you thought it was attractive and you picked it up and you forgot . . . in your vague way you walked off without paying. You know how absent-minded you can be sometimes . . .

ALICIA (*as if she were trying to remember*). I picked it up . . .

THEA (*sharply*). Where did you put it?

ALICIA. I slipped it into my handbag.

(*The telephone rings.* THEA *picks it up.*)

THEA (*into phone*). Yes, Bill – yes, it's Thea . . . darling, I'll be late . . . no, *I'm* all right . . . (*Her voice trembles.*) Oh, Bill, don't ask me now . . . no, no, I swear I'm all right . . . you go, darling . . . I'll come on later. (*She hangs up.*)

ALICIA. Thea – you're going out, aren't you?

THEA (*shrugging it off*). It doesn't matter. It isn't important . . . we must think. (*Calls upstairs.*) Roy!

ALICIA (*starting up*). No! Thea!

ROY (*off*). What is it?

THEA. Here a minute.

ALICIA (*firmly*). Thea, this is something I have to cope with myself. He mustn't know yet. Not till his wedding is over!

THEA. You can't carry this on your mind alone! Something must be done!

ROY. Hallo, wanderer! What is it?

THEA. Get through to Louise's parents and put off this dinner tonight.

ALICIA. Thea! I won't have it. I won't have it, I tell you.

ROY. What on earth's the matter?

ALICIA. Thea's gone mad. You'll do nothing of the kind, Roy.

THEA. Mother isn't well. She can't face it.

ALICIA. Face it? You're treating me like an imbecile!

THEA. You can't go through with it. It's better to put it off than to break down in the middle . . .

ROY. Darling, what's the matter?

THEA (*imploringly*). Mummy, we *need* this evening to see what we're going to do. There isn't much time.

ROY. Do? Do what? What are you talking about, in heaven's name? You can't put them off at this time of day!

ALICIA. Certainly you can't.

THEA (*quietly*). Roy, I mean it.

ROY. If I knew what it was all about!

ALICIA (*sharply*). Nothing. Nothing, Roy.

THEA. Mummy, Roy must know.

ALICIA (*slowly*). Roy . . . I've made a very stupid – mistake. A very stupid and embarrassing mistake.

ROY (*with a little laugh*). Well, tell me, darling – out with it!

THEA.  She's ill! Between you, you've torn her in two!

(ROBERT *comes in – dressed.*)

ROBERT.  Well – why haven't you gone to change? What's going on here?

THEA (*desperately to* ROY). Go and phone from the hall! Tell them Mother's ill!

ALICIA.  I'm not ill!

(ROY *goes.*)

(*Hysterically.*) Thea, you've gone crazy!

ROBERT (*his voice raised*). I'm asking what's the matter. Are you ill, Alicia?

ALICIA.  No, Robert.

THEA.  She's in serious trouble.

(*Silence.*)

ROBERT.  What's the matter, Alicia?

THEA.  Mother, shall we go? Would you like to talk alone?

ALICIA (*defeated*). No . . .

(ROY *comes back.*)

ROY.  Louise is going to phone them.

ALICIA.  You tell them, Thea.

THEA (*quietly*). She took something off a counter in Hartman's this afternoon . . .

(ROBERT *and* ROY *stare in bewilderment.*)

She was seen by the store detective.

(*Dead silence.*)

ROBERT.  How did you explain it?

ALICIA.  I didn't.

ROBERT.  You mean they're bringing a charge against you?

ALICIA.  Yes.

ROBERT.  A charge of theft?

ALICIA.  Yes.

(ROBERT *stops suddenly in his walk, and looks up at* ALICIA.)

ROBERT (*quietly and unutterably shocked*). What in God's name made you do a thing like that, Alicia? Haven't you always got enough money? Don't I give you enough?

ALICIA. Yes.

ROBERT. What was it you took?

THEA. Only a nightdress.

(ROBERT *stares at* ALICIA. *Then he slumps into a chair.*)

ROBERT. I'm completely at a loss. What in the world possessed you, Alicia? You must have been mad! . . . Have you any idea *why* you did it?

ALICIA (*obstinately*). I wanted it.

ROBERT. Then for God's sake why didn't you buy it?

ALICIA. I don't know.

ROY (*quietly*). Forgive me, Father, I don't want to interfere. But I don't think you're the right person to question her.

ROBERT. And who would question her? You?

ALICIA (*desperately*). There's nothing I can tell either of you, except what I've already told you.

ROBERT. I don't understand it. I don't understand even the temptation to do such a thing! I don't understand how it ever crossed your mind.

ROY. It didn't, did it, Mother? It was a blackout. You don't even remember it, do you?

ALICIA. Yes. I do.

ROBERT. What made you want it? What sort of thing was it?

ALICIA (*brusquely*). It was black chiffon.

ROBERT. What could you want a thing like that for?

(ALICIA *doesn't answer. There is a brief silence.*)

How could you want a thing like that, Alicia? You of all people!

ALICIA (*defiantly*). Why 'me of all people'? At that moment I wanted it.

ROBERT. You'll get no sympathy in a court for that kind of theft.

ROY (*passionately*). You talk as if it were a crime.

ROBERT. What else is it?

ROY (*curtly*). A breakdown. Thanks to you – and me.

ROBERT. Me? What the hell are you talking about?

ALICIA. Don't start anything! I can't stand it! Call it a crime or whatever else you want to call it!

ROBERT. It is a crime. After years of honourable living one finds oneself on the wrong side of the law. (*Bitterly angry.*) Forgive me if I can't call it by anything but its real name! You with your glib talk of blackouts and breakdowns!

THEA. Daddy!

ALICIA (*very quietly*). I apologise very humbly to you all.

(THEA *bursts into tears and sobs bitterly.*)

Hush. Hush, darling.

Roy – take her home. She shouldn't be here. She shouldn't be upset. Darling, go home and sleep . . . forget it. It isn't your worry. Go home. (*She kisses her.*) Go with her, Roy.

ROBERT. Roy – It's my responsibility to try to get your mother out of this mess. I'll be obliged if you don't interfere. Please understand that none of this has anything to do with you.

(ROY *goes out.*)

(ALICIA *sits.* ROBERT *turns to face her.*)

CURTAIN.


# ACT II

## SCENE 1

SCENE: *Same as Act I. Tuesday afternoon.*

NANNIE *shows in* DR BENNETT HAWKINS. *He is a pleasant, attractive man of about forty-four.*

NANNIE. If you'll take a seat, sir, I'll tell Mr Christie you're here.

HAWKINS. Thank you.

(ROBERT *enters.*)

ROBERT. Dr Hawkins? How are you, sir? I'm Christie.

HAWKINS. Nice view you have here.

ROBERT. Yes. A few years back John Brissing did a painting of it – from where we're standing now . . . There it is, over the fireplace. You'd scarcely recognise it, would you? . . . It was in the 1936 Academy.

HAWKINS. I don't know Brissing.

ROBERT. He wasn't well known. He died about ten years ago.

HAWKINS. I used to have a house full of pictures. When I was a young GP. I put my plate up in the King's Road . . . and I used to get pictures in lieu of fees.

ROBERT. Did you make on that – or lose?

HAWKINS. I've no idea. All I knew then was that I couldn't eat canvas and paint . . .

ROBERT. Can I get you a drink?

HAWKINS. No thanks. You're in a spot of trouble, I hear.

ROBERT. Yes.

HAWKINS. Brook-Williams rang me this morning.

ROBERT. Yes. He's been briefed by my solicitors, I told them – I had to tell them – get the best counsel you can.

HAWKINS. These cases are very tricky – as I suppose they've told you. The courts have had a crop of them. Much of it is deliberate or organised theft . . . (*Casually.*) In this case, no doubt, one could rule out any suspicion of its being organised.

ROBERT (*testily*). Really, doctor . . .

HAWKINS (*calmly*). One has to start from the beginning. I have no knowledge of either you or your wife.

ROBERT. You can see for yourself what we are . . . how we live.

HAWKINS. I see the evidence of comfortable living.

ROBERT. The fruits of hard work, I can assure you.

HAWKINS. I don't doubt it.

ROBERT. My wife shares all I have. She has an ample – even a generous allowance.

HAWKINS. Is she given to extravagance? Overspending?

ROBERT. No. Not at all.

HAWKINS. And her general health? Is there any history of illness?

ROBERT. No. Her health has always been good.

(HAWKINS *is silent for a moment.*)

HAWKINS. But you're of the opinion that this theft can be explained by mental disturbance? Mental illness?

ROBERT. Only because I can think of no other reason for it.

(*Another slight silence.*)

HAWKINS (*talking slowly and quietly*). A well-to-do woman steals a luxury article. Legal and medical aid are immediately organized on her behalf . . . You must see that that will produce an initial scepticism in the court . . . It can be broken down only if her case is a genuine one.

ROBERT (*murmuring uneasily*). Yes. Yes of course. I see that.

HAWKINS. The courts have been inundated with psychiatric evidence which has been too often unscientific – Even unscrupulous . . . A dishonest, greedy woman who happened to be caught in the act of theft would probably find little difficulty in rustling up evidence of some nervous compulsion. Courts have grown weary of it. The Freudian patter that goes on while the whitewashed rabbit is being produced from the hat.

ROBERT. We don't expect magic, doctor.

HAWKINS. Good. If there is evidence of genuine mental stress – or nervous derangement – then it is one's duty to explain it to the court as best one can. If there is no such evidence you will have to rely on the clever tongue of your counsel.

ROBERT. I understand. But don't you want to ask me anything about my wife – what sort of person she is – the general set-up?

HAWKINS. What do you want to tell me?

ROBERT. Nothing much . . . Just that we're a normal – average – happy family.

HAWKINS. Well, I congratulate you on your happiness, Mr Christie. It may be normal, but it isn't average.

ROBERT. I love my wife. And she, I believe, loves me.

HAWKINS. How long have you been married?

ROBERT. Twenty-four years . . . You can imagine, doctor, this is a terrible blow.

HAWKINS (*kindly*). Yes. I'm sorry.

ROBERT. I seem to feel the disgrace of it more than she does. I've been dashing around all day – seeing my solicitors – fixing up counsel – arranging for her to see you . . . but she doesn't seem to appreciate the seriousness of it.

HAWKINS. You mean she isn't interested?

ROBERT. Oh yes, she's interested . . . but I'll tell you something that struck me as odd, doctor. We were sitting here last night – both of us very upset, because I hadn't minced matters with her about her position . . . and suddenly she burst out laughing.

HAWKINS. Hysterically?

ROBERT. No. Quite ordinary laughter that she didn't seem to be able to suppress . . . You see what I mean when I say she doesn't seem to feel the disgrace of it as much as I do.

HAWKINS (*after a slight pause*). Do you often find her behaviour puzzling?

ROBERT. No, not at all. There's nothing difficult or complicated about her. The reverse. You can read her like a book.

HAWKINS. I envy you your powers, Mr Christie.

ROBERT (*eagerly*). I'm safe in saying, doctor, that she's never done

anything unpredictable in her life, and certainly nothing
dishonourable. She couldn't. It wouldn't enter her head – that's
what's so puzzling . . . She lives for her home and her family . . .
She's what you or anyone else would call a good woman.

HAWKINS. May I see Mrs Christie?

ROBERT. Yes, doctor. I'll send her in. (*Pause.*) You want to see her
alone of course.

HAWKINS. I should prefer to.

ROBERT. Oh . . . er . . . doctor. If anything comes out – crops up, I
mean – about my relationship with my son . . .

HAWKINS (*quietly*). Yes?

ROBERT (*smiling rather conspiratorially*). Don't pay too much attention
to it, will you? It's nothing serious. It's just that we're inclined to
get on each other's nerves occasionally . . . you know how it is?

HAWKINS (*quietly*). Yes. I know.

(ROBERT *goes out.* HAWKINS *follows him with his eyes. Waits.* ALICIA
*comes in.*)

ALICIA. Good afternoon, Dr Hawkins.

HAWKINS. Mrs Christie? How do you do.

(*They shake hands.* ALICIA *is nervous and edgy.*)

ALICIA. It's been a beautiful day, hasn't it?

HAWKINS. Yes indeed.

ALICIA. Won't you sit down?

HAWKINS. Thanks.

(*He sits down.*)

ALICIA. Doctor, I feel very awkward about this interview . . . it was
arranged without my knowledge . . . I'm rather at a loss as to what
you expect me to say.

HAWKINS. Have you any preconceived ideas as to what I might
expect?

ALICIA. Probably that I heard voices or something.

HAWKINS. You're not the type who hears voices. It will help, as time is
so short, if you make an effort to be truthful.

ALICIA (*rather sharply*). I am quite truthful as a rule.

HAWKINS. Truth about oneself is difficult . . . It entails effort.

ALICIA (*after a slight pause*). What can I tell you about myself? . . . I
lead a normal uneventful domestic life like thousands of other
women.

HAWKINS.  Except that thousands of other women don't find
themselves in your present predicament.

ALICIA (*softly*).  No . . .

HAWKINS.  Tell me, Mrs Christie, have you ever stolen from a shop
before?

ALICIA (*staring at him*).  No.

HAWKINS.  Have you ever been tempted to?

ALICIA.  No.

HAWKINS.  What were you going to do with this nightdress? Wear it?

ALICIA.  I don't know.

HAWKINS.  Or hide it away somewhere?

ALICIA.  I don't know.

HAWKINS.  What did it suggest to your mind when you first saw it? . . .
Think back.

ALICIA.  Doctor, I'm not a patient. I haven't come to you with a
problem . . . I haven't asked you to help me fight anything or
escape from anything.

HAWKINS (*imperturbably*).  I realize that. But you have quite a pressing
problem – the question of your defence tomorrow . . . It doesn't
only concern you. It concerns your husband and your family.

ALICIA.  Do you think I'm indifferent to that?

HAWKINS.  I don't know.

ALICIA.  I have a son who is getting married in two days' time . . . This
story will become public on his wedding day. How do you think I
feel, doctor? . . . Except paralysed with shame at having inflicted
this on him.

HAWKINS (*gently*).  He's your only son?

ALICIA.  Yes.

HAWKINS.  Come and sit down. This uneventful domestic life you say
you lead . . . family life is seldom uneventful.

ALICIA.  Mine is. We live very quietly. . . If you're opening the
conversational gates to my family affairs, I'd rather you didn't. I
don't discuss them. I never have.

HAWKINS.  It may be you've reached the moment when you can't
avoid it . . . otherwise one would respect your reticence . . . It's my
unfortunate lot to be besieged by women who hang out their
private lives like flags – till one is often tempted to pull them down
to half-mast.

ALICIA (*with a slight smile*).  Yes, I'm sure.

HAWKINS.  But you have a problem on your hands which is real . . .

and don't let us forget that it's also urgent . . . You're not a thief.
You didn't take this thing with some idea of financial gain to
yourself . . .

ALICIA (*quickly*). No.

HAWKINS. Well, let's assume that it was outside your own volition.
That you were impelled by some force or combination of forces . . .
which must have a source somewhere.

ALICIA (*uneasily*). One should have an anaesthetic for this kind of
operation.

HAWKINS. Or a battering ram to break down the wall of defence
you've built around yourself.

ALICIA. I'm sorry.

HAWKINS. . . . and round your family. What are you hiding, Mrs
Christie?

ALICIA. Nothing that I'm aware of.

HAWKINS. Are you deceiving yourself about the uneventfulness of
your life? The quiet of family life is deceptive. There is occasional
contentment but more often intolerable tensions . . .

(ALICIA *goes to a cigarette box on mantelpiece. Takes one and lights it.*)

It's a battlefield, in fact . . . On which the human struggle for
happiness is won or lost.

ALICIA (*with a slight cynicism*). And people like you are the spectators?

HAWKINS. First aid men. We help to attend to the casualties.

ALICIA. The scratches and the black eye.

HAWKINS. Black eyes are easy. They can be left to nature . . . she
invented them . . . your son, you say, gets married on
Thursday . . .

ALICIA. Yes.

HAWKINS (*after a slight pause*). Nice girl?

ALICIA. Yes – charming.

HAWKINS. So Thursday is the end of a chapter.

ALICIA. What do you mean, doctor?

HAWKINS. You know what I mean.

ALICIA. Yes, I suppose I do . . . but it happens to everyone . . . it's the
natural course of events . . . one wouldn't have it otherwise.

HAWKINS. Are they going to live far away?

ALICIA. No. Quite near. They've found a studio.

HAWKINS. They're lucky.

ALICIA (*rather sharply*). I don't think so . . . It was Louise who found
it, so I couldn't say anything . . . I'm feeling my way around this

awkward relationship of mother-in-law and daughter-in-law. You'll admit it's awkward, doctor.

HAWKINS. Yes. It is undoubtedly.

ALICIA. But I'm so anxious it should be successful. Probably overanxious.

HAWKINS (*casually*). You don't like their going to live there.

ALICIA. No, I don't . . . I've only been there once. I went in and out again. I wasn't in the place more than a couple of minutes. I couldn't bear it.

(*She has become rather heated. She turns away and stubs her cigarette out at desk.* HAWKINS *watches her.*)

HAWKINS (*very casually*). Some places have that effect.

ALICIA. Their past clings to them.

HAWKINS. It wasn't just plain distaste for the surroundings?

ALICIA (*firmly*). No. I could have laughed that off. This was quite different . . .

HAWKINS. Your – er – impressions identified themselves with the past?

ALICIA. Naturally – they must have done. If one gets a peculiar feeling about an empty house, it must necessarily be a sense of its past.

HAWKINS. Not necessarily.

ALICIA. What else could it be?

HAWKINS. It could be a sense of its future. It could be a picture of the life that would go on inside its walls.

ALICIA (*quietly*). Their life?

HAWKINS. Their life . . .

ALICIA. But, doctor . . . I can on think of their life together with interest – and warmth – and love for them both.

HAWKINS. Did you mention it to them – this feeling you had about their house?

ALICIA. No.

HAWKINS. Why? If it were a sense of its past, wouldn't it be natural to say 'I don't like this place. It has unpleasant – or unhappy associations . . .'

ALICIA. My opinion was my own. Why bore them with it?

HAWKINS. But your reaction was so strong you couldn't bear the place for more than a couple of minutes.

ALICIA. It was an instinctive thing. There was no reason for it.

HAWKINS. There's always a reason.

ALICIA. I assure you, none that I know of.

HAWKINS. Think about it. Have you ever come across the French
    saying 'If you want to discover the world, close your eyes'?
ALICIA. I've closed my eyes very often, doctor, but I haven't
    discovered the world. Not even my own small world.
HAWKINS. You're very fond of your son, aren't you? (*It is a statement
    rather than a question.*)
ALICIA. Yes . . . we've always been very great friends.
HAWKINS. Now there's an awkward relationship, if you like!
ALICIA. What?
HAWKINS. A mother and her son.
ALICIA. Awkward? No, doctor. Easy. The easiest of all relationships. It
    was close and friendly and very precious.
HAWKINS. Why do you say 'was'?
ALICIA. Did I? . . . Well, it was, and it is.

    (*Brief silence.*)

HAWKINS. Would you say there is an equal – affection – between your
    husband and your son?
ALICIA (*defensively*). Have you discussed this with my husband?
HAWKINS. He referred, casually, to some slight friction.

    (ALICIA *shows signs of stress. She is silent. She passed her hand across
    her forehead.*)

ALICIA. Doctor . . . I . . .

    (*There is quite a pause.*)

    Doctor, forgive me, but I can't go on with this.
HAWKINS. I think it's important that you should, Mrs Christie. I want
    to help you. I don't like to see a woman of obvious courage in this
    sort of mess. There's some resentment between them?
ALICIA (*reluctantly*). Yes.
HAWKINS. On whose part? The boy or his father?
ALICIA. My husband.
HAWKINS. Is it recent?
ALICIA. No. All the time. Since Roy was a baby.
HAWKINS. Would you call it jealousy?
ALICIA. It's so difficult to believe that a father could be jealous of his
    son . . . but it's a long record of misunderstanding and bitterness.
    I've had to make up for the hurts. I've had to be father and mother
    to him . . . which has made the attachment between us stronger
    than it would have been otherwise.

HAWKINS. Yes . . . how does the boy stand in all this?

ALICIA. Now, he's found himself. He's a boy with his girl – and he's delighted with her. I'm certain it will be a happy marriage.

HAWKINS. And your work is finished.

ALICIA. Yes . . . it's the end of a chapter, as you said . . . (*Quietly and calmly.*) But it's even more than that, doctor. In a kind of way it's the end of my life.

HAWKINS. No.

ALICIA. Yes. It is . . . He's the person I've loved most in the world . . . Is that very terrible?

HAWKINS. Only for you.

(*Silence.*)

ALICIA. Doctor – I've been very frightened. There's nothing the matter with my mind, is there?

(HAWKINS *smiles, shaking his head.*)

You find me quite sensible, and reasonable?

HAWKINS. Too reasonable . . . it isn't enough just to turn the light of reason on one's problems. Reason can be plausible, persuasive, fallible . . . anything it wants to be . . . This approaching marriage – you've had to argue yourself into a conventional attitude to it?

ALICIA. But I've done it! I've nearly done it.

HAWKINS. Not quite?

ALICIA. That's what I meant when I asked if my mind was all right. Because there are moments as the marriage, the breakaway, comes nearer, that I can think of it only with panic . . . and I despise myself! The sort of panic that makes you beat your hands against a closed door to get out!

HAWKINS. Or to get in.

ALICIA (*very still*). Why do you make that difference?

HAWKINS. You saw the difference at once.

ALICIA (*very quickly*). We mustn't talk like this. It horrifies me.

HAWKINS. Why? It doesn't horrify me. It's the old battlefield I mentioned before – the family. The bloodiest struggles in the history of the human mind have been fought across it.

ALICIA. But surely, doctor, its purpose and design was for security?

HAWKINS. That doesn't keep out the old primeval loves and hates.

(ALICIA *is restless and nervy.*)

ALICIA. Such as what? (*Her voice rising.*) What are you saying, doctor?

We're a civilized family. What do you know anyhow? Or think you
know? . . . You're a stranger – knocking at the door of my mind.

HAWKINS. The stranger knocking at the door of your mind might be
yourself.

ALICIA. Just how could I be a stranger to myself?

HAWKINS. The woman who stole a black chiffon nightdress and
slipped it in her handbag was a stranger to the woman I am talking
to now.

ALICIA. What am I, then – a monster with two faces?

HAWKINS. Not a monster – but with several faces. You're shocked by
my conception of the family. I should like to believe in pretty
pictures that are handed out to us. Because if I could accept them
my pessimism would be complete and I could go and fish on the
Wye.

ALICIA. Why do you say your pessimism would be complete?

HAWKINS. Because my own private fight is for more truth in the vision
of life. Deeper soil for the mind to grow in. So that its roots can
strike down into the deep unpleasant darkness under the surface.
Into the fertile darkness beneath.

ALICIA. We have different points of view.

HAWKINS. But you're not unacquainted with the darkness, Mrs
Christie?

ALICIA. I've dug down – searching, perhaps, for the life and strength –
but I haven't found it. I've found deeper confusion, that's all.

HAWKINS. Looking back, can you recall anything of your state of
mind? Excited . . . agitated . . . confused . . . defiant?

(ALICIA *is unwilling to answer.*)

It would help if I knew.

ALICIA. It wouldn't help my case, doctor. And I'm unwilling to tell
you . . . I was shaking with laughter. You see, I knew exactly what I
was doing. My mind couldn't have been clearer. I knew it was
theft. I have no excuse to offer either you or the magistrate.

HAWKINS. Why were you laughing?

ALICIA. Do you know, doctor, the dreadful thing is I still want to
laugh. I've brought this awful trouble on my husband and
family . . . I'm deeply ashamed . . . but I still can't think of that
moment without an appalling desire to laugh . . .

(*She is struggling against laughter.* HAWKINS *is quite still, watching
her.*)

(*Serious again.*) You see, it began with laughter. Someone else's . . . another woman. A stranger.

HAWKINS. I'd like to get this a little more clearly.

ALICIA. I'm tempted to tell you the real story of yesterday. When I came into this room I had quite made up my mind not to. I was in a taxi on my way up to Hartman's . . . I was unbearably depressed. It was a mood, doctor. It would have passed . . . But I was seeing for the first time how complete the break was going to be with my son. Something he had said about never coming back . . . It wasn't so much the fact of his going as the fact that he was going for good. I knew he was and that he was glad to go . . . and I knew that I should have been glad for him – but I wasn't. I was devastated. I thought of the long years I had fought to preserve our family unity . . . I blamed them all. I looked back on a long stretch of wasted years and I hated them for it. Sitting there in the cab, I thought – Oh Lord, let me escape. Let me get out of this bondage. Let me get free of every kind of love and the slavery of it. If I could only be alone, I thought, be myself, without ties dragging me this way and that and without emotions that brought so much more suffering than happiness . . . It was real depression, doctor. I was right down in the depths. I caught sight of my face in a taxi mirror. I looked dreadful. And I said to myself – 'That's what you've done to me.' That's how I look and how I felt. Exhausted. Used up . . . It was the – the collapse of the false front of strength and calm that I had always put up. It was down and there I was – exposed and weak and with a wild desire to run away, to be rid of them all. (*She stops.*)

HAWKINS. But the mood changed?

ALICIA. Yes . . . doctor, how much in life is accidental, do you think?

HAWKINS. I don't know the answer to that one.

ALICIA. Because this was sheer accident . . . my noticing this woman, I mean. My taxi was held up in a traffic jam. She was beside me on the pavement. One could see what she was – but she was pretty and pleasant-looking. She had just accosted a young man . . . I was watching her from my depths of gloom – and suddenly she threw back her head and laughed. And d'you know, doctor, it was a lovely laugh. Rich. Infectious and uplifting. It seemed to fill the cab and beat on my ears. I sat up! It came on me like a flash – there am I, the 'good' woman – I don't mean that priggishly – I mean the sort of woman to whom love is synonymous with responsibilities.

HAWKINS. I know what you mean.

ALICIA. Well, there was my kind of woman – in these black depths of
depression – and there she was, with a laugh like that! . . . The taxi
moved off, but behind it, and as if it were following it, there came
another peal of laughter! I can't describe the strange exciting quality
of it. It worked on me like some kind of magic. I couldn't sit still. I
got out of the cab and walked the rest of the way with her laughter
ringing in my ears. (ALICIA *smiles*.) I went into the shop with this
bedazzlement still all around me. I went into the food department,
but I couldn't bring myself to think or care what I had come for. So
I went upstairs . . . I felt reckless – defiant – I can't quite explain. I
was walking through the shop on a kind of gale of laughter – inward
laughter; I wanted to push everybody out of my way.

HAWKINS. Yes.

ALICIA. And then upstairs I saw this thing on a counter . . . I stood
and looked at it. I knew what I was going to do – and I was afraid
the girl would see me laughing. But she didn't . . . maybe I wasn't
laughing, maybe it was all inside me . . . I edged nearer to it and
waited for the right moment . . . then I slipped it into my bag.

HAWKINS. Then?

ALICIA. Then I walked away.

HAWKINS. And this feeling of exaltation lasted – how long?

ALICIA. Right through the shop till I reached the door . . . I
marched . . . I didn't walk . . . as if I was marching to music. Loud
exciting music.

HAWKINS. And then?

ALICIA. And then – outside – a man barred my way. Looking back on
it today, doctor, from my proper surroundings here at home, it
seems utterly fantastic. I wouldn't blame you if you told me you
didn't believe me.

HAWKINS. I do believe you. I don't doubt a word of it . . . did you
mention anything of this when they questioned you?

ALICIA. No.

HAWKINS. You made no excuses?

ALICIA. No. I hadn't any . . . I didn't speak – except to give my name
and address . . . I was overwhelmed with shame . . . I still am.

HAWKINS. Shame is the wrong word.

ALICIA. It's how I feel. Isolated by it. I go around the house as usual –
but I'm separated from everybody in it. I don't feel that I belong
amongst them any more.

HAWKINS. Is your son at home at the moment?

ALICIA. Yes.

HAWKINS. I'd very much like a word with him. Please.

ALICIA. I don't want him involved in this, doctor. Not in any way. It is, after all, nothing to do with him.

HAWKINS. I shan't keep him a moment.

ALICIA. Roy!

HAWKINS. How old is the boy?

ALICIA. He's twenty-two. (ROY *comes in.*) This is my son – Dr Hawkins.

HAWKINS. How d'you do.

ROY. How d'you do, sir.

HAWKINS. I'll see you downstairs before I go – Mrs Christie –

ALICIA. Yes.

(*She goes.*)

HAWKINS. Cigarette?

ROY. Thank you –

HAWKINS. I've had quite a talk with your mother.

ROY. Yes.

HAWKINS. I want to help her. How much of this business do you understand?

ROY. I think – in a vague way – I understand it, doctor. Something of it, anyhow . . .

HAWKINS. Enough to know that you and your impending marriage will have to be mentioned in her defence?

ROY. It has something to do with that, then?

HAWKINS. Yes.

ROY. I knew it. I mean, I guessed it.

HAWKINS. I'm afraid I shall have to use – and even underline her strong affection for you. You may find it embarrassing. I should feel happier in my mind if I had your permission.

ROY. You don't have to ask, doctor.

HAWKINS. I shan't bring you into it more than I can help . . . you're getting married, I hear?

ROY. Yes.

HAWKINS. Your mother's very pleased about it.

ROY. Is she? Is she really, doctor?

HAWKINS. Delighted.

(ROBERT *comes in.*)

ROBERT. I heard that my son was bringing his intelligence to bear upon the problem.

HAWKINS. I asked to see him for a moment.

ROBERT. Having been told what a phenomenon he was, I suppose!

HAWKINS. Goodbye.

ROY. Goodbye, sir.

(ROY *goes out.*)

ROBERT. Well, doctor, have you had any luck?

HAWKINS. Luck?

ROBERT. With your defence evidence?

HAWKINS. I shall prepare a report this evening.

ROBERT (*anxiously*). Is it going to help us?

HAWKINS (*evasively*). It's a little involved. It will have to be simplified.

ROBERT. Surely the more involved the better – tie them up in knots.

HAWKINS. Magistrates don't like knots. They've got a simple remedy. Take out the knife of the law and cut through them . . . You must remember that the law is very clear as regards theft. They may imprison a mother who steals a loaf of bread for her starving child. In cases of theft the motive is not the law's affair.

ROBERT. But here there wasn't even a motive.

(HAWKINS *is silent.*)

(*Uneasily.*) Was there?

HAWKINS (*quietly*). Oh, yes.

ROBERT (*anxiously*). What?

HAWKINS (*rather absently*). A kind of revenge.

ROBERT. Revenge? But against whom? Against whom?

HAWKINS (*in same tone*). You, probably.

ROBERT. Me? . . . but – but doctor, I love her. I've given her everything . . . I've been faithful . . . I've been . . . You can't mean she did it just to bring this scandal round my ears – because I wouldn't believe you.

HAWKINS. No. Nothing like that.

ROBERT. What then? Tell me. It's driving me half-crazy to know my wife has to answer a charge like this. She's got to be acquitted! It's got to be made to appear a mistake! And such a trivial mistake that even the papers take no notice of it.

HAWKINS. It wasn't a mistake. My evidence can only be an explanation or analysis of her present state of mind.

ROBERT. Will it get her off?

HAWKINS.  That I can't say.

ROBERT.  You think she'll be fined.

HAWKINS.  But it's a stiff court. It's right in the heart of the shopping centre. They get a great many cases. And in the last few months they've dealt with them very heavily – I hope she'll be fined.

ROBERT.  You don't think – for a minute – that they could send her to prison?

HAWKINS.  You know as well as I do that they could.

ROBERT.  But a first offence, doctor? No magistrate would sentence her!

HAWKINS.  That's a fallacy, I'm afraid. It depends on the circumstances, but the theft of property is very high on the list these days –

ROBERT.  Doctor, I couldn't bear it. Can you think what it would mean to her – to all of us?

HAWKINS.  The judgement day, Mr Christie, is any day in one's calendar. It crops up when its moment arrives.

ROBERT.  What d'you mean – judgement day?

HAWKINS.  The day when the past catches up with us. When cause catches up with effect . . . It seems fairly clear, as far as this incident is concerned, that in your innocence there is guilt, and in her guilt there is innocence.

ROBERT.  I don't understand.

HAWKINS.  You must try.

ROBERT.  I want to. But you must help me. Show me how.

HAWKINS.  You are aware of her love for her son.

ROBERT (*curtly*).  Yes. Is it that?

HAWKINS.  Partly. Some twisted jealousy in you has driven them together. I mean it – driven! They've been locked together emotionally.

(ROBERT *is silent for a moment.*)

ROBERT.  Are you trying to tell me something – unspeakable – unnatural?

HAWKINS.  Heavens no! It's the most natural thing in the world.

ROBERT.  What might seem natural to you mightn't seem like that to me.

HAWKINS.  It's a profound love. It has its roots, I should say, in a common despair. You might do well to think about that. Don't get up . . . I shall see your wife on my way out . . . and I'm sure I can rely on you not to repeat anything of our conversation to

her. Don't worry too much. We shall do our best for her.
Goodbye.

(HAWKINS *goes.* NANNIE *comes in.*)

NANNIE. The nights are drawing in, sir, aren't they? That's what
comes of putting the clocks back.

(LOUISE *looks in.*)

LOUISE. Has the doctor gone?
NANNIE. Yes. I think he has, Miss.

(*Exits.*)

LOUISE. Oh, I wanted to see him –
ROBERT. What is it, Louise?
LOUISE. I wanted to tell him something.
ROBERT. About Alicia?
LOUISE. Yes.
ROBERT. If it's important I'll pass it on to him.
LOUISE. I don't know if it is or not. It might only be a coincidence.
But he may make something of it that might help.
ROBERT. What is it?
LOUISE (*hesitantly*). Well, the night before last, I woke up and she was
standing at the foot of my bed.
ROBERT (*frowning*). Alicia?
LOUISE. Yes . . . I didn't speak . . . I thought she was walking in her
sleep . . .
ROBERT. Never.
LOUISE. Well, she was standing looking at me.
ROBERT. Didn't she say anything?
LOUISE. No. Just looked. Then she went away . . . but the strange
thing about it is that . . . I was wearing a black chiffon nightdress.

*Quick* CURTAIN.


SCENE 2


NANNIE (*off*). I've just made the tea, Thea.
THEA (*off*). Thank you, Nannie. Tea's ready, Louise!
LOUISE. I'm going to tea with Mummy, I shan't be long . . . I've told
Roy.
THEA. Well. If you hurry you'll just catch my taxi –

(ROBERT *still sits.* THEA *comes in, in her outdoor clothes. She is carrying a hat-box.*)

Hallo, Daddy . . . I've collected Mother's hat for the wedding – where is she?

ROBERT. She'll be here in a minute.

THEA. What's the matter, Daddy? Has Dr Hawkins been?

ROBERT. Yes.

THEA (*anxiously*). What does he say? Is everything going to be all right?

ROBERT. I don't know.

(ALICIA *enters.*)

ALICIA. Hallo, darling – oh, tea's in . . .

(*She pauses at door.*)

(*Calling.*) Roy! Louise! Tea.

(ROY *comes in.*)

THEA. I collected your hat, Mummy – I can't wait to see it . . . shall I take it out?

ALICIA. If you like.

ROY. Louise has gone to tea with her parents. We're going to a theatre tonight, Mother. I wish you'd come.

ALICIA. Who's going?

ROY. Louise and I and her parents . . . Would you like to come, Dad?

ROBERT. Tonight? No thanks. There's too much to think about.

ROY. You, Mother? You'll only sit here and mope.

ROBERT. Thanks.

(THEA *has unpacked the hat. It is an elegant hat with ospreys.*)

THEA. Oh! Mummy! It's heaven. Do put it on.

ALICIA. Not now, darling.

THEA. You must. I must see what you're going to look like.

ALICIA. Not now, darling –

THEA. It's beautiful. You're going to steal the picture, of course.

(ALICIA *tries to smile but suddenly breaks down.*)

(*There is silence in the room.*)

ROBERT. Thea, put the God-damn thing away!

(THEA *packs it away without a word.*)

ALICIA. I'm sorry.

ROBERT. Our nerves, Thea, are rather on edge. We've had a trying day.

THEA. Yes. It was silly of me. I'm sorry.

ALICIA. This time tomorrow it will be over. Then perhaps we can relax again.

THEA. Yes. Darling – what did Hawkins say?

ALICIA. Nothing much.

THEA. But he thinks it's going to be all right?

ALICIA. Yes. Of course.

THEA. I knew it would.

ROBERT (*intensely edgy*). Thea, it would be a very good thing if you could take your glib talk somewhere else.

THEA. What's glib about it? I *know* it's going to be all right!

ROBERT. Then you're very fortunate.

ALICIA. Robert, what did Hawkins say? (*Tensely.*) Robert! What did he say?

ROBERT. I don't know which is the worst to endure – the scandal or the reason for it. He knows the reason . . . He told you, Roy, didn't he?

ROY. No.

ALICIA. I had no reason. I told him so.

ROBERT. What you tell him, and what he gathers from what you tell him, are two different things.

ALICIA. I told him the whole circumstances – and that I had no reason – no motive. Nothing beyond a sudden impulse.

ROBERT (*tormented – his voice thick with pent-up emotion*). Didn't he give you any explanation of it?

ALICIA. No . . . (*Her voice rising to the edge of hysteria.*) How could he explain something that wasn't there? (*Slowly and emphatically.*) I had no reason, I tell you, Robert.

ROBERT. Tell the magistrate that and you'll go straight to prison.

(*This falls on them like a bomb.*)

ROY. Prison!

ROBERT. Yes. And, by God, it will be you who have landed her there.

ALICIA (*in agony*). Robert!

ROY (*hotly*). Can't you see Mother's going through hell! It doesn't help to add to it – to frighten her with talk about imprisonment when you know very well that will never arise!

ROBERT. Don't talk like an idiot. When I mentioned prison I mean it.

The possibility is there. And you don't have to defend your mother against me.

ROY. If the possibility is there, it's so remote it doesn't matter.

ROBERT. You don't know what you're talking about – Do you think you're a man with forty years' experience and I know nothing? Mind your own business –

ALICIA. Please will you stop this!

(ROY *walks quickly and angrily from the room.*)

THEA. I'm going home, darling – I'll ring you later.

(THEA *goes out.*)

ALICIA. These scenes are absurd, Robert. They're bewildered and worried – as I am and you are. Except that I'm devastated at being the cause of it.

ROBERT (*obstinately*). Roy is the cause of it.

ALICIA. Listen, Robert. You've ruined what might have been a very happy family by this jealousy of Roy. You've never left him alone. What twist it is in you or where it comes from I don't know. But it's been there like a frightening presence in this house right through his adolescence till now.

ROBERT. Because I know you've always loved him more than you loved me.

ALICIA (*quickly*). It isn't true! I haven't!

ROBERT. He's had all your love.

ALICIA. I had to give him that much more because you gave him so little.

ROBERT. You've spoiled him all his life.

ALICIA. Is he spoiled? He's kind – he's good – he works hard. He leads a straight honourable life.

ROBERT. And don't I?

ALICIA. Yes, of course you do. Why do you ask for comparison? I never, even in my mind, measure him against you or you against him.

ROBERT (*drily*). I'm obliged to you.

ALICIA (*earnestly: pause*). Look, Robert, the years when we might have been happy with a young family have gone. But we've still a lot of time ahead of us. Why don't you try to clear your mind of this – poison – and let's live the rest of our lives in peace.

ROBERT (*sharply*). Poison? In *my* mind? . . . How about yours?

ALICIA. Mine?

ROBERT. Hawkins said it was through your love for Roy that you landed in this.

ALICIA. Through Roy? What utter nonsense!

ROBERT. It's God's truth.

ALICIA. Don't say God's truth. Who knows what God's truth is? If we had any idea, we mightn't spend our lives in such confusion.

ROBERT. Hawkins says – and these are his very words – that you're locked together emotionally – you two – and because he's going out of your life, with Louise, you go and do this thing.

(*She shakes her head slowly, unable to speak.*)

ALICIA (*quietly, slowly*). But that is the most monstrous lie . . . you must be wrong. Hawkins would never have said that.

ROBERT. Could I have made it up? Would it ever have occurred to me? You talk about poison in my mind – there might be more peace in our future lives if we make a clean sweep while we're about it. Did you know you went into Louise's room?

ALICIA (*startled*). When? I often go into Louise's room.

ROBERT. A couple of nights ago – during the night.

ALICIA. Never.

ROBERT. Well, the truth is that whether you knew it or not, you did . . . and she was wearing a black chiffon nightdress.

(*Brief silence.*)

ALICIA. I don't believe it! Who said so? I never told Hawkins that!

ROBERT. It's impossible not to connect the two things. One doesn't have to be a mind specialist to see that you had some queer half-witted notion of competing with Louise.

ALICIA (*quiet and harsh*). What you say is quite hideous.

ROBERT. The facts are hideous.

ALICIA. In what would I compete with Louise? For what? Is my mind so confused, or yours so warped, that we can find ourselves in a conversation like this? . . . There's a point at which words must stop, or we shall never be able to speak to one another again. This sort of talk doesn't belong here in this house, Robert.

ROBERT. Nor does theft. Whatever has been uncovered has to be straightened out between the two of us, quite apart from doctors and lawyers.

ALICIA. I can straighten out this idea about Louise now! I like her!

I want her to marry Roy! With all my heart I want them to be happy!

ROBERT. That's what you tell yourself.

ALICIA. I swear it's the truth . . . there are a hundred subtle ways in which a woman who didn't want her son to marry could use her influence. I've never even been tempted to try!

ROBERT. Then ask yourself this . . . You go to Louise's room – she is wearing a black chiffon nightdress. The very next day you go and steal – steal, not buy – the identical object. Ask yourself why – because you have to answer it tomorrow morning from the dock and you can take it that they'll get at you personally for your answer, however strongly you may be propped up by Brook-Williams and Hawkins.

ALICIA (*dully*). It has nothing to do with Louise.

ROBERT. However you explain it to yourself, you must admit it was an abnormal act. It sprang from something abnormal.

ALICIA. But there's nothing abnormal in me, Robert . . . or is there . . . I don't know . . . what?

ROBERT. It's quite obvious to anyone else. Your love for Roy.

ALICIA. Rubbish! Complete and utter rubbish! I've never heard such rubbish in my life! (*Stops.*)

ROBERT. Ask Hawkins. And what's more, it's all got to be revealed. It's your defence . . . it's the story that will be told in court tomorrow, and you'd better prepare yourself to cope with it.

ALICIA (*shocked*). He's going to use that in court? Did he tell you that?

ROBERT. He has to. It's the truth – horrible as it is, and no more for you than for me . . . and it has to be used because it's the only thing that will win any sympathy for your case.

ALICIA (*angrily*). Sympathy! I don't want any sympathy.

ROBERT. For your case, I said.

ALICIA. If that is put forward in an open court, then where do I stand for the rest of my life with Roy – *and* Louise? Louise couldn't but be suspicious of me. It would raise such a barrier between us that we could never mix as ordinary people again! I'd be shut off for ever from them and their children.

ROBERT. That might be a good thing.

ALICIA. For whom?

ROBERT. For you and me.

ALICIA. If I were a possessive mother it would be a good thing. But am

I? Have I tried to keep Roy from marrying? Haven't I received
Louise into my house as my own daughter? If there were anything
abnormal in my love for Roy, surely I would have been up to
something destructive, some undermining –

ROBERT. What you forget is that you've proved it abnormal. It's gone
beyond what you can prove to yourself or try to prove to me. It's
got you into a dock answering a charge in public – and your sole
defence is that it was an abnormal act, springing from an abnormal
state of mind.

ALICIA. I shall deny it with my whole strength.

ROBERT. You can't deny it. You won't be in a position to. Don't
imagine that I like the revelation of this any more than you do; my
whole object in making you face this now is so that you'll be better
able to face it tomorrow.

ALICIA. Face it? Stand by while I'm acquitted of theft and quietly
accused of something unspeakable?

ROBERT. You won't be accused.

ALICIA. But I shall be defended by an insinuation that I'm in love with
my son!

ROBERT. They won't say that. They won't put it that way.

ALICIA. They'll make it sound that way. (*Hysterically.*) I'd rather die
than have him hear it! And it's lies! Lies! Complete and absolute
lies!

ROBERT. He's got to hear it! It'll put an end to this nonsense.

ALICIA (*shouting*). He won't hear it! It isn't true, I tell you.

ROBERT. It is true! It's always been true!

ALICIA. And you want him to hear it. A distorted story that will make
him ashamed. I can't bear this, Robert. I love him. He's my only
son and I've loved him all his life . . . is that so terrible – is that
something for which I should feel guilty?

ROBERT. It's terrible (*Rises.*) in this, that it brought about a crisis that
threatens to wreck the lives of all of us. You must see what you
have done?

ALICIA. What were the words Hawkins used – locked together
emotionally? Is that what he will say tomorrow?

ROBERT. Something like that.

ALICIA. It's a pleasant discovery to present to a boy on the eve of his
marriage!

ROBERT. That's his lookout.

ALICIA. I shall prevent it. I shall protect him from it somehow.

ROBERT.  Protect him? It's yourself you'll have to protect. You'll be
  standing there in the dock fighting for your own reputation – and
  mine.
ALICIA (*very quietly*). I shan't hurt yours, Robert.

CURTAIN.


# ACT III

## SCENE 1

*Same as Acts I and II.*

*The next morning.*

ALICIA *is dressed in dark outdoor clothes. Her bag and gloves are on table
beside her.* NANNIE *is in the room.* ALICIA *is dialling a number.*

ALICIA.  Hallo . . . oh, good morning, Mrs Barnes . . . it's Mrs
  Christie . . . Yes, I am early, but I have to go out . . . would you
  send me the usual amount of potatoes and two pounds of cooking
  apples . . . a cauliflower, and some parsley? . . . What fresh fruit
  have you today? . . . No, I prefer pears . . . yes, I think that's all . . .
  oh, have you, well, perhaps you'd let me have a couple of
  pounds . . . yes, thanks, goodbye. (*She hangs up.*) Well, that's taken
  care of, Nannie. Now what else have we to think of? You could
  make a curry for lunch with that cold meat, and for dinner we shall
  just have to have fish. I know everybody's sick of it, but what can
  one do?
NANNIE.  When do you think you'll be back?
ALICIA.  We've got to be at the court at ten . . . I really don't know,
  Nannie dear . . . but I should think we shall be back by lunch-time.
NANNIE.  I'll get it ready for the usual time, one o'clock.
ALICIA.  Yes.
NANNIE.  You remember when my sister Ellen died and I had to go to
  her funeral? Well, I stood there and I swore blind to myself that it
  wasn't Ellen at all. And anybody looking at me might have thought
  I was a stranger.
ALICIA.  Yes, Nannie.
NANNIE.  It's a good idea, when you've got to face something that

takes you all your time, just to pretend it's somebody else it's happening to – not you. Especially in a public place with a lot of eyes on you –

ALICIA. Yes, dear.

NANNIE. Would you like me to make you a nice cup of coffee before you set out?

ALICIA. No thanks, Nannie.

NANNIE. Well, is there anything else that I can see to this morning? I was up early. I'm nearly through with my work, so I've plenty of time.

ALICIA. There are a few people coming in for a drink tomorrow evening after the wedding reception – perhaps you could make a few cheese straws and things.

NANNIE. And how about flowers? You won't have any time tomorrow.

ALICIA. Yes. You might call in and order some.

(THEA *comes in.*)

THEA. Hallo, darling. Hallo, Nannie.

ALICIA. What are you doing here at this time of the morning?

THEA. I just came round to see if I could borrow some tea. We've run out.

NANNIE. You'll never learn to spin out your rations, will you?

THEA. No, Nannie. I thought you might like me to come to the court?

ALICIA. Court? Whatever put that idea into your head?

THEA. Daddy's going.

ALICIA. He's only driving me down. I don't want him to come in.

NANNIE. Well, madam, if I don't see you before you go – good luck.
(NANNIE *cries.*)

ALICIA (*gently*). Nannie dear, I'm so sorry to upset you.

NANNIE. Remember what I said.

ALICIA. Yes. Oh, Nannie, I'm expecting Dr Hawkins – bring him up here the minute he comes, will you?

(NANNIE *goes out.*)

THEA. I like your hat.

ALICIA. It's got a thickish veil that I can pull down to cover my face.

THEA. You think of everything, don't you?

ALICIA. Nannie will never learn that I don't like ornaments at angles . . . You shouldn't have got up early. Didn't you sleep?

THEA. Yes, of course, darling. I slept like a log . . . Did you?

ALICIA. Yes, thanks, dear.

THEA. What's Hawkins coming to see you about? Um?

ALICIA. Nothing much. Some last-minute details.

THEA. Well – it will be a relief when it's behind us. It won't be long now.

ALICIA. We shall be back for lunch. Will you be here, Thea?

THEA. Bill sent you his love. He told me to tell you he'd keep his fingers crossed for you.

ALICIA. That was sweet of him . . . You shouldn't have had this worry, Thea – at this time.

THEA. Darling, don't give it a thought. I'm not worried, I know everything's going to be all right . . . I only wish I could come and hold your hand in the . . . in the court.

(*There is a strained silence between them.*)

It's like waiting for the train to go, when one's going back to school.

ALICIA. Yes.

THEA. Mummy, would it help you to think of the future for a bit? It's very bright! There will be the baby . . . and all the excitement of a new life . . . And I'm sure he'll be a boy.

ALICIA. But, darling, why should it matter – boy or girl – it will be equally sweet. It will be yours.

THEA. It will be a boy. I promise you.

ALICIA. Thea – Thea, my darling. I know you so well – and what you're getting at. I don't know what I've done to deserve you.

(THEA *breaks down and weeps in her mother's arms.*)

THEA. Oh, Mummy – Mummy – I can't keep it up. I'm so frightened about you!

ALICIA. Thea! Stop it! Listen to me! I will not have you upset yourself! Now stop it!

THEA (*choked but controlled*). It's all right. I've stopped. Oh dear. I came round here full of advice from Bill to be gay and bright; he'd be furious with me . . . what can I do when you're out? Is there anything you need for tomorrow?

ALICIA. No. No, darling, I don't think so.

THEA. Shall I order you a spray of orchids?

ALICIA. Yes, dear.

THEA. What colour?

ALICIA. I don't mind. And get some for yourself.

THEA. I'm too pregnant for orchids.

ALICIA. What would you like? Sunflowers?

(NANNIE *shows in* DR HAWKINS.)

NANNIE. Dr Hawkins.

ALICIA. Oh, good morning, doctor.

HAWKINS. Good morning, Mrs Christie.

ALICIA. My daughter, Thea.

THEA. I'll leave you. You haven't much time.

ALICIA. Thea, see we're not interrupted for a moment, will you?

THEA. Yes, of course.

(THEA *goes out.*)

ALICIA. Thank you for coming round so quickly, doctor. I phoned you
because I had to see you before we went to the court. I had to . . .
Do sit down. I don't know how to apologise to you. But yesterday
when I talked to you I was . . . overwrought. I didn't tell you the
truth.

HAWKINS (*smoothly*). No? . . .

ALICIA. No, I led you completely astray in my desire to hide the real
truth from you. I'm sorry. I had reason enough. I was ashamed of
the real truth . . . you believed what I told you yesterday, didn't
you?

HAWKINS. Yes.

ALICIA. And you made your diagnosis on it . . . a mother clamped
emotionally to her son . . . locked together was the phrase you
used.

HAWKINS (*after a pause*). Not to you . . . I used it to your husband.

ALICIA. Well, no matter. Your memory must be better than mine. But
it's your picture of the situation. The one you're going to use, isn't
it?

HAWKINS. More or less.

ALICIA. What I want to tell you is that it's entirely false! The real
picture is quite discreditable, you'll probably wash your hands of
the whole affair.

HAWKINS. Are you anxious that I should, Mrs Christie?

ALICIA. No, but you must hear what I have to say.

HAWKINS. Yes, yes, I'm listening.

ALICIA. My motive in stealing that thing, doctor, was as clear-cut as
that of any other person who steals deliberately. I wanted it . . . I
was going away . . . after all the fuss of the wedding I was going
away – with someone who wants me to go away with him. I was
ashamed, at my age, to buy an exotic piece of nonsense like that.

But I wanted it. So I took it – it seemed so much easier. So you see
why I lied. It's a disorderly little story, isn't it?

HAWKINS. Yes.

ALICIA. It puts rather a different face on the defence.

HAWKINS (*quickly*). Who is this person you were going away with?
What is his name?

ALICIA. Why should I answer that?

HAWKINS. Please don't stall, Mrs Christie. What is his name?

ALICIA. Brissing . . . If you must know – John Brissing.

HAWKINS. What does he do.

ALICIA. He's an artist.

HAWKINS. You've given me a very difficult problem.

ALICIA. Because I've upset your defence at the last moment?

HAWKINS. More complex than that . . . you see, Mrs Christie, when I
first came into this room I said something about the view, and your
husband pointed out that picture by an artist called John Brissing.
He added that he had been dead for ten years.

ALICIA. You're laughing at me –

HAWKINS. No . . . I'm not an enemy, Mrs Christie.

ALICIA. I know. I'm sorry.

HAWKINS. So I can discount the whole story of your going away? I can
discount it as a desperate invention dictated by a desperate
dilemma which I'm just beginning to see?

ALICIA. Doctor, I can't face your defence! I will not have the
relationship between my son and myself manhandled in a court.
You know that is what would happen. You know that it could be
torn to shreds. And where would *he* stand afterwards? Where,
particularly, in his new young delicate relationship with his wife?
And my husband – where would he be? A father jealous of his son?
Cruel – hard – unkind, they'll say – and he isn't, doctor. He isn't!
Whatever sort of woman I am, or whatever they think I am, I have
some sense of values. I've lived long enough to decide what is
important and what isn't so important . . .

HAWKINS. What is important to you is that nothing should be made of
your love for your son – or the friction between him and your
husband.

ALICIA. Not a word. No suggestion of it, or any mention even that I
have a son.

HAWKINS. But your whole defence rests on it.

ALICIA. I can't help that.

HAWKINS. Mrs Christie –

ALICIA. I'd rather be tried for a petty crime and accept their
    judgement on it than have the secrets of my heart explored in
    public.

HAWKINS. When did you first come to this conclusion?

ALICIA. During the night – you see, doctor – in the last twenty-four
    hours, I've learned that when these strange human secrets are
    dragged out, they assume a new shape, they take on a life of their
    own. I find it terrifying.

HAWKINS. What in particular are you afraid of?

ALICIA. Their power of destruction. I haven't your knowledge. I've got
    nothing to go on except my own instinct. I see this as a serious
    incident in my life and my husband's, but more so in my son's. Put
    yourself in his place. On the eve of his wedding there is a public
    discussion – perhaps a heated intensive discussion – on the
    relationship between his mother and himself. If it starts being
    thrown about, if it becomes a battle of wits between the defence
    and the magistrate, neither *you nor I* will have any *power* to put a
    limit on it. To say where it must end. Doctor . . . that is so, isn't it?

(HAWKINS *is silent.*)

The defence, at the least, would be an attack on his privacy – on
the privacy of my whole family. To save myself it would mean
tearing down a wall of my house and exposing all these years of life
inside it . . . that would be a terrible thing to do. Also, doctor, and
this is what matters most – words and phrases will be used.
Because of what I've done there might be the suggestion that in my
love for my son there was something – abnormal.

HAWKINS. But that is nonsense, Mrs Christie, there's nothing
    abnormal in your love for your son –

HAWKINS. There isn't?

HAWKINS. No, nothing, I should never dream of using the word.

ALICIA. No, you wouldn't – but they might.

HAWKINS. No one who knew the whole facts of this case would use it.

ALICIA. It has only to be mentioned once to do infinite harm to him
    and his wife.

HAWKINS. That is something we shall have to risk. You can't be
    allowed to discard your whole defence because of words and
    phrases that might or might not be mentioned.

ALICIA. Forgive me, doctor, but that is exactly what I mean to do –
    *discard* the *whole defence.*

HAWKINS. Mrs Christie, please listen to me – because time is very short. If you're tried for theft without the background of mental stress and strong emotional disturbance you might, if you're lucky, get off with a fine . . . on the other hand, you might not.

ALICIA. I knew there was that possibility.

HAWKINS (*urgently*). It's more than a possibility! If I had known why you wanted to see me I should have brought Brook-Williams along to tell you what he told me last night. The magistrate is Sanderson. Only a couple of weeks ago he made public his views on this sort of theft. The only way to deal with it, he said, is by imprisonment . . . We have had to build you up a very strong defence.

ALICIA. Around my son?

HAWKINS. Yes. Because it's the truth. The whole strength of the defence lies in its truth. It's sufficiently strong to break down even this magistrate's objection to psychological evidence. You'll leave the court a free woman.

ALICIA. Not at that cost, doctor.

HAWKINS. Mrs Christie . . . please . . . I can't allow this to happen.

ALICIA. Doctor – I know exactly what I'm doing.

HAWKINS. Have you ever seen the inside of a women's prison?

ALICIA. I could recover from a prison sentence, doctor.

HAWKINS. And your family?

ALICIA. They will recover from it too – much more quickly and more easily than from the – indignity – of the defence.

HAWKINS. I – don't – know – quite – what – to – do. I ought to call your husband and stop you from doing this.

ALICIA. But you're not going to, doctor . . . because *you see* what I'm doing – and why.

HAWKINS. I'm up against something I can't argue with. The formidable reasoning of the heart . . .

ALICIA. Only when it has to fight to keep its own secrets where they belong.

HAWKINS. You may be right . . . in the long run you probably are right. (*Gravely*.) I must get along to the court to see Brook-Williams. What do you want me to tell him?

ALICIA. Tell him that I shall plead guilty.

HAWKINS. And if you're asked for any reason why you took this thing?

ALICIA. I took it because I wanted it.

HAWKINS. You realise that after that there will be no more to be said?

ALICIA. That's all I want, doctor . . . that no more shall be said.

HAWKINS. Very well . . .

ALICIA. You'll see to it that nothing can go wrong?

HAWKINS. I'm at your service, Mrs Christie . . . and if you will allow me to say so, at this moment I'm also at your feet. . . . Good luck.

(*He goes out quickly, closes door.* ALICIA *sits on sofa. Starts to pull on gloves.* ROBERT *comes in.*)

ROBERT. Hawkins was a long time – What has he been saying?

ALICIA. Not much, I did most of the talking.

ROBERT. Wouldn't you like a glass of brandy?

ALICIA. No thanks, Robert.

ROBERT. Do you good, Alicia – steady the nerves.

ALICIA. No thanks, Robert – I have to keep my wits about me.

(ROY *comes in.*)

ROY. If you'll give me the key of the garage, I'll get the car out for you –

ROBERT. No, I'll get the car. You stay with your mother.

(*Exits.*)

ROY. Have you got the shakes, darling?

ALICIA. A little.

ROY. Don't worry. It will soon be over . . . Did you sleep?

ALICIA. Yes, thanks. And you?

ROY. Yes, rather . . . Mother, isn't it silly, I don't known what to say to you.

ALICIA. There's nothing to say, darling.

ROY. If I could go there instead of you . . .

ALICIA. Don't let's think about it.

ROY (*bursting out*). Mother, I wish I didn't feel so tongue-tied.

ALICIA. I know.

ROY. If I could tell you how much I love you, without feeling an ape about it.

ALICIA. You don't look like an ape to me.

ROY. You carried a torch for me away back as far as I can remember. And since I grew up you've been such a friend – such a great friend, Mother.

ALICIA. Darling – thank you.

ROY. Have I staggered you by my eloquence?

ALICIA. Roy, we've only got a few minutes . . . I want to talk to you about tomorrow.

ROY. Why tomorrow?

ALICIA. Because I don't want to talk to you about today . . . Get
    yourself ready in good time, won't you? Don't turn up at the
    church looking untidy . . . and rushed.

ROY. No.

ALICIA (*smiling tenderly*). You'll look very handsome . . . and Louise
    will look lovely . . . I shall be terribly proud of you.

ROY. What you mean is – whether you are there or not.

ALICIA. Yes, darling.

ROY. Oh, Mother!

ALICIA. There is always the chance that the case may go against me.

ROY. I'm not even going to begin to think about that.

ALICIA. It's only a remote possibility, Roy – but there it is. If it does,
    promise me that everything will go on as if nothing had happened.

ROY. Mother, how could it?

ALICIA. It must, Roy. Promise me that.

ROY. All right, I promise . . . but why even think about it? Hawkins's
    evidence will put everything right for you, won't it?

ALICIA. He's done his best to uncover some 'emotional disturbances',
    as he calls it. But it's difficult for him, because you see, there's
    nothing there. After all, I should know, and there is nothing there.

(THEA *enters*.)

THEA. Darling, Nannie insists that I give you this.

(*She hands* ALICIA *something*.)

ALICIA. What is it?

THEA. Some beastly little Chinese idol . . . with him in your pocket
    you're insulated against everything.

ALICIA. Good.

ROY. The car's at the door.

ALICIA. Where have I put my bag?

THEA. You'll be back for lunch.

ALICIA. I think so. If we're late – don't wait for us. And darling . . . I
    just want you to know how sorry I am to have brought this – worry
    on you.

THEA. Oh, Mother!

(*They embrace*.)

ALICIA. Goodbye, Roy.

(*He embraces her*.)

ROY. Goodbye, Mother.

ALICIA. It's a lovely morning – why don't you both go for a walk?

(*She goes out very quickly without glancing at either of them.*)

BLACKOUT.


## SCENE 2

*When the lights fade in again, it is three hours later.*

THEA. I wish now we'd gone to the court. We could have waited outside. It would have been better than sitting here.

(NANNIE *enters.*)

ROY. It can't be long now.

THEA. It must be over. It's after one! Why doesn't Daddy telephone?

ROY. There may be a fine to pay. Perhaps it's that that's taking the time.

NANNIE. Are you going to have your lunch or will you wait?

ROY. We'll wait, Nannie.

NANNIE. It can't be long now.

THEA. We've been saying that for the last hour.

(*Silence.*)

NANNIE. The flowers have come. Would you like to arrange them?

THEA. Presently, Nannie.

NANNIE. Give you something to do.

THEA. I've plenty to do keeping myself from going crazy.

NANNIE. I salted the potatoes twice. I had to pour all the water out and boil them up again.

THEA. What is it, Roy? It's the car – it's Father and Hawkins.

(NANNIE *goes quickly.*)

Roy . . . I'm terrified.

ROY. We'll know in a minute.

THEA. I've never felt so terrified in my life.

(HAWKINS *comes in.*)

ROY. Is it over?

HAWKINS. Yes. I'm very sorry to have to be the bearer of bad news.

THEA. Where is she?

HAWKINS. Your father asked me to break it to you.

ROY. What?

HAWKINS. They gave her three months' imprisonment.

THEA. O-o-oh! (*She breaks down, sobbing bitterly.*)

HAWKINS. Hush . . . don't give way too much. You mustn't. You really mustn't.

THEA. It's cruel! It's brutal!

ROY. Three months! I can't believe it! Are they mad? Have they no understanding? Couldn't they see?

THEA. Where is she? Where have they taken her?

HAWKINS. Holloway.

THEA. She'll never be able to stand it.

HAWKINS. She'll be all right. She was very calm . . . She heard the sentence and walked down from the dock without any emotion; you see, she expected it.

ROY. But what about the defence?

HAWKINS. There was no defence; she pleaded guilty.

ROY. But what about your evidence?

HAWKINS. She refused to call me. There was nothing we could do.

THEA. But what could have possessed her?

HAWKINS. Your mother is a woman with a fastidious mind and an eager heart . . . it makes for a sort of obstinacy.

ROY. Obstinacy?

HAWKINS. Yes, the obstinacy with which a bird will freeze to its nest. I must go. I'm terribly sorry. Don't worry too much. I hope the time will pass quickly for you and for her.

ROY. I'll come down with you, doctor.

HAWKINS. Your father will see me out . . . I hope your marriage will be a very happy one.

ROY. Thank you, sir.

(HAWKINS *goes out.*)

THEA (*after a pause*). I shall have my baby and she won't be here.

ROY. I shall be married and she won't be there.

THEA. Even the room looks strange. Empty and horrible . . . I shan't come here while she's away.

ROY. We must, Thea. We both must. Things must be right for her to come back to.

(ROBERT *comes in.*)

ROBERT. Hawkins has told you?

ROY. Yes.

ROBERT. I don't know what we're going to do.

THEA. Wait, that's all, Daddy.

ROBERT. There was a change of plan at the last moment . . . I wasn't told . . . I didn't know.

THEA. Tell us about her, Daddy. Did you see her?

ROBERT. Yes, they let me see her before they took her away. She sent you both her love . . . she was so anxious about the wedding tomorrow . . . I told her not to worry . . . I knew you'd help me, Thea . . . take her place. I assured her that everything would be all right. Nannie said that lunch was ready. Shall we go down?

(THEA *goes out.*)

Roy, we must get things straight before she comes home. Will you help me?

ROY. I'd very much like to try.

CURTAIN.